European Communication Council Report

E-MERGING MEDIA

Communication
and the Media Economy
of the Future

Axel Zerdick · Arnold Picot
Klaus Schrape · Jean-Claude Burgelman
Roger Silverstone

MANAGING EDITORS

Valerie Feldmann
Christian Wernick
Carolin Wolff

E-MERGING MEDIA

Communication
and the Media Economy
of the Future

With 48 Figures
and 6 Tables

Springer

Translator: Rupert Glasgow

Cataloging-in-Publication Data applied for
Library of Congress Control Number: 2004113936
A catalog record for this book is available from the Library of Congress.

Bibliographic information published by Die Deutsche Bibliothek
Die Deutsche Bibliothek lists this publication in the Deutsche Nationalbibliografie;
detailed bibliographic data available in the internet at *http.//dnb.ddb.de*

ISBN 3-540-23138-2 Springer Berlin Heidelberg New York

Springer is a part of Springer Science + Business Media

springeronline.com

© Springer-Verlag Berlin Heidelberg 2005
Printed in Germany

The use of general descriptive names, registered names, trademarks, etc. in this publication does not imply, even in the absence of a specific statement, that such names are exempt from the relevant protective laws and regulations and therefore free for general use.

Cover design: Erich Kirchner, Heidelberg
Prduction Editor: Helmut Petri
Printing: Betz-Druck, Darmstadt

SPIN 11323631   42/3130 – 5 4 3 2 1 0 – Printed on acid-free paper

Editorial

European Communication Council Report

E-Merging Media

Communication and the Media Economy of the Future

The Editors:

Fellows:

Axel Zerdick (1941–2003), Prof. Dr., Institute for Journalism and Communication Science, Free University of Berlin

Arnold Picot (born 1944), Prof. Dr. Dres. h.c., Institute for Information, Organisation and Management, Ludwig-Maximilian University of Munich, Email: picot@bwl.uni-muenchen.de

Klaus Schrape (1946–2001), Prof. Dr., Prognos AG Basel, Media and Communication Department

Jean-Claude Burgelman (born 1957), Prof. Dr., Institute for Prospective Technological Studies (IPTS), Joint Research Centre – European Commission, ICT Unit, Seville, Email: jean-claude.burgelman@jrc.es

Roger Silverstone (born 1945), Prof., PhD; Chair of Media and Communications, Department of Sociology, London School of Economics, Email: R.Silverstone@lse.ac.uk

Managing Editors:

Valerie Feldmann (born 1974), Dipl.-Kffr., M.A.,
Email: feldmav@gmx.de

Christian Wernick (born 1978), Dipl.-Kfm.,
Email: wernick@bwl.uni-muenchen.de

Carolin Wolff (born 1976), Dipl-Kffr., MBR,
Email: cwolff@bwl.uni-muenchen.de

Supported by: SevenOne Media GmbH
Webpage: www.sevenonemedia.de

The ECC would like to thank those experts who gave their valuable time for interviews with us and for discussions in our workshops:

Name	Function	Organisation
Beck, Klaus	Research Assistant Communication Sciences	Chair of University of Erfurt
Couldry, Nick	Lecturer in Media and Communication	London School of Economics
Goldhammer, Klaus	Owner and Manager GoldMedia	Berlin
Groebel, Jo	Professor, Chair of Media Psychology	University of Utrecht
Haddon, Leslie	Research associate in the Media and Communications Department	London School of Economics
Hamm, Ingrid	Manager, Media Department	Bertelsmann Stiftung
Hummel, Johannes	Project Manager at the Institute for Media and Communication Management	University of St. Gallen
Liebenau, Jonathan	Professor, Department for Information Systems	London School of Economics
Latzer, Michael	Deputy Head of Research Centre for Institutional Change & European Integration	Austrian Academy of Sciences
Lauber, Hans	Owner and Manager	LauberProject Medienberatung Cologne/Munich
Lehmann, Michael	Professor, Lecturer in Commercial Law	Max Planck Institute
Löffelholz, Martin	Professor, Institute for Media and Communication Sciences	Technical University of Ilmenau
Maier, Matthias	Professor, Faculty of Media	University of Weimar
Mansell, Robin	Professor, Dixons Chair in New Media and the Internet	London School of Economics
Paterson, Richard	Director of Information	British Film Institute, London
Pichler, Katja	Director Press & PR	SevenOne Media GmbH

Name	Function	Organisation
Schorr, Angela	Professor, Department of Psychology	University of Siegen
Slater, Don	Department of Sociology	London School of Economics
Sjurts, Insa	Professor, Chair of Media Management	University of Flensburg
Tambini, Damian	Senior Research Fellow, Media and Communications Programme	Institute for Public Policy Research, UK

The European Communication Council (ECC) is an independent group of scholars and scientists from different European countries and the USA. For each new report, communication experts from diverse academic backgrounds are invited to participate in research and production as either Fellows of the Council or authors. The ECC's objective is to discuss trends and issues in European communications for leaders and visionaries in communication companies and for leading policymakers.

ECC Reports concentrate on key trends and issues in media, telecommunications and information technologies, which are expected to be predominant for the future development of communication industries, and which deserve higher profile in future debates.

The European Communication Council is organised as an independent research project at the Free University of Berlin and the Ludwig-Maximilian University of Munich. It is fully funded by non-government resources from SevenOne Media GmbH.

Fellows, editors and authors who have contributed to this and previous reports:

Name	Function	Organisation
Artopé, Alexander	Managing Editor 1998/99	Free University of Berlin
Bechtold, Stefan	Author 2003/2004	University of Tübingen
Bogdanowicz, Marc	Author 2003/2004	Institute for Prospective Technological Studies (IPTS), Sevilla
Burgelman, Jean-Claude	Fellow and Author 2003/2004 Fellow 2003 /2004	Institute for Prospective Technological Studies (IPTS), Sevilla
Carlton, Jim	Author 1998/99	The Wall Street Journal, San Francisco
Chyi, Hsiang Iris	Author 2003	Chinese University of Hong Kong
Claisse, Gérard	Author 1997	Laboratoire d'Economie des Transports, Lyon

Editorial

Name	Function	Organisation
Cole, Jeffrey	Author 2003/2004	University of California Los Angeles
Coleman, Stephen	Author 2003/2004	University of Oxford
Compaine, Benjamin	Author 2003/2004	Massachusetts Institute of Technology, Cambridge
Cringely, Robert X.	Author 1998/99	Journalist und Autor, San Mateo
Dreier, Hardy	Author 2003/2004	Hans Bredow Institute for Media Research, University of Hamburg
Ducatel, Ken	Author 2003/2004	Institute for Prospective Technological Studies (IPTS), Sevilla
Feldmann, Valerie	Author and Managing Editor 2003/2004	Free University of Berlin
Frey, Siegfried	Author 2003/2004	Gerhard-Mercator-University of Duisburg
Frissen, Valerie	Author 2003/2004	Information & Communication Department, TNO-STB, Niederlande
Funk, Jeffrey	Author 2003/2004	Kobe University
Gaster, Jens	Author 1997	European Commission, Brussels
Goldhammer, Klaus	Author 1997 Managing Editor 1998/99	Free University of Berlin
Hass, Berthold	Author 2003/2004	Ludwig-Maximilians-University of Munich
Heger, Dominik K.	Author and Managing Editor 2001–2003	Ludwig-Maximilians-University of Munich
Hess, Thomas	Author 2003/2004	Ludwig-Maximilians-University of Munich
Jones, Steve	Author 2003/2004	University of Illinois, Chicago
Kelly, Kevin	Author 1998/99	Wired Magazine, San Francisco
Kleinsteuber, Hans J.	Author 1997	University of Hamburg
Kridel, Donald	Author 2003/2004	University of Missouri, St. Louis
Lange, Ulrich T.	Co-ordinating Author 1997, Author 1998/99	Free University of Berlin
Lehr, William	Author 2003/2004	Massachusetts Institute of Technology, Cambridge
Leijten, Jos	Author 2003/204	Institute for Prospective Technological Studies (IPTS), Sevilla
Lessig, Lawrence	Author 2003/2004	Stanford Law School

López-Escobar, Esteban	Fellow 1998/99	University of Navarra, Pamplona
Martinoli, Mario	Author 1998/99	Databank Consulting, Milan
Mattern, Friedemann	Author 2003/2004	Federal Institute of Technology (ETH), Zurich
McKnight, Lee W.	Author 2003/2004	Syracuse University, New York
Negroponte, Nicholas	Author 1998/99	MIT Media Lab, Boston
Noam, Eli M.	Author 1997	Columbia University, New York
Paterson, Richard	Author 1997	British Film Institute, London
Pavlik, John	Author 2003/2004	Rutgers University, New Brunswick
Picot, Arnold	Author und Fellow 1998–2004	Ludwig-Maximilians-University of Munich
Pilati, Antonio	Author 1997	Instituto di Economia dei Media, Milan
Pitroda, Sam	Author 2003/2004	Chairman and CEO WorldTel, London
Rappoport, Paul	Author 2003/2004	Temple University, Philadelphia
Richeri, Giuseppe	Author 1997	University of Bologna/University of Lugano
Rosenbach, Marcel	Author 1997	University of Hamburg
Scapolo, Fabiana	Author 2003/2004	Institute for Prospective Technological Studies (IPTS), Sevilla
Schlesinger, Philip	Fellow 1997	University of Stirling
Schrape, Klaus	Author and Fellow 1998–2001	University of Basel/Prognos AG
Seufert, Wolfgang	Author 1997	Deutsches Institut für Wirtschaftsforschung
Shapiro, Carl	Author 1998/99	University of California at Berkeley
Siegrist, Hannes	Author 2003/2004	University of Leipzig
Silj, Alessandro	Fellow 1997	ROMA – Research on Media Associates/ Consiglio Italiano per le Scienze Sociali, Rom
Silverstone, Roger	Author and Fellow 1998–2004	London School of Economics
Tannenbaum, Percy	Fellow 1997	University of California at Berkeley
Taylor, Lester	Author 2003/2004	University of Arizona
Thorngren, Bertil	Author 2003/2004	Stockholm School of Economics
Tuomi, Ilkka	Author 2003/2004	Visiting Scientist at the Institute for Prospective Technological Studies (IPTS), Sevilla
Varian, Hal	Author 1998/99	University of California at Berkeley

Vierkant, Eckart	Author 1998/99	Free University of Berlin
Waesche, Niko	Author 2003/2004	IBM München
Wattenberg, Ulrich	Author 1997	GMD Forschungszentrum Informationstechnik, Berlin
Wernick, Christian	Managing Editor 2004	Ludwig-Maximilians-University of Munich
Weber, Martin	Author 2003/2004	Technology Policy Unit, ARC Seibersdorf Research, Austria
Wolff, Carolin	Managing Editor 2003/2004	Ludwig-Maximilians-University of Munich
Zerdick, Axel	Author and Speaker 1997–2003	Free University of Berlin

Contents

About the ECC and This Report   15

E-Merging Media: The Future of Communication   19

Valerie Feldmann and Axel Zerdick

1   Changing Media
Diversification and Individualisation   31

1.1 Disintegration and Reintegration
in the Media Sector:
How Business Models are Changing
on Account of Digitalisation   33

Berthold Hass

1.2 Media Companies between
Multiple Utilisation and Individualisation:
an Analysis for Static Contents   57

Thomas Hess

1.3 Multimedia and Multidimensional:
Concepts of Utilisation
in the "Age of Digitalisation"   75

Hardy Dreier

1.4 New Technologies, New Customers
and the Disruptive Nature
of the Mobile Internet:
Evidence from the Japanese Market   97

Jeffrey L. Funk

1.5 Journalism in the Face of Developments
in Digital Production   117

John Pavlik

Contents

1.6 **Spellbound by Images**   127

Siegfried Frey

2   **Changing Technology**
     Ubiquity and Miniaturisation   143

2.1 **Ubiquitous Computing:**
     Scenarios from an Informatised World   145

Friedemann Mattern

2.2 **Wireless Internet Access:**
     3G vs. WiFi?   165

William Lehr and Lee W. McKnight

2.3 **That's What Friends Are For –**
     Ambient Intelligence (AmI)
     and the Information Society in 2010   181

K. Ducatel, M. Bogdanowicz, F. Scapolo, J. Leijten and J-C. Burgelman

2.4 **Evolutionary Perspectives**   201

Klaus Schrape

3   **Changing Society**
     Individual and Collective Life Options   213

3.1 **Virtual Communities,**
     Space and Mobility   215

Ilkka Tuomi

3.2 **Towards a Sociological Theory**
     of the Mobile Phone   235

Hans Geser

3.3 Mobile Europe: Balancing a Fast-changing Society and Europe's Socio-economic Objectives 261

Martin Weber and Jean-Claude Burgelman

3.4 The Myth of the Digital Divide 271

Valerie Frissen

3.5 The Vanishing Digital Divide 285

Benjamin Compaine

4 Changing Rules
Deregulation and reregulation 301

4.1 Regulation and Law 303

Ilkka Tuomi

4.2 The History and Current Problems of Intellectual Property (1600–2000) 311

Hannes Siegrist

4.3 Digital Rights Management: Between Author Protection and the Protection of Innovation 331

Stefan Bechtold

4.4 Does the Internet Need a New Competition Policy? A Global Problem from a German Point of View 339

Arnold Picot and Dominik K. Heger

4.5 Towards an e-Connected Europe 357

Stephen Coleman

4.6 Regulation, Media Literacy and Media Civics 367

Roger Silverstone

Contents

Author Curricula   381

References   387

Index   411

Introduction

About the ECC and This Report

The present, third ECC report, "E-merging Media: Communication and the Media Economy of the Future," describes the potentials of long-term developments for communication systems and the media economy. The associations of a digitalised, greatly changing media landscape include the transformation of the media themselves, changes in information and communication technology, implications for society, and alterations to the regulatory framework.

The development of new media (emerging media), the growing together of media considered incompatible through the media-neutral storage of contents (merging media), and the advancing digitalisation of all elements of the media economy indicate a change in paradigm (e-merging media), which calls into question whether the fundamental principles of communication and the media economy valid today will still be workable tomorrow. Within this context the third ECC report outlines changes and trends that can serve as a relevant basis for decision-makers in the communication and media economy both in constructing visions and formulating strategies.

The idea of the "European Communication Council" was born in 1996 on the initiative of Michael Wölfle and Hans Lauber from MEDIAGRUPPE MÜNCHEN. It was conceived as a small group of predominantly European communication scientists faced with an unusually appealing task. This was to bring contributions from European (and international) communication science on the development of the media and communications industries to the notice of the decision-makers, identifying in particular themes of special relevance for future development. Various scientific fields concerned with developments in the communications industries and countless research institutions in many countries have recently witnessed the emergence of new lines of discussion in the area, some of which are highly specialised, many of which are exceptionally interesting. It is hard enough for specialists to keep an overview of the contributions that have come about from these discussions, and just about impossible for decision-makers and visionaries in politics and business, whose work leaves no time for reading and digesting such a diversity and multitude of scientific texts. This is where the European Communication Council comes in. Its task is to sound out the broad field of current scientific discussion and to filter out and examine those trends and themes which seem of special relevance for the future development of the media and communication industries and which should be a basis for discussion among visionaries and decision-makers.

Introduction

Calling the European Communication Council "European" is in certain respects something of a challenge. On a pragmatic level things are clear-cut enough. "European" here means that the focus will be on the key communications markets in Europe, but also on other European countries (both inside and outside the European Union) where interesting and significant developments can be discerned. The term is also meant to denote a European viewpoint, in contrast to narrower national perspectives and with the claim of observing developments in other countries (mainly the United States and Japan) from a specifically European point of view.

The relation of the European Communication Council to other European institutions is in three respects a complementary one. Firstly, we have built upon the important and successful work performed by European institutions such as the European Commission, the European Audiovisual Observatory, the European Information Technology Observatory (EITO) and the European Institute for the Media (EIM). Our activity is in turn intended to direct more attention to these institutions. Secondly, the work of the ECC is complementary to the European Union in that the ECC is financed entirely by private funding – not a single EU-euro has been spent on this volume. Visible independence from economic and political interests is thus a central objective in

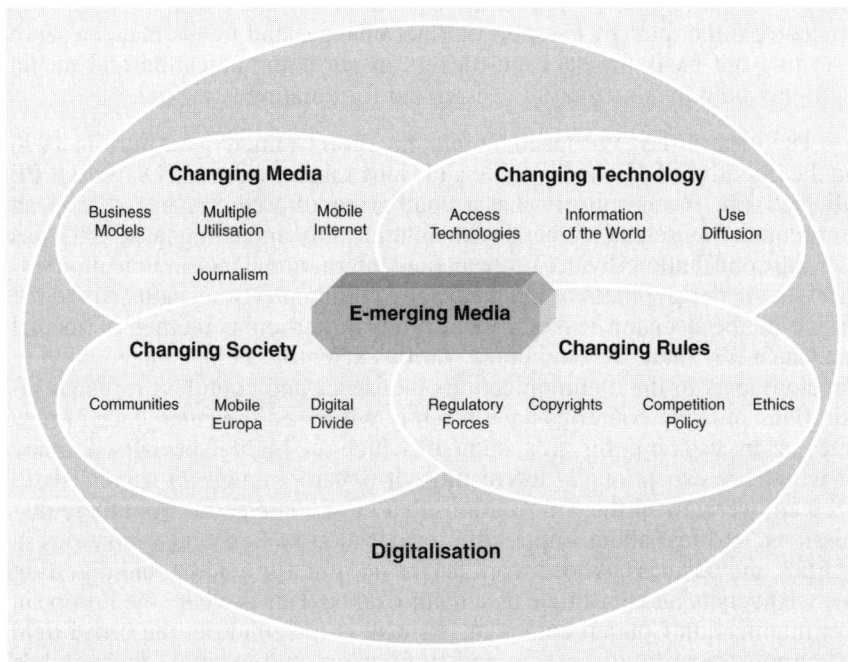

Fig. 1 Frame of reference for the digitalisation of the media economy and focal points of the changes under consideration

the work of the ECC. Thirdly, the ECC reports are complementary to official EU reports in that the ECC is not obliged to reflect Europe as a political entity – neither the Europe of the EU in its entirety, nor the range of interests and perspectives of the member states. These two aspects are necessary and correct for official European reports. The European Communication Council treats its subject matter independently of these considerations, thus giving itself the opportunity to produce stimulating thought that is international, interdisciplinary, and rooted in an intellectual exchange between theory and practice.

The first ECC report, "Exploring the Limits – Europe's Changing Communication Environment," contained a number of views, analyses and suggestions relating to the Internet. Yet the future of the Internet was by no means clearly marked out. "Internet years," as the rule of thumb in the communications industry has it, "are like dogs' years: they pass seven times as quickly." Today, no area of the economy can escape the pull exerted by networking. The significance of the Internet is becoming apparent everywhere, not just in the predictions of research institutes on e-commerce but in new work procedures in many companies from totally different branches. Now the initial euphoria is over, however, the necessary rational approach to this theme has established itself in the economy.

Yet the potentials of the Internet are evidently difficult to tap, and it seems to be bound up with high risks. The usual laws of classical economics do not appear to be entirely valid: it seems that the rules of play, the strategies and perspectives, are different in the Internet business from those we have known until now. Because these new rules are decisive for competition for almost all branches of the economy but above all for the media, information and telecommunication industries, the European Communication Council directed its second report, published in four languages and entitled "E-conomics: Strategies for the Digital Marketplace," at the question of which economic laws accompany and determine the evolution of the Internet.

The third ECC report, "E-merging Media: Communication and the Media Economy of the Future," builds on the second book and carries the analysis further, investigating how the progressive digitalisation of communication technologies is changing society and the corresponding branches of the economy.

The third ECC report is part of the legacy of Prof. Dr. Axel Zerdick who passed away in November 2003 shortly before the publication of this report's German version. Axel Zerdick was the heart and motor of the European Communication Council and accompanied the creation and publication of all three ECC reports with brilliant ideas and great dedication. We keep him in our memories with highest gratitude.

" ...now, if I turn up the volume, then you have to pay royalties...?"

Khaleil having his hand on the auto-radio to the shooting film crew
in the documentary picture "startup.com"

E-Merging Media

E-Merging Media: The Future of Communication

Valerie Feldmann and Axel Zerdick

Changes through the Internet

Many of the assumptions made about the consequences of the Internet for the nexus of economic relations, societal developments and the processes of political participation are today being revised or at least toned down. Following the sudden end to the dot-com boom (there are those who speak of dot-cons), the question to be posed now is whether the Internet economy – to invert a well-known turn of phrase – does not in fact constitute the tunnel at the end of the light. Yet even though short-term developments may have fallen short of some expectations, the Internet will in the long run change patterns of communication and economic, political and social processes. Indicative of this is not least the high level of Internet penetration in households, businesses and public institutions, which is increasingly reaching all sectors of the population. Yet considered from a macro-perspective as well, it is possible to interpret the collapse of the stock market and the bankruptcy of countless start-up enterprises as a turning-point on the way to genuinely far-reaching and long-lasting developments (see figure 1). Seen against the background of historical analogies such as the development of the rail industry in the 19th century, institutional adjustments in relation to the players

Dot-coms or dot-cons?

The crash as a turning point?

> "New technologies is a historically relative term. We are not the first generation to wonder at the rapid and extraordinary shifts in the dimension of the world and the human relationships it contains as a result of new forms of communication, or to be surprised by the changes those shifts occasion in the regular pattern of our lives."
>
> *Carolyn Marvin (1988)*[1]

---

1 Marvin, Carolyn (1988), When old technologies were new. Thinking about electric communication in the late nineteenth century, Oxford University Press: Oxford, p. 1.

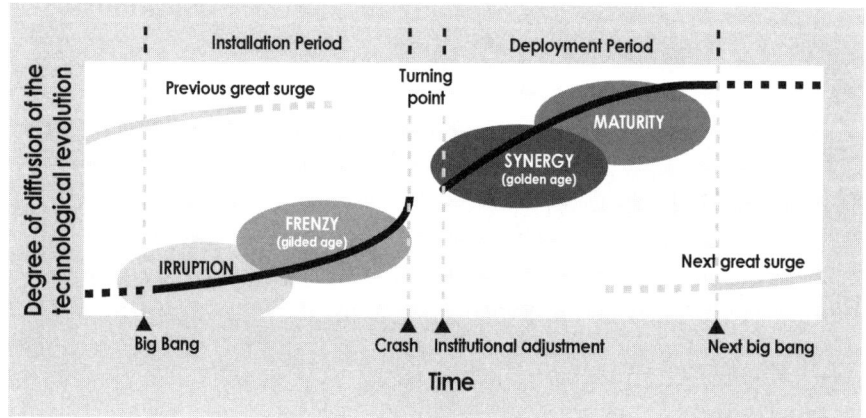

Fig. 1 The crash as a turning point? (Following Perez, 2002, p. 48, and The Economist, 8 May 2003)

involved, their roles and the regulatory context point towards major changes on a long-term basis.

There are also Internet-driven developments, however, that have been distinctly underesstimated. These include on the one hand the sweeping – some say exaggerated – extension of rights to intellectual property and on the other hand the success of commercial monopolies, which have consolidated their market dominance with the aid of long-term customer-relationship and price strategies. It is in this context that the foundations of the Internet economy will here be reappraised and analysed in terms of strategic implications for (media) enterprises.

Underestimated developments: copyright law and commercial monopolies

Foundations of the Internet economy revisited

A central feature of the Internet is its nature as a network, which fosters the emergence and development of positive externalities. Many expectations as regards changes in the Internet economy have been derived from the argument that positive externalities contribute to the increased value of network goods and networks whereby the increase in value is exponentially (or alternatively: ... that positive externalities contribute to the exponentially increased value of network goods and networks). Indeed, what has come to be called the network economy gains in significance on account of the Internet. More discriminating reflection, however, leads to the conclusion that not every enterprise that offers products or services (also) over the Internet can automatically realise network effects just because the Internet is a network.

Discriminating reflection on the Internet economy

The realisation of network effects is closely bound up with what is offered by the business in question. The rapid attainment of a critical mass as a first mover is a further network effect that in retrospect calls for critical analysis. As it happened, numerous established firms – reverting to their own strengths and the competitive advantages specific to their company – invalidated the argument that early market entry and the rapid attainment of critical masses might represent a lasting basis for entrepreneurial activity.

A second central feature of the Internet that continues to hold great potential for further processes of transformation is the opportunity it presents for expanding essential basic functions of communication. The Internet unites within a single technical medium two communication possibilities that up to now have been clearly separated: its publication function (as in newspapers and radio) and individual communication (as in letters and the telephone). On top of this, it permits an organisational orientation that spans between professional and non-professional content-production. Within this frame of reference, extended and new forms of communication can develop and influence one another. Professionally produced online media offers, for example, are thus expanded by means of communication platforms that allow for communication between users. Mass-media content production and distribution as well as interpersonal communication – both between users and content-producers and among users – as a result become possible simultaneously and through a single medium, and this can also be broadened to include transaction offers via e-commerce. Not only the Internet, however, but also intranets as a new form of communication internal to a company are assuming an increasingly significant role in businesses, organisations and public institutions alike.

Recombination and expansion of communication

While in the professional and institutional realm it comes as no surprise that new information and communication technologies are being deployed with a view to increasing effectiveness and efficiency, the Internet is also becoming increasingly important for the non-professional organisation of publication and communication. Private email use is an essential motivation for the diffusion of Internet connections in private households. Furthermore, the oft-cited "information overload" of the Internet can be attributed, among other things, to the opportunity it provides not only for private persons but also other non-commercial organisations and associations to produce homepages and websites and publish them on the Internet. A fascinating hybrid development in collective publishing, combining professionally and non-professionally produced contents, is the spread of web logs (or "blogs"). In these web-based "diaries" users contextualise online media contents available on the Internet with their own commentaries, in some cases adding publications of their own making. The communicative and organisational functions of the Internet in this way give rise to a whole host of opportuni-

Non-professional content-production profits from the Internet

Web logs as a hybrid form of collective publishing

ties for the recombination and expansion of economic, political and social communication.

What emerges is that the foundations of the Internet economy need not be called into question in fundamental terms, but that we can observe a continuous shift in the weight attached to individual assumptions. This supports the argument of the evolutionary development of the Internet.

Strategic consequences for enterprises

Paid content and versioning models as Internet revenue forms

Among the fundamental assumptions underlying changes in competition and business strategy in the Internet economy are that the Internet economy promotes the formation of business webs, that new forms of versioning for information goods lead to further differentiation within price discrimination strategies, and that combining a variety of revenue sources constitutes the basis for Internet business models. The experiences learnt from the wave of new enterprises set up in the 1990s show that Internet business models based primarily upon advertising income or commissions are limited in their viability. Yet it is equally difficult for so-called "paid content" models for information goods, which imply use-dependent charges for consumers, to find acceptance in an Internet culture perceived by most users as available free of charge. It is for just this reason that versioning models, which can use various formats of the information or entertainment offer, are gaining in significance. Spatial extensions of versioning, for example, are conceivable: the willingness to pay for use of an online newspaper might correlate with spatial distance from the media offer. With the increasing mobility of training and labour markets, there are more and more people seeking contact with the local media through the Internet.

The Internet facilitates contact with local media

Finally, it is not the case for every industry that cooperation and competition are necessarily closely linked. On the one hand, online providers of business-to-business platforms in particular have learnt that enterprise-sensitive information, for example concerning companies' purchasing behaviour or relationships with the supply industry, is not willingly shared with competitors. On the other hand, processes of vertical integration suggest that a disproportionately large number of business webs may be just a transitional phenomenon in maturing industries.

Global production and services with the help of ICT

Nevertheless, through Internet-based information and communication systems business webs and production sites are being used increasingly globally. Examples are found both in the 24-hour production (e.g. of software or translations) that takes place across different continents and in customer services carried out by countries with lower wage-cost levels. Parallel to the globalisation strategies of companies, however, markedly regional or locally-oriented strategies are also developing, for example with regard to regional product and price differentiation. Media enterprises too are developing in both directions, interested as they are both in international and in local contents and customer groups.

Developments of the Media

The development of the media under the influence of the Internet has taken two specific forms: an overlap ("merging media") and an expansion ("e-merging media") of classic media categories. Broadcasting is extended to incorporate forms of webcasting; hyperlinks create added value for Internet newspapers; even an appliance such as the PC develops into a cross-media reception device.

E-merging media: expanding classic media categories

One special feature in this changing media landscape is the development of the meso-media (see figure 2). Through the Internet, the meso-media, which address small target groups of between a hundred and a hundred thousand participants, offer high potential for development in the realms of both communication and publication, and the Internet further provides them for the first time with an economically viable base. Lower acquisition costs for digital production and processing equipment provides the amateur so inclined with virtually professional work conditions. Yet professional low-budget productions too, for example in the film and music branch, find new publics through the Internet, which with skillful marketing can potentially expand to become a mass public. In addition to this there is the expansion of the production and utilisation possibilities of other meso-media, such as local television, on-demand book printing, as well as intranets or DVDs: these permit new forms of convergence of existing and developing communication channels and broaden the diversity of media categories. Conversely, the integration of specific meso-media elements within existing media offers provides new possibilities for traditional media providers as well. Daily papers such as the San Jose Mercury News, for example, include integrated web-log functions in their online offer: particularly prominent journalists can run a web log on the pages of the online paper. Web logs are in this way used as a new and innovative customer-relationship tool for online newspapers.

Meso-media gaining ground

Development opportunities for individual media

The Internet broadens in particular the development potentials of the communication offers made by traditional media providers. Print media such as newspapers and magazines make special use of the opportunities presented by the Internet. The availability of e-paper editions, for example, results in

Users can control the depth of focus of media

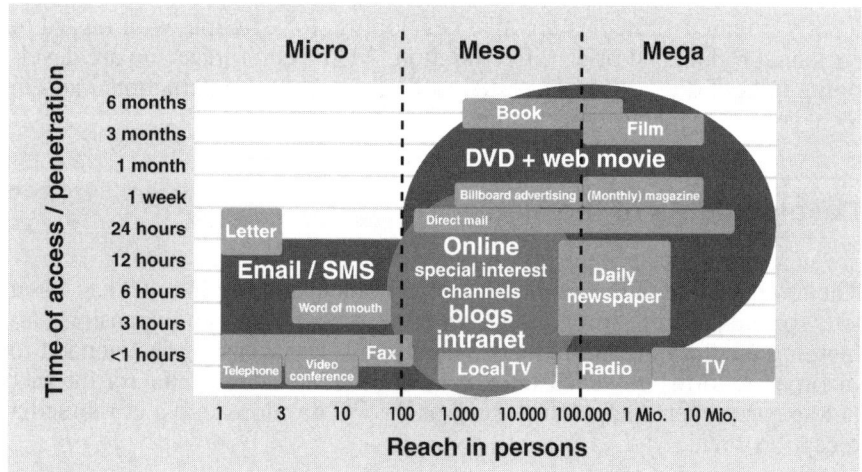

Fig. 2 The development of the meso-media

some subscribers no longer receiving the paper physically, but only in digital form. This is feasible in particular when it comes to opening up new regional submarkets where distribution – for example to other continents – no longer represents a barrier or even produces a delay. Professional journals such as the MIT Technology Review or newspapers such as The New York Times in this way find new subscribers. Yet the advantages of online editions are immediately evident even to the readers of physical editions: additional external links and access to archives and databases make possible a depth of focus that can be controlled by the user. Many newspapers are going over to administering particularly this added value with paid content payment models and in return making the bulk of their texts and images freely available on the Internet. The farthest-reaching changes for print media enterprises, however, are taking place in the realm of the advertising business. Database queries and search masks in the Internet permit a clear reduction in the search costs for classified ads for the reader or user in question. If papers then also enter into cross-regional joint operations combining their databases, it will be possible to achieve further network effects that go considerably beyond the capacity of the classified ads hitherto printed in newspapers. The conclusion for media enterprises must thus be to rethink the mixture - that is a characteristic of revenue models in the media industry - of individual revenue forms. In the long term, it is conceivable that – presumably with the exception of death notices – a great deal of the job, property and motor vehicle ads will go mainly through the Internet.

In the realm of broadcasting, Internet radio and Internet TV have not produced any significant substitution effects, although Internet radio in par-

Advertising markets shifting into the Internet

> *" In media use especially there are many moments of rational passivity. "*

ticular has interesting potential as a networked jukebox. The introduction of digital terrestrial television, however, will open up new opportunities when synchronised TV and Internet contents are broadcast and a broadband quasi-television is engendered: a permanent IP connection for "point-to-point" television in conjunction with demand aggregation models might then indeed allow for hybrid TV-online applications transmitted via the television set. TV companies are also extremely keen to activate their programme archives and try out new paid content models in broadcasting as well.

"Point-to-point" TV via DVB-T

A third exemplary branch of the media industry subject to major changes on account of the Internet is the film business. Digital film production permits additional versioning, whether through potential HDTV Home Theatre versions or a full-blown launch in the Internet. With skill, small, independent film producers in particular can use the Internet for marketing and distribution purposes, as a result of which the diversity of so-called low-budget productions may gain from the Internet. Digital distribution to cinema operators, for example by satellite, will also foster further changes in the processes in this part of the film value chain. Additional marketing flexibility is produced, for example, by the fact that films can be added to or removed from the cinema programme at short notice without incurring the costs of transporting the film reel or quality-loss through use. While previous cost barriers may be overcome by digitalisation, however, it may also lead to increased insecurity for film producers regarding the use of their films if target returns are not met as soon as the film is released. One way of supporting large-scale film projects is to underline their character as an "event." Film industry measures here include, for example, the simultaneous launch of accompanying video games.

Digitalisation in the film industry reduces costs but increases uncertainty

Facets of possible overall development

The diffusion of the Internet has attained a critical mass that means it now pervades countless areas of life on a lasting basis: the demographic data of users are coming closer and closer to the demographic distribution of population as a whole. Even so, the masses still to be reached are critical too. These are the people who are neither technophile early adopters nor come into contact with the Internet through work experience. This second "critical mass" has different priorities and interests and also, to a certain extent, different expectations of everyday technology. When it comes to technology, they are interested more in results that make everyday life easier and are less driven by a (healthy) play instinct than technophile users.

Two critical masses

In order to reach these users too, it is important and necessary to convey clearly the added value of Internet use. Yet with respect to the major lines of development of communication, two central misconceptions hold sway: (1)

Misconceptions about the development of media and communication:

communication is desirable; (2) interactivity is good. In fact, the opposite can often be observed. In an age when the ubiquity of information and communication technologies makes many people feel under pressure to be reachable everywhere and at all times, strategies of de-communication are a rational choice. Times of non-reachability have thus become a new scarce good. Protection from communication through systems of variable contact and communication management that allow a simultaneity of ubiquity and inaccessibility may as a result become a new symbol of power and influence. In everyday life as well, communicative restraint in public spaces is a form of de-communication that is not only socially accepted but may even be regarded as socially desirable: witness the conscious denial of communication on public transport, where people prefer to turn to a newspaper or fix their gaze upon the screen provided rather than make eye contact with the person opposite.

An oft-cited feature of improvement in new media is the increase in their possibilities for interactivity. Yet this argument ignores that in media use especially there are many moments of rational passivity. Relaxation, entertainment and restfulness can be interpreted as forms of rational passivity: rational inactivity, rational listening and the rational marking of time. Interactivity may even be interpreted as an imperfect engineering achievement: the more questions have to be answered in interaction at the man-machine interface, the more negative the assessment. Even though some new media, such as the rapidly growing video game segment, are based upon the principle of interactivity, this does not necessarily mean that opportunities for interaction are judged or viewed positively for all uses of media. On the contrary, one of the central functions of the media is to take on selection decisions. New possibilities for interactivity through return channels may address specific target groups as an optional added value. To address this market, media enterprises can provide self-selection mechanisms to achieve more discriminating market cultivation.

Along with misconceptions about communication and interactivity, there are further limits to media use that must be overcome. Both time and the attention of users are scarce goods, for which more and more information and entertainment offers are competing. Parallel media-use is a way for users to surmount limits with respect to time. To be able to use offers more selectively in return, one might imagine putting a price on attention: one idea to be developed, for example, might be for users to sell their attention to direct marketers of product and service providers through a "personal 1-800 number." As one possible reaction to media advertising, this inverse mode of value added services would allow consumers to inform advertising companies of their interest in a telephone call and be rewarded for their attention on a monetary basis.

-"communication is desirable"

-"interactivity is good"

Interactivity is an optional added value

Inverse mode of added value service

The Future of Media Communication

The digitalisation of vast areas of media production, bundling, distribution and use, together with the development of the Internet, has contributed to the dissolution of previous limits to the media and the forms of communication associated with them. In their various manifestations spanning interpersonal and mass-media communication, professional and non-professional content production, and involving a variable yet cost-efficient number of communication participants, online media provide the user with extended and new communication offers. It is also to be expected, however, that online media will pervade daily life to an even greater extent than hitherto through the development of numerous wireless transmission possibilities. Against the background of increased diversity in the platforms, contexts and occasions for using online media, these will become increasingly crucial for media enterprises when it comes to decisions about offer and price discrimination models for audience and advertising markets.

Previous limits to media are being overcome

Cross-media and mutual reinforcement

The online offers of traditional media can be used especially to broaden their functions, motivating existing reader, listener or viewer groups to make additional use of the media offer online. The mass media in particular, with the reach they offer, can set incentives to Internet use. Yet also new – e.g. younger – customer groups can be introduced to traditional media through their online offers. This sort of cross-media offer serves the mutual reinforcement of various distribution channels, reception situations and user needs. Daily newspapers, for example, can react immediately to up-to-the-minute news in their online versions, thus countering the structural weakness of print media, which is to appear only once a day as an information source about the events of the previous day. However, these functional extensions may also lead to shifts in the competition structures of the media market. Radio and television, traditionally regarded as immediate sources of information for "breaking news," acquire new competitors. Even so, analyses of user behaviour in response to disaster or emergency reports show that the majority of people still switch on the radio or television first when trying to get information. These situations also reveal the strength of broadcasting for reaching large numbers of people simultaneously, whereas the Internet at times of great demand has difficulties managing such peaks in use.

Internet functions counter structural weakness of print media

The strength of broadcasting for emergency communication

Yet it is not only considered from the supply side but also from the user side that cross-media functional extensions permit greater choice in terms of the scope and depth of the media offer that is used. In addition, the diversity of access possibilities to the Internet – at the workplace, at home, and increasingly via wireless local networks in public spaces as well – facilitates the rapid pursuit of the contents one is interested in.

Media enterprises that joined forces with online specialists in business webs during the first phase of the market development of online media offers now integrate their online offer within existing organisational structures and pursue multiple-utilisation strategies with the aid of content management systems. Yet when it comes to developing innovative contents, for example for mobile personal receivers, media enterprises once more revert to the strategy of active partnership with new intermediaries.

Chances for media development

Predicting future media development is difficult, if not impossible, owing to the unclear technological advances, the dynamic, complex evolution of market structures and competition, as well as uncertainty regarding future user needs. The evolution of the long-discussed interactive television, for example, is thus currently taking an unexpected course, in particular under the influence of hybrid DVB-T/mobile telephony applications. The aim of describing facets of media and communication development is not, therefore, to make predictions but to pinpoint fundamental lines in the development of media-use.

Under the influence of digitalisation and the Internet, media enterprises can and should be in the vanguard of communication developments. For a start, the media are themselves network goods: their value increases with the number of users able to communicate about media contents in the process of social connectivity. Media enterprises can thus turn to account the advantages of the Internet network economy. Media companies also have strategically vital experiences for the Internet economy, such as versioning, the combination of distinct revenue sources, and above all the organisation of communities based around contents. Even users looking for a forum for their web logs or self-produced contents can find a target public in communities for specific media contents, in this way using the power of the media to bundle attention and in turn contributing to the competence of media enterprises in building up communities. New possibilities for media use are produced not least by the development of wireless transmission channels that allow for personal mobility without precluding access possibilities to the information and communication infrastructure. Mobile data communication options, wireless local Internet access and digital terrestrial broadcasting make three scenarios of media-user mobility possible: at home, at work and out and about.

Vertical integration and active partnership in business webs

Media are network goods

Media as organisers of communities

Personal mobility broadens media use

One example of the development opportunities for the media that take on new dimensions through the Internet is the possibility of using fictionality for brand management. Opportunities lie above all in the construction of brand myths. Brands can lose much of their mythology through practical use. This can be put down to product weaknesses or the lack of occasion to try out the communication myths of the media, as with the exhilarating cross-country drives of the adverts. However, the reasons for disillusionment may also be grounded in a realisation of one's own limitations, as occurs with the use of sport equipment. Yet the disappointment induced by use can be absorbed by the media if these apply the possibilities of virtuality as a central element of myth management. The BMW films available on the Internet as "branded content" are a clear example of this. The professional short films produced by BMW permit outstanding directors and actors to tell stories which skilfully incorporate the cars manufactured by BMW, not as an end in themselves but in the service of a story with a plot and a message that are the focus of attention. The myths created by the medium of film for the brand BMW in the Internet counter the myth-loss through use. Virtuality and the construction of fictional components of the branded offer can thus be consciously utilised as a formal element to counter the erosion of the brand myth. In this process media enterprises with their (Internet) competences may also offer their services to other industry branches, as a way of using development chances through the Internet.

Fictionality as an opportunity for development

Media as services for myth management

Even though there may be some substitution processes in the long term, traditional media and the Internet will reinforce one another. The central challenges in this process at present include the issue of copyright law in the face of developments in digital rights management and the question of consumer protection in the face of developments in commercial monopolisation. In these areas there is an increased need for policies to provide a framework for strategic business decisions. However, the growing diversity of use options offered by the Internet in its manifold aspects – in future also wireless and ubiquitous – provides media enterprises with a broad, dynamic space for innovation.

Regulatory challenges of digital rights management and consumer protection

Chapter 1   Changing Media

Diversification and Individualisation

The developments in the media in the course of the progressive digitalisation of media production, aggregation, distribution and reception constantly pose fresh challenges to all the players and participants involved in the processes of value-creation in the media economy. In the following chapter, the authors investigate some of the changes in business strategies that are taking place, the development of new distribution platforms for media contents, as well as the resulting changes in the conditions of representation and reception for media offers and the opportunities for innovative forms of contact and recipient integration.

In the first article, *Berthold Hass* describes the changes in business models produced by disintegration and reintegration. Disintegration leads to the opening up of new levels of freedom in the configuration of media products in terms of the way the information is put together, the arrangement of the characteristics of the media used, and the corresponding revenue model. Also to be expected, moreover, is a turning away from media-oriented forms of specialisation and a greater focus on specific information contents or customer groups.

Thomas Hess examines the changes to which this gives rise for media enterprises, discussing in particular the two formal options of multiple utilisation of contents and the individualisation of media products. *Hess* argues that individualisation is not just a matter of availability in time, but also the putting together of contents. Moreover, individualisation in the sense of the flexible compilation of product contents itself presupposes multiple utilisation. The direct integration of the customer into the production process and the multiple utilisation of customised contents demonstrate that cost leadership and price differentiation are no longer necessarily mutually exclusive as fundamental business strategies. Instead, in *Hess*'s opinion, the Internet for the first time provides media enterprises with the option of combining the two strategies.

Hardy Dreier describes multiple utilisation in the form of licensing and the changes in use-options for consumers. The new use-options opened up by digital products include, for example, the wider range of supplementary material available on data carriers through the bundling of offers. Furthermore, licensing makes it possible to increase the attention received by content, which is aired via various distribution channels both in the media and through the licence products that pervade everyday life. *Dreier* emphasises that licensing not only contributes to the financing of media productions but

Berthold Hass

Thomas Hess

Hardy Dreier

cooperation between production and marketing can also lead to a spreading of risks for the providers.

Jeffrey Funk

The mobile Internet as a disruptive technology and a new platform for contents, portals, traders and navigation services is the focus of the contribution by *Jeffrey Funk*, who describes current developments in the Japanese market and puts forward the thesis that the success of the mobile Internet in Japan is not based on distinctive cultural features but on having correctly identified the target group in conjunction with the right services and contents. *Funk* shows that the market leaders in the mobile Internet in Japan are different from those in the PC Internet.

John Pavlik

Taking newspapers to be the editor's medium and broadcasting to be the producer's medium, *John Pavlik* declares the Internet to be the journalist's medium. He describes the changes in storytelling as a consequence of on-line environments that allow for forms of contextualised journalism. New modalities include, for example, the 360-degree camera, hyperlinks, object-oriented multimedia, heightened recipient involvement and the customisation of contents.

Siegfried Frey

In his paper entitled "Spellbound by Images," *Siegfried Frey* looks into the influence of visual perception on the way people form impressions of one another. Fathoming the role played by nonverbal communication will prove essential if the human sciences are to make a contribution to an understanding of the process of communication.

Chapter 1.1

Disintegration and Reintegration in the Media Sector: How Business Models are Changing on Account of Digitalisation

Berthold Hass

> *In the information and entertainment industries, bits and atoms often are confused. Is the publisher of a book in the information delivery business (bits) or in the manufacturing business (atoms)? The historical answer is both, but that will change rapidly as information appliances become more ubiquitous and user friendly.*[1]

In the media economy more than virtually any other traditional sector, digitalisation and networking are leading to new challenges and deep-rooted structural changes. The reason for this is that the value proposition of media enterprises is itself information and thus immaterial. Improvements in information and communication technology, therefore, not only influence the organisation and management of media *enterprises*, but also exert a lasting effect in particular on the production, composition, distribution and consumption of media *products*.

An important – if not the most important – theme of the current changes in the media branch resides in the transition to the digital, non-physical production and distribution of information content: while traditionally information was unambiguously and firmly coupled to particular media, now one and the same content can be circulated through a variety of media configurations. This increasing separation of medium and information will here be referred to as *disintegration*.[2]

Disintegration as the separation of medium and information

This article investigates the repercussions of this disintegration of medium and content for the business models of media enterprises. With this aim in

---

1 Negroponte 1995, p. 13

2 Also to be found in the literature are the related concepts of dematerialisation (Quah 1996) or deconstruction (Schwartz 1998, pp. 33; Evans/Wurster 1997; O'Brien/Charron/Grimsditch 2000). The phenomenon also falls within the frame of reference of Rayport/Sviokla (1994), who discuss the disaggregation of a transaction's content from its context and from the infrastructure required for its production.

mind, Section 1.1.1 starts by examining more closely the phenomenon of disintegration. Section 1.1.2 presents a general scheme for business models, which serves as the basis for the analysis of the changes in the product architecture, revenue model and value structure then undertaken in Section 1.1.3.

1.1.1
Desintegration of Medium and Content

Dual character of media products

A specific feature of media products is their dual character: they consist of a combination of medium and information in the form of a good or service that can be marketed. The actual core utility is created by the information, yet this requires a medium as a "means of portraying or representing facts or contents capable of being communicated."[3] To this extent there is an important difference between the news to be transmitted (the information) and the transmitting signal (the medium). To adopt an image used by Barlow,[4] the information can be described as "wine" that is transported by means of "bottles" (the medium).

Analysis of the emergence of new media products in recent years shows that the essential effect of technological developments up until now has not been the creation of new content forms. Compaine thus established at an early stage:

Greater development in the media than the content

Changing information technologies are most important today in expanding accessibility to information. That is, the content of messages is not changing so much as the range of alternative conduits by which they can be processed and transmitted and the variety of formats in which they can be displayed.[5]

The common denominator of these new media possibilities can be understood to be the disintegration of medium and information: what was previously sold by means of specific, physical carrier-media can now also be transmitted through the universal medium of Internet; "atoms" are being replaced by "bits," as Negroponte puts it.[6]

---

3 Szyperski 1999, p. 5. For this and further possible conceptions of the concept "medium" see Faulstich 1998.
4 Barlow 1996
5 Compaine 1981, p. 135. For a similar account see also Shapiro/Varian 1999, p. 8
6 See Negroponte 1995, pp. 11

Considered from a historical perspective, the basis for the disintegration of information and medium is on the one hand telecommunication, which in the course of the 19th century facilitated the separation of channels of information and commerce through the non-physical transport of contents. In the mass media, however, this for a long time only affected the production stage: agencies delivered their news reports by telegraph to the newspapers, but these then delivered the contents physically in paper form to the final customers. In the next phase, the introduction of radio and television added new media of telecommunication, which altered the significance of the old media such as books and newspapers, but not fundamentally the process of value-creation.

Dimensions of disintegration

It was only with increasing digitalisation that this came about. Digitalisation broke up the fixed assignment of contents to specific media. The process of value-creation (production, editing, distribution) all takes place on an immaterial plane and is thus media-independent. At the same time, digital information permits the use of compression procedures and consequently the transmission of more extensive and varied contents.

These two dimensions of disintegration – non-physical information transport and digital data-processing – are illustrated in Figure 1.1-1 using the example of the marketing of music.

In the course of this process of disintegration, there has been a trend for the fixed coupling of information to a specific medium to be shifted further and further towards the customer. Newspapers, for example, were formerly produced using hot-metal setting procedures and were dependent upon the medium (see Figure 1.1-2). With the growing utilisation of information technologies in publishing from the 1970s onwards, texts were prepared, edited and structured increasingly independently of their media, but the distribution

Trend towards coupling information to the customer

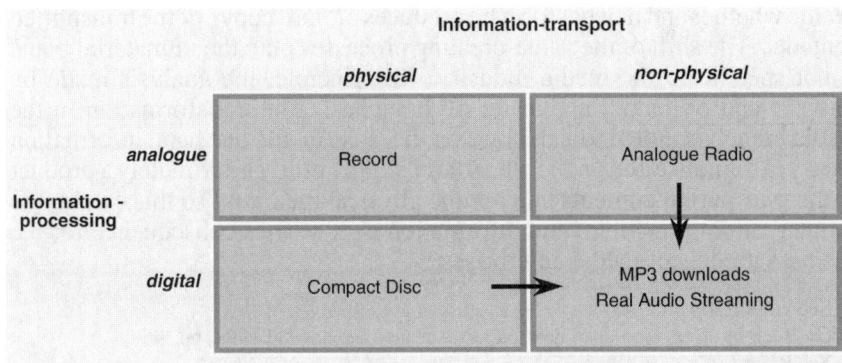

Fig. 1.1-1 Disintegration as exemplified by the music market (Hass, 2002, p. 83)

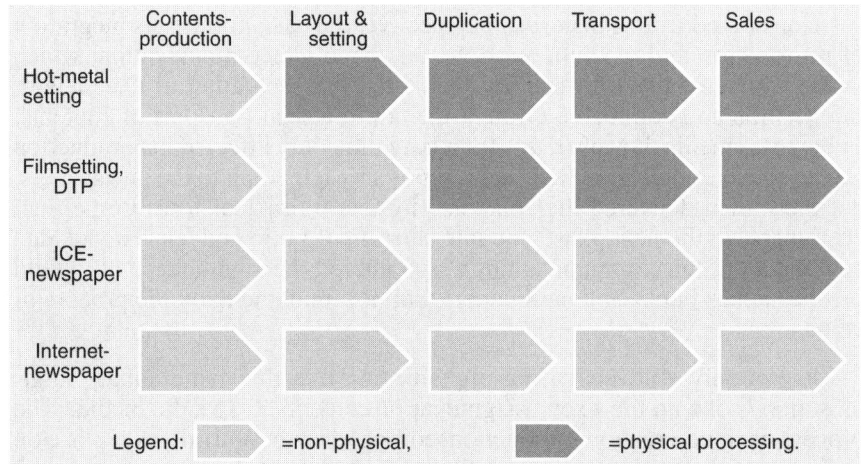

	Contents-production	Layout & setting	Duplication	Transport	Sales
Hot-metal setting					
Filmsetting, DTP					
ICE-newspaper					
Internet-newspaper					

Legend: =non-physical, =physical processing.

Fig. 1.1-2 Disintegration as exemplified by the newspaper market (Hass, 2002, p. 84)

continued to take place in physical form on paper.[7] To save distribution costs and time, it is today normal for the production of national newspapers to be spread over various sites (most obviously, for the customer, in the case of the "ICE-press" transmitted by fax to German Intercity Express trains and duplicated on board). Finally, the Internet has permitted a media-independent, disintegrated value chain from the news agency correspondent all the way through to the end customer.[8]

The possibility of disintegration is an essential element in the transition from the traditional "market place" to "market space."[9] The upshot is that the value chain becomes less and less physical, as it is up to the customer to decide whether and in what form he produces a "hard copy" of the transported contents. The shift of the value-creating processes onto the immaterial plane is not specific to the media industry. In principle, the analysis made by Rayport and Sviokla[10] applies to all branches. The transformation in the media branch is more radical, however, because on the one hand information is easy to digitalise and on the other the customer utility is ultimately a product of the transported contents and not the physical medium. To this extent, the disintegration of medium and information is of serious consequence for the business models of media enterprises.

Media-independent, disintegrated value chain

7 See von Prümmer 1998
8 On Internet offers similar to newspapers, see also Sennewald 1998, pp. 96
9 See Rayport/Sviokla 1994
10 Ibid.

1.1.2
Business Models as a Frame of Reference

Although business models play a crucial part in the development of viable strategies not only for media enterprises, scholarly discussion of the concept is still in its infancy.[11] Basically, a business model can be understood as an abstract description of the enterprise as a combination of production factors in the making and marketing of goods, with various definitions each spotlighting different of these aspects. The definition proffered by Mahadevan is: "A business model is a unique blend of three streams that are critical to the business. These include the value stream for the business partners and the buyers, the revenue stream, and the logistical stream. The *value stream* identifies the value proposition for the buyers, sellers, and the market makers and portals in an Internet context. The *revenue stream* is a plan for assuring revenue generation for the business. The *logistical stream* addresses various issues related to the design of the supply chain for the business."[12] Starting from Mahadevan's conception, three fundamental aspects of business models can be pinpointed:

- The product point of view brings the "value proposition" of the enterprise to the fore, i.e. the problem solution that the customer is offered. In marketing terms, one might speak of a *product architecture*, which it is the object of the product management to design.

- The revenue point of view considers the sources that go to make up the enterprise's revenue. The representation of the sources of revenue is termed a *revenue model* or revenue architecture.[13] This corresponds to the choice and segmentation of the market and the establishment of a pricing policy.

- The value-creation point of view analyses the way production is organised, dividing the enterprise into a sequence of production stages in the sense of a value chain internal to the firm or a business chain specific to the branch.[14] At issue here is the problem of shaping the *value structure* in terms of a theory of organisation.

Three fundamental aspects of business models

    The various forms of product architecture, revenue models and value structure relevant to media enterprises are briefly elucidated below.[15]

---

11 For an overview see Schoegel 2001, Stähler 2001, and Hass 2002.
12 Mahadevan 2000, p. 59 (my emphasis)
13 See ECC 2001, pp. 24, as well as Skiera/Lambrecht 2000
14 See Porter 1985, pp. 33
15 For an exhaustive account see Hass 2002.

Information as the core utility
of a media product

Quality and bundling of
information determine the
utility of a media product

Product architecture

Basically, the notion of product architecture denotes the design of the product that the supplier offers the customer.[16] For marketing, it is crucial to base the product definition not on material objects but the promise of utility.[17] This is especially valid in the media branch since media products, as already explained, have a dual character. From this perspective, it is the information that forms the core utility of a media product. To use the information, however, a medium is required. From this the media product – i.e. the combination of information and medium – is created as a generic product that can actually be traded.

Accordingly, it is on the one hand the type and scope of information and on the other the character of the medium used that in principle constitute the two dimensions of product architecture for media products. The utility derived from a media product depends in particular upon two factors: the quality of information (premium vs. commodity content) and the way it is bundled.

By contrast with the information transmitted, the medium is fundamentally just a means to an end, even though certain characteristics of the medium utilised may on occasion create an added value, as occurs with special booklovers' editions of books. Nonetheless, the nature of the medium does determine what information can in principle be transmitted and the forms in which it is represented (writing, fixed image, moving image, sound, etc.). The medium further determines the customer's use possibilities, especially with respect to the accessibility of the information and the comfort of access.

Revenue models

The notion of revenue refers in general to the payments made for the products put on the market.[18] In principle, there are three different revenue sources possible for media enterprises: the direct sale of the media products to customers, the sale of customer contacts (advertising), and the marketing of customer data that have been generated.[19] A special feature of the media branch is that advertising is not infrequently a more important source of revenue than the direct sale of media products to customers.

16 The concept of product architecture is borrowed from Timmers 1998.
17 See Kotler/Bliemel 1995, p. 659
18 See Plinke/Rese 2000, p. 700
19 See Skiera/Lambrecht 2000

The revenue from each source can be distinguished according to the form in which it is obtained. In terms of use-dependency, it is in general possible to differentiate between direct variable (e.g. pay-per-view TV) and direct fixed (e.g. pay-TV subscription) revenue forms.[20] In addition, there are further indirect revenue forms that do not involve a direct transaction but where fees are charged for the medium in question by collecting societies such as the German Copyright Society GEMA (*Society for Musical Performing and Mechanical Reproduction Rights*), a proportion of which is then distributed to the authors.

Distinguishing revenue sources

Value structure

The concepts of product architecture and revenue models refer first and foremost to the marketing side. The value structure, by contrast, designates the organisation of production within and between enterprises. For media products this in principle comprises three stages within the value chain: production, editing / bundling and distribution. In analysing value chains, two viewpoints can be differentiated: one vertical, i.e. looking along the flow of goods; the other horizontal, i.e. focusing upon connections between distinct value chains. The central parameters of the value structure are the level of vertical integration, the design of the various stages of trade from producer to final customer, and not least the degree to which the customer is integrated into the value chain.

1.1.3
Changes in Business Models Owing to Disintegration

With the threefold division of the business model into product architecture, revenue model and value structure, we now have a framework that can be used to sketch the fundamental changes that have occurred for the media branch through the disintegration of medium and information.

---

20 See ECC 2001, pp. 26

Product Architecture

Information

The basic need to position the information product in the market on the basis of its quality is unaffected by technological change. In many areas, however, technological progress causes a reduction not only in the marginal costs of information reproduction, but also in the fixed costs of producing the master copy. In the music branch, for example, modern digital technology today makes it possible even for amateurs to achieve well-nigh professional results. Very good results can likewise be attained in image-treatment, desk-top publishing and web design even with simple means. On the other hand, increasing possibilities frequently entail a rise in the demands of consumers too, as has happened with animations and animated sequences in feature films, as well as video games. Moreover, the fixed costs for creative work remain largely unaltered, as the activities of this production stage – unlike skilled craftwork in typesetting or animation – can hardly, if at all, be substituted by the use of technology.

Completely new perspectives are opened up by the greatly increased possibilities for customisation. By nature, the better a product is adapted to a customer's specific needs, the greater the utility the customer can derive from this product. Firstly, this includes customized offers, as made possible by personalisation: in this case users are given distinct information products that vary with the customer data available or explicitly expressed customer desires. Also conceivable, moreover, are context-dependent information offers, since one and the same person's information requirements can take a very different form depending upon the situation.

Yet personalised offers of this sort require adjustments in the value structure. Low-cost implementation is only possible if the content base is sufficiently classified and archived to make customer-specific queries relatively simple. Nonetheless, such operations are in principle possible through new information and communication technologies, making such strategies of variety in the new media notably easier to carry out than was previously the case.

An essential effect of the disintegration of physical media and information is the reduction of indivisibilities. The capacity of media such as paper or compact discs is either fixed or "step-variable" (e.g. 650 MB in the case of CDs). For non-physical distribution as through a server over the Internet, such capacity limitations only exist in the aggregate, through the registered server or network capacity, but not with respect to transactions with individual customers. This results in a clear reduction in economies of scope on a media level, which ceteris paribus should lead to unbundling.

Digitalisation opens up the market for amateurs

Increased utility through customisation

Reduction of indivisibilities

Medium

A key feature of new media is the increasing degree of freedom in the arrangement of the media characterisation.[21] Whereas properties of the medium such as interactivity, encryption, etc. used to be fixed, these characteristics have become a variable in the design of the new media: as the information is on principle digital, it is possible to market it in very different media forms.

Regarding the process of distribution, the trend towards disintegration can be seen to have brought about a transition to transmission media (often in conjunction with local storage, as with the downloading of contents from the Internet). From the provider's perspective, the advantages of this over carrier media reside above all in the lower marginal costs and the more rapid scalability, allowing potential economies of scale in media production to be exploited more swiftly. From the customer's point of view, advantages accrue through the greater utility often produced by increased topicality, the variety of information and the possibilities for interaction (particularly personalisation and communication in communities).

From carrier to transmission media

One factor in favour of carrier media, however, continues to be that they facilitate the enforcement of copyright law, because being physically bound to a carrier medium makes it more difficult to pass on information. This applies in particular to contents in analogue form such as printed newspapers and books. Yet even in the case of digital information, misuse can be prevented by tying rights of use to the physical carrier. This principle is applicable above all in the realm of software, where video games, for example, are designed in such a way that they can only be played if the corresponding CD-ROM is also available in the drive. However, such strategies only make sense if the retail price of the information is in proportion to the additional costs resulting from the physical as opposed to the non-physical sale. Along with production costs for the carrier medium, these also include the transaction costs at the stages of wholesale and retail trade and with the final customer.

Advantages of carrier media

Moreover, carrier media are also more significant when it comes to information contents with a high data volume, such as feature films, since given currently available bandwidths it is still relatively expensive to download them from the Internet. Here too, however, further growth in network capacity and/or greater data compression will increase the use of Internet, as is already happening with music files. In general, therefore, there will be a continued shift in emphasis towards transmission media in the sale of information. Yet this does not rule out the possibility of the customer storing

---

21 On characteristics and types of media, see in detail Hass 2002.

" **As a self-decoding medium paper is simple and convenient.** *"*

non-physically-acquired information on material carriers in accordance with his planned use or reuse or even for archiving purposes.

Paper continues to be important as a carrier medium

For the foreseeable future paper too will play a major role as a carrier medium. Yet this is less due to its nature as a physical medium per se than the simplicity and convenience of its use as a secondary medium. Paper is one of the self-decoding media that can be received without the further application of technology. Given its near-universal usability independent of technology, paper will continue to be important even once current restrictions on screen media in terms of reading comfort and display size or weight have been overcome.

Online media must create added value

It thus becomes clear that from a customer's viewpoint the transition from paper to media that require decoding such as online media only makes sense if it creates an added value that more than compensates for the disadvantages of the technology use it requires. The general advantages of media that require decoding reside in the much greater number of forms of representation they support (moving images, sound, etc.), as well as in additional functions in information-processing, such as search or possible hyperlink functions, etc.[22]

A further element of the concept of disintegration is that recipients increasingly choose not only their contents interactively but also the corresponding media type. The starting point here is generally transport via transmission media such as the Internet, allowing the customer to be reached virtually everywhere quickly, cheaply and individually. On the other hand, carrier media at one's "point of use" provide the user with advantages in terms of robustness, user-friendliness and often greater adaptability to forms of representation. A customer might first receive a certain piece of news in reduced form over his mobile telephone, for example, before then investigating further over his VDU and storing the contents. As a rule, however, extensive reading on the computer is (still) too uncomfortable, in which case the user may print certain contents and then read them in paper form. In this context, Groebel[23] cites the so-called "PSF" formula, according to which the concrete choice of a medium depends upon $personal$, $situational$ and $functional$ factors.[24] For the information provider, this gives rise to the challenge of keeping contents available in as media-neutral a form as possible in order to be able to meet customer needs for diverse media use, as illustrated in Figure 1.1-3.

"PSF" formula to determine the choice of a medium

---

22 See Baubin/Bruck 1996, pp. 140
23 Groebel 1997
24 On the thesis of multimedia use, see also Neumann-Bechstein 1996

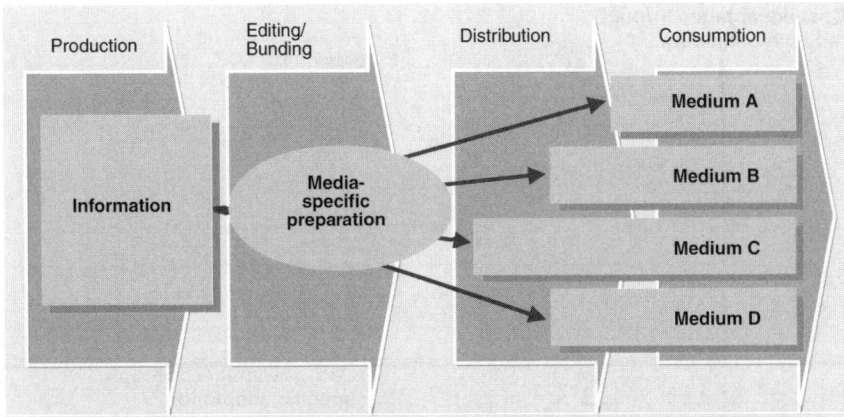

Fig. 1.1-3 Interactive media choice (Hass, 2002, p. 116)

However, the value of the resulting media product also depends upon how far the final format of the contents satisfies the specific nature of the medium of reception used. Transmitting a lengthy newspaper article unaltered over a mobile phone with a typical maximum representation capacity of 160 characters, for example, leads to a loss of utility. The capacity of the medium is in principle enough for an advert, but such use is more than uncomfortable and ultimately not suited to the medium.

By contrast with unmodified multiple utilisation of already-produced contents, however, the media-specific preparation of contents does result in additional costs. When choosing optimal product architecture, therefore, there is a trade-off between optimal multiple utilisation on the one hand and optimal adaptation of the information to specific media on the other (Figure 1.1-4).

Compared with the media-specific production of contents, the multiple, cross-media utilisation of information results in lower costs on account of economies of scope. However, a standardised product has use disadvantages in that the contents are not adapted to the specific features of particular media and the devices they involve. These disadvantages can be partially circumvented by a subsequent reworking of the content, as when a newspaper article is shortened for mobile-phone use. Even so, utility still falls short of media-specific content-production, which even at the production stage facilitates an optimal adaptation of the contents to the medium concerned. When production is completely specific to the media form, however, economies of scope can hardly be attained, so cost disadvantages ensue.

Additional costs through
media-specific preparation

Economies of scope of
multiple utilisation

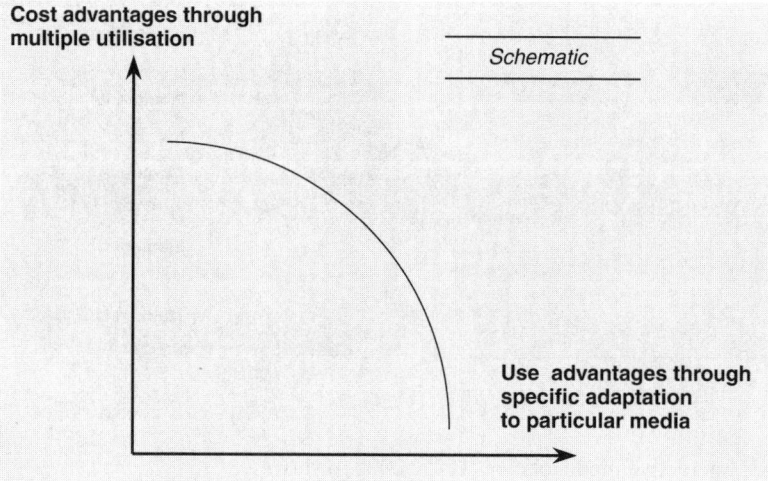

Fig. 1.1-4 Trade-off between cross-media multiple utilisation and media-specific adaption

Ultimately, optimal product architecture depends upon how high the adaptation costs are and what utility can be generated by media-specific adaptation in each case. The adaptation costs within one and the same representational format, e.g. drawing or fixed image, are generally lower, whereas modification across distinct formats is highly complex. As a result, the potential for the multiple utilisation of contents within one representational format is much greater than between different representational formats.

Revenue models

The search for viable
revenue models

The search for viable revenue models is at present one of the most difficult tasks faced by media enterprises, as the characteristics of new media and especially the Internet are producing changes in the competition for media products. The rise in competition is due in particular to the even lower marginal costs entailed by non-physical distribution, the increased number of providers on account of globalisation, as well as the tendency towards greater market transparency. Yet opportunities for designing innovative revenue models are also arising.

No One Would Pay for it? Web Content as Inferior Goods

Hsiang Iris Chyi

The economic concept of an "inferior good" refers to a good for which an increase in income leads to a decrease in consumption, ceteris paribus.

In a focus group study of the economic nature of online news and the feasibility of the subscription model for news-oriented websites, none of the participants – overseas students at the Chinese University of Hong Kong – showed any intent to pay for online news, even though most of them ranked the Internet as their no. 1 information source. Do these findings reveal anything about the economic nature of online news? The focus group participants' descriptions of their use, perceptions and purchasing intent regarding online news seemed to match – to a certain extent – some of the traits characteristic of inferior goods.

First, inferior goods often serve as replacements for normal goods. Most participants said they relied more on offline media such as TV, newspapers and magazines back home. After coming to Hong Kong, the Internet became the best alternative information source for news from home because of its accessibility – just as people consume instant noodles when a balanced meal is not available.

Second, compared with normal goods, inferior goods are often perceived as of lesser quality. Some participants said online news was not as good as print newspapers for the lack of in-depth information. But the overall "lesser quality" perception does not mean that inferior goods have no strengths over normal goods. For instance, many people find instant noodles convenient and accessible, just like online news.

Third, inferior goods have to be very inexpensive when compared with their normal counterparts. This may explain why users are so reluctant to pay for online news. While many other news media – TV, print newspapers, magazines – offer news either for free or at a comparable price, online news services would easily seem overpriced in users' minds once any subscription scheme were adopted. To get a better understanding of online news economics, further investigations should follow up on these findings in a systematic way.

Hsiang Iris Chyi is Professor at the School of Journalism and Communication of the Chinese University of Hong Kong.

Online news has the characteristics of inferior goods

Revenue sources

The classic revenue structure of media enterprises as a mixture of advertising revenue and revenue from the direct sale of media products was on the one hand a consequence of the capacity of information to generate attention. On the other hand, this mixture was also largely an outcome of the technological features of the media concerned, since media characterisation has repercussions both for the cost structure and in particular for possibilities of enforcing copyright law. In future, new technological possibilities will produce changes in the significance of the revenue sources constituted by the media product, customer contact and customer information.

Lower complexity with direct
marketing of media products

The direct marketing of media products to the customer has the advantage of being less complex than the triadic exchange involving customer contacts and customer information. However, this way of earning revenue often founders on account of prohibitive transaction costs, in particular the costs of initiation, administration and copyright protection.

New information and communication technologies generally reduce the costs for a particular transaction. This comes to light especially in the initiation costs, where the possibilities for seeking and processing digital information as well as interactive information offers considerably diminish search costs. Cost reductions likewise occur in administration, because new technologies facilitate both the billing of customers and encryption as protection against misuse. Especially when it comes to billing, further possibilities arise through price differentiation given appropriate knowledge of the customer through interactive media.[25] In principle, the financial settlement of small sums should be made easier in the form of micropayments, even though – despite the general technical possibilities – no such payment system has hitherto been able to establish itself on the market.[26]

In general, therefore, the opportunities for direct marketing increase on account of the lower marginal costs of production and reduced transaction costs. Even in future, however, it will only be possible to market media products themselves if the gross utility of the information is sufficiently high for the customer. This applies especially to exclusive, time-sensitive and personalised contents. In terms of targeted information, the model here is the much-cited *Wall Street Journal Interactive Edition*. Conversely, where there is very valuable information (e.g. studies), there is the danger of product piracy, which in turn must be taken into account in the context of the product architecture.

25 See Varian 1996
26 On payment procedures in the Internet see for example Henkel 2001.

The increase in information offers and their greater accessibility also influence customer contacts as a revenue source. Attention itself is a scarce resource, for which media enterprises compete by making suitable offers. This competition is tending to rise as improved information and communication technology increases capacities for information transmission both in qualitative and above all quantitative terms, making information more easily accessible.[27] As the range of information produced is also growing, moreover, the overall offer of available information is on the rise. If the time spent using media does not increase proportionally, the competition among information-providers will necessarily go up and attention will become progressively more fragmented.

However, new media are often better suited for mediating contacts.[28] On the one hand, if the appropriate customer data are available, advertising contents can be personalised relatively cheaply in terms of one-to-one marketing, increasing the accuracy with which the customer is targeted by the advert message.[29] Ideally the media user actually comes to perceive such a message as "consumer information" and no longer as advertising.[30] On the other hand, the relevant link in the hypertext can shorten the path from the advertisement to the point of sale (i.e. the online shop) to the click of a mouse, thus increasing the probability of a transaction.

Furthermore, Internet-based forms of advertising are not only more effective but also more efficient, as the link between the advert and the transaction allows the effect of the advert to be measured more accurately. This also makes it possible to go from a fixed revenue form to one dependent on success (i.e. commission-based). The media enterprise thereby moves towards a role as a trade mediator, often making it difficult to differentiate between a content-oriented media provider and a transaction-based e-commerce concern.

For many content providers in the Internet, customer contacts are frequently the only source of revenue, for example because their information is unsuitable for direct marketing to the recipients. Yet the competition for available advertising budgets is relatively intense. In addition, media agencies prefer large web sites so as not to fragment their advertising expenditure excessively. As, moreover, the attention of Internet users is distributed rather unevenly – just a few sites such as those of portals, search engines or well-known print and radio brands have a disproportionate number of users, while the remaining attention is severely fragmented – further consolidation is to be expected in the sphere of advert-based information offers. This will apply

> Additional fragmentation of the scarce resource of attention

> One-to-one marketing as "consumer information"

---

27 See Shapiro/Varian 1999, p. 9
28 See for example Bruck/Selhofer 1996; Wamser 2000
29 See Shafer 2001
30 See Scheirer et al. 2000b, p. 10

particularly once the available technological possibilities of new media can be transmuted more effectively into advertising success.

Revenue forms

The classic revenue forms in the media sector were not only a product of marketing and in particular pricing considerations, but also a result of limited technological possibilities. New media have at least partially overcome these restrictions. Direct revenue forms are altered above all by the easier measurability of content-use. In the case of indirect revenue forms, moreover, changes in the possibilities for protecting copyrights should be taken into account.

New media make content-use easier to measure

An essential feature of new media is the increasing interaction between transmitter and receiver. Such return channels permit not only a choice of contents specific to the user, but also easier measurement of information use. Variable revenue forms thereby become viable even for media products or customer contacts where hitherto only fixed revenue forms have been possible.

While direct revenue forms have always been usual for carrier media, such revenue models have only recently become possible for transmission media. For a long time it was not technically feasible, for example, to guarantee exclusivity or to bill customers according to time of use. Inventions in the field are making such revenue forms at least technically feasible. An example of this is one of the developments in the sphere of television, where coding has permitted the exclusion of recipients who are unwilling to pay and thus facilitated first subscription pay-TV and now also pay-per-view offers.

Use-dependent revenue forms for transmission media too

Accordingly, use-dependent revenue forms are in principle also conceivable in the future for music or video games, for example, provided that there is the requisite bandwidth for such contents to be transmitted and that the transaction costs for such billing procedures sink enough to be economically viable even for lower-value contents such as feature films.[31]

---

31 The application service provider *Yummy Interactive* is already offering a one-day licence for video games, which could serve as a foundation for a time-based price model. See Patrizio 2000

> **Fixed prices are often preferred due to 'mental' transaction costs.**

The example of television also shows, however, that technological feasibility in itself says nothing about the economic rationality of a particular business model, as in the television market advertising-based free-TV continues to be widespread. In analysing the advantages of particular forms, the relevant information contents and their characteristics are especially worthy of investigation.[32]

Fixed revenue forms are favoured above all by the transaction costs that continue to exist. From a technological perspective, these transaction costs could sink considerably once electronic payment procedures have also gained acceptance for small and very small sums. Alongside monetary costs, however, non-monetary costs for the information-processing must also be taken into account. These transaction costs are incurred especially in decision-making, i.e. the question of whether a transaction is to be realised in the first place (as with Pay-per-View).[33] To avoid such costs, users frequently prefer fixed revenue forms. Such a fixed fee further has an insurance effect in that uncertain variable expenses are replaced by a secure fixed sum, and one's expenditure thus has an upper limit from the outset. As well as such transaction-cost argumentation, private customers in particular seem to overestimate how much they actually use an offer, which also contributes to the continued significance of fixed revenue forms. New media thus make variable, use-dependent charges possible, but in many cases consumers still prefer fixed prices due to "mental transaction costs" and their aversion to variable bills.[34]

User preference for fixed revenue forms

From a longer-term perspective, however, it is perfectly possible that even here there may be changes in behaviour. This seems all the more plausible since in the mobile field such revenue forms are not only easier on account of the simpler billing procedures permitted by the technology, but are already common and accepted by customers.[35] Via the circuitous route of mobile contents, therefore, it is possible that in the long term there will increasingly be use-dependent pricing for the Internet and digital radio as well.

Long-term acceptance of variable revenue forms is likely

In the case of customer contact as a source of revenue too, the new media make variable revenue forms more easy to implement than has been the case with previously prevalent advertising forms. The billing is now done according to the effect achieved by the advertisement.[36] To determine how prices are graded, the following criteria are conceivable:

---

32 An analysis of the economic rationality of various business models, specifically in the sphere of television, is to be found in Dietl/Franck 2000.

33 See Fishburn/Odlyzko/Siders 1997

34 See Cohen 2000

35 Nevertheless, even with mobile contents revenue problems still exist. See Brooks et al. 2001

36 See Scheirer et al. 2000b, p. 9

"Pay per click"

"Pay per sale"

- contacts actually established (measured, for example, in clicks on the web page of the company advertising, also known as "pay per lead" or "pay per click");

- proportional participation in the transactions actually realised (commission or "pay per sale").

Such forms of advertising raise the efficiency of direct marketing, as the transaction-seeker only pays for the successful initiation of a contact, reducing the risk involved. This "affiliate marketing" has spread in the Internet particularly in the form of partner programmes.[37]

The need for indirect revenue forms such as copyright society fees has its historical roots in the problem of effectively implementing copyright law for information. As shown by *Napster* and its successors, the new media in principle lead to increased opportunities for product piracy, as digital technology permits the production of perfect copies. At the same time, however, there is also an increase in the technological possibilities for ascertaining the misuse of information or preventing it from the outset with the appropriate encryption.[38]

Optimal protection of copyright?

The net effect of these two opposed developments is not easy to assess. Yet the question of optimal encryption is increasingly becoming a part of the architecture, so in this respect the significance of indirect revenue forms could tend to decrease: whereas for the old media the effective protection of copyrights was often virtually impossible in purely technical terms, it is now up to the author himself to decide what security measures he takes to maximise the realised value of his information contents.

Value structure

The use of new information and communication technology not only permits new forms of organisation but also alters the tasks to be dealt with by the organisation.[39] This applies in particular to the media branch, as in principle the whole process of value-creation and purchasing can be digitalised.

Vertical value structure

Integrating the customer into the value chain

Like other sectors, the media sector has developed fundamental possibilities for reducing vertical integration and eliminating marketing stages. The in-

---

37 See also ECC 2001, p. 169
38 See Detering 2001, pp. 89
39 See Picot/Hass 2002

creasing integration of the customer into the value chain plays a greater role in the media industry than in other industries.

Possibilities for reducing vertical integration are arising in particular at the stage of distribution. Whereas before – in the newspaper industry, for example – the reproduction and distribution took place internally, with disintegrated media these activities can be outsourced, especially since media enterprises lack the competence and the telecommunications infrastructure needed for the non-physical sale of contents. Instead, network-like structures can be seen to be emerging, characterised by the close interconnection of the individual players.[40] This is especially due to the system character of new media. This system character calls for standards that can only be successfully imposed if there is a synchronous marketing of contents and the user-technology required by this.

Reduction of vertical integration at the distribution stage

In contrast to this partial trend towards "marketisation," one can also observe processes of concentration with which media enterprises try to cover several stages of the value chain. This is less for organisational reasons than as a measure to diversify their market and competence portfolio in what is a highly uncertain environment, especially as far as the attractiveness of the individual stages of the value chain is concerned.[41] Nonetheless, this phenomenon is characteristic of an experimental phase within media development. Accordingly, increased consolidation can be expected to bring in its wake a tendency to reduce vertical integration through a greater focus on core competencies.

The economic rationality of classical marketing structures resides in the saving on the transaction costs that would be produced by direct marketing. New information and communication technologies reduce the costs of initiation, agreement, etc., resulting in principle in the possibility of disintermediation, i.e. the elimination of intermediary stages. This applies to media products in particular, as the immateriality of information means the whole purchasing process can be carried out non-physically. In this way, the classic trade functions such as storage and transport cease to be valid, as illustrated in Figure 1.1-5 by the example of the music market.

In classical marketing, the customer buys a compact disc from a trader. With music-on-demand, this middleman is eliminated.

Also conceivable in principle is direct marketing from the artist to the consumer. In this case the record company (major) is also bypassed. Perhaps the best-known example of such a procedure was the attempt by the musician *Prince* to sell one of his albums directly to the customer.[42] Yet the failure

Direct marketing as disintermediation becomes an option

40 See Middelhoff 1998, p. 57
41 See Middelhoff 1997, p. 419
42 See Cavanaugh 1998

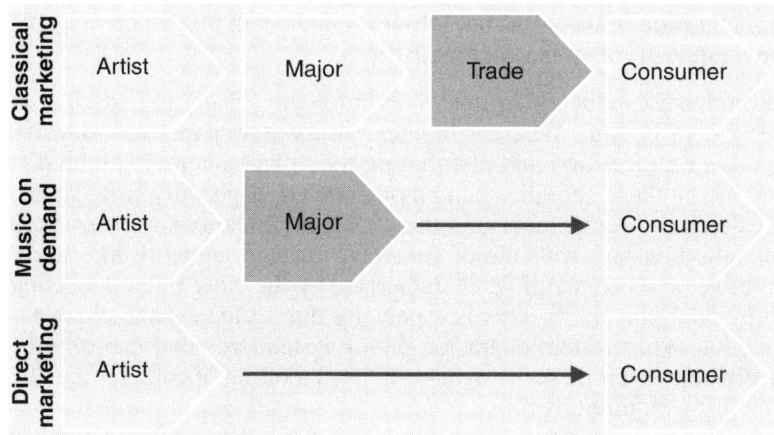

| | Artist | Major | Trade | Consumer |

Fig. 1.1-5 Disintegration as illustrated by the music market (following Buhse and Thiem, 2000, p. 183)

of this experiment shows that such extreme disintermediation is unlikely to catch on because editing/bundling and especially the marketing of contents continue to be activities that create utility for the customer and are rewarded accordingly.

Even so, such direct marketing represents an alternative for artists who do not have a contract with a record concern. To create the contact between the consumer and the artist, however, an intermediary in the form of a specialised music portal such as *BeSonic.com* is required. Such providers are a central point of reference for interested musicians and customers alike, further offering additional research functions that facilitate the search for a particular musical style.

Integration of the customer through the return channel

A key feature of the new media is the great increase in possibilities for interaction between information-providers and consumers. This is made possible by the transition from carrier media to transmission media with a return channel. This technical infrastructure means that consumers can be integrated into the value chain to a much greater extent than previously, changing the character of media products.[43] This then raises the question of the optimal integration not only of those companies before and after them in the value chain but also the customer.[44] With the new media, the integration of the customer can in principle take place at any stage of the value chain.

The most important factor here is still the interaction with the customer at

43 See Smith/Bailey/Brynjolfsson 2000, p. 124
44 See Hardt 1996, pp. 67

the level of editing/bundling, i.e. the selection of contents. Unlike the classical media, however, new technologies now permit strategies for customisation and above all personalisation. If there is ample information available to the media enterprise, the customer is supplied with a tailor-made media product on the basis of his user profile. If the customer's information need is more focused, by contrast, a research solution is plausible whereby the consumer uses the appropriate search technology to filter out contents that interest him from the content basis.

Interaction possibilities also allow for the customer to be integrated within the production stage. The consumer is thus turned into a producer of contents. This is exemplified most strikingly by the virtual communities in the Internet, where the contents are in large measure user-generated, with the media enterprise playing what is essentially the role of a moderator (editing/bundling stage).[45] Yet production activity on the part of customers is now even found in journalistic offers or in the form of discussion forums based on professionally produced contents.[46] A further example are the extensions of commercial video games produced by private individuals using the appropriate software.

The consumer as producer of contents

At the distribution stage, customer activity is frequently less desirable, as with the unauthorised transfer of information contents via peer-to-peer file-sharing systems such as *Napster* and its successors.[47] Yet here too business models are conceivable that make long-term sense once the issue of copyrights has been satisfactorily resolved for providers and customers alike.

Horizontal Value Structure

Classic media enterprises in principle focused upon individual carrier and transmission media.[48] This was because of the differences between the individual stages of distinct value chains. Moreover, the control of individual media in production and distribution was a highly specific matter of major strategic import.

Convergence of previously separate segments of the media-contents industry

The increasing use of information and communication technology is tending to reduce the differences between distinct media, as the production, editing and distribution now take place partly or wholly digitally. In technical terms, this disintegration has led to a convergence of formerly separate segments of the media-contents industry. The appropriate data integration thus makes it theoretically possible for contents of different representational

---

45 See Armstrong/Hagel 1995
46 See anon 1999
47 See anon 2000 and Scheirer et al. 2000a
48 See O'Brien/Charron/Grimsditch 2000

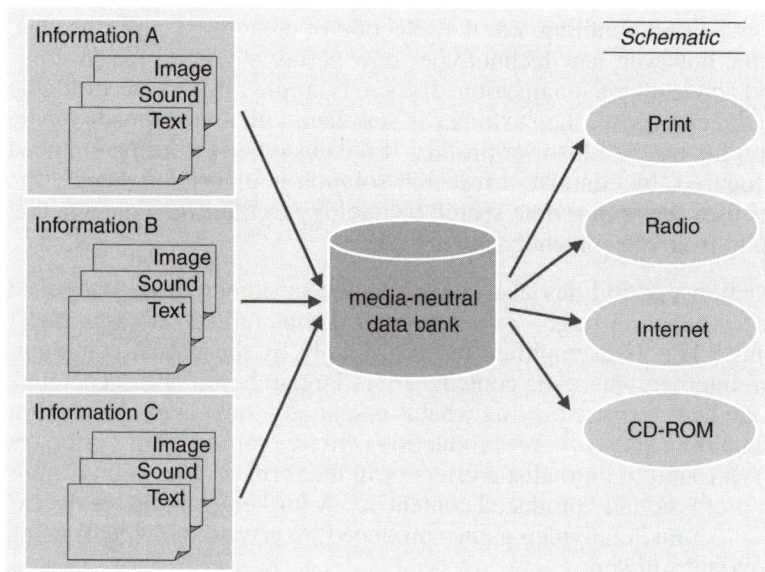

Fig. 1.1-6 Content management and media-neutral data storage (following Schumann and Hess, 2000, p. 117)

formats to be processed in the same way using standardised data types, as shown in Figure 1.1-6.

Convergence of this order gives rise to potentials for synergy across various media. Instead of the focus being upon particular media and the corresponding representational formats, the orientation of media enterprises shifts to contents and target groups.[49]

Focus upon contents and/or target groups

However, such strategies are not easy to implement, because even with media-neutral production the differences between media do not disappear for the consumer. As explained before, this results in a trade-off between the gains in efficiency of media-neutral multiple utilisation and the gains in utility of media-specific production and preparation of contents.

As well as such horizontal network strategies at the level of media technology, content-driven cross-media strategies are also of significance. Unlike the technology-driven strategy, the point is not to achieve cost advantages through the use of a variety of distribution media, but rather to maximise the value of a particular format by using the optimal medium of distribution in

Cross-media strategies maximise the value of formats

49 See ibid.

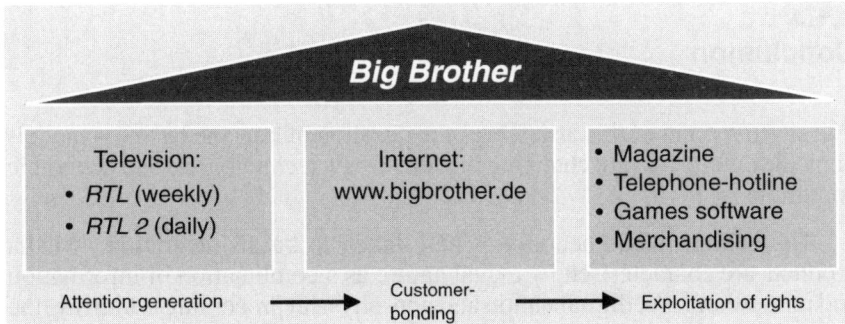

Fig. 1.1-7 Cross-media strategies, as exemplified by Big Brother (Hass, 2002, p. 155)

each case.[50] An example of such a strategy was the marketing for the reality soap *Big Brother,* as illustrated in Figure 1.1-7.

The starting point was the generation of attention to get the content-format known and talked about, in turn giving rise to the network effects of information consumption. Television is the most suitable means for attracting such attention on account of its reach and its synchronous, simultaneous utilisation by a large number of users.

For especially interested recipients, the Internet represented a means of satisfying additional, more fragmented information needs. Its asynchronous character further provided the Internet with possibilities for offering new contents outside the fixed broadcasting times.

The real commercial exploitation of the contents so created – i.e. *Big Brother* as a brand – then ensued through a magazine, a telephone hotline, and complementary products of a licensing and merchandising nature.

Exploiting the value of a brand

The network strategy thus allowed the specific features of diverse media forms to be optimally used in order first to create a brand and then turn its value to full account.

50 See Reinhard-Karlmann 2000

1.1.4
Conclusion

The starting point of this article was the question of how the business models of media enterprises are changing in today's new technological and economic conditions.

Disintegration as a moment of change in digital media

The central phenomenon was here taken to be disintegration. Media products are characterised by a dual nature as a combination of information and its medium. Yet digitalisation and non-physical processing is blurring the formerly fixed assignment of particular information contents to a particular medium. In the course of this development, specific media are in general losing in significance, while the typical features of information (such as non-rivalry and economies of scale) are coming more and more to the fore.

New levels of freedom in the configuration of media products and organisation

Disintegration is opening up new levels of freedom in the configuration of media products, be this in the compilation of the information, the arrangement of the characteristics of the medium used, or the corresponding revenue model. Ideally, the combination of information and its medium should adapt to the context in such a way as to produce an optimal product bundle for the customer. Such a focus on the recipient makes it possible to produce tailor-made premium content with an added value that should in turn be reflected in a higher willingness to pay on the part of the customer. This strategy of differentiation is thus an effective way of coping with the pressure of competition resulting from the availability of free contents.

The reformulation of media products makes it vital for media enterprises to adjust the way they are organised accordingly. In general a move away from media-oriented forms of specialisation and towards a focus on particular information contents or customer groups can be expected. In terms of organisation, therefore, there will be an uncoupling of content providers from specific media.

As has become clear in the course of this article, technological developments are leading to lasting changes in the management of media enterprises. Yet many media concerns are having trouble building successful businesses from the underlying potential of the new media. The reason for this is frequently that the business model applied is inconsistent in terms of the formal parameters of the product architecture, revenue model and value structure. In this respect, the media branch still finds itself in a phase of experimentation with new media and innovative business models.

Chapter 1.2

Media Companies between Multiple Utilisation and Individualisation: an Analysis for Static Contents

Thomas Hess

The Internet poses various challenges for media enterprises, both internally and regarding their position in the value chain of their branch.[1] The new medium makes it possible to integrate various medium types (such as text, image, audio and video), new services (e.g. in support of communication), and offers in several media (e.g. television and Internet). New sources of revenue emerge (for instance by directing recipients to e-commerce providers), while others, such as the retail sale of contents in the music industry, are problematic. Within the value chains, the role of intermediaries such as the traditional publisher has been especially called into question. The integration of the formerly separate net products of the media, telecommunications and software industries has been another theme in recent discussions. In general, two especially important thematic fields can be identified: multiple utilisation and individualisation. There is scarcely a media company that in the last few years has not attempted to utilise existing contents in various products by means of a media-neutral databank, albeit with varying degrees of success. Another attraction is doubtless to reduce the target groups of information offers and thus in the end increase the product utility for the customer. Many information providers therefore give customers the option of specifying their personal preferences for particular subject fields, which then flow into the production of the contents. Not all are successful however, and some have already reduced such offers again. Although these two phenomena have been discussed for several years now, the discussion has so far proved in many respects fragmentary. The goal of the following article is to give an overview of the current state of the discussion, focusing more on an economic assessment of the new technology and less on questions of technical implementation. The focus is on static contents, i.e. text and image information. Consequently, it is the print sector, i.e. newspapers, magazines, books and the online-utilisation of corresponding static contents, that will here assume greatest significance. In addition, examples from other segments of the media branch will also be drawn upon. The two themes of

Central challenges for media enterprises

1 See Hess 2002

multiple utilisation and individualisation will first be looked at separately. Along with a short summary, the article concludes with an analysis of the interaction between the two issues.

1.2.1
Multiple Utilisation of Contents

Idea

The development of a media product can traditionally be broken down into three stages.[2] In the first stage the original contents, e.g. text, images, videos or pieces of music, are produced. In the second stage these contents are packaged into products ready for the market. For example, various pieces of music are combined on a CD; articles and advertisements are bundled up into an edition of a daily newspaper; or a range of different types of media go to create a multimedia CD. Put together in this way, such products serve as the starting point for the third production stage. Not until the third stage does the distribution of the contents to the recipient take place, be it through conventional print, through data carriers such as CDs, over the radio, or through the Internet. Typically,[3] in the print industry over 50% of the costs are incurred in the first two stages – in the radio sector it is over 90% – and thus independently of the quantity distributed. This in turn leads to the progressive reduction of unit cost characteristic of the media industry, which is known as the "first-copy cost" effect.[4] In other words, media concerns must take special pains to utilise contents repeatedly in the second production stage or to market products repeatedly in the third production stage.

First-copy cost effect

A variety of examples of the multiple utilisation of products can be found in the media industry. The utilisation chains for films are exemplary.[5] A film is often first shown in cinemas, then sold or rented as a video film, and finally shown on pay-TV and regular TV. In this way it is possible to maximise the proceeds from a film, especially through a consistent focus on the variations in the recipients' willingness to pay. A typical utilisation chain can also be found in the book segment. A novel is frequently first offered in a hardcover version, then as a paperback, and finally in an anthology. Here too, the sequence of the utilisation chain corresponds to the potential for revenue. It is less common, however, to come across the multiple utilisation of contents,

Utilisation chains in the media sector

2 See Schumann/Hess 2000, p. 9
3 Ibid., p. 21
4 See Shapiro/Varian 1999, p. 20; Wirtz 2001, p. 26
5 See ECC 2001 p. 56

i.e. the use of already created contents in several products.[6] It is true that regional newspapers often receive the transregional section from a central editorial office or from another publisher. Also, on CDs songs are frequently put together in different combinations. However, this multiple utilisation always remains restricted to one medium or to few contents.

If one considers the new opportunities arising from digitalisation and networking it seems reasonable to assume that the possibilities for multiple utilisation will tend to increase. From a production-oriented view, it is to be expected that the costs for further use are slight once the contents are available in digital form. In addition, a trend towards product integration across various media can also be recognised from a sales-oriented perspective. In terms of the individual product, more and more information providers are going over to no longer providing isolated offers for individual media, but combining traditional offers from print or radio with Internet offers suitable for specific target groups. Thus, many newspaper and magazine publishers, for instance, coordinate their print and online offers by providing further information in the Internet to supplement the static print content (for example through archives, lavish tables, links, or just access to classified ads). Newspaper publishers especially are thus reacting to the erosion of their customer basis among 14-29 year-old consumers. In like fashion, television stations offer in the Internet training for quiz shows or participation in soap operas. This very combination of various media on the product side makes a multiple utilisation of content on the production side very important. This trend will become even greater if media concerns switch more vigorously from making a product-oriented offer to making a customer-oriented offer. Here too, the multiple utilisation of contents seems to suggest itself.

Product integration across various media

It should be further pointed out that the multiple utilisation of components has already been under discussion in at least two other industries for some time now. In particular, the Volkswagen company was the first provider to realise clear synergy potential through the deliberate multiple utilisation of parts above and beyond the boundaries of make.[7] Other manufacturers such as Daimler-Chrysler are in the process of following this example. In the software industry too, the multiple utilisation of modules has been intensively discussed for years.[8] It is still unclear, however, whether the increase in efficiency hoped for at first will actually end up being achieved.

Increased efficiency through modularisation

6 See Wirtz 2001a, p. 503
7 See Piëch 2000
8 See Turowski 2001

Technical options for multiple utilisation

With regard to the multiple utilisation of contents, two development stages can be distinguished. Where the multiple utilisation is limited to one medium, efficient, specialised databanks have long since become available, in which content (of any kind) can be stored or easily looked for.[9] At issue here are usually not object-oriented databanks, but rather object-relational ones.

In the context of the above-described requirements for multiple utilisation in various products and/or media, however, media databanks are now restricted to a very narrow area of application. Of greater significance is use-neutral and modularised storage. An aid for static contents, especially for text, that is frequently discussed at present is the so-called mark-up language XML (Extensible Markup Language). XML[10] has its historical and technical roots in the Standard Generalised Markup Language (SGML). XML forms a subset of SGML and is suitable especially for the Web. As with HTML, text elements in XML documents are characterised by so-called tags. Tags can also be nested within one another and in this way hierarchically structure the document. Unlike with HTML, the number of the elements and attributes is not fixed, but can instead – decisively in this context – be bindingly determined for a class of documents in the form of a Document Type Definition (DTD). In addition, a DTD also allows the hierarchical dismantling of the contents in the module. XML documents are representationally neutral, i.e. the representation of the contents is not determined by the XML mark-up. Style sheet languages are used to achieve a representation suitable for human addressees in a particular medium. With these, representations can be derived from the XML structures in rule-based form. This illustrates a central concept of XML: the division between data and output format. An example of a style sheet description language is the Extensible Stylesheet Language (XSL), which has now come to replace the W3C standard as the standard for the conversion from XML to HTML (and other formats structured by tags). Figure 1.2-1 shows the interplay of DTD and style sheet language in a schematic overview. It should be further pointed out that XML is especially suited for text-based contents. All other media types can be integrated, but not modularised.

For editing XML documents there are special XML editors that take special account of the specifics of XML, unlike simple text editors or word processors. XML-specific practicalities include, for example, structure controls, support in the choosing of elements (i.e. the display of the elements and attributes admitted in the context), and various document views (flow text, source code, tree structure). Furthermore, the structure editors partly

Use-neutral storage with XML

Separation of data and output format

---

9 See Merten/Grauer 1999, pp. 51-67
10 For an overview see Tolksdorf 1999

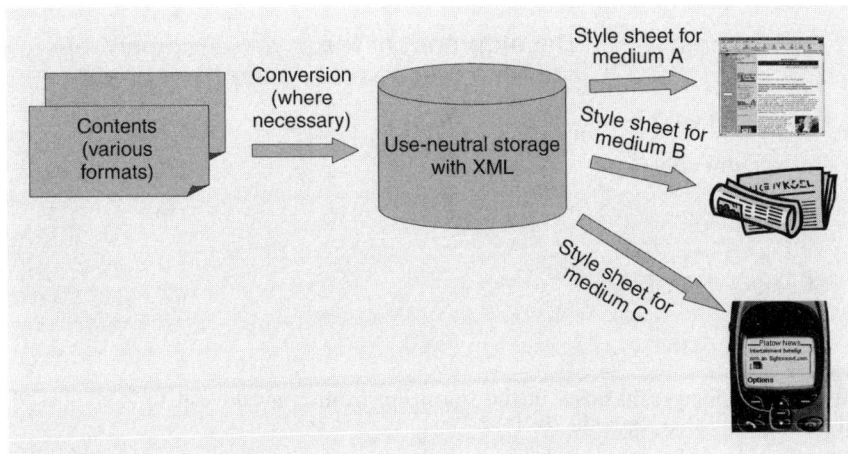

Fig. 1.2-1 The use of XML for the multiple utilisation of contents

support the development of DTDs. Tools of this kind offer the user, as a rule, a graphic surface in which the hierarchical structures can be displayed as attributed trees and manipulated. Saving XML documents can be done with (text) files as well as with special databank management systems.

To clarify the possible uses of XML in the context of the multiple utilisation of contents, the fundamental concept of XML can be elucidated with the example of a pilot project that was carried out as early as 1999.[11] Up until this time, the publisher Heinrich Vogel in Munich had supplemented its loose-leaf collection of the German traffic laws, which contained a total of approximately 1,900 pages, four to five times a year with addenda of 50 to 100 pages. The aim of the publisher was now also to offer the product through CD-ROM and the Internet and thus meet the expected demands of the market early and efficiently. First, working together with a provider of print and type services, a special DTD was developed, since there was no existing standard-DTD for the description of legal texts that satisfied the demands of the publishers concerning the semantics to be depicted. In order to increase the reusability of parts of the DTD for other publications as well, an important objective was to construct the DTD as modular as possible. The DTD that was developed today consists of a total of eleven modules, which describe various classes of text such as law texts, flow texts, tables, keyword indices, and tables of contents. As soon as the documents were present in a syntactically and semantically correct form, work could be started on the development of style sheets, which to a large extent automatically produce

Pilot project based on the concept of XML

11 See Rawolle/Hess 2000a

Type of cost	Development of the variable unit costs	Development of the fixed costs
Data capture costs	↑	↑
Conversion costs	↓	↑
Revision costs	↓	↑
Structure definition costs	–	↑

Fig. 1.2-2 Changes in costs in the transition from conventional to XML-based publishing (cf. also Rawolle 2001)

the representations necessary for the relevant media. In this case, a style sheet in XML was made for the CD-ROM publication, and the typesetting system 3B2, tried and tested in the SGML environment, was used for the print edition. With the help of a processor a section from the traffic laws was generated within a short time as an HTML interface. The XML documents were stored in text files.

Bilateral exchange of contents on the basis of XML

There is wide agreement today concerning the technical feasibility of XML solutions. But the question of the profitability of such solutions has by no means been conclusively settled.[12] For a cost-oriented analysis, one approach is to focus on the steps taken in converting contents between various media. It is here possible to distinguish the costs of capturing the contents, of actually converting the contents into new media, and then of revising them as necessary. In general, structural costs also arise, especially for constructing a DTD. Assuming stable structures, no adaptation of contents during conversion and no revisions of the layout specific to target groups, the changes in the cost structures will be as described in Figure 1.2-2. As the cost driver, the number of converted documents was chosen. The only surprising element is that the variable unit costs of capturing data rise with the introduction of XML. The reason for this is principally that the editors are now forced not only to capture the contents, but also – in accordance with the guidelines of the DTD – to structure them.

Profitability of XML solutions

12 On the following see Rawolle 2001

Taking into account the magnitudes observed in practice, it can be ascertained that in this greatly simplified analysis the use of XML may be profitable, though only once a not inconsiderable number of converted documents is exceeded. The use of XML is completely unprofitable if any of the aforementioned conditions cannot be met. This is especially true if the structures are not stable. This situation applies in particular to layout-oriented publications such as magazines.

Multilateral exchange of contents on the basis of XML

In the previous section it was implicitly assumed that the conversion of data is carried out on the basis of an individual standard agreed upon by the communication partners taking part. If contents of the same kind are repeatedly exchanged between the same communication partners, then the introduction of communication standards must be considered, i.e. in the case of XML the use of a uniform DTD. The establishment of such a standard must be investigated from an economic point of view. For this purpose the groundwork done by general standardisation theory can be used. If one follows the easily upheld approach propounded by Buxmann and König,[13] the standardisation problem can be analysed from a graph-theoretical perspective. According to this approach the nodes in the graph are to be interpreted as communication participants. These communication participants are assigned standardisation costs $K_i(i = 1, ..., n)$. The communication costs that accrue from the transfer of information from participant i to participant j are modelled as weights of the accompanying edge and labelled as $c_{ij}(i = 1, ..., n; j = 1, ..., n)$. In the proposed model the costs c_{ij} accrue to the sending node i. It is also assumed by way of simplification that the common use of communication standards by two participants i and j causes the communication costs c_{ij} to fall to zero; c_{ij} can therefore also be interpreted as the cost reductions brought about by standardisation. Figure 1.2-3 illustrates the use of this simple model with a clear example, in which two publishers pass on contents to two so-called aggregators for further utilisation.[14]

For an individual communication partner, the introduction of a standard makes sense whenever $K_i < \Sigma c_{ij}$ is valid. This cannot be achieved alone, however, but is dependent on whether the other communication partners also introduce this same communication standard. In other words, the more communication partners also introduce this standard, the more profitable its introduction will be. This phenomenon has already been discussed in the literature for some time now under the generic term of "network effects."[15]

Multiple utilisation and profitability

Reduction in communication costs through standardisation

13 See Buxmann/König 1998
14 See Rawolle/Hess 2001
15 See Katz/Shapiro 1985

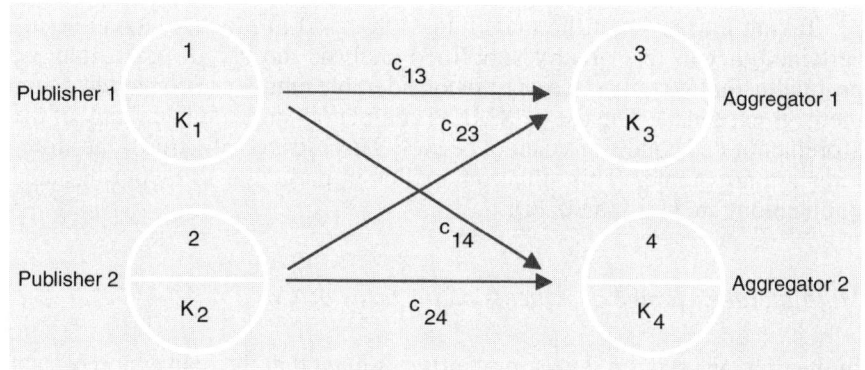

Fig. 1.2-3 Modelling the standardisation problem using an example

De jure versus de facto
standards

This problem can be solved on three levels. It would naturally be ideal if national or even international standards could be created. Yet this was not even achieved with the classical standards, for example the exchange of data to order, or only at the cost of very broadly based standards. There are signs of a similar development when it comes to standards in the exchange of contents. Proposals for such standards, e.g. the News Industry Text Format (NITF) or XMLNews, have existed for some time now, but these standards have not yet been able to gain wide acceptance, not least because of their broad orientation and in spite of worldwide attempts at standardisation. Of greater significance, however, are standards created within business groups or networks. Within a business or business group (i.e. one corporate group) there is the possibility of centrally promoting the development of a standard, for example by financing investments or compensating for individual disadvantages ("side-payments"). This approach was tested in a pilot project with the specialist publishing group BertelsmannSpringer in 1998 and 1999.[16] Figure 1.2-4 shows the configuration in this case. The project had to start from completely different formats in the individual publishing houses, not at least because of the very different products in question. Rough calculations – based on the types of costs portrayed in Figure 1.2-2 and on the model outlined above – had shown that a standardisation of content exchange was economically viable for the business group as a whole. This profitability would not be achieved by all the participating organisations, however, especially not by those publishing companies with strongly layout-oriented contents. With the appropriate advances from the business group, however, the investment was realised, and as a result an economic advantage was gained for the group as a whole.

---

16 See Rawolle/Hess 2001

EUROPEAN COMMUNICATION COUNCIL

Chapter 1.2
Utilisation and Individualisation

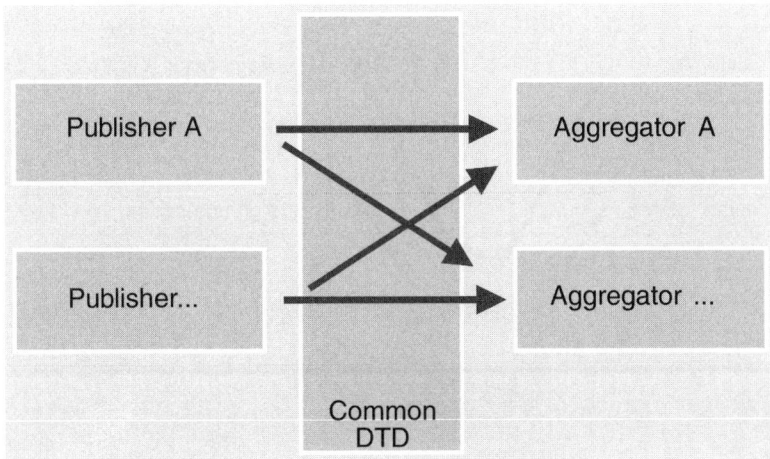

Fig. 1.2-4 Decentralised exchange of contents with XML

Firm cooperations, especially in the form of firm networks, also offer interesting conditions for the use of standards. A key feature of firm networks[17] is that the three or more participating companies maintain their legal independence while at the same time working together on commissions with a view to enhancing the marketability of their product. To achieve this cooperation on specific projects, the participants coordinate to construct a common basis. This basis may consist, for example, in the coordinated build-up of resources (e.g. specific training profiles in their employees), the setting-up of common software for managing commissions, or – as here – the establishment of a standard for the exchange of data. From a theoretical perspective, a business network can be classified as a hybrid between the organisational forms of market and hierarchy.[18] Through the aforementioned networking and digitalisation in the media field, the costs of electronic data exchange are reduced. At the same time, however, the participating firms must have the tendency to make more specific investments more frequently, especially in standards for the exchange of content. According to transaction cost theory, this leads – along with high uncertainty in the handling of the transaction – to the exceptional profitability of firm networking.[19]

Besides a reduction in the production costs, the use of standards can also lead to an increase in turnover for information providers. Known as Content Syndication, this new sales method for media enterprises has been

Standards within business networks

Content Syndication as a form of increasing turnover

17 See Hess 1999
18 See Picot/Reichwald/Wigand 2001, p. 55
19 See Picot/Reichwald 1994, p. 552

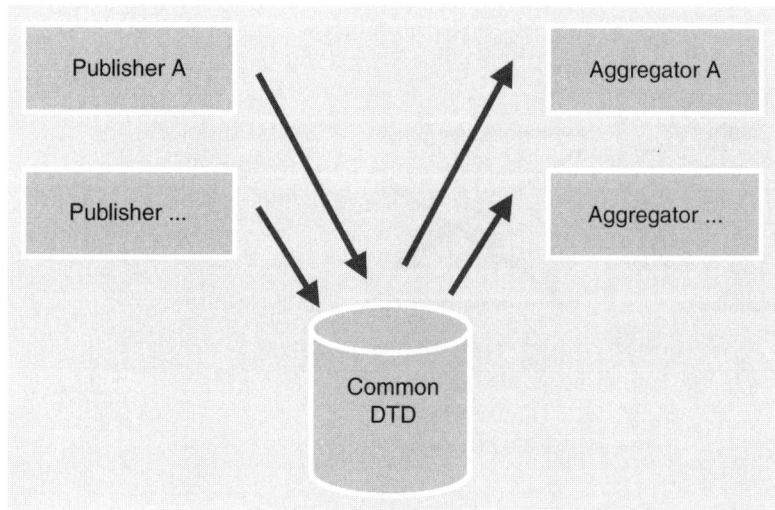

Fig. 1.2-5 Centralised database on the basis of XML

The role played by
intermediaries

intensively discussed for some years now. Basically, two assumptions underlie this approach. On the demand side it is expected that the demand for contents significantly rises through the increasing integration of externally obtained contents into the offers of intranets and e-commerce. A good example is the integration of product tests into theme portals.[20] Simultaneously, the marginal costs of production can be substantially reduced through digitalisation and networking. The networking presupposes in particular a standardised and thus, under certain basic conditions, a more economical exchange of data. The anticipated result is that the demand for reusable contents will significantly increase. It is still too early to say whether these expectations will be fulfilled. In any case, what can be observed is that many media providers are for the first time taking an interest in selling contents to commercial customers for re-utilisation. Also of interest in this context is the role of intermediaries. It is thus feasible that intermediaries, along with their traditional functions, might take on conversion as a service. However, it has been observed up to now that such intermediaries are hardly successful in the market.

Assuming that contents are exchanged on the basis of a standard, the question that then arises is whether or not the bilateral exchange of contents should be replaced by a central database. Figure 1.2-5 shows this variant in a simple example, again on the basis of XML.

---

20 See, for example, www.autouniversum.de.

Comprehensive analyses of the use of centralised databases are not yet available for this type of context. Nonetheless, two points can be ascertained even now. On the one hand, a centralised database facilitates the search for contents and thus contributes to a reduction in the search costs. This is especially relevant when the demand is discontinuous, i.e. when different contents are asked for at different places in the company. On the other hand, a centralised database requires a considerable outlay in advance, since an appropriate system must be constructed and maintained, and the contents needed for applications of all sorts must be edited and described. These two factors must be weighed up in each individual case, and very different decisions may be the result.

Cost effects of centralised databases

If a centralised database is decided on, then the organisational integration must be considered. In doing so, one must distinguish between a product-neutral and a core-product-centred production of the contents.[21] With product-neutral production the contents may be captured at any particular place and are put into the central, media-neutral database, while the product-specific extraction, bundling and structuring of the contents proceeds in the corresponding company units. In contrast to this, core-product-centred production begins with the creation and structuring of the contents for the core-product, e.g. a newspaper. In the process, special formats are used that especially support the desired target medium. Not until the following stage are the media types extracted from the initial product and put into the central databank. At first sight, the redundant storage of data, the possible delay, and the lack of obligation to provide the central supply speak against core-product-oriented production. Nevertheless, this solution is frequently seen in practice, for which there are two essential reasons. First of all, it must be taken into consideration that this approach only requires minor changes in the organisation of a media company and is thus relatively easy to implement. At the same time, the experience and training of contents producers today still focus in large measure on one medium.

Organisational integration: product-neutral or core-product-centred

In the music industry, file swapping has been intensively discussed lately, a good example here being Napster.[22] Such file swapping is based on what are called file-sharing systems, in which the users of the system make certain parts of their hard-disk space available for Internet access and in this way swap data directly with other users. For this purpose a central server has a directory of users and the data files they offer, in turn enabling the users to find providers of the data file they are looking for. The data transfer then takes place directly between the two users, giving rise to the notion of "peer-to-peer" file sharing. The use of such an approach also suggests itself for the exchange of contents, as a middle course between a centralised and a

File swapping as a middle course between centralised and decentralised data records

---

21 See Rawolle 2001
22 See Hummel/Lechner 2001

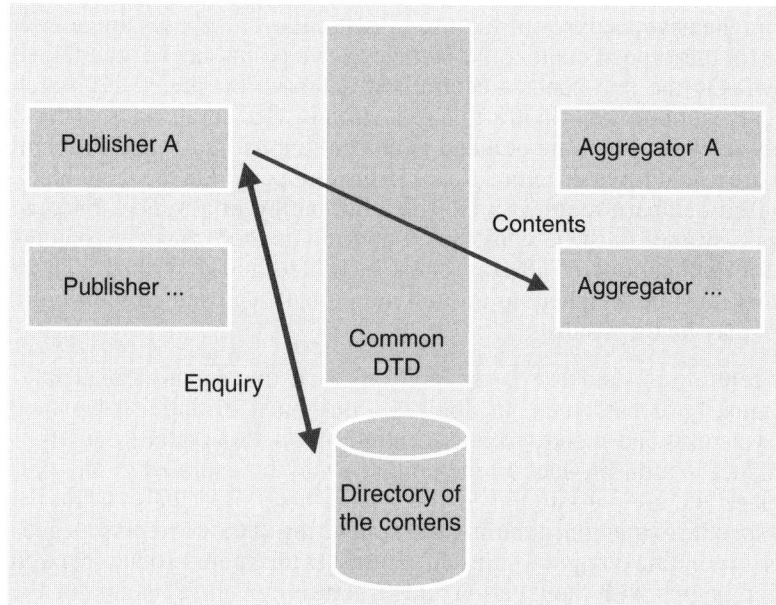

Fig. 1.2-6 Data swapping on the basis of XML and the concept of file-sharing

decentralised approach. For this, a directory of all possible sources would have to be maintained in the central server, while the data remain with the producers. The user who has made use of the central directory to identify contents of interest would then be able to obtain these contents from another user (on the basis of a standard, of course). Figure 1.2-6 shows a summary of the fundamental idea. This method seems especially attractive since it could keep search costs to a minimum without having to pay large sums in advance for the central data storage. The extent to which this approach can be realised in practice is being tested at present.

It should finally be pointed out that the question of judicial administration in multiple utilisation still remains largely unanswered, both in material and in technical terms. In many cases there are no corresponding regulations with the authors of the contents. Many products that are today offered as media-neutral databanks are not capable of billing for the multiple utilisation of contents.

The issue of judicial administration in multiple utilisation

1.2.2
Individualisation of Contents

Idea

Media enterprises with predominantly commercial goals must always endeavour to ensure that their products and services create as great a utility
as possible for their customers. The more precisely the individual needs
of the customer are met, the better this can be achieved. Up until now the
individualisation of products in the media industry has been quite limited,
due especially to the abovementioned first-copy cost effect. According to
this, in the print industry as well as the broadcasting industry a substantial
minimum circulation or reach had to be attained for an offer to be economically feasible in the first place. In the wake of increasing networking and
digitalisation, it can now be observed that the "compulsion to mass-produce"
is no longer absolutely valid. A detailed analysis follows below. It should
be pointed out at this stage, however, that the relevance of these reflections
on the individualisation of products in the wake of the Internet is by no
means limited to the media industry. The customised production of traditional industrial goods has been intensively discussed for some years under
the catchword "mass customisation."[23] One of the first practical examples
was in the clothing industry, where customers could put together their jeans
individually via the Internet. Some car manufacturers have recently also
offered the configuration of cars over the Net.

*Customised media
production through
networking and digitalisation*

*Changes in the basic technical conditions for the individualisation of
contents*

An immediately obvious factor is the changes in the media of communication. Here, changes in two directions can be observed.[24] On the one hand,
the wishes of recipients can be directly discerned by the provider, and on
the other, products can be made available in accordance with these wishes in
terms of content and timing. A prerequisite for this is interactive networks,
which, alongside the already intensively used telephone network, are now
also based on existing television cable networks or through satellites. The
latter media, which were traditionally used only for the transmission of information from provider to customer ("unidirectional," "broadcasting"), are
here expanded to incorporate a return channel, in part on the basis of the
telephone network, in this way allowing for the return of information to the
provider – an essential condition for ascertaining customer preferences and

*Differentiation in
communication media and
terminals*

23 See Piller/Schoder 1999
24 For an overview see Rawolle/Hess 2000b

Direct and indirect methods
of identifying customer
wishes

providing individualised compilations of the available contents. In addition, new broadband technology, be it on the basis of the telephone network or cable networks, fixed or mobile, is for the first time permitting the transmission of multimedia contents in large quantities. Closely associated with the media of communication is the differentiation that can be observed among terminals. In the last few years personal computers have acquired the capacity to represent multimedia contents. Another line of development is the television-based terminal. In particular, progress in the miniaturisation of electronic components has in recent years made it possible to offer the consumer not only traditional, stationary terminals, but also portable systems. These include first and foremost notebooks, personal digital assistants, and mobile telephones.

In this context, moreover, the technical changes on the side of the provider should be considered as well. As regards the modularised storage of data, which is an indispensable prerequisite for its customised compilation, reference should be made to the considerations outlined in the previous section. From a technical viewpoint, the question of how to identify the concrete wishes of the customer is especially interesting.[25] One must here distinguish the direct from the indirect method. Customer demands are ascertained directly through an active statement of preferences (e.g. through online-questionnaires). A good example of this is the newspaper "Rheinische Post," which lets prospective customers choose their interests from a list in its daily newsletter. In contrast to this, the indirect way of ascertaining customer wishes is based on a technologically supported analysis of customer behaviour, for example using data on products requested or websites visited (web-tracking). The term "collaborative filtering" here brings together technologies that assign individual customers to particular groups and then infer the characteristics of individual customers on the basis of the group characteristics. The online bookseller BOL is exemplary in this respect. If a customer is interested in a certain book he is then recommended further books that have also been bought by the buyers of the book in question. By means of the customer's search conduct, his interests are analysed (with the help of the search terms used), and on his next visit to the website the corresponding books are immediately offered. Cookies are often used, allowing the provider to store a customer's transaction data locally on the customer's computer and to use these data the next time the customer visits the website. Of vital importance here is the customer's acceptance of this indirect method. The observation and storage of transaction data can provoke fears of the "visible" user and is therefore frequently undesired.

The compilation of individual products by providers is done by matching the customer information obtained with the characteristics of the product

25 See Brenner/Zarnekow 1999

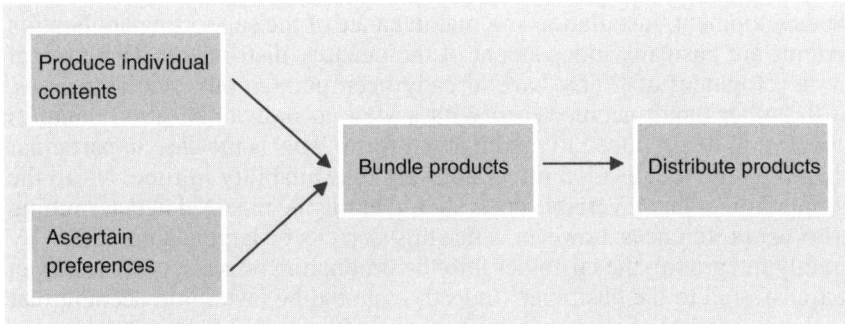

Fig. 1.2-7 Changed production process in the wake of individualisation

modules that have been constructed – usually on the basis of predefined categories, which are added to the products as meta-information. The degree of specification of these categories is of immediate importance for the exactness of the individualised compilation. It should be explicitly pointed out here that individualised compilation by no means always entails a completely digitalised product. Given improvements in printing technology, it is nowadays possible to make books of good print quality on an individual basis. The English provider BookTailor thus offers the customised production of travel guides, into which notices of current events, for example, may also be incorporated.[26]

The profitability of the individualisation of contents

While from a technical standpoint an almost complete personalisation of content-offers is conceivable, this does not always make economic sense, nor is it always feasible even in the long run. From an economic point of view, the costs and the benefits of individualisation must be weighed up against one another.

In analysing the costs one must first examine the production process more closely. The "classical" production process of the media industry has already been outlined above. When it comes to the individualisation of the data, a production stage "ascertain preferences" must be added, which is to be carried out in parallel with the creation of the original contents. Figure 1.2-7 gives an overview of the corresponding changes in the production process.

Individualisation gives rise to additional costs throughout the whole production process, partly fixed in nature and partly variable. The costs of

26 See Hess/Tzouvaras 2001

Matching of customer
information and product
modules

Costs and benefits of
individualisation

the development, installation and maintenance of the supporting application systems are basically independent of the quantity distributed. The costs of the development of DTDs have already been pointed out. Variable costs, on the other hand, accrue when with a view to individualisation contents first have to be produced in modularised form. This is the case in particular when the individualisation refers not only to availability in time, but to the compilation of data. Variable costs should hardly be incurred in determining customer preferences, however, since this step can be largely automated. By directly integrating the customer into the production process, costs can even be transferred to the customer. Indeed, it should be taken into account that the determination of customer preferences – from a strictly economic point of view – is an investment on the part of the user. At what point the costs for this pay their way through increased benefits is a matter to be assessed in each individual case.

The benefits of the individualisation of information products may be either direct or indirect. Direct benefits refer to the contents requested by the customer. Additional benefits can be generated if customer preferences are targeted more accurately, or strictly speaking if this is what the customer's assessment leads him to expect. In the simple case, this leads to him being more willing to pay, and this willingness to pay – thanks to near-perfect price discrimination – can be completely skimmed. In the more complex case of integrated products, short-term or long-term improvements can be expected, though it is in practice very difficult to assess them. For a practical analysis of such effects, the "effect-chain analysis" can be used, as it already has in similar cases.[27] As shown in the following example, the effect-chain analysis makes it possible to assess the effects of the online offer of a daily newspaper on its sales revenue in the print sector.

The average recipient structure for the online offer of a daily newspaper as a rule differs from that of the print offer. For instance, the average age of recipients of online offers is less than that of conventional newspaper readers. It can thus be assumed that an online offer makes the newspaper more attractive to new groups of readers and consequently opens up new market segments. In this way, new subscribers can be won over by addressing new target groups. For already existing subscribers, the online offer provides an added value compared to the conventional print edition. This includes background information or price reductions for the use of chargeable services in the supplementary online offer (e.g. provider services). It is here assumed that the rising attractiveness of the newspaper generates a stronger reader-newspaper bond, and in this way the online offer results in the duration of an average subscription being extended.

Ascertaining customer preferences is an investment on the part of the user

Effect-chain analysis as an assessment tool

Addressing new target groups through online media

27 See Böning-Spohr/Hess 2001a

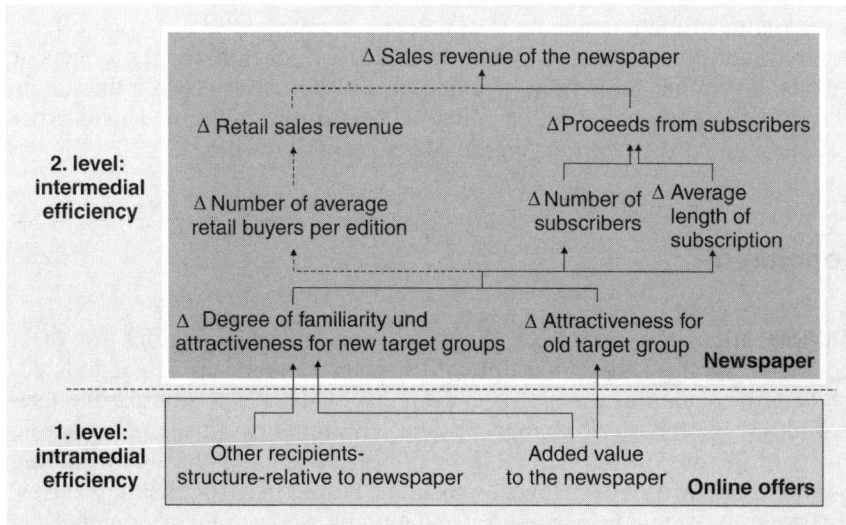

Fig. 1.2-8 Chain of effects in the target area of sales revenue (Böning-Spohr/Hess, 2002: 110)

Both individual effects – the change in the length of average subscriptions and the change in the number of subscribers – lead to an increase in subscription revenue and thus also in sales revenue. In sum, the individual effects on the sales revenue are positive. The effect upon the number of individual buyers of the newspaper in the example is less; the left branch in Figure 1.2-8 is therefore represented as a broken line.

Similar analyses of effect-chains are also conceivable for individualisation and multiple utilisation in print and online media.

Individualisation tends to make sense from the point of view of the customer whenever contents are provided frequently and on the basis of defined, stable (!) preferences. The abovementioned newsletter service of the "Rheinische Post" fulfils this demand, since the newsletter is provided daily and the preferences are stable. In this context it comes as no surprise that the individualised offers from search engines receive rather slight attention: the preferences here are especially prone to change. The aforementioned provider BookTailor also had problems imposing a supplementary charge for the individualisation of data.

Besides direct benefits, the indirect benefits of individualisation also deserve attention. Indirect benefits arise whenever supplementary revenue can be generated beyond the contents being offered. For example, higher advertising revenues are possible on the basis of individualised advertising, or additional incomes through the offer of products from other branches, as

Stable preferences as a prerequisite for individualisation

in the realm of merchandising.[28] The concrete assessment of such effects requires analyses that are no longer oriented towards individual products or periods, but rather the whole lifecycle of a customer.[29] Within the media sector, such approaches can be found at best in the traditional mail-order business, but hardly at all for digital offers up until now.

1.2.3
Conclusion

Multiple utilisation and individualisation as structuring options

Multiple utilisation have been discussed as structuring options for print providers. With regard to multiple utilisation, the mark-up language XML has been presented as an approach currently under discussion for the use-neutral and modularised storage of data. Building on this, the economic effects of the use of this technology were discussed. Assuming the simple case of a bilateral data exchange, for example between two publishing houses, what emerges is that the use-neutral and modularised storage of contents can make sense once a certain amount of data is exceeded. If, on the other hand, several firms are exchanging contents between one another, then standards can be a good idea for this exchange, and if the lines of communication are unstable it can make sense for these data to be stored centrally. An outline was given of the as yet unrealised variant of mixed central/decentralised storage where the data storage is decentralised, but a directory with the data providers exists centrally. The second part of this article started by describing the changes in the basic technological conditions that make the continuing individualisation of information products possible or economically feasible in the first place. Of particular significance are the possibilities of interaction over the Internet, as well as new approaches for obtaining information about individual customer preferences. From an economic viewpoint, the aim was to analyse in particular increases in fixed and variable costs resulting from individualisation as well as the possible increases in benefits.

Unilateral dependence between multiple utilisation and individualisation

Combination of cost leadership and differentiation

In conclusion, there are two general points still to be mentioned. First, it should have become clear that between multiple utilisation and individualisation there exists a relation of one-sided dependency: individualisation in the sense of a flexible combination of services offered presupposes multiple utilisation, since the contents in products generated around the customer are inevitably used more than once. In addition, this indicates that cost leadership and differentiation by no means necessarily cancel one another out as mutually exclusive basic strategies of a company. On the contrary, the Internet gives media companies the option of combining both strategies for the first time.[30]

---

28 See ECC 2001, p. 47
29 See Böning-Spohr/Hess 2002
30 See also Fleck 1995

Chapter 1.3

Multimedia and Multidimensional: Concepts of Utilisation in the "Age of Digitalisation"

Hardy Dreier

1.3.1
Phases in the Development of an Information Society in the Age of Digitalisation

It is not just since the triumph of Internet that the use of digital technology has played a vital role in the development of the information, communication and media branches. Even beforehand, digital technology was a constant component in the manufacture and distribution of media. The motivation for the use of digital technology was to improve the economic and media productivity of media companies. The results of using digital technology are varied. They range from gains in quality in the presentation of images and text through improved printing technology, gains in topicality through optimised work cycles, to cost reductions through rationalisation.[1]

One of the advantages that arise from preparing content in digital form is, for example, the easy transmutability of the products. The scientific publisher Springer has thus established an offer with LINK that makes journal articles available online as well as in print form.[2] In this way, costs can be reduced with respect to traditional analogue production. Yet this advantage is at the same time a disadvantage, since it makes possible undesired intrusions that can bring about identical copies, manipulations and forgeries. The example complained about by industry is the copying of music CDs. It is a development that not only since the emergence of the first DVD-burners has also affected the medium of film, for which this data carrier is gaining in importance.[3] There is a dynamic process of coding and marking tech-

Improvement in economic and media productivity

---

1 See Sihn/Klink 2000, p. 19
2 See de Kemp 1999, pp. 263
3 See Turecek et al. 2001, p. 270

" **Television as the number one medium for attracting attention.** *"*

nology going on, which will always involve competing with new copying programmes.[4]

Diverse forms of distribution for digital contents

For the distribution of digital or digitalised contents, data carriers are no longer absolutely necessary, because there are many different networks available. Besides broadband cable and telephone networks, there are networks with varying transmission capacities and performance features in the form of radio, electric or satellite networks or the terrestrial transmission of digital signals. The advantages of digital distribution are, amongst other things, the good use of transmission capacities, the high quality, and the reduction in costs, which is achieved in part through the passing on of transmission costs to the user, e.g. in the form of telephone charges. This advantage can also be a disadvantage given the existing business models: in the case of the Internet, the removal of geographical borders in such networks means that regionally structured sales networks, as in the music branch, are called into question. In addition, unwillingness to pay, together with the difficulties of user exclusion, are problems for content providers. The various swap markets for digital media products show the loss of control in the area of distribution. On top of this, the expansion of the Internet leads to bandwidth bottlenecks for the transmission of content: Internet TV of an acceptable quality is still not ready for the mass public.

Conditions for the use of digital contents

For the use of digital media offers, the public is expected to invest in hardware and software and be willing to make continuous expenditure. In terms of the terminals, this means purchasing devices for the digital reception of radio and television, investing in network access and reception equipment – from the satellite dish and cable connection through to online access – and, finally, buying software to operate the devices. The software includes the technically necessary programmes for operating the devices, as in the case of the d-box, as well as the contents that are used.

> *"Even today, after the growth of the Internet, television still is the only mass medium that can attract the entire nation's or world's attention at the same time."*
>
> *Jeffrey Cole (2001)[5]*

---

4 See Erb 2001
5 The UCLA Internet Report: Surveying the digital future, http://ccp.ucla.edu/pdf/UCLA-Internet-Report-2001.pdf.

1.3.2
Transformation of Use Options

Central to the debate concerning the development of the information society is the spread of the Internet among the general public. About 40 percent of the German populace has now had experience with the Internet.[6] An ever greater share of online use is shifting from the workplace to the home: in 1997 more than half of online activity took place exclusively at the workplace or school, but this amount has since dropped to under one fifth.[7] The share of persons who have Internet access both at the workplace and at home is continuously increasing. As a result of this change in the place of access, different forms of use are developing which will also have an effect on the uses of traditional media. Thus, some online users maintain that they use other media less intensively than before, even though this impression has yet to be verified through data on use.[8]

Whether computers will still play the main role in online access in the future remains to be seen. The television is another screen present in households, which is used more than other current media for entertainment.[9] Even at the present time, this is the screen that has gained importance in the use of digital products such as video games and DVDs. The Sony PlayStation 2 and the Xbox from Microsoft are two devices that can combine various functions: with a hard drive the game console becomes a personal video recorder; with the corresponding drive a DVD player; and with a cable modem it can access the Internet. Given the multi-functionality of the playing devices there are more options for the design of DVDs and CDs, which can be expanded with multimedia accessories. Thus, video clips can be found on music-CDs nowadays, and film-DVDs contain a range of additions from music and images to games. With the game consoles and computers, the hardware in part already has online access, and even pure DVD players will presumably in the future be technically equipped for linking up to the Internet. The content of the DVDs could then be expanded with HTML pages through links to the homepages of film studios. The DVD owner could receive access to special offers through client/server technology and with conditional access have premium offers at his disposal. It would also be conceivable to use DVDs to strengthen e-commerce by having access codes for certain offers available on the DVD. The last two options could also help to make protecting the original relevant to the owner: if particular individual access codes were to

Forms of use dependent upon place of access

Multi-functionality as a broadening of functions for storage media

---

6 Ridder 2002, p. 121
7 Working group formed by the advertising companies of Germany's public broadcaster ARD 2001, p. 88
8 See Oehmichen/Schröter 2000, p. 363; Ridder 2002, p. 124
9 See Dreier 2002, p. 48

be usable only within a certain period of time, for example, this could lead to competition between the owner of the original and the owners of the (bootleg) copy, making it more important for the buyer to be able to identify his copy as the original.

Internet Use and the Parallel Use of Media

Jeffrey Cole

Development of multitasking

The issue of different media usage between users and non-users is also complicated by multitasking, the concurrent use of the Internet with other media. Since only users of the Internet can multitask it with other media, it is important to compare multitasking by new users of the Internet with that of more experienced users. From the very beginning, new users of the Internet seem to be multitasking the online experience with another use of media or some other activity (see chart). While most other media began as solitary activities, Internet users seem to gravitate toward multitasking almost instinctively.

Looking at the newest users of the Internet, over one-quarter of them (27.5%) listen to music on their computers while involved in some other activity on the Internet. The most common multitasking activity among new users is to listen to the radio (whether online or offline) while on the Internet. Over 40% have some sort of radio on while on the Internet, while close to a third are instant messaging while connected to the Net. Over a quarter are watching television while on the Internet and just under a quarter are on the telephone.

Looking at experienced users, not surprisingly, multitasking is even more pronounced. Close to half of those online listen to music on the radio or talk on the telephone while online. Almost 40% listen to music on the computer or instant message or chat while online. And almost a third of experienced Internet users watch television while connected.

Multitasking is an important part of the Internet experience, and it is interesting that from the beginning so many users gravitate toward multiple uses. Some users report that they are multitasking with three or at the same time. All this multitasking calls for some way to measure comprehension to see the ways in which multitasking may

When you are using the Internet, do you typically do any of the following activities at the same time?

■ Very New Users (<1 Year)   □ Very Experienced Users (≥5 Years)

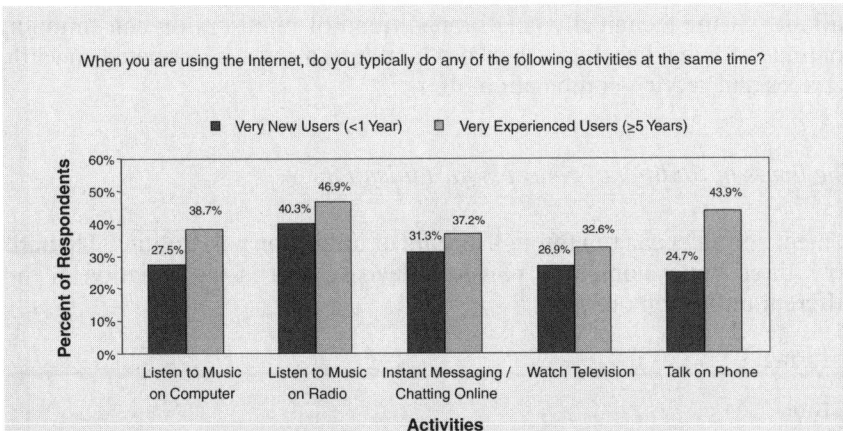

Fig. 1. Surveying the digital future (UCLA Internet report 2001)

more media be affecting understanding. Clearly, whatever the impact, multitasking is an important part of the Internet experience and may be an aspect of the larger picture of what captures people's attention and in what ways.

Jeffrey Cole is Professor at the Center for Communication Policy of the UCLA

Multitasking as an important part of the Internet experience

The increase in use-options for terminals, in connection with the situations in which the use of the media actually takes place, will play an important part in the selection of media offers.[10] In addition, the question of actual media use must be asked anew. A great number of the media offers that are purchased are not actually used, or not fully so: print media are not completely read; video films often gather dust in the bookcase next to the video recorder.[11] This is of relevance for the future development of offers, for the number of possible variations of devices, places and situations presents media companies with the question of what form they want to make their offer available in and what business and financing models are promising in the various contexts. Accordingly, current developments require media companies to develop variations on their traditional offers, while traditional utilisation strategies must be re-examined with this in mind to see how functional they

10 Ibid., p. 44
11 Turecek et al. 2001, p. 268

still are. If the technically conditioned trend of multi-option consumption continues for media offers, then product design must be oriented towards services and service-combination offers.[12]

The limits of traditional concepts for utilisation

A media product can run through a chain of utilisation possibilities. Up until now, three dimensions have played a decisive part in the variation of the different utilisation options:

- format

- time

- geographical region.

In addition to the variations that arise from these three dimensions for the media product, there are possibilities for utilisation in the form of licensing and merchandising rights, concerning which only an indirect link exists to the original product. In connection with media offers for children, for example, these are frequently clothes and shoes with depictions of the corresponding products.

The utilisation of films, for example, has until now followed the three dimensions mentioned above: if the film is a cinema film it is exploited in this format in the various countries for a varying time of up to ten months. The next stage is the release of the film as a rental video and then as a video for sale. If technically possible, the film appears in the next stage as a pay-per-view and then as a pay-TV offer. In the last stage of utilisation, after at least two years it is shown on commercial or public television. This traditional process of utilisation is termed windowing.[13] The length of the different stages of utilisation varies in Europe from country to country. The target figures for the duration of the individual stages are determined in the respective guidelines of the film-promotion institutions or by the corresponding associations. Departing from this time schedule is possible in principle, although skipping a stage of utilisation can entail a financial reimbursement to the rights-owners for the lost revenue from the stage in question.[14]

Windowing as the revenue model

In the course of the different stages of utilisation, many changes in format also take place. The cinema film turns into the television film and the video film or DVD. The following diagram shows the development clearly: the

12 Meffert/Giloth 2002, p. 120f.
13 Owen/Wildman 1992, pp. 26f.
14 See, for example, the German Film Promotion Act (FFG) § 30.

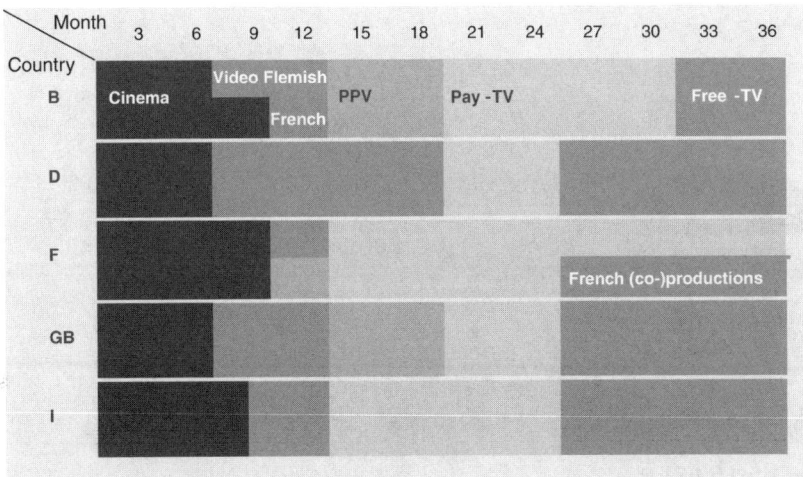

Fig. 1.3-1 Windowing with films[15]

starting-product appears first as a cinema film in the USA, then in Europe. It goes through the various utilisation windows for film, from the cinema via television and then on to video. During this process, the film changes its technical format from the spool of film to the video cassette. In addition, there are products that are related to the film and are either marketed as independent components such as soundtracks, or open up further possibilities for revenue in the form of merchandising and licensing to refinance the initial product. With skilful time planning, the idea is to bring off an additional project that uses the attention generated and the public interest and confidence earned by the starting-product. How this is realised comes to light in the numerous "mini-series" of cinema films: there is hardly a successful film that does not have a sequel, and in many cases the shooting of the sequel is now started irrespective of the success of the first part. Two sequels of "Back to the Future" were filmed parallel to one another. In like manner, all three parts of the film adaptation of Tolkien's "Lord of the Rings" were filmed simultaneously. In this way, the marketing activities can be comprehensively planned for the several films of such a series.

With this expansion of the marketing activities for a chain of products over a longer period of time, the standards in this field rise. However, this is not the only development that contributes to making the marketing of media products more complex. Along with the expanded options on the supply side, the new options for the user also have consequences for these strategies. Global communication networks hinder the use of regional concepts in

Changes in format through windowing

Productive use of attention and confidence

15 See Screen Digest 2000, p. 124

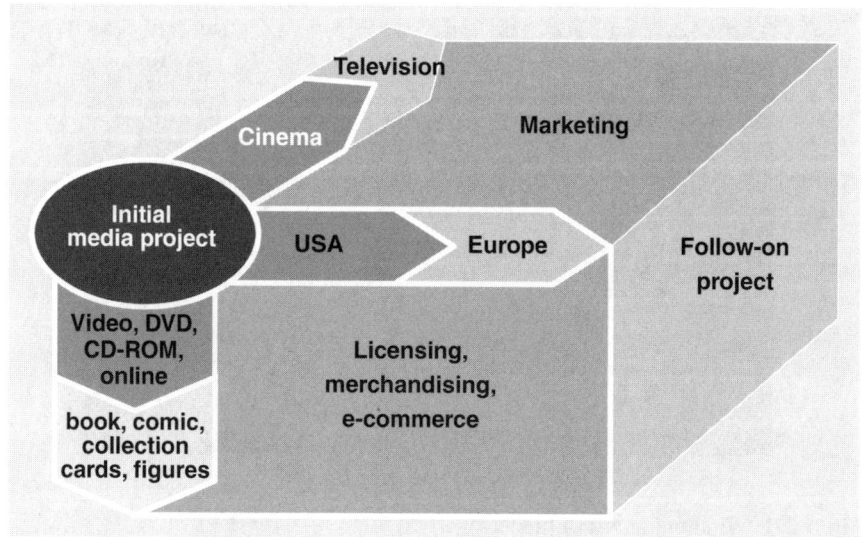

Fig. 1.3-2 Diagram of dimensions of utilisation

Regional factors in the
introduction of products

introducing products. If every movie-goer with online access can get information over the Internet about film content and reviews from the American premiere of a film, the marketing campaign will at the launch of the film in Europe three months later already be confronted with informed and educated public opinion, which can become a problem during marketing. The possibilities for marketing the film as "new" are thus restricted with so much information available. In the past there have been attempts by the public to bypass regional differences in film premiere dates using the Internet. For example, a copy of the American version of a "Star Wars" movie filmed in the cinema was put on the Internet ready for downloading. This was certainly an exceptional situation, but it called into question above all the rationale for the regional differentiation of media releases. Furthermore, in subsequent windows too utilisation is affected by the digitalisation of the products offered. Over the Internet, digital data can be dispersed worldwide. As soon as the film can be recorded or is present on a data carrier, the provider's control over the distribution of the offer dwindles.

The consequence of this technical development on the distribution level is that a greater readiness to take risks is required on the part of the providers. To carry out such a project, not only is investment in the actual film necessary but also considerable investment in the infrastructure for the marketing. In order to cover the capital requirements arising from setting up such an infrastructure, there are many new variations in the utilisation of films besides the traditional utilisation through windowing, which yields proceeds with a corresponding time delay. One element of film financing that is gaining in importance is the selling of licensing rights. Licensing is the profit-oriented concession of rights of use.[16] Licensing is thus distinguished from primarily sales-oriented merchandising. Along with licensing and merchandising, which must be coordinated for the cinema film as well as for all the elements connected with it, three levels can be distinguished on which the activities take place: first, the classical utilisation through the cinema and as a cinema film; secondly, the utilisation of the product or components of the product in digital media for private use; and thirdly, utilisation through online offers. The publicity triggered by marketing also allows products not directly linked to the digital offer to make a profit. Thus, the boom surrounding the cinema films based upon the best sellers "The Lord of the Rings" and "Harry Potter" caused the books themselves to win back or reinforce their position at the top of the best sellers list. Of the first volume of the "Harry Potter" books, 50,000 copies were sold in October 2001; in November, the month of the film premiere, 200,000 books were sold.[17]

Licensing as a tool for financing

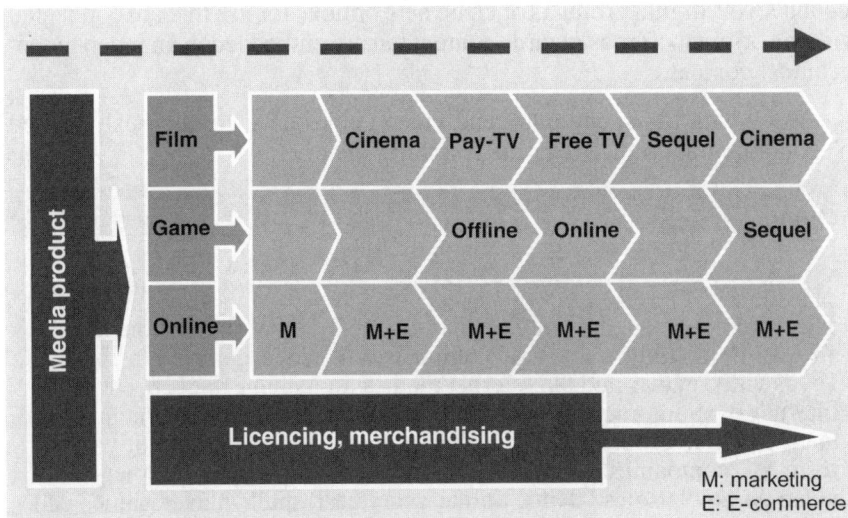

Fig. 1.3-3 One source – many rivers

16 See Böll 1999, p. 5
17 See Manz/Fröhlich/Holowaty 2002, p. 62

" **Logical marriage of video and computer games with the Internet.** *"*

1.3.3
Developmental Perspectives for Concepts of Utilisation

With the release of a cinema film as a video or DVD, the consumers have the option of determining the place of use and possibly obtaining their own copy of the film. Relevant to the debate over the problem of bootleg copies is the fact that many consumers acquire a pirate copy to have an option for use in their bookcase, possibly without ever using it. If they had to pay the actual costs for this option they would probably do without it. The value of the option of use apparently does not justify the purchase of the authentic product in the opinion of most consumers. Enlarging the offer on DVDs with additional material such as bonus scenes, games, etc., on the other hand, creates an added value that can lead to a decision to buy the product. This bundling of offers on a data carrier or in a retail unit can result in an attractive offer for the customer. Consequently, DVDs that besides the original film contain additional material and possibly new functions such as online access or a character data bank are located at the threshold of the second level: digital products open up new options for use that are connected with the original offer as regards content but are embedded in an independent technical context.

Along with films, computer and video games have continuously gained in economic importance over the last thirty years.

Additional contents as use-options

Online gaming

Steve Jones

The emergence of the Internet has opened a new dimension for the already flourishing market of computer and video games. In the late 1990s video games and the Internet made a logical marriage, because the Internet is an interactive medium, and games, by their very nature, are interactive. Internet games have become so popular that major gaming software companies (Nintendo, Sony, etc.) produce Internet-ready video game consoles. Thus, unlike years past, multi-player games can be played online as well as offline. While quickly adopted by gamers in the USA, console penetration in Europe has lagged behind the use of mobile phones and PCs for online gaming. Datamonitor (2001), however, predicts that by 2004 consoles will become the predominant stream of online gaming revenue in Europe. Datamonitor also forecasts that wireless gaming alone Europe by the year 2005, with four out of five mobile phone users playing games on their phone. However,

Increasing popularity of cross-media games

will account for US $6 billion in they note that in 2001, 87% of wireless gaming revenue came from the Asia-Pacific region. Importantly, in the USA adoption of online gaming consoles has correlated with adoption of broadband, and thus an increase in consoles in Europe may portend a significant rise in demand for always-on broadband Internet access in Europe.

During the last several decades, video, computer and Internet games have emerged as one of the most popular forms of entertainment, particularly among adolescent youth. Young people in the USA spend an average of 20 minutes per day playing video games.[18] This figure compares to Drotner's finding of the same average for U.S. children but of 57 minutes per day for children in Denmark, 44 minutes per day for children in the U.K., and 36 minutes per day for children in Spain.[19] For many children around the world, video games have become a large part of educational, social and cultural experience.

And, just as clearly, video games have emerged as one of the most popular forms of entertainment in the United States. In 2000, 35 percent of U.S. residents surveyed identified video games as the most entertaining activity (television came in second at 18 percent); over 219 types of computer and video games were sold in the United States; and the video game industry reported sales of over US $6.5 billion.[20] These figures are expected to grow as high-speed broadband Internet access facilitates networked game play.

A reported 60 percent of people in the United States play video games, with 42 percent of game console users under 18 years of age, 37 percent between 18 and 35 years old, and 21 percent over 35 years old.[21]

According to the Pew Internet and American Life Project, 66 percent of U.S. teenagers play or download games online.[22] While 57 percent of girls play online, 75 percent of boys reported that they play Internet-games. This finding contrasts with the adult online population, in which online game playing is generally more popular with women than with men.[23] According to the Interactive Digital Software Association (IDSA), an organisation that serves and surveys the gaming industry, a remarkable 79 percent of online gamers are age 25 or older.[24] Online gamers are not only more likely to be women than men, but they are smarter and richer than the average Net user according to at least one survey by the IDSA.

"Cross-Age"

18 See Jensen 1999
19 See Drotner 2001
20 See IDSA 2001, as cited in Sherry et al. 2001
21 Ibid.
22 See Lenhart et al. 2001
23 See Walsh 2000
24 See Lindsay 2000

Research deficits in online gaming

The survey shows that more than 88 percent of online-gamers have some college education and that nearly 40 percent have household incomes of at least US $60,000.[25]

Despite the fact that online gaming is one of the fastest growing entertainment industry branches, there is remarkably little data on the development and acceptance of this new medium and even less about its impact on adults. Market research tends to focus on game adoption and revenue and is largely predictive. Research by social scientists tends to focus on spotential social problem areas, such as gaming addiction, social isolation, or emerging violence and aggression, primarily in children 18 years and younger. So far, studies dealing with everyday use and the integration of gaming in children's social lives are still neglected, as are studies into the aesthetic, commercial and technological elements of online gaming. As a medium, online gaming is already superseding television viewing among children and adults in some corners of the world, and if only for that reason demands serious attention.

Steve Jones is Professor and Head of Communication at the University of Illinois at Chicago

In the year 2001, computer and video game sales again exceeded the turnover of the whole film industry.[26] By coordinating the marketing activities for games and films, the effects of one product can be passed on to another. Thus, in the case of the trilogy of the film version of "The Lord of the Rings," a release policy was agreed upon by the game and film companies for a period of three years (the films premiered at Christmas each time). After the film has left the cinemas and the retail copy appears on DVD, the first game is put on the market in versions for PCs and game consoles. The game is also playable in networks. The DVD and the games are two offers that make it possible to lead the consumer thematically into the Internet. In addition, when it comes to selling the product there are numerous options available for combining diverse products with one another and selling them together. A demo version of a video game on a DVD could be a freebie that grabs the attention of people who do not usually play. Melodies for mobile phones could also be an attractive free gift on a music CD. The compilation of the package contents can be oriented towards the new terminals: owners of a multifunctional terminal like the Xbox or PlayStation2 can use packages that contain DVDs, video games and music CDs; computer users might be won over by the combination of a DVD, a computer game, a print studio with film motives for making T-shirts, and access to online offers.

---

25 Ibid.
26 See IDSA 2002

As the third level, the Internet plays an important part in the utilisation of media products. At the start of the utilisation of a film in the cinema, the online appearance as a theme portal serves above all marketing purposes. Such an appearance is excellent in building or maintaining a community and, over a longer period of time, in creating excitement without yet investing heavily in classical advertising. The online appearance of "The Lord of the Rings" was already well-known among fans more than a year before the film reached the cinemas. The casting of the characters was intensively discussed there, and as the first images of the mystery-shrouded project became available for downloading the website visits quickly increased in number. The marketing function of the online appearance remains intact during the whole project, yet it also acquires another function: besides being a theme portal it also becomes a theme shop. It is at this address that customers are most likely to be found for the licence-owners. These addresses are also attractive for providers of DVDs and computer games because they here come into contact with the interested audience. In using these options, revenue-sharing agreements in the form of commissions with licensees and games-providers for sales successfully made using this platform can generate additional income, which may contribute to the economic success of the project.

Role of Internet in the utilisation of media products

Licensing – En route to new target groups

In the past there have been series of products which have been exploited with the help of licensing. One good example is the "Power Rangers" by Bandai.[27] Through skilful cooperation, the companies Saban International, Fox Kids and Bandai successfully managed to exploit the cartoon series in the form of toys and cinema films with real actors. According to a study of the German licence market, in 2001 licensing revenue totalling US $195 million was raised on a turnover of US $3.9 billion. Of this, US $89 million alone was in the entertainment industry.[28]

Utilisation with the help of licensing

Digital production allows an audio-visual product to be broken down into individual components. This includes images, diagrams and individual scenes, but also pieces of music, dialogues or sounds. This creates a multitude of possibilities for the development of additional offers that are tied to a film. Graphic patterns can be used much more easily than formerly for printing on fabric and objects, while film sequences omitted from the original film and stored in the archives until a director's cut comes out are distributed as bonus material on DVD and in the Internet. Parts of the original film are edited as sequences into computer and video games that are offered by third

27 See Zacherl 2001
28 See anon 2002a, p. 3

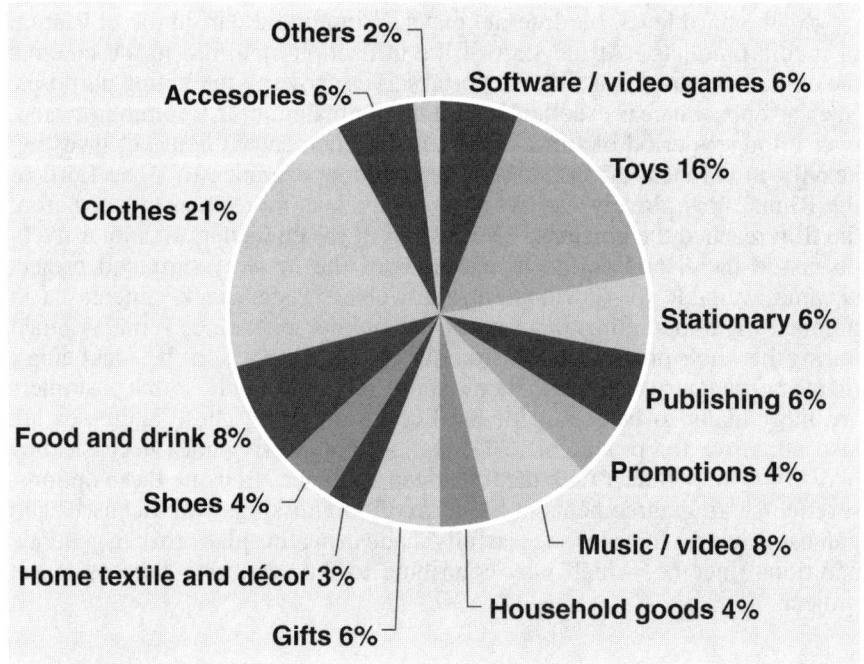

Fig. 1.3-4 The German entertainment licence market[29]

parties, and music and sounds are marketed, for example, as elements of advertisements.

These individual elements can be exploited in the form of licences. The traditional way is to focus on a product to whose success licensing makes a twofold contribution: first, the revenue obtained for the licences is, of course, a decisive factor in the total revenue; secondly, the licensees support the marketing for the starting-product with the advertising for their own product and provide for a strong presence in the market. This additional marketing also taps into target groups of cinema-goers who are not counted as the classical movie-goers.

For this type of audience, the film itself is possibly not the central product: it is more likely that other elements of the package comply with the use preferences of this group. Should irregular movie-goers nonetheless feel the urge to go to the cinema due to interest sparked in this way, this is made easy for them: because of the multiple function of marketing for film and licence

Smaller utilisation
possibilities in shorter time
periods

---

29 See anon 2002b, p. 14

products and the fact that instead of one big profit window for the product cinema film many smaller utilisation possibilities are now realised in short time periods, the film's run in the cinemas is shortened, but in compensation for this the number of copies significantly increases. Already, more than a thousand copies have been exceeded with the film version of "Harry Potter" and "The Lord of the Rings," and the films and their contents are ever-present in daily life through various channels both in the media and through their licensed products. The utilisation and control of the publicity created by the film is now a marketing objective that can break away from the starting-product. An example of how such a concept can develop is "Pokémon" from Nintendo. The successful toy for the GameBoy was "translated" into other formats. The "pocket monsters" were also successful as cartoons, cinema films, music-CDs, videos for retail sale, online games, collectors' cards, etc. The three cinema films had a box-office intake of US $138 million in the USA; in Germany more than 5 million movie-goers saw the film.[30] With "Yu-Gi-Oh," the game provider Koname is trying to repeat the success with a similar principle.[31]

Under these conditions, early cooperation between the participants in the various levels of utilisation presents new options in developing digital media products. Extensive cooperation, for example, between providers of games and film production makes possible an optimisation of marketing that plays an important part in the success of the product. Even before the first media product is released the licences must have been sold. For one thing, this contributes to the financing of the project in that the licences are paid for, and secondly, the licensee profits from the marketing for the media product. On this basis, skilful product development can lead to optimal results with a theme concept based on the film and around which a large family of products is grouped. The use of different media also results in a spreading of risks for the providers. A theme that as a cinema film was interesting only for a small audience can be economically successful as a computer game for another target group. The success of the film "The Lord of the Rings" has attracted new readers for the book and contributed to its rise up the international best seller list. This development is appropriately summed up by a quotation from Tim Burton, the director of "Batman Returns" from 1992: "The making of the film is now almost secondary to the merchandising."[32] A transformation is thus taking place as regards media projects. An investment in licences for such a project means first of all a share in the risks. The distribution of risks in production is no longer carried out just through the conjunction of several film projects where one successful film cross-subsidises several less successful ones. Now, in addition to this traditional form, the development

Cooperation between the players

Licensing as a tool for spreading risks

30 See Fröhlich 2002a, p. 84
31 See Fröhlich 2002b
32 Böll 1999, p. 55

of various modules in different utilisation variations also contributes to the risk-sharing.

Film title	Production costs	Box-office proceeds	Licensing turnover
Batman	50	600	1,000
Batman Returns	75	1,000	3,000
Jurassic Park	65	913	3,000
Jurassic Park II	75	800	1,000
Titanic	180	1,200	600
Star Wars	30	780	1,000

Fig. 1.3-5 The relation between production costs, box-office proceeds and licensing proceeds[33]

The consequences of this development for the film industry and the media market as a whole are difficult to assess, since the development of tremendous projects also means the chance of a tremendous failure. Central to the development is the question of what its consequences are in view of the increasing concentration of the media.

Think big?

The demand for capital arising from the planning and realisation of big film or game projects involves a great risk for investors. For this reason, it tends to be material that is already successful which is used for such extensive concepts. "Star Wars" is an example of this, along with the film versions of successful books such as "Harry Potter" and "The Lord of the Rings." In the past, the comic heroes Batman and Superman also showed themselves to be ready for the silver screen. Spiderman too has recently attracted fans in a cinema film, computer and video game, comic, etc., and the comic hero "The Incredible Hulk" has been filmed as well. Along with successful figures from literature, comics are also a good source because their target group partly belongs to the cinema public and because the graphic design can be better rendered with the help of digital technology than was previously the case. It is here quite possible to cast the cartoon characters with real actors. Along with

Reuse of media hits as a way of reducing risks

---

33 In million US dollars, cf. Böll 1999, p. 55

Title	Production year	Attendance Germany	Box-office proceeds USA
Pokémon – The Film	1999	Ca. 3,200,000	Ca. 86 Mio. $
Tomb Raider	2001	Ca. 2,400,000	Ca. 131 Mio. $
Pokémon 2	2000	Ca. 1,835,703	Ca. 44 Mio. $
Final Fantasy	2001	Ca. 1,091,000	Ca. 32 Mio. $
Pokémon 3	2001	Ca. 701,000	Ca 8 Mio. $
Street Fighter	1994	Ca. 820,000	Ca. 33 Mio. $
Mortal Combat	1995	Ca. 385,000	Ca. 70 Mio. $
Super Mario Bros.	1993	Ca. 290,000	Ca. 21 Mio. $
Wing Commander	1998	Ca. 109,000	Ca. 13 Mio. $

Fig. 1.3-6 Film versions of games and their success[34]

comics as an easily digitalised source, computer and video games are also gaining in importance: Lara Croft from the game "Tomb Raider" was also a success as a film heroine. With the filming of games like "Final Fantasy" and "Resident Evil," other computer games have already been made into films for the cinema.

In realising these extensive digital media projects the participants are forced to construct large networks and to communicate and coordinate the activities in these networks. This is done successfully above all by big corporations such as Vivendi Universal, Disney or Time Warner-AOL, which combine a multitude of stages of utilisation and production steps under one roof and have at their disposal a multitude of regional partnerships that they can use for such projects. Nonetheless, media concentration counteracts one of the advantages of this concept: when a lot of partners in such a project belong to one media company, the risks will naturally not be distributed. For this reason companies that do not belong to the corporation are more attractive as partners in competition with the corporation's own companies in order to spread the risks.

Advantages of media conglomerates

---

34 Fröhlich 2002a, p. 84

Service combination in business webs

Smart is beautiful!

Aside from major projects, the traditional business and finance models still retain their importance, even though they have to be partly modified and adjusted due to the current developments. For media products and media offers, service combinations will gain considerably in importance and thus contribute to the increased demands on communication between the partners. As a consequence of the growing need for communication and coordination, increasing importance is accruing to integrated and fixed trade systems that are used by several partners and in this way serve as a platform for more or less stable networks.[35] An important element in the development of these networks is the reliability of the partners involved as regards their offer. Current developments show, at least in licensing, a move towards longer-term contracts of greater scope, which increases the ability to plan and guarantees the quality.[36]

The individual companies that are specialised in their fields must develop adequate interfaces to these networks in order to do justice to the demands within such a business web. Only then can they participate in costly and risky projects. In the process special problems arise, especially as regards the German film industry: in order to develop and maintain such competence permanently, a company must have continuity and be of a minimum size allowing partnerships to develop and projects to be managed on a longer-term basis. Such companies are not very numerous in the German film industry.[37] A European network, appearing as an already functioning utilisation network, could pave the way for a more comfortable position in negotiating in such a partnership, since the position of the licensees in competition is weak under the current conditions. Besides the choice of German marketing partners, a large media company also has the choice of cooperating with another company, choosing the most attractive partner in a particular national market or looking for a partner for a larger region by bundling licences for several countries.

When swarms spin webs ...

The power of the (decentralised) swarm

Under the new conditions, in some areas the image of the consumer who loses his freedom of choice in the marketing network of a single provider is substituted by the image of the swarm which coordinates and follows an objective in common.[38] It emerges, however, that the value of utilisable

35 See ECC 2001, p. 150, Ahlert 2001, p. 50
36 See Anon 2002a, p. 14
37 Pätzold/Röper 2002, pp. 181
38 See ECC 1999, p. 209

contents is still very important for such a network, and the individual work done by the players participating in the network is likewise to be regarded as highly significant. Also important, of course, is the orientation of the different partners within their cooperation. The target groups of different films, for example, differ from one another considerably, and this factor in itself might result in a varied choice of partners.

The basis for a successful utilisation network is of course the network participants who have the rights of disposal over the contents. In contrast to classical utilisation, however, it must be kept in mind with this structure that the dividing up of labour, risks, and revenue perspectives is a central factor for success in competition with other networks. The quality of the content only partially determines the success of the products and the network. The efforts of the various participants in the network are decisive for the economic success of the entertainment production. The development in the film industry towards a dominance of networks that are supplied with American films is being passed on to other areas of media more than ever before. The networks will in future be oriented more strongly towards individual projects, so as to take advantage of all revenue possibilities.

"Rational Exuberance"
Reflections on the theme of know-how in the German multimedia and Internet industry

Niko Waesche[39]

Financial euphoria on the stock markets and the ensuing sharp correction were decisive influences upon the perception of the times in the years around the turn of the century. As the upswing of the stock market was attributed to the spread of Internet and other digital technologies and to the positive effects these had on economic productivity, a connection was made. The financial developments were equated with the wave of new Internet companies being set up. It was believed, indeed, that it had been the stock market euphoria that had triggered the boom in founding Internet enterprises.[40] This was not so. Though Alan Greenspan had coined the term "irrational exuberance" as early as 1996 as a warning against a dangerous development on the stock markets, the first generation of Internet enterprises had already come into existence by then. The Internet software company Netscape had been floated on the NASDAQ in 1995. And even before the first Internet companies

No parallel between financial euphoria and the wave of new businesses

---

39 For an extensive consideration of the theme of Internet entrepreneurship in Europe, see Waesche 2003
40 For an ex-post description of the illusions and realities of Internet euphoria, see Litan/Rivlin 2001

were founded, entrepreneurs had been looking into digital production and online technologies necessary for the multimedia and commercial Internet to come. This was the case in Germany too. The spectacular growth of the new technology segment of the German stock exchange, the Neuer Markt, towards the end of the 1990s overshadowed company-founding activity in the new media that went back right to the beginning of the decade. Furthermore, the imitation of U.S. Internet business models seemed to substantiate the claim that Internet technologies and the concomitant financial euphoria had been "imported" from the United States.

As the example of the German multimedia branch makes clear, a long run-up phase was necessary before the commercial "take-off" of the Internet technologies could come about and the theme be taken up by the finance markets. The history of technology has already shown on many occasions how fundamental technical innovations are accompanied in parallel by social changes. The entrepreneur must help impel these social changes. The work of an entrepreneur in the early phase of establishing a technology is radically different from entrepreneurial activity in later stages. Faith in a new technology is born before the technology has reached maturity and is ready for commercial use.[41]

Evangelism or rational exuberance?

In the context of innovations in information technology (IT), a sort of "missionary" activity with a view to developing market demand has frequently been observed in the USA. This has been termed "evangelism," a concept with positive connotations in American English. Following Greenspan, one might also speak of "rational exuberance." The know-how of the evangelist is distinguished from specialist technical expertise, such as knowledge in system integration, but also from general management experience in the running of fast-growing technology firms. Evangelists proclaimed the potential of a new information technology for social transformation. The original motivation for the creation of new markets was closely bound up with a message of fundamental social change, a democratisation sparked off by technology. The graphical user interface shifted to the focus of attention: its continued development was to foster the mass-use of the computer and boost networking. The evangelist drew upon the computer "subculture" and a heterogeneous elite of cultural, artistic and technological sources, and transferred this knowledge into the economy. Evangelism was a transfer of knowledge, but it was also a business.

It is not possible to speak of "the" evangelism of information technology. Different bursts of IT innovation were accompanied in part by different evangelists. Yet the message of the democratisation of the means of production was always to the fore. The concept of "evangelism" itself came into being in the course of the development of the personal

---

41 See Christensen 1997

" The masses become more devout believers than their preachers. *"*

computer in the late 1970s and early 1980s, promulgated by workers at Apple. Apple Computer had a special place in the various waves of evangelism,[42] as indeed it did in Germany. Yet new messages of social change also came from outside the IT industry, and were then taken on board by the industry.

It is important to distinguish evangelism, which always has to do with establishing markets for new technologies, from the alternative computer culture. Evangelism was the selective transfer of knowledge from elite cultural and technological circles to society in general and the economy. Important stimuli for computer culture came from the subculture of hackers, influenced as this was by science fiction. Apple Computer had its origins in the hacker scene in Berkeley. Yet artists and media theorists too were in intensive dialogue with hackers about social aspects of computer technology.

Evangelism as a transfer of knowledge

One of the most important groups of evangelists in Germany were the early multimedia entrepreneurs. As in the United States, of course, in Germany too it was a heterogeneous group of people who spread the tidings of social transformation and contributed to the creation of new markets for multimedia and the Internet. Yet in the USA there were more formal and better developed points of contact between the economy and the cultural and technological elite.

The end of the evangelists came when the masses became more devout believers than the preachers themselves. Initially, multimedia entrepreneurs could not afford to be excessively euphoric. They were reliant on the expectations that they aroused with their projects actually coming to fruition. Accordingly, there were distinct approaches among evangelists. While some of them were able to speak of long-term prospects and comprehensive social transformation, the multimedia entrepreneurs had to stick relatively close to the technical possibilities of the time and the market. The multimedia entrepreneurs believed in social change, but knew how difficult it was to turn offline into online behaviour. They put the brake on the expectations of their customers.

At present in public discourse there exist two viewpoints with respect to the so-called "new economy" of the 1990s. Some see this time as an era of waste, a waste of resources, in which excessively young entrepreneurs took on positions of leadership for which they lacked the necessary experience and knowledge. Others used the decade of the 1990s to found their own firms or to get round hierarchical structures.

"New economy" – an area for innovation

---

42 There is an exhaustive Internet site on Apple at: http://library.stanford.edu/mac/. One Apple worker, Guy Kawasaki, himself came to monopolise the role of "Chief Evangelist."

They justify their activities with the learning experience this permitted them to glean. Some show greater sensitivity and intelligence in their justifications than others.

Interestingly, the issue of knowledge is prominent in both interpretations. What sort of knowledge was it that the founders lacked? Why was it seemingly the least experienced people who founded the early firms, and what exactly was motivating them? Where were the "old" experienced managers at the beginning of the 1990s?

Many multimedia entrepreneurs who opted for expansion in the 1990s did not succeed in building up genuine expertise in industry-specific strategic consultancy or IT system integration within their company. In the 2000s this was their undoing.

In spite of the poor economic situation and cuts in the IT budget, the starting position for digital business models in Germany has improved: access costs for the Internet have fallen in the early 2000s, and Internet penetration in Germany has gone soaring. It is the customers of the multimedia founders – well-established companies such as Deutsche Telekom, Bertelsmann or KarstadtQuelle – who will possibly profit most from the new technologies, the rising barriers to entry, and the increasing Internet penetration in Germany. Nor should one forget the few U.S. Internet firms that seem to have found their feet worldwide on a long-term basis, firms such as Yahoo!, eBay and Amazon.com.

With the example of the 1990s, the thesis is here being put forward that "rational exuberance" is necessary at the outset of bursts of IT innovation and for the creation of new IT markets. The development of information technologies in recent decades has already gone through several such bursts. There will be further ones in the future. The comment made by a multimedia entrepreneur is telling: "The great vision of a departure into a virtual world is not dead; only the small vision is, where you get to be a millionaire in three years."[43]

Niko Waesche is employee of IBM Germany

Rational exuberance as an enabler for innovations

---

43 Telephone interview with Harald Neidhardt, co-founder and Chief Executive Officer, Cardmine, Inc., 510 LaGuardia Place, New York 10012, 15 August 2001.

Chapter 1.4

New Technologies, New Customers and the Disruptive Nature of the Mobile Internet: Evidence from the Japanese Market

Jeffrey L. Funk

The parallel growth in mobile phone and Internet usage throughout the 1990s has suggested to many people that the market for mobile Internet service is potentially very large. Penetration rates for mobile phone usage now exceed 60% in most European countries, and fixed-line Internet penetration rates appear to lag phone penetration rates by only a few years. Many predict that the portable and personal nature of mobile phones will lead to greater Internet access from mobile phones than PCs by 2005.

This paper uses models of technology management to analyse the current state of the mobile Internet. Although there is a broad range of these models, most of them are based on the general idea that designs and market concepts evolve simultaneously. Following a technological discontinuity,[1] uncertainty about design and customer preferences leads to a diversity of technology in the products vying for customer acceptance. Actual customer usage generates information about the real customer requirements. And the logic of problem-solving in design and the formation of concepts that underlie choice in the marketplace impose a hierarchical structure on the evolution of the technology.[2]

Technological uncertainty despite high penetration rates of mobile phones

Different types of technologies and markets lead to differences in the evolution of the designs and market concepts. In many cases, the lead users of the old technology are the initial users of the new technology and thus define the evolution of the designs and market concepts. These types of technologies are easy to understand, and incumbents are often the winners since they can use their existing processes and business models to introduce products that are based on the new technology.

---

1 See Abernathy/Utterback 1978; Tushman/Anderson 1986; Utterback 1994
2 Clark 1985; Nelson/Winter 1982

Chapter 1.4
Funk

Disruptive technologies
appeal to new sets of
customers

On the other hand, a special class of technologies called disruptive technologies operates differently. These technologies improve some aspects of product performance while sacrificing others, thus making the new technologies appropriate for a new set of customers.[3] For example, each generation of new computing technology has first been used by a set of new customers. Mini-computers, PCs, and PDAs initially each offered lower computing capability at a much lower price and appealed to a new set of users. It was these new users and their requirements that initially defined the evolution of these computing technologies and this is one reason why a new set of firms like DEC, Wintel, and Palm came to dominate the hardware and software markets for these new technologies.

"The Internet, like its network predecessors, has turned out to be far more social than television, and in this respect, the impact of the Internet may be more like that of the telephone than of TV."

Robert Kraut et al. (1998)[4]

The PC Internet is also a disruptive technology for many firms. Due to the initially low richness available in the PC Internet it was a new set of customers that were initially interested in buying books, travel and financial products, and computers and in participating in auctions on the PC Internet. Like the various computing technologies, these new users and their requirements initially defined the evolution of the PC Internet, and this is one reason why new entrants like Amazon.com, Travelocity, Charles Schwab, Dell, and E-Bay moved faster to develop Internet businesses than leading incumbents like Barnes & Noble, travel agents, Merrill Lynch, Compaq, and Lloyds of London. There are some successful incumbents, and in many of those cases they created independent units to identify the appropriate customers and develop the appropriate technology.

Young people put mobility
above richness

It appears as if the same thing is happening all over again in the mobile Internet. The disruptive nature of the mobile Internet makes it initially appropriate for a new set of users, young people, and a new way of accessing information – opt-in mail over contents. The mobile Internet has higher reach (portability) but provides lower richness (small screens and keyboards) than the fixed-line Internet. Young people place more emphasis on reach (portability) and less emphasis on richness than older people because they are more

---

3 Christensen 1997
4 Kraut, Robert et al. (1998): Internet Paradox: A Social Technology That Reduces Social Involvement and Psychological Wel-Being? In: American Psychologist, vol. 53, no. 9, p. 5.

mobile (higher reach) and less specialised (lower richness) than older people. Opt-in mail compensates for the small screens and keyboards on the mobile phones by having the information come to the user as opposed to the user searching for the information.[5]

The mobile Internet is far more successful in Japan than in the West, and a major reason is that the mobile Internet is less disruptive for Japanese service providers and manufacturers than for their counterparts in the West. The mobile Internet is disruptive for service providers and phone manufacturers who have traditionally focused on business users since the mobile Internet is initially more appropriate for young people. This makes the mobile Internet more disruptive to Western than Japanese service providers since Western service providers and manufacturers have historically focused on business users more than their Japanese counterparts. As of mid-2002, there were almost no users of mobile Internet service in Europe or the USA while there were more than 50 million mobile Internet users in Japan, and they were spending an average of $15 a month on packet, content and other charges.[6]

> Wrong definition of target groups in the West

However, the more interesting story is how the mobile Internet is more disruptive for some Japanese firms than others and how this is causing dramatic changes in the Japanese Internet and software industries. A reorganisation of Japan's Internet and software industries is already underway, and it is quite likely that similar changes will occur in the West. Thus the advanced state of Japan's mobile Internet can tell us a lot about what to expect in the West. But before we look at these changes in four areas of Japan's mobile Internet, let's look at the concepts of disruptive technologies and network effects.

1.4.1
The Disruptive Nature of the Mobile Internet

Figure 1.4-1 shows the trade-off between reach and richness in both the pre-Internet and Internet economies. The Internet was supposed to "blow up" the existing trade-off between reach and richness[7] whereas it has actually created a new trade-off between them.[8] The mobile Internet provides higher reach but lower richness than the PC Internet, the classic case of a disruptive technology. This is why simple entertainment such as screen savers, ringing tones, games and horoscopes initially and to some extent still dominate the traffic in the Japanese mobile Internet.

> Trade-off between reach and richness

---

5 For more details see Funk 2001a
6 Ibid.
7 Evans/Wurster 2000
8 Funk 2001a

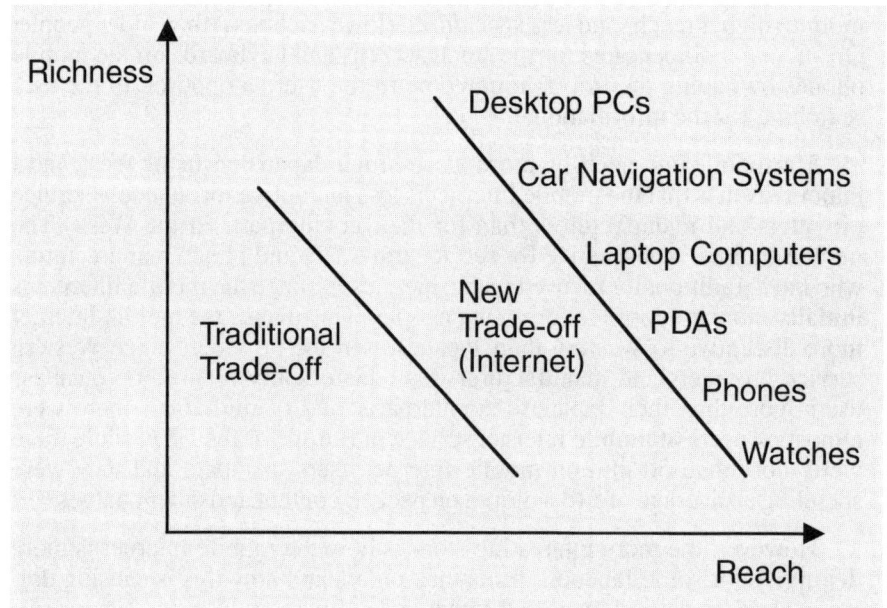

Fig. 1.4-1 The new trade-off between richness and reach

Young people are the initially appropriate users for the mobile Internet since they value reach more than richness to a greater extent than business people. High school and college students and even recent graduates spend more time outside their offices and homes than business people because they often do not have offices, spouses and kids. Further, they place less emphasis on rich information since they are less specialised than business people. This is why young people were initially dominant among users of the Japanese mobile Internet and still use the mobile Internet more than business people in Japan.

Of course, the users and applications will expand as the capabilities of mobile phones improve. Small and cheaper electronic devices have reduced phones to the size of candy bars, and now manufacturers are busily using smaller and cheaper electronic devices to introduce phones with larger and better displays, better input methods (e.g. voice recognition) and higher data rates. These developments are causing the applications and users of the Japanese mobile Internet to expand, and new developments like wearable computing may eventually eliminate many of the mobile Internet's deficiencies with respect to the PC Internet.

The Demand for Broadband: An Analysis of Access and Content

Paul N. Rappoport, Donald J. Kridel and Lester D. Taylor

In general, we here analyse the demand for broadband from three interwoven perspectives: the form of access (i.e. narrowband or broadband), sites visited (as a reflection of a user's choice of content), and time spent at an Internet session (as a measure of the value of time). Two primary questions guide our analysis of click-stream data. First, does usage – such as the hours per month online – help distinguish broadband users from narrowband users? Second, what measures of usage are most useful for classifying households?

Households with high-speed access show more intensive usage as well as greater variation of usage than households with lower-speed access (see Table 1).

Minutes of usage per month	Narrowband access	Broadband access
Average	1,013	1,536
Median	495	870
Standard deviation	1,563	2,261

Tab. 1 Average minutes of usage by type of access (Plurimus, August 2001)

On average, broadband users spend 50% more time online than their narrowband counterparts. Both the narrowband and broadband usage distributions are long-tailed distributions, indicating that there are users who consume large amounts of time independent of type of Internet access. Two points are worth emphasising. First, about 55% of narrowband subscribers were online less than 10 hours per month. For broadband users, the comparable percentage was about 40%. The fact is that independent of the type of access, a large number of Internet users fall on the lower side of the usage distribution. Second, two percent of the narrowband users were online over 100 hours per month as compared to 4.6% of broadband users. This presence of long tails is expected for the broadband group, but probably less so for the narrowband group, given the hypotheses associated with opportunity cost and the implicit value of online activity.

More intensive use and greater variance in broadband users

Broadband users visit more web sites but for shorter periods

Another indicator of usage is found in the number of sites (specific URLs) visited. The differences between narrowband and broadband users in the number of sites visited is even more striking. Broadband users visit, on average, 90% more sites. They also tend to spend 23% less time at a site (see Table 2).

Number of sites visited per month	Narrowband access	Broadband access
Average	434	824
Median	207	466
Minutes per site	2.75	2.12

Table 2 Average number of sites visited by type of access (Plurimus, 2001)

More intensive use between 6 pm and midnight

Does hour of the day help differentiate narrowband from broadband users? This question is explored in Figure 1, which displays the percentage of all minutes spent online for each user group by time of day. Interestingly, broadband customers are heavier users from midnight through 6 a.m., while dial-up customers are heavier users from 6 a.m. through noon. Afternoon and evening usages are very similar for both types of customers.[9]

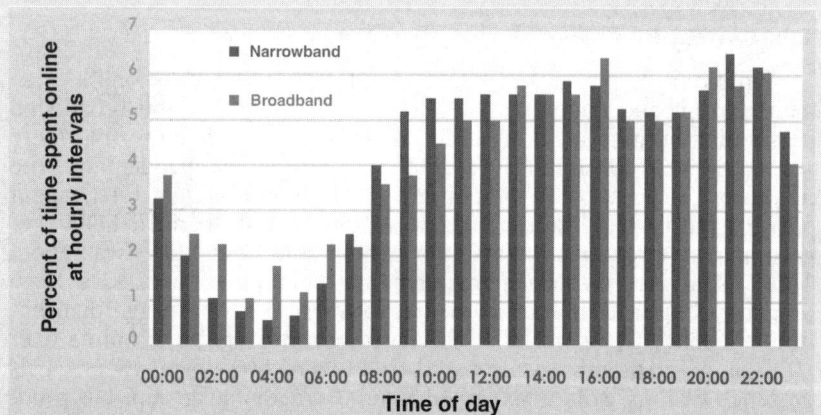

Figure 1 Distribution by type of site (Plurimus (August 2001))

---

9 Average minutes online for households who were online for at least 10 minutes in that hour and who have visited at least two sites.

There is observed to be a difference in terms of the type of sites visited (see Figure 2). For example, we observe that broadband users spend twice the amount of time at entertainment sites, on average, as their narrowband counterparts whereas broadband users spend less time on the category Internet services than narrowband users. The Internet category includes email and chat, both low bandwidth activities. These results suggest that more differentiation may be found as one drills down to more micro levels of detail.

Broadband users spent more time on entertainment services

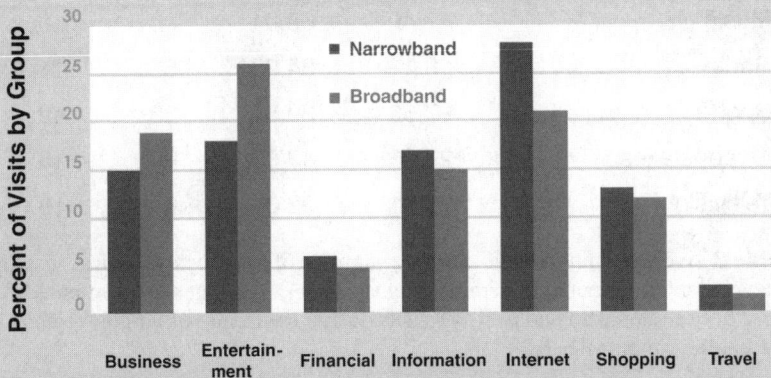

Figure 2 Distribution by type of site (Plurimus, August 2001)

Table 3 supports the view that entertainment sites are more intensively used, both with respect to minutes and number of sites visited.

Broadband users spend more time at specific sub-categories such as gambling and music. However, the difference in terms of average number of minutes is small for adult services, music and sports. In general, broadband users tend to be above average users of those sites that are associated with intensive use. This use could be measured in terms of the number of bytes downloaded or the time required to finish a task (games, music, software).

	Minutes		Sites	
	S	B	S	B
Adult services	112.84	126.43	51	124
Arts	13.34	7.43	6	4
Gambling	15.20	47.04	3	6
Games	79.27	109.24	22	48
Movies	14.65	10.69	5	5
Music	47.40	68.01	10	15
Radio	18.11	34.92	6	11
Sports	67.52	89.51	23	42
Sweepstakes	25.06	42.00	9	18
Television	21.01	32.01	6	13

Table 3 Average minutes and average number of sites by type of access for category entertainment (Plurimus, August 2001). Averages are computed for those households who had positive visits during the month of August to at least one entertainment site.

Paul Rappoport is Associate Professor in the Economics Department of Temple University, Philadelphia; Donald Kridel is Associate Professor in the Economics Department of the University of Missouri, St. Louis; Lester Taylor is Professor in the Department of Economics of the University of Arizona.

Figure 1.4-2 uses the concepts of reach and richness to show how the mobile Internet can also be disruptive for PC Internet content providers. PC content providers must simplify their contents for the small screens and keyboards of the mobile phone, thus creating a discontinuity with the previous services. The degree to which it is possible for content providers to simplify their services for the small screens and keyboards of mobile phones determines the degree of the disruptiveness from the mobile Internet. As is discussed below, some contents are easier to simplify than others.

Further, most Japanese content providers have also introduced personalised mail and to a lesser extent site customisation services in order to realise the "potential reach" of the mobile phone.

The need to adapt contents to the mobile format

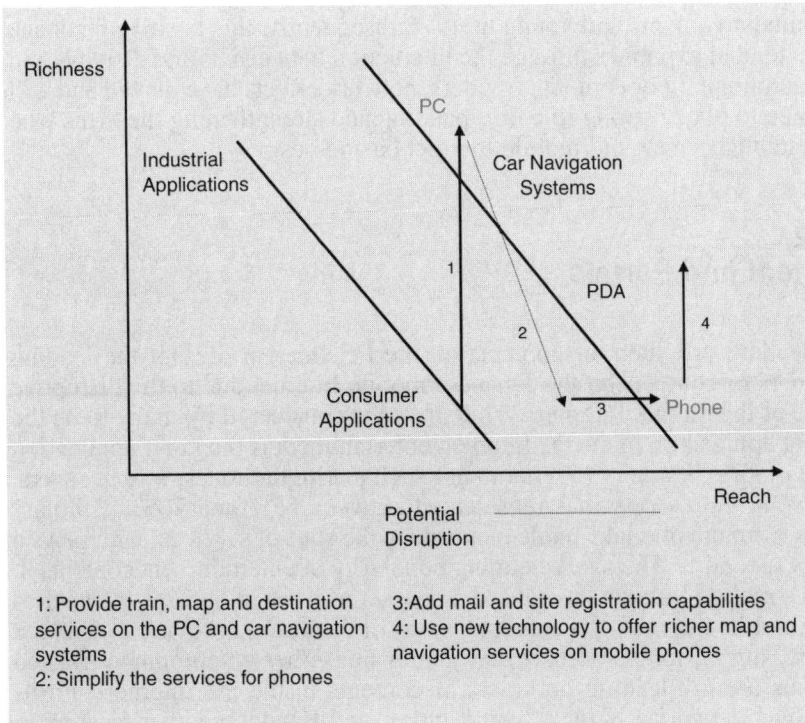

1: Provide train, map and destination services on the PC and car navigation systems
2: Simplify the services for phones
3: Add mail and site registration capabilities
4: Use new technology to offer richer map and navigation services on mobile phones

Fig. 1.4-2 The potential disruptiveness of mobile internet: example of navigation services

Both of these personalised services enable users to partly avoid the small keyboards and screens of mobile phones to search for specific information on the site. Mail services make the information more accessible to the user, since they make it unnecessary for users to remember and actually access the site. And while mail services are slightly more expensive than site customisation services to the content provider, successful content providers have found that mail click rates are very high and thus rates for advertisements placed in mail have not experienced the same reduction as banner advertisements on the PC.

A second key concept in the mobile Internet is network effects. When the value of a product to one user depends on how many other users there are, the product is said to exhibit network effects or network externalities. Communication technologies such as telephones, email, and the PC and mobile Internet are prime examples of products that exhibit network effects. The early success of entertainment contents in NTT DoCoMo's i-mode service in mid-1999 led to the emergence of positive feedback between these en-

Personalised services: success despite cost intensity

Network effects in the mobile Internet

tertainment contents and young users. Subsequently, this positive feedback was extended to phones through the interaction between colour displays and colour contents. For content providers, network effects have played and will continue to play a strong role in expanding and strengthening the firms who first establish successful mobile Internet businesses.

1.4.2
Content and Portals

Different leading content providers in fixed-online Internet and mobile Internet

The leading providers of contents on the PC Internet are not the leading providers of contents on the Japanese mobile Internet due to the disruptive nature of the mobile Internet. While travel is considered by many to be the leading application in the PC Internet, entertainment is the killer application in the mobile Internet. Entertainment such as ringing tones, screen savers, games and horoscopes has represented between 55% and 70% of the accesses from the official i-mode menu since the start of services, with news a distant second.[10] The overwhelming popularity of entertainment contents in Japan's mobile Internet has caused a new set of firms to become the leaders in the mobile Internet. For example, many of the leading providers of screen savers, ringing tones, horoscopes, games and other entertainment-related contents are not leading providers of contents in the PC Internet. Firms like Giga Networks, X-ing, Cybird, Index, and Bandai together have more than 10 million subscribers paying 100 to 300 Yen a month through micro-payment services offered by the service providers. And some of these firms, in particular Cybird and Index, have used their success in providing these simple entertainment contents to become leaders in providing entertainment and mobile commerce solutions to other firms.

Simple entertainment services are more popular than news

Similar things are happening in news. While business news, in particular news about information technology, is the most popular news on the PC Internet, weather and sports are the most popular news on the mobile Internet due to the small size of the screens and the large number of young users. Table 1.4-1 summarises the leading PC and mobile Internet sites in Japan. Most of the leading providers of news on the PC Internet, which are business news providers, are not leading providers of news on the mobile Internet. Impress (no. 1 on the PC Internet), Nikkei BP (no. 2), Nikkei (no. 4), ZD Net (no. 5) and Ascii24 (no. 9) are not leading providers of news on the mobile Internet. Instead, the most successful PC news providers on the mobile Internet have focused their news on sports; this includes Sankei, Asahi, and Yomiuri. These firms along with Mainichi News and the weather news providers have

---

10 Ibid.

PC Site Traffic Ranking		Mobile site Traffic Ranking	
Site name	Field	Field	Firms
1) Impress	IT	1) Weather	WNI, All Nation Weather, i-Weather, DWP
2) Nikkei BP	Business	2) Newspapers (all sports except Nikkei)	Mainichi, Asahi Nikkan, Sankei, Yomiuri, Nikkei
3) Asahi	General	3) Regional Newspapers	32 newspapers sites
4) Nikkei	General	4) News	News Service Center, Jiji Communication News, Asahi/Nikkei, Kyodo News
5) ZD Net	IT	5) Foreign Media	7 sites
6) Sankei	General	6) Business Info	Pocket Ascii, BizTech News (Nikkei BP), Imperial Data, Diamond, Nikkei, TSR, Impress
7) Asahi Nikkan	Sports		
8) Yomiuri	General		
9) Asccii24	IT		

Tab. 1.4-1 Leading providers of PC- and mobile internet news in terms of traffic[12]

several millions of subscribers who are paying between 100 and 300 Yen a month.

Even more dramatic changes have occurred in independent portals that offer information on so-called unofficial contents and mail magazines. These contents and mail magazines are not available on NTT DoCoMo's official i-mode menu, and already traffic to these unofficial sites far exceeds traffic

Unofficial portals are leaders

12 Japan Access Rankings (http: //www.istinc.co.jp/jar/jar_sum/jar2001.html) for PC Internet data i-mode official menu. The mobile Internet services offerd by the leading PC news providers are underlined

on the official i-mode menu. The importance of mail in the mobile Internet has caused two relatively unknown portals, Girls Walker and Magic Island, to become the leading independent portals in the mobile Internet. While the leader portal in the fixed-line Internet, Yahoo! Japan, has focused on making its PC contents accessible to its PC customers, Girls Walker and Magic Island have focused on mail magazines and homepage creation services respectively; the latter is important because young people like to put links to these homepages in their mobile mail. Neither of these firms has advertised its services, and instead they have relied on viral marketing to promote their portals. All of the mail sent by Girls Walker's mail magazines and homepages created on Magic Island's site contain links to the places in the sites for creating new mail magazines and homepages.

Girls Walker now offers 17,000 types of mail magazines that are written by 1,700 independent and unpaid writers; it has 75,000 sites registered on its contents portal; it receives 8.4 million page views each day; and it has used the strength of its portal and mail magazines to become one of the leading providers of mobile shopping in Japan's mobile Internet. Magic Island's users have created 1.4 million homepages, and the Magic Island site and its homepages receive 22 million page views per day. Both firms make money from sending opt-in mail to their many millions of unique users.

1.4.3
Retailers and Manufacturers

The importance of the mobile phone also extends to retailers and manufacturers. Retailers and manufacturers are using mobile Internet mail to send discount coupons and surveys due to the low cost, fast turnaround and high response rate of mobile mail. For example, the most successful retailer in the mobile Internet is Tsutaya Online, which is the leading provider of video and music rentals and sales. It has increased the number of visitors and sales by sending mail containing discount coupons to its online members. Tsutaya's success first caused other retailers that sell to young people like Jeansmate and Fast Kitchen to offer these discount coupons in opt-in mail services, but now Japan's largest supermarkets and department stores like Seiyu, Odakyu, Tokyu and Yuni along with many online restaurant sites and fast-food restaurants also offer these discount coupons on various sites and in mail services.

Powerful portals and content providers are using their strength to provide discount coupon and survey services to retailers and manufacturers. The largest provider of these discount coupons and surveys is D2C, a joint venture between NTT DoCoMo and Dentsu. NTT DoCoMo uses the strength of its

Attracting users by means of homepage creation services and mail magazines

Discount coupons through the mobile Internet

portal to send discount coupons and surveys to consumers from a broad set of retailers and manufacturers. It has more than 2 million registered users who have elected to receive information about discount coupons and/or participate in surveys.

Further, Japan's newest mobile phones contain short-range infrared communication technologies that will enable phones to exchange data with other devices. Retailers would like to use this technology as a form of point card to obtain individual consumer data and reward heavy shoppers. More interestingly, they would like to combine this data with the data collected by bar code scanners. Although this has been the goal of credit card companies in their development of smart IC cards for many years, it is possible that infrared technology will soon provide similar results at a fraction of the cost.

The effect of the disruptive nature of the mobile Internet on retailers and manufacturers provides some retailers like Tsutaya Online with an opportunity to expand their retail presence in the Japanese market and the new providers of discount coupons and surveys with an opportunity to challenge the leading providers of customer-relationship management software and services. The leading providers of these software and services focus on the integration between the telephone and computer, particularly the Internet. Customer-relationship management in the mobile Internet focuses on a different set of technologies, such as discount coupons, surveys, mail, short-range infrared communication, and bar code scanners.

1.4.4
Mobile Shopping

The disruptive nature of the mobile Internet is also having a dramatic effect on mobile shopping in that it is causing the products, selection methods and leading firms to be different from those of PC Internet shopping in the West. The leading products are relatively simple and are popular with young people. They include CDs, DVDs, concert tickets, game software, fashion and accessories (see Table 1.4-2), and they are quite different from the PC Internet, where travel, computers and books dominate the market.

Users also select products very differently on their mobile phones than on their PCs. While sophisticated search engines were a major reason for the early success of Amazon.com and other major dot-coms, in the mobile Internet most products are purchased through opt-in mail services. The next most popular products are those that are advertised at the top of the first page, in the new releases section, or in product rankings. It is too difficult to use search engines on the mobile Internet, and it seems that many young people

Exchange of data from one device to another

Data-mining among mobile services

Customers purchase different products through mobile opt-in mail

Sub-Category	Leading Content Providers
CDs,DVDs,Games and Books	Tsutaya Online (all), HMV Japan (music and videos), Playstation (games), Kinokuniya (books), Honya-san (books), Book Service, Amazon.com, CD &DVD Neowing, TV Panic Game Store
Convenience Stores	Lawson, Family Mart, 7-11
Tickets	Ticket Pia, Lawson Ticket, E-Plus
Fashion	f-mode, Perfume (Index), Shibuya 109, Uniqlo, Magaseek (Itochu),
Flowers	Flowers (Index), I-Flower Shop

Tab. 1.4-2 Order of traffic by sub-category and content-provider in the i-mode official shopping category

just want to get the most popular CD, video or game software before their friends do.

These different methods of selection also cause the type of CDs, DVDs, concert tickets and other products that are purchased on the mobile Internet to be different from that on the PC Internet. For example, HMV Japan categorises music as pre-order, current and past popular, and "deep catalogue." While the percent represented by pre-order sales is almost the same for the PC and mobile Internet, the percent represented by current and past popular is 50% higher on mobile than PC, and the percent represented by deep catalogue is *six times* higher on the PC than on the mobile Internet. Most people find it far too difficult to search for deep catalogue music with the small screens and keyboards found on the mobile phones.

Opening up customer groups
with little experience in
e-commerce

As with other disruptive technologies, the different products, customers and experiences with purchasing methods have caused firms that are relatively weak in the PC Internet like Tsutaya Online, convenience stores, Girls Walker and Index to become the leaders in mobile shopping, a market that exceeds US $20 million a month. Tsutaya Online has used its strength in mail services and discount coupons to become the leader in CDs and DVDs. Convenience stores have used their proximity to train stations to promote in-store pick-ups of music and video-related products, including the sale of concert tickets. Girls Walker has used its mail magazines to become the leader in shopping services for fashion and accessories. Index sells perfume that is used by leading entertainment celebrities and organises this site in terms of these celebrities.

" Multi-channel integration by combining TV programmes and the mobile Internet. "

The concepts of reach and richness also tell us something about why and how firms are combining different media. Firms are compensating for the low richness of the mobile Internet by integrating their contents with other media like magazines, and radio and TV programmes. On the surface, since firms may not have to sacrifice reach or richness when they combine different media with the mobile Internet, the mobile Internet may not be disruptive technology for these firms.

Compensating for low richness through media integration

However, it may not be easy for some firms to quickly integrate different media in a short period of time, and thus it may be best for some firms to create independent units that are responsible for handling their mobile Internet activities. Radio stations appear to face the least disruption from the mobile Internet, and this may be why they have not created independent units to handle their mobile Internet activities. Mobile Internet mail has already become their main source of music and free concert ticket requests, replacing telephone calls and facsimiles. These stations are now trying to integrate information on their mobile Internet sites about on-air songs with online CD sites. Nevertheless, it is the radio stations with young listeners that have moved faster than those without young listeners.

Low disruption for radio, greater disruption for print media

The integration of magazines and the mobile Internet appears to be a bigger challenge. Several content providers now enable consumers to purchase products that are advertised in magazines, thus dividing up the consumer's purchasing process between searches in magazines and purchases on the mobile Internet. For example, one of Japan's largest trading companies created an independent unit called Magaseek, which sells products that are advertised in women's fashion magazines that are published by young people. The challenge for Magaseek is to increase the number of sales without substantially increasing the search time for users. In the current hierarchical search process offered by Magaseek, increasing the number of items offered on the site would increase the search time. It would probably be useful for Magaseek to rank products and provide mail services, methods that have proved useful for other sites.

Clearly the integration between TV programmes and the mobile Internet represents the largest potential market for so-called multi-channel integration. Already, many of Japan's major TV stations have created independent business units to sell their programme theme songs as ringing tones, popular animation and celebrities as screen savers, and games and horoscopes that are based on their TV programmes all over the mobile Internet. They are also experimenting with doing real-time surveys in non-prime-time television and providing information on actors, actresses and programme locations on their mobile sites. These surveys and information could provide a simple version of interactive television at a fraction of the cost of digital televisions and special digital programming.

Potential for integrating TV and mobile Internet

It is interesting that many TV stations are creating independent units to manage what in the long run will require effective integration between TV programmes and mobile contents. However, the independent units believe that it is more important for them to bring in independent revenues in order to demonstrate the viability of the mobile Internet. Thus, they are more concerned with introducing games that obtain paying subscribers than games that increase the number of TV viewers. On the other hand, it is likely that eventually TV stations will need to implement a new form of organisation to promote effective synergies between TV programmes and mobile contents.

1.4.5
Navigation Market

Navigation or so-called location-based services were supposed to be the killer application on the mobile Internet. People were expected to use the location capabilities of phones to find the restaurants, bars, hotels and parking lots that are near them. Location-based ads were also expected to become a big market as restaurants and other firms began sending mail-based advertisements to people near them.

Location-based services – a killer application?

This has not yet happened due to the *current* technological and cost problems of putting GPS in phones but also due to the key role of network effects. Network effects play a strong role in destination-information services. Few people want to visit these sites until there is information about a large number of restaurants, bars, stores, hotels or parking lots on the site. And restaurants and other firms do not want to participate in such services until there are a large number of users of these sites.

The existing business models exacerbate these problems. Currently, these sites charge restaurants money to put information about the restaurants on the sites since users are unwilling to pay for the services. But these charges make it even harder for restaurants to justify participation in these sites until there are a reasonable number of visitors to these sites. Of course, U.S. dot-coms tried to solve this problem by spending large amounts of money on marketing, and many of them ended up in bankruptcy proceedings. Destination-information sites must find the critical set of users, services and data that will start the positive feedback in the system.

The concept of disruptive technologies tells us something about why some firms are currently winning, and the combination of disruptive technologies and network effects can also tell us something about who will eventually win (see Table 1.4-3).

The mobile Internet is far less disruptive for train/bus and destination-information (e.g. restaurant information) services than for map services. It is easier to input train stations, bus stops or food types into your mobile phone than it is to look at a map on the mobile phone displays, which are currently small and have poor resolution. This is why the train and bus information services have almost one million paying subscribers and 10 million page views a day while the map services have less than a tenth of these numbers. The destination-information services have more than 10 million page views per day.

Network effects are working against the map providers. They are now giving away free maps to the train, bus and destination-information services in order to advertise their map services to mobile Internet users. But this only increases the attractiveness of the latter services, thus causing more firms to want their information placed on the latter sites, particularly the train and bus information site offered by the leader Toshiba. Toshiba is trying to conquer network effects by offering destination information and maps only around the train stations. It hopes that phones with GPS capabilities, which have just begun to appear, will allow Toshiba to provide its users with the capability to get from the train station to that hard-to-find restaurant.

Differences in the viability of various mobile services

On the other hand, the map services may find success in the new car navigation systems that are starting to appear through a joint venture (Xanavi) between Hitachi and Nissan. While the existing car navigation systems use expensive DVD-ROMs to store map information, the new systems, which cost about 50,000 Yen ($400), download the maps and optimal routes using Internet technology from proprietary servers. This is definitely a disruptive technology for the leading manufacturers of car navigation systems, since the

Ranking	Type of Contents
1	Train route information
2	Restaurant information
3	Vehicle traffic information
4	Maps
5	Airline information
6	Rental car information
7	Hotel information

Tab. 1.4-3 Ranking of navigation contents by traffic

new systems are slow and cumbersome. But as processing and transmission speeds increase through better electronics and 3G services, these new systems may eventually replace the existing car navigation systems.

1.4.6
Discussion

Japan's success in the mobile Internet confirms the initial predictions made by many Westerners about the importance of the mobile Internet. More than 80% of Japan's mobile phone subscribers own an Internet-compatible phone, and the high average mobile Internet revenue use per person suggests that many Japanese utilise this capability. Although entertainment and weather and sports news represent the majority of the traffic on the Japanese mobile Internet, there continues to be strong growth in new applications like mobile shopping and navigation services.

Mobile entertainment for young target groups

Of course, the mobile Internet has evolved very differently than many people expected (both in Japan and elsewhere). The popularity of entertainment for young people has caused technology development initially to focus on colour displays for screen savers, games and horoscopes, cameras for mail, polyphonic ringing tones, and Java for games. Contents for third generation services focus on entertainment and also news, but there has been little growth in the demand for these third generation services. GPS-compatible phones have also just been released, but the poor maps suggest this function may not play an important role in the near future.

This article argues that the concept of disruptiveness explains why the mobile Internet has evolved differently than expected. The increased portability at the expense of screen size has made the technology appropriate for a new set of users, young people. They favour personalised services like screen savers and ringing tones, simple entertainment like horoscopes and games, weather and sports news, and mail. The concept of disruptiveness also explains why mobile shopping and navigation services are evolving differently than expected.

And as with previous disruptive technologies, the markets and margins for these young people in the mobile Internet are small when compared to the established technologies. Mobile commerce (not counting packet charges) was only 7.2% of total e-commerce in Japan in fiscal 2001,[12] and as Vodafone and other leaders like to report, the margins for young users are much smaller

---

12 Ibid.

than for business users. But mobile commerce is growing faster than e-commerce and so are the capabilities of mobile phones when compared to PCs, which may have already exceeded many consumer needs.

The evolution of Japan's mobile Internet has important implications for Western service providers like Vodafone, Verizon and AT&T Wireless, manufacturers like Nokia and Motorola, and content providers like Yahoo! Unfortunately, they and the Western press are following the classic pattern of disruptive technologies. They keep focusing on those technical developments that will enable the mobile Internet to be meaningful for their targeted users, when they should be finding those users who will put up with the limitations of the mobile Internet. Western manufacturers[13] and service providers have focused and still focus on business users; they did this with their WAP services and phones and are still doing it with their GPRS services and phones. Of course, it is true that business users have always played a more important role in Europe and the USA than in Japan due to differences in roaming. Roaming does provide high margins in the USA and Europe, and business people incur most of these roaming charges. Japan has had the equivalent of national licence for at least ten years, and this is part of the reason that NTT DoCoMo never got hung up on business users.

The decisions to focus on business users have made it easy for Western firms to ignore Japan's mobile Internet's success. But recently it has become harder to do this. On the one hand firms say that the Japanese market is different, and on the other hand they say that they do not want to cannibalise their SMS (short messaging services) market, where young people are the major users and screen savers and ringing tones are playing an important and expanding role in this and next generation SMS. Both cannot be true. The message for the West is clear. It is not differences in culture; it is differences in targeted customers and the appropriate services, phones and contents for those targeted customers.

To what extent does Japan's experience in mobile Internet apply in the West?

---

13 See Funk 2001b

Chapter 1.5

Journalism in the Face of Developments in Digital Production

John Pavlik

1.5.1
A Journalist's Medium

It has been said that newspapers are an editor's medium and that broadcasting is a producer's medium. To the extent that either of these statements is true, today it can be said that the Internet is a journalist's medium. The Internet not only embraces all the capabilities of the older media (text, images, graphics, animation, audio, video, real-time delivery) but offers a broad spectrum of new capabilities, including interactivity, on-demand access, user control, and customisation. Thus using the new media tools available via the Internet, online journalists can tell stories using whatever modalities and communication features are needed and appropriate for a particular story. Moreover, each audience member can receive personalised news that places each story into a context meaningful to her or him. The only real limits on the Internet as a journalistic medium are bandwidth, connectivity, and credibility of content. All three of these are likely to become much less constraining over time, as bandwidth and connectivity increase (i.e. as transmission speeds increase, allowing for easier access to quality multimedia content, and as the number of citizens connected to the Internet increases) and as citizens become more familiar with the Internet and develop new media literacy skills that allow them to recognise reliable, authentic online sources. Bandwidth and related network congestion are periodically a heightened problem for all online news providers whenever there is a breaking story of particularly great audience interest.

Internet as a journalist's medium

Contextualised Journalism

This article examines the fundamental nature of the storytelling transformation of journalism in an online, electronic environment and argues that a new form of news is emerging, perhaps best described as contextualised

Contextualised journalism as a new form of news

journalism. Contextualised journalism has five basic dimensions or aspects: (1) breadth of communication modalities; (2) hypermedia; (3) heightened audience involvement; (4) dynamic content; and (5) customisation.

1.5.2
Communication Modalities

First, and most obviously, news in this new media environment can take advantage of the full range of communication modalities, including text, audio, video, graphics and animation, as well as emerging capabilities such as 360-degree video. These capabilities enable the journalist to tell each story in a way uniquely suited to it, no longer constrained by the limited modalities available in previous analogue media. A variety of fixed media publishing enterprises have demonstrated the value of the enriched storytelling capabilities of multimedia.

Multimedia possibilities in online journalism

Unfortunately, online journalism has only slowly begun to incorporate many of these multimedia capabilities. There are several reasons for this. First, except for many television network-based sites, most online news operations (with a parent newspaper or other print operations) do not have extensive traditions in creating multimedia content; neither do they have a culture or set of resources to begin producing such multimedia content easily. Some innovative sites are beginning to produce more original multimedia content, however, and this will grow in the months and years ahead. Second, some news operations tend to view online reporting as merely an extension of their existing activities, and if they are print based, they tend not to view video and audio as terribly relevant. Third, many operations do not have staff with multimedia capabilities and backgrounds and are likely to hire reporters similar to those who have worked for the parent print operations, where the emphasis is on the written word; graphics, images, audio and video are not part of their training.

A room with an omnidirectional view

Visual storytelling

Dating to the work of the Lumière brothers in 1890s' Paris, the constraints of limited-field-of-view photography have provided the fundamental structure of visual storytelling, especially news and entertainment on television and film. Video- and photojournalists, cinematographers, and other videographers have used the frame of the photographic lens to define the linear narrative of visual storytelling. Now, three fundamental developments have made possible a paradigmatic shift in visual storytelling. First, digital video, although not new, has matured and is set to become important not just in production but also in storytelling, as viewers at home and elsewhere will have direct access to video in digital form. Second, a new generation of image and sound acquisition devices (e.g. new 3-D cameras and microphones, high-resolution remote sensing satellite imagery, etc.) will open up the possibilities available to those creating images and video, offering options ranging from panoramic views to three-dimensional immersive environments. Third, the growth of networked media, including today's Internet and tomorrow's digital television, will furnish a wide range of creative and interactive alternatives to visual storytellers.

Possible applications of omnidirectional imaging are substantial and wide ranging. Surveillance and security systems will be profoundly altered by the introduction of 360-degree video. An omniview camera can survey an entire scene with virtually no blind spots. Supplanting robotic mechanisms and controls, an omnicamera permits multiple viewers to survey different parts of a scene. It involves a miniature 360-degree camera mounted on a gyroscope and encased in a plexiglass sphere. The sphere, which also contains a microphone for capturing sound and batteries for power, can be rolled into areas unsafe for a person to enter, such as a nuclear power plant where there has been a radiation leak, or a burning building, or even a hostage or terrorist situation. The camera can then transmit a 360-degree video of the location via a wireless transmitter. Another version of this "Cyclops" has a motor and system of locomotion that allows an operator in a remote location to steer it around objects or corners. The implications for firefighters, police or even journalists are profound, since such devices would enable safe remote observation of hazardous or inaccessible areas. When linked to the World Wide Web, parents anywhere in the world with Web access could monitor their children's activity.

Possible applications of omnidirectional technologies

The real risk in the deployment of omnidirectional technology is that the omnicamera will become little more than a technological gimmick employed by local (or network) news operations that will be showcased for its own sake rather than as an enhancement to storytelling. There is little to prevent this from happening; indeed, it already has happened with various preceding technologies, such as live transmissions from remote locations, helicopters, and infrared cameras. In a business driven more by commercial interests than the public interest, perhaps the only two things that could help ensure the appropriate use of omnidirectional cameras or any other new media tool would be (1) a clear set of standards for the appropriate use of new media tools, articulated by leaders in journalism and the news industry (and adopted by the leading news organisations, such as the Radio Television News Directors Association); and (2) media news startups to a certain degree free of the constraints and traditions of long-standing news organisations and

Risks in the use of omnidirectional technologies

thus able to define their news standards in a fresh manner that could serve as a competitive advantage.

The omnicamera could also be a valuable tool for journalists who find themselves in hazardous zones, such as in a military conflict. Rather than stand up and pan the camera around the battlefield, putting himself at serious risk of injury or death from enemy or friendly fire, a reporter could simply set an omnicamera on a tripod and crouch down.

Even outside a war zone, omnidirectional technology might have important uses, say, at live events, such as protests, political rallies, sporting events, or busy traffic intersections. Or imagine putting an omnicamera on the dashboard of a police cruiser. News reports have sometimes provided dramatic video of a suspect and police officer captured by a dashboard camera, only to have the suspect move to the side of the squad car and a critical moment pass unrecorded. With an omnicamera on the dash, nothing would be lost from view.

A second broad application of the omnidirectional camera involves the transformation of storytelling. In many ways, omnidirectional video represents a changing imaging paradigm, one fundamentally different from the achievement a century ago of the Lumière brothers, who invented the first motion picture camera and projected the first motion picture, documenting scenes from daily life ("Man Hammering Wall" was among the Lumière brothers' first films and evokes the documentary model of modern television journalism).

Consider this in the context of the historical roots of omnidirectional imaging. The concept is derived from 17th- and 18th-century panoramas or panoramic paintings and murals depicting scenes, often found in the castles and palaces of Europe.

The panorama, frequently a full 360° cyclorama, was the brainchild of the English artist Robert Barker, who developed the correct perspective approaches to give the appearance of all-round vision. He was granted a patent for his process in 1787. The first exhibition space was not large enough to hold the full 360° painting, which was not displayed in its entirety until 1793, when the first purpose-built panorama building in the world was constructed in Leicester Square. Panoramas became all the rage for the rest of the century and well into the 19th.

A few years later the panorama made its way to the New World. Steamboat skipper Robert Fulton introduced the panorama to Paris in 1799 and shortly thereafter to the United States. John Vanderlyn's 1819 panoramic depiction of the Versailles gardens is on exhibit in the Metropolitan Museum of Art in New York. Panoramic images were also used in reporting the Civil War. One famous three-camera photograph was taken in 1864, just after the

Union Army had captured the city of Chattanooga, Tennessee, from Confederate forces. Almost two centuries later the first digital panorama appeared on the *Star Trek* CD-ROM, which allowed circular tours of the chambers of the Starship Enterprise.

Often, technologies are invented for explicit purposes and applications, in the case of journalism to improve the efficiency, accuracy and speed of some aspect of communication. And as important as these intended effects are, the unintended or unexpected consequences are often more significant. The panorama is such a case. When King George III visited one of London's first panoramas in 1794, he was intrigued by the imagery surrounding him, a detailed painting of a naval fleet moored near the Isle of Wight. The reaction of his wife, Queen Charlotte, was somewhat more visceral: she became mildly seasick, which may explain why the work was retitled the *Nausorama* when it was displayed in Hamburg in Germany a few years later.

Cultural resistance

One of the biggest factors causing relatively limited use of omnidirectional imaging among news organisations up to 2000 has been the slow development of a new storytelling paradigm suited to 360-degree images. Taking a good omnidirectional image is even more complex than taking a good conventional still image (because one must consider the entire field of view). Moreover, most news organisations that have used the technology successfully, such as the "New York Times on the Web," "CNN.com" or "MSNBC.com," have provided interesting-looking 360-degree views of news events, frequently for features, but rarely have they used the images to tell a story. Instead they use them as novel complements to accompanying text reports. A development that may advance the storytelling of omnidirectional imaging is the incorporation of object-oriented video or hot spots (hypertext links), as well as the addition of audio tracks to omnidirectional still images. In this second case, the reporter will report accompanying facts and context for the image in an audio narration with ambient sound, while using a Java applet to pan, tilt or zoom throughout the 360-degree view automatically. In this way, one might tell a story and create a dynamic, moving picture from a single, 360-degree still image, minimising the bandwidth and processing power for a high-resolution video report.

Although iPIX and the other 360-degree imaging systems are in some news use, most have significant limitations, such as being large and complex to use, thereby limiting their potential in online journalism, especially by freelancers or one-person news crews, or require multiple images that must

Slow development of a new storytelling paradigm

Disadvantages of omnidirectional imaging from a journalistic perspective

be stitched together to create the 360-degree effect. From a journalistic perspective, this is a significant problem since breaking news events rarely pause to let the camera operator take multiple pictures so as to create a composite image: it is difficult if not impracticable to stop a moving train, a speeding bullet or a nightstick-wielding police officer. Thus a camera that can capture an entire field of view in a single instant offers significant advantages journalistically, although other devices might be useful in other applications, such as architecture, fashion or nature photography. This is one of the most important advantages of the ParaShot omnicamera. It takes in the entire field of view through a single lens, whereas most alternative products use multiple cameras, multiple mirrors and multiple CCDs requiring the user or photographer to piece together the images. In early 2000 iPIX introduced a system using a double-lens system attached to a single camera to create 360-degree images; this enables the iPIX system to see the entire field of view in a single moment.

1.5.3
Hypermedia

The use of hyperlinks in storytelling

Stories told online (including via television linked to the Internet or other network-based digital technology) can make connections much more easily than in any other medium. This is done primarily through the use of hyperlinks, or clickable pointers to other online content, although other tools for making such links or associations are now emerging.

Implications of hyperlinks for journalism

Although hyperlinks are familiar to anyone who has ever surfed the Net, there is not a great deal of research on the implications of hyperlinks for journalism. A leading programme of research on hyperlinks, and hypermedia in general, in journalism has been developed by Eric S. Fredin and Prabu David at Ohio State University. Fredin and David write, "While the integration of audio, video, graphic, and textual information is often perceived as the exciting benefit of hypermedia over traditional media, the more substantial benefit may be the links between electronic pages, such as the links connecting any one news story to related news stories and other sources of information." Such links are ubiquitous in news stories reported at Internet news sites.

This represents a new form of journalism that places stories in a much richer historical, political and cultural context. "The fact that massive repositories of information are only a few mouse clicks away offers a richness to hypermedia that set it apart from traditional media," conclude Fredin and David. At the same time, they point out, hypermedia require or at least enable a much more active and participatory audience.

Object-oriented multimedia

A complementary new media storytelling technique with significant implications for journalism is object-oriented multimedia. Object-oriented multimedia refers to the creation of digital objects in full motion video and audio.
Using MPEG-4 or even next-generation Web technology, storytellers can
create items that incorporate both linear and multilinear narrative forms by
making every image within a video stream a digital object. Each object,
such as a person, place or building, can be encoded with layers of additional
content, such as textual description, interactive graphics and animation, additional motion video or audio, or links to other sites on the World Wide Web,
all retrievable or accessible with a mouse click. Thus a reporter might create
a standard two-minute report for the evening news but also encode another
hour or more of content accessible to viewers interested in more depth but
not forced on viewers who prefer more passive acquisition of news.

Object-oriented multimedia is essentially the extension of digital objects
from relatively static Web pages (e.g. clickable hyperlinks) to digital video,
which is now entering the market both in the United States and around the
world. It permits journalists and other content creators to layer in additional
content and create interactive elements and hyperlinks in motion video. Consider another example. Say that a political reporter might produce a story
about a candidate for U.S. president. In analogue television, a typical report
might provide a 90-second linear narrative that all viewers would watch in
similar fashion. Using object-oriented multimedia, a digital video report
might contain the same 90-second linear narrative but also many layers of
additional content. These additional layers might include a detailed statistical profile of the candidate's voting record, complete with graphics and
animations illustrating the candidate's campaign contributors and their relationships to his or her voting record on various bills, as well as links to
the candidate's own Web site. These additional video elements could be
accessed by a mouse click, a remote-control click, or even voice command.
Not all viewers, however, would obtain this content, only those who were
interested. Similar applications could be effectively used in a wide variety
of stories, ranging from weather reporting to sports and the arts. All could
benefit from the additional context.

Object-oriented multimedia
applications use multiple
layers of content

1.5.4
Audience Involvement

Use of immersive storytelling
to increase audience
integration

The third aspect of contextualised journalism is audience involvement. Audience involvement is potentially much greater online, since the Internet is an active medium of communication rather than a passive medium like traditional analogue print and broadcast media. One way involvement is increasing is through the use of immersive storytelling. Immersive storytelling is largely a new format for presenting and interacting with the news in a three-dimensional environment. Today, most work involves producing three-dimensional representations of actual locations in news stories, which are produced digitally and then transferred back to analogue format for distribution on television. But as television converts from analogue to digital format in the next decade, three-dimensional news presentations will become common. At "CBS News," for example, 3-D "extrusions" are routinely used in a variety of news reporting, ranging from stories about conflicts in Iraq to environmental stories set in the Brazilian rain forest to President Clinton's 1999 State of the Union Address (where a 3-D fly-through was created for Washington, D.C.). These three-dimensional animations are far more than virtual environments. They are precisely rendered 3-D representations of actual buildings, cities and regions based on 2-D images acquired via high-resolution remote sensing satellite imagery and other image acquisition devices and built from precise databases known as geographic information systems (GIS). Recent advances in computer processing power have made it possible to create these 3-D extrusions using desktop computers rather than massive parallel-processing supercomputers. As digital television makes its way across the country, 3-D news reporting will become available to all viewers for their own navigation and interaction.

Will geographically based news, information and entertainment find a willing audience? Rent a car with a GPS mapping system and drive to an unfamiliar part of town. The answer is obvious.

1.5.5
Dynamic Content

News in real time

The fourth aspect of contextualised journalism is dynamic content. News content is much more fluid – dynamic – in an online environment, which enables better representation of events and processes in real life. People want and get their news on demand and in real time. Audiences are not willing to wait for the evening news or the next day's paper for developments in a breaking story. They want to know right now, and they want their information as current as possible, and via the Internet they can find it. This represents something of a double-edge sword for journalists, who now not only can but must provide continuously updated news for an audience increasingly accustomed to having access to the latest news developments. The journalist A. J. Liebling once observed, "I can write better than anyone who can write faster. And I can write faster than anyone who can write better," but today's journalist must write both faster *and* better. The problem is that few journalists have time for thoughtful analysis before they issue their reports.

1.5.6
Customisation

Finally, news in an electronic, digital environment can be customised, or personalised, in a way not possible in other media. Coupled with the first four dimensions, this personalised nature of online journalism potentially offers audiences a view of the world that is much more contextualised, textured and multidimensional than stories told in the worlds of print and broadcast analogue media. Although some sceptics would argue that personalised media will bring even further audience fragmentation, this is a red herring. While it is true that the so-called multi-channel universe has unarguably brought an end to the dominance of the three network newscasts and the Internet is offering a burgeoning array of news choices, this diversity represents more inclusiveness of alternative viewpoints, not an exclusion of them. In fact, early research suggests that younger audiences value the diversity of news perspectives made available via the Internet. Personalisation as it is manifesting itself on the Internet today is more a matter of obtaining news customised to an individual's life situation than a screening out of important news.

Personalised storytelling

1.5.7
Conclusion

Contextualised journalism can bring a variety of potential benefits to the citizenry and to democracy, including more engaging reporting, more complete information, and news that better reflects the complexities and nuances of an increasingly diverse and pluralistic society. Democracy depends on an informed citizenry. Traditionally, the press, whether online or off, has served as information provider to the citizens of a democracy. Increasingly, however, the press and journalism in all media have slipped in their performance of this vital duty. Consider the following words from Carl Bernstein, the *Washington Post* reporter who, along with Bob Woodward, broke perhaps

Contextualised journalism as fostering democracy

the greatest news story of the second half of the 20th century, the break-in of the Democratic headquarters at the Watergate hotel:

> *"[Journalism] is disfigured by celebrity, gossip and sensationalism. I believe it's the role of journalists to challenge people, not just to mindlessly amuse them. In this culture of journalistic titillation, we teach our readers and our viewers that the trivial is important."*

The idea of reporting the facts in context is certainly not a new notion; journalists throughout history have sought to place stories into better and more complete context. The problem has been that for the most part the media used to publish journalism have not provided the means to achieve this. The space and time limitations of analogue print and broadcast media have foreshortened the news and led to a newsroom culture in which most stories are reported in truncated form, telling each story from a single point of view and providing the audience with reports that purport to be the truth. But despite the claims of many traditional journalists, the truth is not easily encapsulated into a single linear narrative of 1,500 words or less in print or three minutes or less of video and audio. Only in an interactive, broadband online medium can context be provided for complex, multidimensional news events where perspective and point of view are centrally important in understanding the complete truth behind the news.

Taken as a whole, these new media developments are transforming the very nature of news content and storytelling. In the 21st century, we may see the world through a computer-mediated reality and become empowered participants in the process of contextualised journalism. What is beginning to emerge is a new type of storytelling that moves beyond the romantic but unachievable goal of pure objectivity in journalism. This new style will offer the audience a complex blend of perspectives on news stories and events that will be far more textured than any single point of view could ever achieve.

Objectivity and truth in storytelling?

Offering a single perspective necessarily furnishes only a limited view of the reality of what occurred. Thus, whether achievable or not, objectivity and truth can best be pursued through a storytelling medium that supplies the texture and context possible in an online, multimedia and interactive environment. Because it is impossible for any human being to lay aside completely all his or her personal beliefs and present a culturally and bias-free account of any event, process or set of facts the best one can do is to reveal to the reader one's biases and provide a balanced accounting of the facts, circumstances and context surrounding a story. Intelligent readers can then reach their own conclusions as to reality.

Journalists now need to think about a global audience that not only reads what they write and report but can comment, provide perspective, and offer new insight into the complexities of an increasingly global society. This is the essence of the contextualised journalism possible in the digital age.

Chapter 1.6

Spellbound by Images

Siegfried Frey

Some 350 years have passed since the mathematician, physicist and inventor of the calculator, Blaise Pascal, first raised the question of the influence of nonverbal stimuli on the cultural and political happenings of the world. With his famous dictum "If Cleopatra's nose had looked different, the face of the world today would be different," he drew attention – as concisely and succinctly as anyone has before or since – to the enormous implications that even thoroughly banal nonverbal stimuli can have, especially in a political context.[1] Nevertheless, research work in this area was slow to get going. And for a long time it was not human scientists but physicists and political commentators who were the ones behind the progress in what was known.

In the 18th century Pascal's perspective was expanded upon by no less a figure than Georg Christoph Lichtenberg, the first holder of a chair in experimental physics in Germany. In a now famous paper entitled "On Physiognomy – against the Physiognomists," he explained that our external appearance may not only earn us the *affection* of our interlocutor, but also trigger an *aversion* to us, and that the irresistible tendency we all harbour to interpret what is known as "body language" is one of the main reasons that prejudices come about. He had been prompted in his enterprise by a monumental work entitled "Physiognomic Fragments to Promote the Knowledge and Love of Mankind," written by the Zurich pastor Johann Caspar Lavater together with Goethe, which had made the practice of judging character from facial features and bodily physique fashionable throughout Europe.[2] And as though he almost suspected that one day "reading the surface" of faces would provide the scientific accompaniment to the spectral danse macabre jigged by the racial dementia of the 20th century, his commentary upon the physiognomical practices being pursued by his

Cultural and political influence of nonverbal stimuli

---

1 The passage in question in Pascal's *Pensées* runs verbatim: "Qui voudra connaître à plein la vanité de l'homme n'a qu'à considérer les causes et les effets de l'amour. La cause en est un je ne sais quoi (Corneille), et les effets en sont effroyables. Ce je ne sais quoi, si peu de chose qu'on ne peut le reconnaître, remue toute la terre, les princes, les armes, le monde entier. Le nez de Cléopâtre: s'il eût été plus court, toute la face de la terre aurait change" (Pascal 1972 p. 79).

2 See Frey 1993

contemporaries up and down the country was that "if physiognomy becomes what Lavater expects it to become, children will be hanged before they have committed the deeds that deserve the gallows."[3]

Irrational nature of the interpretation of body language

A century later it was the outstanding physicist Hermann von Helmholtz, acclaimed as a "universal genius" on account of the variety of scientific disciplines to which he contributed,[4] who took a decisive step forward in the understanding of the phenomena highlighted by Pascal and Lichtenberg, for the first time describing the mechanism of the brain responsible for the deeply irrational nature of interpretations of body language. In the course of his pioneering investigations into the psychophysiology of the optical apparatus, Helmholtz had noticed that at the sight of other people we automatically make judgements – akin to rapid-fire verdicts – about their characteristics, moods and likings, judgements that make a mockery of all rational explanation, but that nonetheless "impose themselves upon our consciousness, as though they were produced by a compulsive, almost external force against which our will is powerless."[5] Helmholtz saw the cause of such "*unconscious conclusions*," which came about without the least cognitive effort, as lying in a pre-rational mechanism of visual stimulus-processing dating back to primeval times, which behaved with the utmost insubordination towards the "cleansing and testing work of conscious thought" made possible by the development of the neo-cortex, and which in this way sought to wield its imperious power over human reason.

Images have a decisive influence upon public opinion

In the 20th century it was the U.S. political commentator Walter Lippmann, the man who coined the concept of a "stereotype," who laid the theoretical foundations for a deeper understanding of the "nonverbal" dimension of processes of communication. In his classic *Public Opinion*, first published in 1922, the author who has been hailed as the most gifted and influential political journalist of the 20 century[6] pointed out that images influence public opinion far more than words do. "Photographs have the kind of authority over imagination to-day, which the printed word had yesterday, and the spoken word before that," was the sober and realistic appraisal of a journalist whose editorials and newspapers columns were avidly read four days a week throughout the USA for more than 36 years. And he left no doubt that *moving* images would substantially consolidate the dominance of the image over the word even further. Indeed, at a time when the film camera had only just been invented, Lippmann drew attention to the fact that moving pictures in particular foster an unreflective, stereotyping form of information-processing in that – more than any other medium – they entice the recipient into mental passivity:

3 Lichtenberg 1980, p. 532
4 See Krüger 1994
5 Helmholtz 1867, p. 449
6 Curtis 1998, p. xi

They are the most effortless food for the mind conceivable. Any description in words, or even any inert picture, requires an effort of memory before a picture exists in the mind. But on the screen the whole process of observing, describing, reporting, and the imagining, has been accomplished for you. Without more trouble than is needed to stay awake, the result which your imagination is always aiming at is reeled off on the screen.[7]

1.6.1
Ascribing Characteristics in Milliseconds

The profound influence exerted by the cerebral mechanism responsible for visual stimulus-processing upon the process of ascribing characteristics and the emotional attitude adopted towards one's interlocutor has only emerged in full, however, through the experimental investigations carried out over the last two decades. It was thus shown in a series of experiments in the late 1980s, in which people were asked to assess portraits we showed them tachistoscopically for just a few milliseconds, that just a vague perception of human features is enough to provoke in the observer a firm opinion about the personality traits of the stimulus-person in question. Jendraczyk[8] then carried out an investigation in which she presented 16 application photos submitted by students at a drama school to be judged by a group of 19 people, varying the time of exposure from case to case. It emerged that an exposure time of 250 milliseconds is sufficient to produce a highly sophisticated image of the other person, where judgements are made, for example, as to whether the person in question is "authoritarian," "pleasant," "emotional," "underhand," "intelligent" or "boring." On the basis of such optical impressions founded upon unconscious conclusions, attitudes are formed just as quickly ascertaining whether one would like to have the person in question as a "colleague," a "superior," a "partner" or an "acquaintance."

The enormous powers of suggestion of nonverbal stimuli are further underlined by findings showing that unconscious conclusions reached in fractions of a second hardly change when the person making the judgement is given the opportunity to look at the images for as long as he wants. It thus emerged from Jendraczyk's study that the judgement-forming processes triggered by nonverbal stimuli were virtually completed within a quarter of a second: the impressions recorded by the observers concerning the stimulus-person they had seen for a time-span of just 250 milliseconds correlated with the judgements made on being permanently exposed to the images at an average level of $r = .92$. A replication study using a total of 45 portraits

Moving images induce mental passivity

Influence of visual stimulus-processing on the formation of opinions

Judgement-forming processes are rapidly completed

7 See Lippmann 1922/1997, p. 6
8 See Jendraczyk 1991

of politicians taken from an intercultural investigation into the media effect of nonverbal communication, which the author made in conjunction with the U.S. political scientist Roger Masters and the French linguistic researcher Alfred Raveau at the Maison des Sciences de l'Homme in Paris,[9] produced almost identical results: the judgements of personality made after a quarter of a second correlated with the ones that could be permanently considered at an average level of $r = .89$.[10]

1.6.2
The Significance of Movement
for the Spontaneous Formation of Impressions

Movement behaviour guides
spontaneous
quality-ascription

The currently available results from dummy experiments with moving images first made possible by *Scriptanimation*, a procedure for the computer modelling of natural movement behaviour based on the *Berner System*,[11] suggest that the psychological apparatus that deals with the formation of unconscious conclusions attaches greatly varying importance to the different aspects of human appearance. Even at the present stage of enquiries, it can be established that a person's movement behaviour influences the process of spontaneous quality-ascription to a much greater extent than the person's static, physiognomic appearance. Figure 1.6-1 illustrates this point with the aid of an experiment in which we made the same computer-animated doll imitate the movement behaviour of various politicians and in this way eliminated the influence of the physiognomic aspect of their appearance.

The importance of movement
behaviour

As becomes clear from a comparison of the personality profiles that were established on the one hand for the original person and on the other for the doll imitating the movements of the original person, the observers reached virtually the same judgement on the basis of movement-information alone as when they saw the politician in person.

Both the rather insipid, undifferentiated impression made by the U.S. politician Smith (upper diagram) and the highly positive opinion formed of Madame Barzach (middle diagram), and even the decidedly negative characterisation produced by Jesse Helms, were reflected virtually unchanged in the judgements given by the group asked to comment on the personality profile of the doll. Indeed, the consensus surprisingly even stretched to judgements concerning the "beauty" of the stimulus-person: the doll that imitated Madame Barzach's movements was found to be fairly attractive (though not quite as attractive as the original), yet when it moved like Helms

---

9 See Frey et al. 1993; Frey 2000
10 See Frey 1999
11 See Kempter 1999; Frey 2000

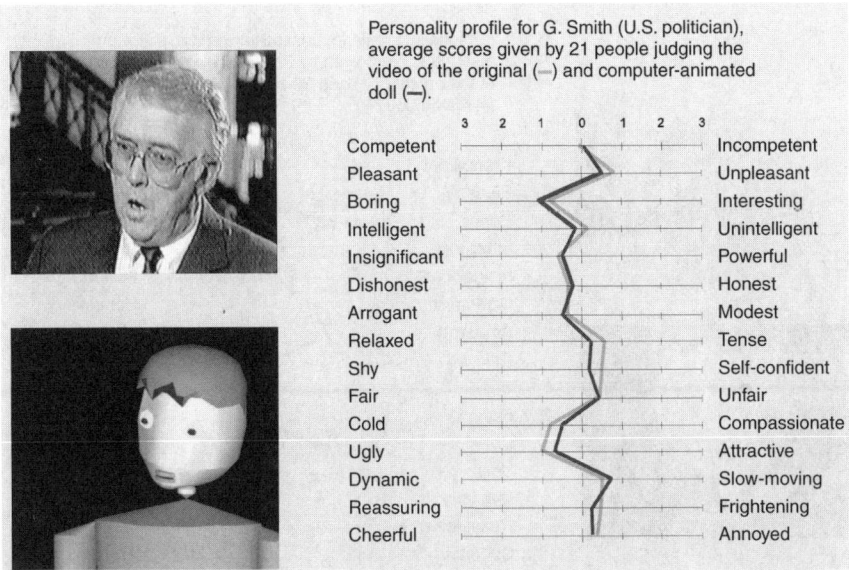

Personality profile for G. Smith (U.S. politician), average scores given by 21 people judging the video of the original (—) and computer-animated doll (—).

Competent — Incompetent
Pleasant — Unpleasant
Boring — Interesting
Intelligent — Unintelligent
Insignificant — Powerful
Dishonest — Honest
Arrogant — Modest
Relaxed — Tense
Shy — Self-confident
Fair — Unfair
Cold — Compassionate
Ugly — Attractive
Dynamic — Slow-moving
Reassuring — Frightening
Cheerful — Annoyed

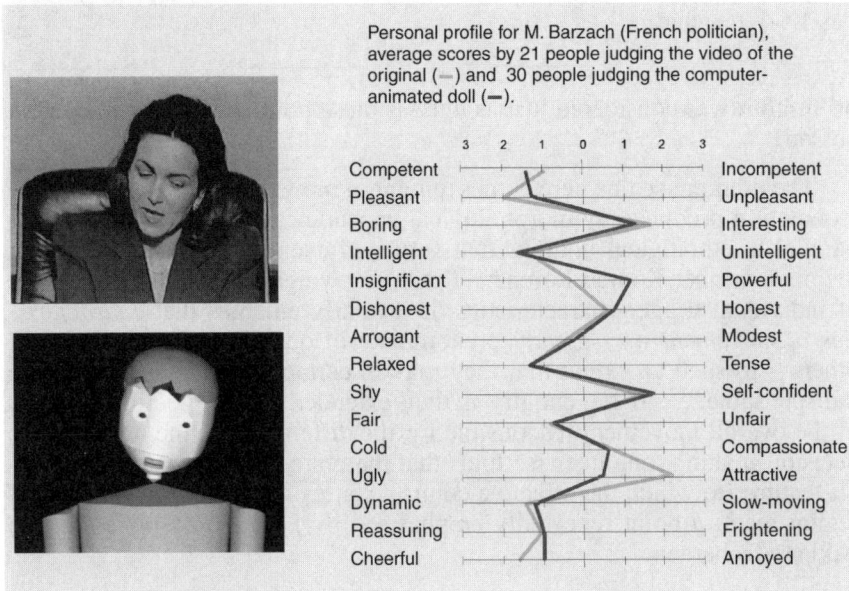

Personal profile for M. Barzach (French politician), average scores by 21 people judging the video of the original (—) and 30 people judging the computer-animated doll (—).

Competent — Incompetent
Pleasant — Unpleasant
Boring — Interesting
Intelligent — Unintelligent
Insignificant — Powerful
Dishonest — Honest
Arrogant — Modest
Relaxed — Tense
Shy — Self-confident
Fair — Unfair
Cold — Compassionate
Ugly — Attractive
Dynamic — Slow-moving
Reassuring — Frightening
Cheerful — Annoyed

Fig. 1.6-1 The influence of movement for the spontaneous formation of impressions

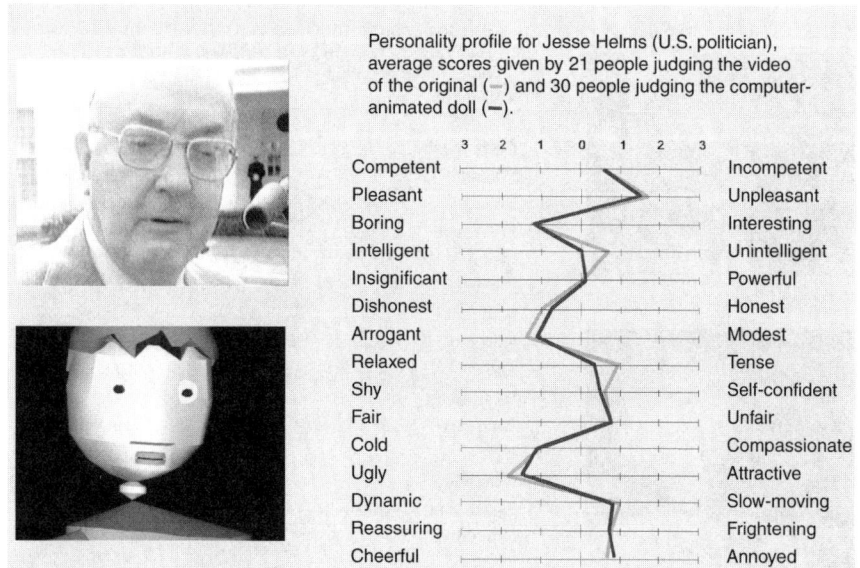

Personality profile for Jesse Helms (U.S. politician), average scores given by 21 people judging the video of the original (–) and 30 people judging the computer-animated doll (—).

Fig. 1.6-1 (continued)

or Smith it was considered just as ugly as these politicians had appeared in person.

The dominance that here comes to light of movement behaviour over the stimulation produced by morphological appearance suggests an interesting parallel to ethological findings that surprised even the ethologist and Nobel prize-winner Konrad Lorenz: "If one ... weighs up the relative effects of individual trigger-characteristics, it regularly emerges that *characteristics of movement* ... greatly predominate in quantitative terms over all others – to such an extent that they may in certain circumstances become indispensable."[12] If the enquiry is then extended to the specific elements of the overall movement responsible for the differences in the unconscious decision-making, one likewise finds that there are typically very few stimuli features to which the affective control centres located in the subcortical region react, a point repeatedly emphasised by Lorenz and his colleague Niklaas Tinbergen.

12 See Lorenz 1968, p. 45

A comparison of the behaviour patterns of the politicians who had been categorised in particularly positive terms with those who had been evaluated very negatively thus revealed that observers responded very strongly to one highly specific aspect of nonverbal behaviour: the way in which the agents brought into play the sideways inclination of the head. For reasons that have as yet only been partially elucidated, our optical apparatus attaches enormous importance to changes in the lateral dimension of the way people hold their head. Even the earliest dummy experiments we carried out in the 1980s (with a view to explaining the effect exerted by static elements of posture upon a person considering a work of art) had shown that this apparently trivial aspect of nonverbal communication has a decisive influence upon the impression we are given of a person (see information box). The same people who had initially been perceived as "pleasant, sensitive, tender, honest and modest" were suddenly regarded as "unpleasant, cold, deceitful, arrogant, hard and aloof" – for the simple reason that they were holding their head slightly differently.

The sideward inclination of the head as a central aspect of nonverbal communication

The Power of the Image: The Influence of the Lateral Flexion of the Head upon our Judgement of Others

Pre-rational nature of visual information-processing

Not only beauty, but also character lies in the eye of the beholder. The fact that we "cannot help" having such-and-such an impression of a person resides in the pre-rational nature of visual information-processing. It is often quite simply structured stimuli that determine our image of the other. The "Madonna del Magnificat" by Sandro Botticelli (left image) is transformed before our very eyes from a meek and humble woman into a self-confident mistress simply by straightening her head, which was bent to one side.

In the case of Elisabeth-Louise Vigée Le Brun's "Self-Portrait" (left), if one removes the sideways inclination of the mother's head to the child and of the child to the observer, mother and child suddenly seem to be shrinking back from the observer in fear.

The Secret of the Mona Lisa

From the notebooks of Leonardo da Vinci it becomes clear that the artist who worked as the architect, general engineer and weapons expert of Cesare Borgia underestimated neither the power of the image nor that of the creator of images. More than anyone else, wrote the universal genius of the Renaissance in one of his many sketch pads, the painter is "the master over people of all sorts and over all things." Painting, he said, seduces people into falling in love with a dead portrait consisting of strokes of paint and dashes of colour "which does not even represent a living woman. ... It incites nations to turn to the images of the gods with fervent vows. ... Even animals are taken in by it. I once saw a picture that deceived a dog with the appearance of its master. ... I have seen how swallows have flown up and wanted to settle on painted iron bars of the sort found in front of windows." Indeed, he had even had the strange experience of painting "a picture that represented something holy, and a man in love with it, who had bought it, wanting to have the representation of divinity removed and taken off so he could kiss it without inhibition. In the end, however, his conscience prevailed over his yearning and desire, and it was necessary for him to remove the picture from his house."[13]

Leonardo's notebooks likewise reveal just how fine a feeling he had for the stimuli that provoke such overwhelming emotional reactions in the onlooker. The lasting effect exerted upon us by the sideward flexion of the head had thus by no means escaped his attention. "Women," he wrote in his sketch pad, should always best be presented "with their head inclined to one side."[14] In the case of the Mona Lisa, he did not himself keep to this rule. Yet consciously or unconsciously he used his knowledge of the cognitive and affective effects produced by the tilting of the head to one side to create that unfathomable, mysterious smile that still intrigues and unsettles the onlooker.

"Each time we go back to her," wrote the great art historian Ernst Gombrich, articulating the experiences of countless visitors to the Louvre, the Mona Lisa looks "a little bit different. Even in photographs of the painting we experience this strange effect, but faced with the original in the Louvre it is quite uncanny. Sometimes she seems to be making fun of us, and then once again we seem to catch a sort of sadness in her smile." The onlooker, according to Gombrich, is thus simply unable to be certain "what mood Mona Lisa is really in when she looks at us." Indeed, even as we stand before her, she seems to "change like a living being before our very eyes."[15]

Lateral flexion of the head by Leonardo da Vinci

---

13 For all quotations, see da Vinci 1909, pp. 15
14 See ibid., p. 122
15 Gombrich 1978, p. 227

To achieve this mysterious effect, Leonardo's genius turned to account the fact that the pragmatic interpretation of the sideways inclination of the head is completely different depending on whether the figure's head is tilted towards or away from a person of reference.

If the tilt is towards the partner (who need not even be present in the picture, but whose position can be deduced from the figure's line of vision), the unconscious conclusion – in a word – is of "affection," in the opposite case "aversion."

Leonardo has opted for the Mona Lisa to hold her head in such a way that there is an absolutely minimal lateral flexion which can hardly

"aversion"

be made out for certain with the naked eye (see upper image). This ambiguity clearly produces a sort of "see-saw phenomenon," a sense of precarious equilibrium, in the onlooker, which in turn causes a constant vacillation in the quality-ascription on the part of the person interpreting nonverbal stimuli. If the Mona Lisa's head is tilted counter to the direction in which her eyes are looking (and thus also away from the observer), it seems as though the smile on her face disappears and the mocking, derogatory manner referred to by Gombrich, whereby she seems to be sizing us up, comes clearly to the fore (middle image).

"affection"

If, by contrast, her head is tilted in the direction in which her eyes are looking (and thus towards the observer), as in the lowest image, one is given the sensation of a gentle, rather sad person, whose dreamy face now has a sweet smile that is suddenly no longer mysterious at all.

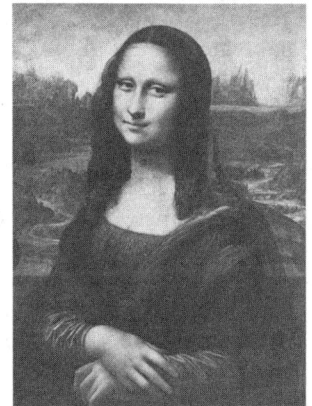

Precarious equilibrium in the way the Mona Lisa holds her head

Very much in the sense of Helmholtz's unconscious conclusions, this impression came about quite spontaneously, was absolutely compelling for onlookers from the most diverse of countries and cultures, and could not even be shaken off once the experimental subjects had clearly seen the comparatively flimsy reason that had induced such a fundamental change in their opinion of the person under consideration.[16]

1.6.3
Perspectives for the Future

Today, at the start of the third millennium, the power of images casts its spell over people more than ever before. And yet the age of enlightenment in the field has not even really begun yet. Indeed, in his book *Four Arguments for the Elimination of Television*, Jerry Mander wrote: "Western society ... tends to be blind not only to the power of images but also to the fact that we are nearly defenseless against their effect."[17]

The power of images holds people spellbound

Defenceless? Does that go for Pascal, Lichtenberg, Helmholtz, Lippmann and Lorenz too? And for Shakespeare, who told us that beauty lies in the eye of the beholder? Hardly. Yet the involuntary interpretation of gestures and facial expressions, of physique and posture, continues to trigger – as it has done since time immemorial – emotional reactions that develop within us in the form of sympathy or antipathy quite independently and without the least cognitive effort as soon as we catch sight of a person. It also constitutes the basis for the quick-fire judgements on which the proverbial "man in the street," following his rise to ascendancy in the course of the 20th century, founds his opinions of the characteristics of others and in the process forms an impression he can as a rule "hardly help" but form.[18] Given the fundamental incorrigibility and the unwavering nature of visual perception emphasised time and again from Pascal through to Lorenz, therefore, the question must surely be asked what benefit we can hope to gain by tracing the secret causality governing our involuntary "reading" of nonverbal stimuli.

At the latest since "the Copernican worldview came to form a part of every child's upbringing," as the political scientist Thomas Meyer[19] has expressed a paradox already noted by Helmholtz, it has been common knowledge that our visual sense leads to misconceptions about the geographical facts of the world. And yet "even in the fourth century after Copernicus," writes Meyer, for us the earth "does not turn away at night. To the eye, the worldview and

16 See Frey et al. 1983
17 Mander 1978, p. 257
18 See Frey 2003
19 See Meyer 1992, p. 44

the heart it is still the sun that goes down."[20] So what good does it do us, we may ask with a shrug of shoulders, to crack the secret code that produces the stereotyped "images in our heads," if there is ultimately nothing we can do to alter the impression that imposes itself upon us on the basis of nonverbal stimuli?

To find an answer to this question, centuries after the inception of the Age of Enlightenment, we need no longer look much further. We may still see the things of the world with the same eyes as our Stone-Age forefathers. And we are no more able to shake off the pre-judgements imposed upon us by our optical apparatus than they were. Yet unlike Stone-Age man, for whom the images produced by his unconscious conclusions necessarily formed the basis for his entire way of living, the people of today no longer – at least insofar as they have a better understanding of things – have to base their *actions* on them. The visual perception of civilised human beings may continue to be dominated by the Ptolemaic, geocentric worldview, yet their behaviour is geared towards the Copernican, heliocentric worldview. Accordingly, the modern human being is not only better able in purely external terms to cope with the world in which he lives. The much more valuable benefit is the higher level of inner, psychological autonomy he is granted by the greater processing depth of conscious thought. Unlike his ancestors in whose upbringing Copernicus was yet to feature, 21st century man – though the earth may still appear "flat" to him – is no longer gripped by the dull fear of falling off the edge of the world into nothingness when he boards a ship today.

The issue cannot, therefore, be to "eliminate television," in the sense implied by Jerry Mander above. And even less is it possible for science to set itself the task of issuing normative instructions in an almost bureaucratic capacity. Its job is to penetrate the hidden connections between things. If it is successful in this, the rest will fall into place. The issue must thus be to bring about "enlightenment" if we do not want to succumb in the "war of images against citizens' powers of judgement."[21]

The Enlightenment was given its decisive definition by Kant as "man's emergence from his self-incurred immaturity."[22] The suggestive power with which we are governed by appearances seems, as Helmholtz recognised, to make "maturity" in this field particularly difficult to attain. Lichtenberg himself at times felt the compulsive nature of the visual to be such a burden that he once joked: "Nothing grieves me more, in everything I do, than having to look at the world as the common man does, for I know scientifically that he looks at it wrongly."[23] Yet Helmholtz and Lichtenberg themselves

Pre-judgements through visual perception

The compulsive nature of the visual

20 Ibid., p. 49
21 Ibid., p. 93
22 Kant 1991, p. 54
23 Lichtenberg 1991, p. 405

provide the best example of just how great a degree of sovereignty can be achieved precisely by *refusing* to rest content with the "physiognomic world-view" automatically delivered by the visual sense, which at bottom amounts simply to getting bogged down in the infantile perspective that – normally as a merely transitional phase in the development of personality – governs childlike thought and experience.

If things were as they seem to us, there would be no need for science. As Konrad Lorenz so forcefully made clear, animals whose sensory apparatus is in many respects comparable to ours always feel – precisely because they are unable to doubt – perfectly in the picture. Whatever the form taken by the unconscious conclusion drawn by their inferential system from their sensory input, it is as it were the final word on the matter. Nor did Lorenz forget to point out that this is precisely why animals again and again fall into the traps set by human beings. We are the first and so far only species equipped with the option of not allowing the unconscious conclusions that our sensory apparatus imposes upon us unasked to *determine our action*. Of course, we can only turn the resulting vast potential for autonomy and innovation to account to the extent that we succeed in overcoming the false knowledge produced by unconscious conclusions – and to the extent that we are brave enough to free ourselves from the comfortable pseudo-certainty that all too often prevents us getting to the bottom of things. As André Gide once put it, "you don't discover any new continents unless you have the courage to lose sight of all coasts."

Sensory information need
not determine behaviour

1.6.4
The Reorientation of Research Work

At a time when the entire communicative process is shifting more and more into the realm of the visual, the human sciences can no longer afford not to examine the questions of the formation of visual impressions if they wish to make a relevant contribution to the understanding of communicative action. In the near future the study of the processes involved in human communication will once more gain substantially in practical significance. Not only for understanding media effects but also for the developments already taking shape in the field of dialogical forms of man-machine communication, a close knowledge of the conditions present on the side of the recipient is a vital precondition. Indeed, the design philosophy underlying the conception of modern information and communication technologies excludes the recipient to the extent that it fails to account for the pragmatic dimension of information-processing, i.e. "the relation between the signs and their in-

Conditions within the
recipient as a vital factor for
understanding the effect of
media

terpreters."[24] Of course, the classical *sender-receiver model* conceived by the telecommunications scientist Claude Shannon has proved of outstanding value in technical communication. However, as soon as it is called upon to explain the processes of human communication, where it is the pragmatic dimension that is of central importance, the account it provides is a distorted one. It is hardly surprising, therefore, that information technology still elicits a groan from so many people or makes them back off completely – notwithstanding the "user friendliness" constantly invoked by software developers. Here too, rethinking will be necessary.

There still remains the question of which discipline – when it comes to clarifying the role of nonverbal communication – is supposed to bring about our "emergence" from an immaturity that is indeed, as the history of science shows, self-incurred. Philosophy, ethology, anthropology and linguistics, disciplines that through the works of Morris, Grice, Lorenz, Hall, Goffman, Sperber and Wilson,[25] etc. have in recent years contributed so much to the progress in the theoretical understanding of communicative action, come upon what seem to be almost insuperable limits in investigating the pragmatic effects of nonverbal stimuli, limits that are first and foremost methodological in nature. Yet even psychology, the discipline most likely to be competent to undertake investigations into the cognitive and affective processes in the recipient, seems ill-equipped to cope with the questions on the agenda, at least for the moment.

The underlying conditions for a comprehensive empirical clarification of the pragmatic interpretation of nonverbal stimuli are undoubtedly more favourable today than ever before in the long history of this research area. The same technological developments that have flooded us with visual information in our everyday life have also put us in possession of the highly powerful tools needed for throwing light on the psychological effects produced by the nonverbal component of communicative behaviour.[26] Yet as far as the theoretical understanding of the subject is concerned, the discipline continues not to make any headway. The few psychologists who addressed in the issue following the decline of the "psychology of expression" in the 1940s[27] did not even participate in the attempts undertaken in allied disciplines to provide the research work with a new intellectual orientation. Instead, they remained trapped in the established psycho-diagnostic way of thinking and thus – as Lichtenberg reproached the "physiognostics" of the 18th century – simply cast "new glances through the old holes." The task of the science of "human communication" that is only now emerging will

Theoretical understanding must shake off the psycho-diagnostic approach

---

24 Morris 1938, p. 30
25 See Morris 1938; Grice 1989; Lorenz 1942; Hall 1958; Goffman 1959; Sperber/Wilson 1986
26 Frey 2000; Frey/Möller 2002
27 See, for example, Ekman 1993; Watzlawick et al. 1972

thus be to usher in the necessary rethinking and to open up the new paths we shall need to take if we wish – in the sense conceived by Helmholtz – to emancipate ourselves from the trickery of the senses and attain a deeper understanding of what is happening within ourselves and in the surrounding – ever more strongly visualised – world.

Chapter 2   Changing Technology

Ubiquity and Miniaturisation

The potential applications of a new generation of networked and "intelligent" technological systems are considered to be more or less infinite, but these are still only at the very early stages of being realised. Images of the future are shaped by ubiquitous computer and network technologies, ubiquitous communication systems, and intelligent interfaces that surround human beings at all times and in all places.

Yet what are the fundamental possibilities for daily human life that are opened up by the constantly accelerating process of technological development and the convergence of key technologies or the increased efficiency of important technological parameters? What effects will be produced by the progress in microelectronics and nano-technology? What new fields of application will all this engender? How do human beings behave in a context in which the intelligence of information and communication technologies is embedded virtually everywhere.

The following chapter seeks to get to the bottom of such questions and others raised by changes in media technologies. In the process it identifies important drivers and trends in use-diffusion and unearths technological tendencies and developments.

The first contribution, "Ubiquitous Computing: Scenarios from an Informatised World" by *Friedemann Mattern*, sheds light above all on the social and political challenges posed by the era of ubiquitous computing, an era characterised by an increasing dependence upon technology and in which the greatest task will be to protect the private sphere. The vision of ubiquitous computing presents a world where it is possible to enrich and enhance the environment with which people are familiar by means of discreet, unobtrusive forms of technology. The first indicators of such a "post-PC era" featuring near-total networking are in evidence today in the form of mobile phones with Internet connections, localisation and voice-recognition capabilities, as well as smart cards and PDAs that communicate with their environment via radio.

Friedemann Mattern

In their paper *William Lehr* and *Lee McKnight* compare two technologies that permit wireless broadband Internet access: 3G and WiFi. Even though the two technologies reflect fundamentally different aims, origins, and concepts of service, branch and architecture design, each has recently attracted considerable attention as a candidate to be the predominant platform for providing wireless broadband access to the Internet. The question of how

William Lehr & Lee McKnight

far these two technologies will compete with or possibly complement one another remains as yet unanswered. In the wireless future, heterogeneous access technologies will coexist side by side, so equipment manufacturers, service providers, customers and political decision-makers should not expect to be faced with a wireless future that is linear in nature.

A further example of a user-friendly information society is Ambient Intelligence, as described by *Ken Ducatel et al.* in their paper, "That's What Friends Are For. Ambient Intelligence and the Information Society in 2010." AmI stands for ubiquitous networking and communication technologies and intelligent interfaces that are integrated within everyday objects and interact with human beings. To meet with acceptance among users, AmI must be driven by human and not technologically determined concerns, and win people over through the utility and relevance of its applications for citizens and consumers. An especially significant factor is that AmI must also be something that the ordinary person can control.

To be successfully put into practice, however, technological visions such as the AmI vision cannot simply be left to their own devices, as *Klaus Schrape* – the ECC Fellow who has sadly died far too early – shows in his paper on "Evolutionary Perspectives." Technological maturity is not to be equated with market maturity; market maturity is not market diffusion; and market diffusion is not the same as use diffusion. Rather, the implementation and acceptance of technological visions depend upon a whole variety of cultural and social preconditions that still have to be realised. This contribution focuses on an investigation into the tension between technological-scientific progress and social-cultural evolution. New technological media that go far beyond merely replacing physical labour and whose potential applications lie in the realm of human intelligence will be the decisive feature of the future.

Ken Ducatel et al.

Klaus Schrape

Chapter 2.1

Ubiquitous Computing:
Scenarios from an Informatised World[1]

Friedemann Mattern

2.1.1
From Internet Mobile Phones to Wearable Computers

The effects of rapid progress in microelectronics, the convergence of communications and information technology, and the trend toward computerising and networking everyday objects can best be demonstrated using the example of mobile phones. A few years ago, mobile phones were still so big, expensive, and limited in their functionality that they did not sell well and were often used more as a status symbol than a practical tool. This has changed very rapidly (Figure 2.1-1). In Europe, there are now more mobile phone users than car drivers. Many users have grown so accustomed to them and adapted their professional and even private lives to them to such an extent that they cannot imagine life without this technology.

Parallel to this development, within a short period of time the mobile phone has become a device that offers more than just the pure functionality of voice transmission. It has developed into a piece of equipment for which the German expression "Handy" is much more appropriate – not only has it become smaller, but it has also acquired new "handy" functions. The SMS short messaging system has become a completely unexpected success, especially with young people. Specifically for this target group, coloured displays which permit the use of more attractive computer games as well as the viewing of forwarded photos and video clips are now being integrated into the most up-to-date generation of mobile phones. The same applies to MP3 players, which offer high-quality music reproduction and could replace the classic "Walkman."

Mobile telephones have become widely accepted

Mobile phones have become multifunctional

---

1 This article is based on the study "From Mobile Phone to Ubiquitous Computer," which the author wrote by request of the Friedrich Ebert Foundation.

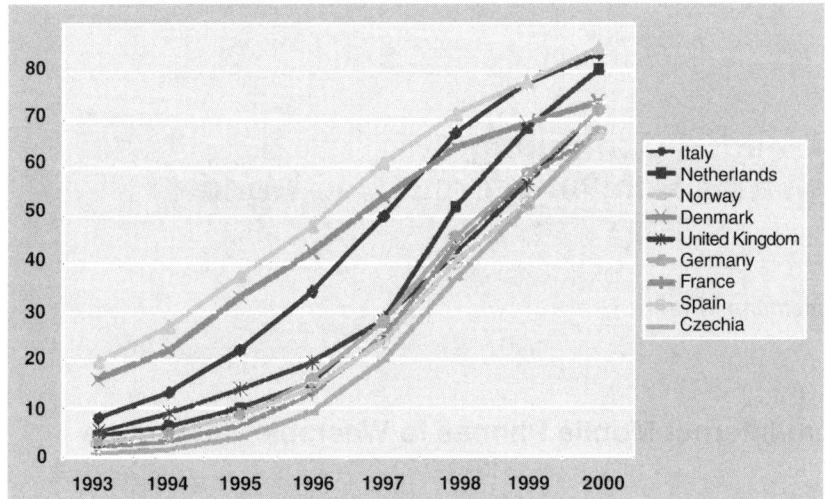

Fig. 2.1-1 Percentage of people who have ever used a mobile phone (Eurescom 2001)

Another additional function is connection to the Internet. In Europe this has been implemented using the WAP system, through which you can access Web sites from your mobile phone.

However, this functionality has not been widely accepted in its current form, firstly because the transmission technology on which the system is based was not sufficiently well developed in 1999 / 2000 (for example, it was not "always on," which meant long waits whilst connecting, making it awkward to use). Secondly, it is clear that the WAP system was not appropriately marketed. Expectations were too high, and consequently users were disappointed. The development of the i-mode system in Japan was a totally different experience: here, it was not mobile commerce that was marketed as an application area as in Europe, but the system was intentionally targeted at twenty-to-thirty-year-old women as a lifestyle feature. The term "Internet" does not appear in the advertising, the focus instead being on services for specific target groups (such as local events, horoscopes, weather forecasts and even karaoke). Strict quality control, a clear pricing structure, and lots of free services, as well as the ability to be "always on" without any explicit connection set-up, are further characteristics of the i-mode system, which is now beginning to gain ground in other countries, including Germany. In Japan at least it has been enormously successful: in the year 2001, it attracted more than ten thousand new customers a day.

The reception of mobile Internet has varied from country to country

" **The mobile phone becomes a personal base station and control centre.** *"*

Mobile phones are now fully functional computers with the capability to execute Java programmes, even those they receive "wirelessly." This opens up a whole new world of application possibilities. Even with the Japanese i-mode system, however, these mobile computers are not fully integrated into the Internet with all its services. They offer only highly limited functionality by accessing Web information via the conventional mobile telephony network. However, this may soon change, since prototypes of mobile "Internet appliances" already exist. Consequently, it will be possible to use a much broader range of services and options.

WWW goes mobile

The functionality of mobile phones is currently expanding in different directions. One option, for example, is to add localisation functionality: using radio direction-finding and other positioning methods, mobile phones can already be localised to within a few hundred metres. By using satellite-supported GPS systems, localisation can be as exact as about ten metres outside buildings. Providing mobile phones with an additional short-range radio interface (a range of about 10 metres can be covered with a thousandth of the usual transmission energy, as with the Bluetooth standard currently on the market) means that other personal devices belonging to the user can also profit from the communication and localisation abilities of the mobile phone. The mobile phone implicitly becomes a personal base station and control centre for a variety of other devices and "smart objects" nearby, which only have to be equipped with a simple, low-energy (and therefore very cheap and small) short-range communications module in order to be used for Internet services and other functions.

Localisation functions turn the mobile phone into a personal control centre

Another development is the so-called smart phone, which in addition to the usual mobile phone functionality also takes on the role of a PDA ("Personal Digital Assistant"), with notepad and appointment scheduling functions, for example. Conversely, PDAs are taking on additional telephone functions. This can result in synergies: for example, the portable appointment scheduler can now be synchronised largely automatically with its counterpart in the office via mobile radio communications technology.

Integrating additional functions into mobile phones typically leads to an increase in size. This might be necessary because the display must be a minimum size, or because a means of input has to be provided. In contrast to this development is the trend towards the decomposition of the conventional mobile phone: you might only wear a light headset or "earpiece" (perhaps even as a piece of jewellery), with the microphone disappearing into a shirt button, both parts communicating wirelessly with the actual mobile phone worn on a belt or in a wrist watch, which would also enable short messages and control functions to be displayed. Communications services, controls, displays, and additional functionality such as localisation services, Internet

Communications technology is integrated within accessories

access, and digital support can therefore be distributed across different personal "devices" (or rather, fashionable "accessories") that cooperate with each other. This might even go as far as spectacles that look perfectly normal, but that display information over your normal view or even blending into it, which might some day make possible the virtual red carpet that the personal navigation system rolls out in front of your eyes to help you find your way in an unknown environment . . .

These aspects are often subsumed under the somewhat diffuse term "wearable computing." From a technical viewpoint, however, this is not about utopian cyborg visions where humans and computers merge into a single entity. The expectation is very simple – that computer functionality and the devices that incorporate it should not only be "portable," but also, to a certain degree, become part of our clothing and be worn more or less directly on our bodies. An appropriate comparison might be between a "portable" pocket watch, which has to be taken out and opened up if needed, and a "wearable" wristwatch, which can be read at any time. Since its sensors are located close to the body, a wearable computer is also suitable for monitoring its user's health (and, if necessary, reporting values of vital functions via telemetry to a medical call centre) or for reinforcing his sensory perception. In this respect, the proximity to the body leads to the development of new qualities and functions which a normal mobile phone could never achieve.

The reason such ideas are only now partly being realised is quite simply that technology has not been sufficiently advanced until now. On the one hand, semiconductor technology has had to be developed in such a way that complex functions could be integrated in a very small space, so that size, weight and energy consumption were acceptable; on the other hand, it is only now that adequate communications technologies for use at very short range (for example "body area networks") are coming within reach. Last but not least, components such as miniature microphones and high-resolution small-format displays have not been available as low-cost mass-produced products until now. Since technical progress has slowly overcome these obstacles, we can soon expect to see such products.

Experiments are also being carried out on mobile phone voice recognition, which would simplify operation whilst driving, for example. In a broader sense, voice recognition always makes sense in situations where there is no room for controls: this would be the case with future devices that were "integrated" into clothing or worn as small fashion accessories. When it comes to highly restricted areas of conversation, voice recognition is already relatively good. In the future, higher processor speeds will also deliver sufficiently high recognition rates to enable other digital auxiliary functions (such as navigating in an unknown environment or querying timetables) to be used. We can also expect further increases in quality with the output

Proximity to the body makes new functions possible

Voice recognition remains a complex problem

of synthetic speech. It is a different story with functions that require the "comprehension" of spoken language within a context, such as language translation. Although research results are encouraging, this continues to be a tricky problem, where only slow progress can be expected.

Functions requiring a high computing capacity, large databases or large storage volumes do not have to be implemented "locally" in the IT accessories themselves. For example, if a mobile phone or advanced digital auxiliary device is connected more or less permanently with sufficient speed to the Internet and its servers and services, the storage of data (e.g. photos or music) or information processing (e.g. automatic language translation) can also take place elsewhere "on the Net" where sufficient capacity, space and energy are available. Only input and output data would have to be transferred wirelessly between mobile phones and background systems in order to give the user the illusion that his device was doing all this itself. Storing data on the Net also makes sense because if the small IT accessories are lost, the data will not be lost as well.

Virtual storage of data in the Internet takes the load off IT accessories

Which of these innovations will be first to arrive, and how successful it will be, depends, of course, on a variety of circumstances and is not easy to predict. Technical factors (such as the available bandwidth for wireless communications), economic factors, and above all acceptability play an important role. From a technical viewpoint we can already estimate what in principle appears to be feasible in the next few years by extrapolating Moore's Law (the doubling of processor power every 18 months and the associated reduction in size and decrease in costs for the same level of performance). What makes sense from an economic viewpoint – for example, regarding the construction of an infrastructure or possible business models – is a far more complicated question to answer, as was recently demonstrated by some of the bizarre results of the various UMTS frequency auctions. It is equally difficult to predict how personal information and communications technology will be accepted: satellite telephone systems turned out to be a failure (initially at least), whereas the short messaging system has been a totally unexpected success, given its scale. Whether innovations develop into something useful and acceptable for citizens can often only be decided with hindsight.

Development depends both on technical progress and acceptance

2.1.2
The Trend towards Computer Technology
That Is Both "Invisible" and Ubiquitous

The post-PC era has
dawned!

Mobile phones with Internet connections, localisation and voice recognition capabilities, or smart cards and PDAs that communicate with their environment via radio are the first indicators of the dawning of a "post-PC era," in which the computer no longer appears primarily in the form of a personal computer and which was once described by IBM Chairman Lou Gerstner as follows: *"A billion people interacting with a million e-businesses through a trillion interconnected intelligent devices."*

Processors become
ubiquitous

What can we expect in this regard from such rapidly growing technical progress? It is becoming ever clearer that we are on the brink of a new era of computer applications that will radically influence our lives. In recent years PCs, the Internet and the Web have already changed much, especially in business life. Today we are seeing indicators everywhere of a major convergence of entire industries in the fields of media, consumer electronics, telecommunications, and information technology. But the approaching wave of the technological revolution will affect us more directly, in all aspects of our lives: it is becoming apparent that our future will soon be full of tiny processors communicating spontaneously with each other, which will be integrated into the vast majority of everyday objects thanks to their small size and low price.

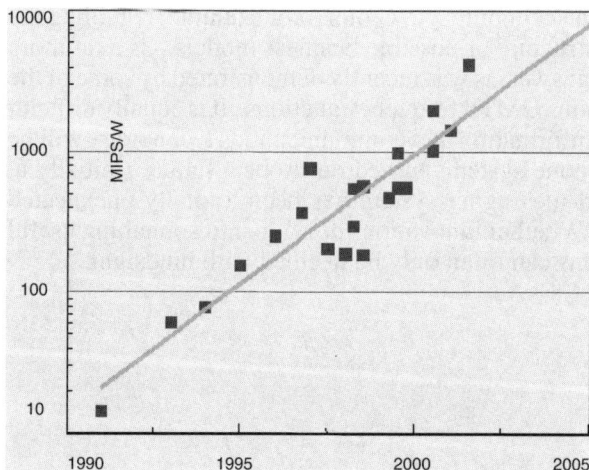

Fig. 2.1-2 Parameter MIPS/W for selected processors

One reason for this is to be found in the long-term trend of microelectronics. Moore's Law,[2] drawn up in the late 1960s by Gordon Moore, which states that the power of microprocessors doubles roughly every 18 months, has held true with astonishing accuracy and consistency. For the chip-producing industry, this has almost become a self-fulfilling prophecy, and they even produce their future-oriented "technology roadmaps" according to this law. A similarly high growth of efficiency can be observed for some other technology parameters such as energy requirements per computer instruction (Figure 2.1-2 shows the parameter MIPS/W for selected processors), storage density (Figure 2.1-3), and communications bandwidth. Conversely, prices for microelectronic functionality with a given computing power are falling radically over time. Technology experts expect this trend to continue for many years to come, meaning that computer processors and storage components will become much more powerful, smaller and cheaper.

Moore's Law still applies

Recent developments in the field of materials science and solid-state physics could give computers of the future a completely different shape, or even mean that computers will no longer be recognisable as such because they will completely blend into their surroundings. One example in this context is light-emitting polymers ("illuminating plastic"), which enable displays consisting of highly flexible, thin and bendable plastic foils to be created; in the future, you might want to affix your Internet portal to the weather service as an adhesive film on your bedroom window instead of a thermometer or barometer. Laser projection from within spectacles directly onto the retina of the eye is another option currently being investigated as a replacement for traditional computer output media. Research is also taking place into "electronic ink" and "smart paper," which will enable pen and paper to become fully functional interactive and truly mobile input/output media, with a tried and tested user interface. Although there is still a lot of technical development work involved and a broad commercial application may be some years off, prototypes of electronic paper and ink already exist. The practical significance of transforming paper into a computer or, conversely, computers into paper cannot be overestimated.

Computers merge with their surroundings

The results of microsystems technology and, increasingly, nano-technology are becoming more and more important. For example, they are producing tiny integral sensors that can record a wide variety of different environmental parameters. More recent sensors can not only react to light, acceleration, temperature etc., but also analyse gases and liquids or generally pre-process sensor input and therefore recognise certain patterns (e.g. fingerprints or facial forms). One interesting development in this regard is radio sensors that can report their measured data within a few metres distance without an explicit energy source: such sensors obtain the necessary energy from the

Environmental parameters are recorded by radio sensors

2 See Moore 1965

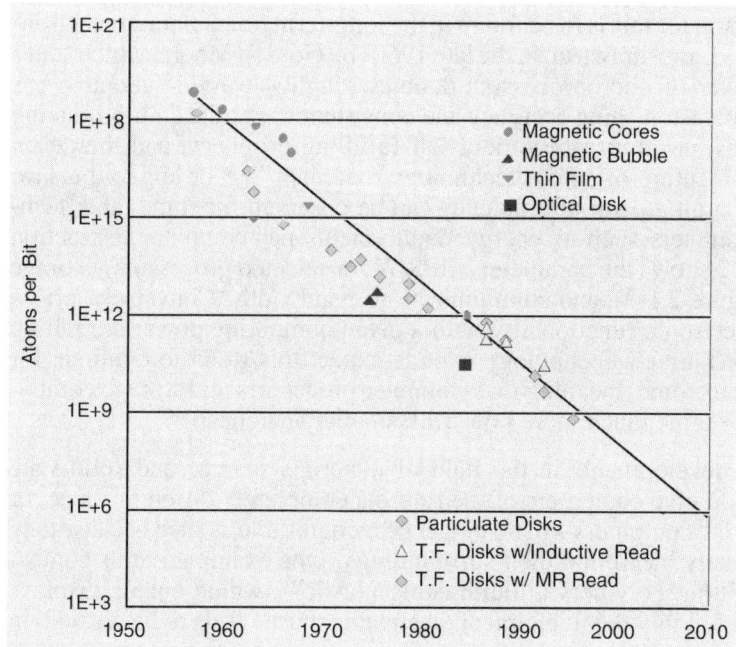

Fig. 2.1-3 Development of storage density

environment (e.g. by being irradiated with microwaves) or directly from the measuring process itself (as with temperature change or pressure).

Electronic labels (so-called passive "smart labels" or RFIDs – "Radio Frequency Identification") also operate without a built-in source of power. Depending on their construction, these are less than a square millimetre in area and thinner than a piece of paper.[3] In the form of flexible self-adhesive labels, these cost between € 0.1 and € 1 each, and therefore have the potential for replacing traditional bar codes for the identification of goods in certain areas. Their great advantages are that they do not have to be placed in the line of sight of the "reading device" (unlike the laser scanners currently used in supermarkets), that individual products rather than whole product groups can be differentiated, and that the electronic label can be used several times by recording different information on it. In a certain sense this is a further development of the anti-theft technology involving security gates in department stores. However, this is not just about the binary information "paid/stolen"; within milliseconds, several hundred bytes can be read and

Smart labels make the environment "intelligent"

---

3 See Finkenzeller 1999

Chapter 2.1
Ubiquitous Computing

written "wirelessly" up to a distance of about two metres depending on the underlying technology.

What is interesting about such remote-inquiry electronic markers is that they enable objects to be clearly identified and recognised and therefore linked in real time to an associated data record held on the Internet or in a remote database. This ultimately means that specific data and information-processing methods can be related to any kind of object.[4] If everyday objects can be uniquely identified from a distance and furnished with information, this opens up application possibilities that go far beyond the original task of automated warehousing or supermarkets without cashiers, as outlined below.

Everyday objects can be read by computers

Significant advances have also been made in the field of wireless communications. GSM mobile phone technology has established itself extensively and has become a so-called third generation system (UMTS) with higher bandwidth and better possibilities for data communications. Especially interesting are recent short-range communications technologies that need much less energy and make smaller and cheaper products possible. At the moment, such communications modules are the size of about half a matchbox, with further integration aiming to reduce their size even further. The price is only a few euros and is expected to fall rapidly.

Another exciting development is the field of "body area networks," where the human body itself is used as a transmission medium for electrical signals of very low current. Simply by touching a device or an object, an individual identification code can be transmitted. (This could, for example, be supplied to the body by a wristwatch). This could be used for access controls, personalised device configuration, or the billing of services. Experiments are also taking place in the field of "wearable computing" with clothing containing conductive fibres. Fibres that can change their electrical resistance when they are stretched or bent will certainly make for interesting man-machine interfaces, allowing body movements to be captured, or triggering functions by gently pulling on an item of clothing.

Body area networks: the human body as the transmission medium

Scientists are also working intensively on improved possibilities for determining the position of mobile objects (e.g. via satellite-supported systems such as GPS or radio direction-finding methods in mobile phones). As well as increased accuracy, the aim is also to make the receiver smaller and reduce its energy requirements. GPS receivers will soon be about the size of a credit card, including the antenna.

Many of these technological developments can be used together or even integrated. In the field of "embedded systems," for example, fully-functioning

---

4 See Want et al. 1999

153   Changing Technology

Chips make everyday objects smart

computers including sensors and wireless networking functionality will be developed on a single chip that can be built into any device or everyday object for control purposes. High processor speed is not as important as producing chips that are small, cheap, and save energy. Such microchips – if necessary in conjunction with suitable external sensors, input and output interfaces, and communications functionality – are the primary components that can make everyday objects "smart."

Technology, trends and developments

Summarising these technological trends and developments – tiny, cheap processors with integrated sensors and wireless communications ability, the attachment of information to everyday objects, the remote identification of objects, the precise localisation of objects, flexible displays and semiconductors based on polymers, electronic paper, and improved voice recognition – it becomes clear that the technological basis for a strange new world has been created: everyday objects that are in some respects "smart" and with which we can communicate under certain circumstances on an almost natural level.

2.1.3
Everyday Objects Become "Smart" and Network Themselves via the Internet

The "single-use" computer

The "creeping revolution" induced by the sustained technological progress that is influencing not only the quantity but also the quality of information-processing capabilities is leading to a situation where there will be a plentiful supply of computing power. Smart cards that become worthless after being used in the form of telephone cards, or electronic labels that act as a substitute for bar codes – and which are on the verge of mass production – are the first indicators of a new wave of "single-use computers."

Everyday objects become "smart" without being "intelligent"

This likely saturation of our world with information-processing capacity heralds a paradigm shift in computer applications: tiny, cheap processors can be embedded into many everyday objects, can detect their surroundings via similarly integrated sensors, and can equip "their" object with both information-processing and communications capabilities. This adds another completely new dimension to such objects: they can, for example, find out where they are, what other objects are in their vicinity, and what has happened to them in the past. They can also communicate and cooperate with other "smart" objects and, theoretically, access all sorts of Internet resources. Objects and devices can thus behave in a context-sensitive manner and appear to be "smart," without actually being "intelligent."

*"*Smart Labels: first step on the way to single-use computers.*"*

The phrase "ubiquitous computing," which is used in this context, was coined more than ten years ago by Mark Weiser, who was chief scientist at the XEROX Palo Alto Research Center until his early death in 1999.[5] Weiser saw technology as only a means to an end, which should take a back seat in order to allow the user to concentrate fully on the task at hand. In this respect, it would be wrong to approach the personal computer as a universal information-technology tool, since its complexity takes up too much of the user's attention. According to Weiser, the computer as a dedicated device should disappear, while at the same time making its information-processing capabilities available throughout our surroundings (ubiquitous computing in a truly literal sense). Intrusive technology should make way for "calm technology": *"As technology becomes more embedded and invisible, it calms our lives by removing the annoyances. . . The most profound technologies are those that disappear. They weave themselves into the fabric of everyday life until they are indistinguishable from it."*[6] It remains to be seen whether this apparent paradox does indeed take place, namely that despite the increasing quantity and increasingly ubiquitous nature of information, this information also becomes easier to use (perhaps due to more intuitive interfaces and more implicit information processing).

Calm technology

While Weiser saw the term "ubiquitous computing" in a more academic and idealistic sense as an unobtrusive, human-centred technological vision that will not be realised for many years yet, industry has coined the term "pervasive computing" with a slightly different slant.[7] Though this also relates to pervasive and omnipresent information processing, its primary goal is to use this information processing in the near future in the fields of electronic commerce and Web-based business processes. In this pragmatic variation – where communications concepts, middleware concepts, and technologies for application-neutral data representation (e.g. XML) play a role alongside various mobile devices (such as smart phones and PDAs) – ubiquitous computing is already gaining a foothold in practice.

Ubiquitous computing – omnipresence without obtrusiveness

When talking about the paradigm of ubiquitous computing, it is interesting to note that, in claiming to bring computers into the world, it appears diametrically opposed to the maxim of virtual reality, that of bringing the world into computers. In fact, the vision of ubiquitous computing is not to isolate itself from the real world and construct an artificial world, but on the contrary to enrich and make more comfortable the natural environment humans are used to by means of discreet background technology. A synthesis of these two viewpoints exists in the form of "augmented reality": this involves overlaying the real world with elements of a virtual, information-

Fusion of the real and the virtual

---

5 See Weiser 1991
6 Ibid.
7 See Burkhardt et al. 2001 and Hansmann et al. 2001

based world, for example by mirroring additional information for the user onto his spectacles, so that the real world is not excluded, but enriched.

As a consequence of objects being able to communicate with each other (e.g. by telling other interested and authorised objects their location or sensor values), the Internet will also undergo an enormous change. Indeed, the growth of the Internet is characterised not only by a rapid – currently almost exponential – increase in the number of computers connected (if the current growth rate continues, more than one billion Internet-enabled computers are expected in the year 2005), but also by its qualitative growth. In the 1980s, it was primarily used for *person-to-person* communication – e-mail was the dominant application at that time – but the 1990s brought a completely new form of usage with the Web: now *people* were communicating via browsers on one side with *machines*, namely Web servers, on the other side. The consequence of this was the multiplication of data traffic, and at the same time this led to the rapid commercialisation and popularity of the Internet. But now another qualitative leap forward has become apparent: the Internet of the future will be used principally for *machine-to-machine* communication, or rather *object-to-object* communication. Since nowadays almost all computers in the world are connected to the Internet, an expansion of the Internet into everyday objects is the next step. Neil Gershenfeld from MIT's Media Lab expressed this as follows:

"In retrospect it looks like the rapid growth of the World Wide Web may have been just the trigger charge that is now setting off the real explosion, as things start to use the Net".[8]

But what exactly does it mean if objects can communicate with each other? Envisioning concrete applications is not easy. However, the potential seems to be great if objects can cooperate with each other, can theoretically access any information stored in databases or on the Internet, and can use any suitable Internet-based service available. An automatic lawn sprinkler will thus profit not only from being networked with humidity sensors in the ground, but also from obtaining the current weather forecast free from the Internet. Another example is pens that digitise everything they write, and communicate this to an appropriate location. Many more applications are imaginable. The limits are less of a technological nature than economic (business models, standards, the amortisation of the infrastructure, costs of information access, etc.).

Localisation technologies also have great application potential. In the future, it may be virtually impossible to lose things, or it may be possible to relocate lost objects, because the objects will know where they are and can communicate this if necessary. Localisation modules that use the GPS

When everyday objects use the Internet…

Person-to-person, machine-to-machine, object-to-object

Localisation technologies in objects

---

8 Gerschenfeld 1999

system, for example, are still too large, expensive and imprecise, and consume too much energy for many applications. But continuing progress is being made on all four parameters, and for larger, more valuable objects, it is already worthwhile: some hire cars, for example, are already secretly equipped with localisation equipment. As technology progresses, simpler things will also profit from this possibility. Parents might appreciate it, for example, if their children's shoes and coats revealed their whereabouts or even raised the alarm if the objects became too far separated outside the home.

In the same way, "tachographs" could be produced for a variety of objects. If an object knows where it is located, then it only needs to store this information regularly together with a time stamp or make a note on its own private (and secure) home page on the Internet. Later on, the "life trace" of this object can be easily reconstructed. By comparing a variety of such life traces, it will be possible to determine the common context of different objects or obtain other information through this history (e.g. the hotel to which a location-sensitive travel bag has been taken).

Internet-based "life trace" of objects

Initially, it will be the higher priced appliances, tools and other objects that benefit from ubiquitous networking and "artefact intelligence" (and therefore contribute to the expansion of technologies and infrastructures). Sensor-supported information-processing and communications capabilities will provide objects with substantial added value. But soon a lot of other, more trivial objects (from calendar schedules to furniture, from toys to tin cans) will use the Internet with its many resources to carry out their tasks, even though their users may not be aware of this. Savvy business consultants have already coined an expression for business transactions that are carried out between machines or objects without human intervention: "silent commerce."

Silent commerce

2.1.4
"Ubiquitous Computing" Gains Great Economic Significance

The new basic functions resulting from the progress of information and communications technology (such as the remote identification of objects, local "intelligence," the networking of objects via the Internet, unconventional man-machine interaction principles, etc.) and the applications made possible as a result are set to gain great economic significance in the medium to long term. This can be illustrated using the example of remote identification.

A whole range of constantly improving techniques exists for identifying objects over a distance of a few metres. In addition to options that are not yet suitable for general use, such as biochemical marking and purely optical recognition (the automated identification of faces and vehicles is already yielding promising results), there are the electronic labels mentioned above.[9] In a more complex and therefore more expensive and larger form, these use batteries to transmit at regular intervals a unique radio signal that can be recognised by the environment. In contrast to this, paper-thin, *passive* electronic labels measuring only a few square millimetres in area can be stuck onto objects or integrated into them during the manufacturing process, but require more complex "detectors," which transmit a radio signal to the labels and recognise their unique radio echoes. Yet the labels themselves are much cheaper and do not need batteries, and are therefore perfect for mass production.

Until now, such "smart labels" have been used as prototypes to increase the forgery-proofing of branded products (as a kind of electronic seal) or to optimise warehousing and production processes. Parts boxes on vehicle assembly lines, for example, can automatically control their own stock and transmit a signal to the warehouse and supplier as soon as they need replenishing. Using this method, suppliers receive precise information regarding the requirements and can deliver the necessary parts just in time. Another example is the pilot application of an English supermarket chain, where electronically labelled recyclable containers for perishable products are resulting in a clear reduction in the supply chain lead time and thus increase the time products can spend on the supermarket shelf. This involves detectors automatically identifying every box and recognising the expiry date of the contents in the interim warehouse and at the retail store.

Most pilot applications for "smart labels" have so far been found in the automobile, logistics and transport industries. Examples of more recent applications come from the life sciences and the retail sector. Simple applications are limited to the basic functions of ubiquitous computing such as identification, localisation and tracing, where only the identifier is stored locally on the object. More complex applications are increasingly using sensors for the decentralised collection of data from the environment and working with what are known as notification services: in other words, smart objects report automatically if a specified condition occurs or if a pre-programmed rule (e.g. regarding permitted temperature or duration of stay) is violated.

Generally speaking, a smart product can on the one hand automatically download (from a database or from its own homepage) the latest information such as a destination or updated user instructions; on the other hand it

Identifying objects by means of radio signals...

... to optimise production and logistical processes

Identification, localisation and tracing

---

9 See Finkenzeller 1999

can independently supply its informational counterpart, which resides some-where on the Internet, with sensor data such as its location. In a certain sense, one might think of the object with its electronic label or radio sen-sors as the "body" of the object, with its informational counterpart being the "soul," storing object-specific data and even acting and communicating autonomously as an active information unit.

The new technologies of ubiquitous computing, therefore, are automat-ing the process of linking the real world of everyday objects, products and means of production with the virtual world of the Internet or e-commerce and supply-chain management systems; in many ways, they are replacing man as the mediator between the real and the virtual world. As a consequence, this is facilitating new business processes that bring additional benefits to man-ufacturers, suppliers and clients. These technologies are helping to reduce lead times, warehouse inventories, risks and error rates. They can contribute to new solutions in the fields of maintenance and repair, security and liability, quality assurance, waste disposal and recycling, and ultimately create a vari-ety of new services such as the consistent individualisation or personalisation of goods throughout their entire lifecycle.

What Peter Harrop, IDTechEx expert, has to say about this is almost alarming:

The next evolution involves fully automated communications on a vast scale. The fast-moving consumer goods industry will be transformed by trillions of one cent smart labels... Many new consumer benefits will be offered such as the food that tells the microwave how to cook it... Many markets for position services will be created such as low-cost gadgets that trace lost children, assets and animals and tags on one million vehicles permitting the be located and their tax, license, etc. verified remotely.

In the longer term, the process of remotely identifying objects along with wireless information access, mobile communications technology and "wearable computing" pave the way for possibilities that go far beyond the optimisation of business processes mentioned above and, to some extent, amount to an informatisation of the world.

To give an example, imagine everyday objects such as furniture, pack-aged food, medication and clothing being equipped with an electronic label that contains a specific Internet address as digital information (a "URL") which, to put it simply, points to the homepage of the object.[10] If you then read this Internet address with a device similar to a mobile phone just by pointing it at the object, the mobile phone can, independently and with no further assistance from the object in question, access and display the corre-sponding homepage via the mobile telephony network.

The Internet soul

Ubiquitous computing as mediating between the real and the virtual world

Informatisation of the world

Everyday objects get a URL

---

10 See Hansmann et al. 2001

The user has the impression that the object itself has "transmitted" the information attached to it, although in fact it has been provided to the mobile phone via the URL from the Internet.[11] The information could for example be instructions for a tool, or cooking instructions for a ready-to-serve meal, or the information leaflet for medication. The details of what is displayed may depend on the "context" – factors such as whether the user is a good customer and has paid a lot of money for the product, whether he is over 18 years of age, what language he speaks, his current location, or which world-explanatory service from which encyclopaedia company he has subscribed to – but also maybe on whether he has paid his taxes on time...

Objects carry and communicate information about themselves

The appliance that we describe as a "mobile phone" may in the future take the form of a special pair of spectacles, or a piece of electronic paper for displaying information, in conjunction with a "pointer." Furthermore, it will not only be human users who are interested in the additional information on objects, but also other "smart" objects. A trash can, for example, may be very curious about the recycling characteristics of its contents, and a medicine cabinet may be concerned about its medication's possible side effects and best-before date. Theoretically, at least from a technical point of view, there is nothing to stop objects (or their informational counterparts on the Internet) exchanging information amongst themselves, i.e. almost speaking with each other, as long as a common basis for communication in the form of a standardised formal language exists. Efforts are already being made to define product-description languages.

Physical products obtain digital added value

Even if a detailed assessment cannot yet be made, it is clear that completely new applications will come into existence based on this multitude of smart objects. The digital added value of a manufacturer's own products can be very different from that of physically similar products marketed by the competition, and can tie clients more closely to its own added value services and compatible products. The maintenance and ongoing development of the global infrastructure necessary for such aspects – including the measures required to meet the increased need for security and data protection in such an environment – might even occupy a whole industry, similar to today's energy and telecommunications enterprises.

---

11 See Barrett/Maglio 1998

2.1.5
Social and Political Challenges

While a technical analysis may be able to predict what the future *could* bring, the question of what the future is *allowed* to bring can only be answered by means of a social process.

If information is attached to "electronically enhanced" objects, in other words physical objects effectively become media, who can or should determine their content? It is no secret that there are often arguments on the Internet over who owns address "xyz.com" and whether you can prohibit someone from adding a link to someone else's home page. There is also the question of which Web pages search engines should be allowed to deliver (instructions for making bombs? pages with pornographic content? racist views?) and who should take responsibility for them, and this is almost becoming a political issue. If, for example, ready-to-serve meals contained an electronic label, would a consumer protection institute be permitted to map this number using its own electronic directory onto information other than that which the producer intended (e.g. to warn of allergies to the ingredients)? Or should this at least be permitted if the "viewer" specifically requests it?

To put this in more general terms: if objects are equipped with information or a means of identification that enables a personal digital assistant, maybe located in a pair of spectacles, to explain the world ("Computer, what's that?"), can real-world objects then be interpreted by the manufacturer of the smart spectacles in any way he likes? World views have often been the cause of disputes. Given a situation where cyberspace is approaching reality, partially overlaying or even merging into it, there are some things we must be prepared for; ultimately, some political questions of a fairly explosive nature must be asked.

Many other questions are generated by the informatisation of the world, only a few of which are touched on here: if many objects can only function properly if they have access to the Internet or a similar infrastructure, this results in a far-reaching dependency on those systems and their underlying technology. If these fail for whatever reason – design errors, material defects, sabotage, overloading, natural disasters, etc. – then it could have catastrophic consequences on a global scale. If the correct functioning of the information-technology infrastructure is vitally important to society and individuals, not only do we need appropriate security mechanisms, but the systems have to be designed from the outset with this in mind.

Another set of questions relates to the socially acceptable design of the technologies outlined and their applications. Using the most important func-

Who controls the interpretation of the world?

Dependence on the informatised infrastructure is critical in the case of system failure

Consideration of aspects
related to competition policy

From online to offline history

Emergence of a surveillance
infrastructure

Informatisation of the world
makes everyday objects
smart

tions should, of course, be simple and straightforward in order to prevent a "digital divide" in society reaching deep into our everyday lives. It is equally important to bear in mind that cartels, monopolies, or power concentrations could develop due to the expansion of the Internet into our everyday world, and to consider how this could be moderated in a democratic society.

Last but not least, we should pay particular attention to the protection of privacy. The vision of ubiquitous computers expands the existing Internet problem of "online history" (in other words, the detailed recording of mouse clicks and Web pages visited) into a comprehensive "offline history": whereas the Web surveillance of a person has previously been clearly limited to computer usage, there will often be no distinction between "online" and "offline" in a world full of smart everyday objects. As a result, this ubiquitous data will become more valuable. Whereas until now only a relatively limited view of a person could be obtained by rummaging around in data, a much more comprehensive picture can be painted of this person and his day-to-day behaviour in the ubiquitous vision.

It seems clear that, without effective data-protection measures, the technology of ubiquitous computing could be used to create a surveillance infrastructure that would render ineffective many existing laws and privacy-protection mechanisms. Therefore basic legal considerations and new technical approaches, as well as much social and organisational effort, will be required in order to prevent this brave new world of smart, interconnected objects becoming an Orwellian nightmare. As Rossnagel would say,[12] Big Brother will be joined by lots of little brothers.

2.1.6
Conclusion

The technological trend is pointing quite clearly towards a continued informatisation of the world, for example through embedding more and more processors into everyday objects and through the increasing connection of all kinds of devices to the Internet. From a technical and organisational viewpoint there are already many challenges to consider: the energy supply for objects, communications standards, and much more besides.

If technical progress means more and more everyday objects are becoming "smart" and therefore behaving unconventionally towards humans, then this will ultimately lead to a totally different world from the one we are accustomed to. The changes will not happen overnight; instead, this process will be more of a creeping revolution. Taken to its logical conclusion, a

---

12 See Rossnagel 2002

world that is literally permeated by information technology will sooner or later bring with it major social and economic consequences, adding a political dimension to ubiquitous computing and the associated future direction of the Internet.

The driving forces behind these underlying technological achievements are microelectronics and computer science, supported by basic research in the fields of physics and materials science. Dynamic development in these areas is continuing unabated, and its effects are increasingly influencing everyday life. It is therefore clear that the 21st century will be characterised less by major technological structures such as moon colonies, underwater cities and atomic cars (as suggested by earlier popular futurologists), than by the application of tiny, practically invisible technology that is thus easy to replicate and distribute. This involves biotechnology and nano-technology as well as microelectronics. And looking further into the future, it is nano-technology that should make a further decisive contribution to smart environments, creating tiny actors that actually make changes to the physical world.

The driving forces of future development

But before the far-reaching expectations of nano-technology can be fulfilled, we can look forward to seeing the effects of ubiquitous computing. It is already worth thinking about the economic and social prospects and the social and legal consequences all this could have, but most of all about what role Europe should play in designing this "Internet of things"!

Chapter 2.2

Wireless Internet Access:
3G vs. WiFi?

William Lehr and Lee W. McKnight

The two most important phenomena impacting telecommunications over the past decade have been the explosive parallel growth of the Internet and mobile telephone services. The Internet brought the benefits of data communications to the masses with email, the Web, and e-commerce, while mobile service has enabled "follow-me-anywhere/always-on" telephony. The Internet helped accelerate the trend from voice-centric to data-centric networking. Data already exceeds voice traffic, and the data share continues to grow. Now these two worlds are converging. This convergence offers the benefits of new interactive multimedia services coupled to the flexibility and mobility of wireless. To realise the full potential of this convergence, however, we need broadband access connections. What precisely constitutes "broadband" is, of course, a moving target, but at a minimum, it should support data rates in the hundreds of kilobits per second as opposed to the 50 Kbps enjoyed by 80% of the Internet users in the USA, who still rely on dial-up modems over wireline circuits, or the even more anaemic 10-20 Kbps typically supported by the current generation of available mobile data services. While the need for broadband wireless Internet access is widely accepted, there remains great uncertainty and disagreement as to how the wireless Internet future will evolve.

The goal of this article is to compare and contrast two technologies that are likely to play important roles: Third Generation mobile ("3G") and Wireless Local Area Networks ("WLAN"). Specifically, we will focus on 3G as embodied by the IMT-2000 family of standards versus the WLAN technology embodied by the WiFi or 802.11b standard, which is the most popular and widely deployed of the WLAN technologies. We use these technologies as reference points to span what we believe are two fundamentally different philosophies for how wireless Internet access might evolve. The former represents a natural evolution and extension of the business models of existing mobile providers. These providers have already invested billions of dollars purchasing the spectrum licences to support advanced data services, and equipment makers have been gearing up to produce the base stations and handsets for wide-scale deployments of 3G

Internet and wireless technologies converge

3G versus WLAN

3G and WLAN – two distinct philosophies

" **Heterogeneous access technologies constitute the wireless future.** *"*

Vertically integrated
service-provider approach
versus decentralised
end-user-centric approach

services. In contrast, the WiFi approach would leverage the large installed base of WLAN infrastructure already in place.[1]

Speaking broadly, 3G offers a vertically integrated, top-down, service-provider approach to delivering wireless Internet access, while WiFi offers (at least potentially) an end-user-centric, decentralised approach to service-provisioning.

We believe that the wireless future will include a mix of heterogeneous wireless access technologies. Moreover, we expect that the two access technologies, 3G and WLAN, will converge in such a way that vertically-integrated service providers will integrate WiFi or other WLAN technologies into their 3G or wireline infrastructure when this makes sense. We are, perhaps, less optimistic about the prospects for decentralised, bottom-up networks. However, it is interesting to consider what some of the roadblocks are to the emergence of such a world. The latter sort of industry structure is attractive because it is likely to be quite competitive, whereas the top-down vertically-integrated service-provider model may – but need not be – less so. The multiplicity of potential wireless access technologies and/or business models provides some hope that we *may* be able to realise robust facilities-based competition for broadband local access services. If this occurs, it would help solve the "last mile" competition problem that has bedevilled telecommunications policy.

2.2.1
How are WiFi and 3G the Same?

Similarity of the services in
the eyes of the user

From the preceding discussion, it might appear that 3G and WiFi address completely different user needs in quite distinct markets that do not overlap. While this was certainly more true about earlier generations of mobile services when compared with wired LANs or earlier versions of WLANs, it is increasingly not the case. The end-user does not care what technology is used to support his service. What matters is that both of these technologies are providing platforms for wireless access to the Internet and other communication services.

1 For example, the Yankee Group estimates that over 12 million 802.11b access points and network interface cards have been shipped globally to date, with 75% of these shipped in the last year. See Zawel 2002

Both are wireless

Both technologies are wireless, which (1) avoids the need to install cable drops to each device when compared to wireline alternatives, and (2) facilitates mobility. Avoiding the need to install or reconfigure local distribution cable plant can represent a significant cost saving, whether it is within a building, home, or in the last-mile distribution plant of a wireline service provider. Moreover, many types of wireless infrastructure can provide scalable infrastructure when penetration will increase only slowly over time (e.g. when a new service is offered or in an overbuild scenario). New base stations are added as more users in the local area join the wireless network and cells are resized. Wireless infrastructure may be deployed more rapidly than wireline alternatives to respond to new market opportunities or changing demand. These aspects of wireless may make it attractive as an overbuild competitor to wireline local access, which has large sunk/fixed costs that vary more with the homes passed than the actual level of subscribership. The high upfront cost of installing new wireline last-mile facilities is one of the reasons why these may be a natural monopoly, at least in many locations.

> Mobility through being wireless

> Wireless technology facilitates rapid scalability

Wireless technologies also facilitate mobility. This includes both (1) the ability to move devices around without having to move cables and furniture, and (2) the ability to stay continuously connected over wider serving areas. We refer to the first as local mobility, and this is one of the key advantages of WLANs over traditional wireline LANs. The second type of mobility is one of the key advantages of mobile systems such as 3G. WLANs trade the range of coverage for higher bandwidth, making them more suitable for "local hot spot" service. In contrast, 3G offers much narrower bandwidth but over a wider calling area and with more support for rapid movement between base stations. Although it is possible to cover a wide area with WiFi, it is most commonly deployed in a local area with one or a few base stations being managed as a separate WLAN. In contrast, a 3G network would include a large number of base stations operating over a wide area as an integrated wireless network to enable load sharing and uninterrupted hand-offs when subscribers move between base stations at high speeds.

> WLAN provides bandwidth, 3G provides mobility

This has implications for the magnitude of initial investment required to bring up WLAN or 3G wireless service and for the network management and operations support services required to operate the networks. However, it is unclear at this time which type of network might be lower-cost for equivalent scale deployments, either in terms of upfront capital costs (ignoring spectrum costs for now) or ongoing network management costs.

> Big differences in initial investments in building up network

Both are access technologies

Difference in the last mile

Both 3G and WiFi are access or edge-network technologies. This means they offer alternatives to the last-mile wireline network. Beyond the last mile, both rely on similar network connections and transmission support infrastructure. For 3G, the wireless link is from the end-user device to the cell base station, which may be at a distance of up to a few kilometres, and then dedicated wireline facilities to interconnect base stations to the carrier's backbone network and ultimately to the Internet cloud. The local backhaul infrastructure of the cell provider may be offered over facilities owned by the wireless provider (e.g. microwave links) or leased from the local wireline telephone service provider (i.e. usually the incumbent local exchange carrier or ILEC). Although 3G is conceived of as an end-to-end service, it is possible to view it as an access service.

3G – end-to-end or access service

For WiFi, the wireless link is a few hundred feet from the end-user device to the base station. The base station is then connected either into the wireline LAN or enterprise network infrastructure or to a wireline access line to a carrier's backbone network and then eventually to the Internet. For example, WiFi is increasingly finding application as a home LAN technology to enable sharing of DSL or cable modem residential broadband access services among multiple PCs in a home or to enable within-home mobility. WiFi is generally viewed as an access technology, not as an end-to-end service.

WLAN as technology for multiple Internet access

Finally, focusing on the access-nature of 3G and WiFi allows us to abstract from the other elements of the value chain. Wireless services are part of an end-to-end value chain that includes, in its coarsest delineation, at least (1) the Internet backbone (the cloud); (2) the second mile network providers (ILEC, mobile, cable, or a NextGen carrier); and (3) the last mile access facilities (and, beyond them, the end-user devices). The backbone and the second mile may be wireless or wireline, but these are not principally a "wireless" challenge. It is in the last mile – the access network – that delivering mobility, bandwidth, and follow-me-anywhere/anytime services is most challenging.

Wireless services are also part of the end-to-end value chain

Both offer broadband data service

Both 3G and WiFi support broadband data service, although as noted earlier, the data rate offered by WiFi (11 Mbps) is substantially higher than the couple of hundred Kbps expected from 3G services. Although future generations of wireless mobile technology will support higher speeds, this will also be

Cable wins the broadband data race

the case for WLANs, and neither will be likely to compete with wireline[2] speeds (except over quite short distances).

The key is that both will offer sufficient bandwidth to support a comparable array of services, including real-time voice, data, and streaming media, that are not currently easily supported over narrowband wireline services. (Of course, the quality of these services will be quite different, as will be discussed further below.) In this sense,[3] both will support "broadband" where we define this as "faster than what we had before."

Both services will also support "always on" connectivity, which is another very important aspect of broadband service. Indeed, some analysts believe this is even more important than the raw throughput supported.

Bandwidth for real-time and streaming media

2.2.2
How are they Different?

Current business models/deployment are different.

As noted above, 3G represents an extension of the mobile service provider model. This is the technology of choice for upgrading existing mobile telephone services to expand capacity and add enhanced services. The basic business model is the telecommunications services model in which service providers own and manage the infrastructure (including the spectrum) and sell service on that infrastructure. End-customers typically have a monthly service contract with the 3G provider and view their payments as a recurring operating expense – analogous to regular telephone service. Not surprisingly, the 3G business model is close to the wireline telephone business. The mindset is on long-lived capital assets, ubiquitous coverage and service integration. Moreover, telecommunications regulatory supervision, including common carriage and interconnection rules, is part of the landscape. The service is conceptualised usually as a mass-market offering to both residential and business customers on a subscription basis. The 3G deployment and service-provisioning model is one of top-down, vertically integrated, and centralised planning and operation.[4] It is expected that 3G services will be

3G – a telecommunications business model

Analogy with fixed-line telephone services

---

2 That is, including fibre optic cables.

3 Defining what constitutes broadband is contentious, and in any case it is a moving target. For the purposes of collecting data, the FCC defines broadband as offering 200 Kbps in one or both directions.

4 Eli Noam has discussed how FCC spectrum policy has fostered the perpetuation of vertically-integrated wireless service models and how different policies might enable the sorts of alternative business models and industry structure discussed here. See Noam 2001

provided as part of a bundled service-offering, to take advantage of opportunities to implement price discrimination strategies and to exploit consumers' preferences for "one-stop" shopping/single bill service.

Voice calls still most important

> Talk, Talk, Talk: So who needs streaming video on a phone? The killer app for 3G may turn out to be–surprise–voice calls
>
> 3G was sold by its promoters as a way to provide mobile Internet access. But the market has figured out that not only will streaming video not be feasible with 3G, it is doubtful whether it would bring in much revenue even if it could be offered. People don't want to be entertained by their cell phones. They want to be connected. The investments being made in 3G may not be necessary, as 2.5G would have been sufficient, but they will provide much greater voice capacity.
>
> *Andrew Odlyzko (2001)*[5]

In contrast, WiFi comes out of the data communications industry (LANs), which is a by-product of the computer industry. The basic business model is one of equipment makers who sell boxes to consumers. The services provided by the equipment are free to the equipment owners. For the customers, the equipment represents a capital asset that is depreciated. While WiFi can be used as an access link, it has not heretofore been thought of as an end-to-end service. Only recently have WLANs been targeted as a mass-market offering to home users. Previously, these were installed most typically in corporate or university settings. End-user customers buy the equipment and then self-install it and interconnect it to their access or enterprise network facilities. Typically, the users of WiFi networks are not charged directly for access. Service is provided free for the closed user-community (i.e. employees of the firm, students at the university), with the costs of providing wireless access subsidised by the firm or university. More recently, we have seen the emergence of the FreeNet movement and several service-provider initiatives to offer (semi-) ubiquitous WiFi access services.

The WLAN business model is pursued by equipment manufacturers

FreeNet movement calls for free use of wireless broadband access services

Participants in the FreeNet movement are setting up WiFi base stations and allowing open access to any users with the suitable equipment to access the base station (i.e. just an 801.11b PC card in a laptop). Participants in this grass-roots movement do not charge for use of the access service (either to recover the costs of the wireless access infrastructure or the recurring costs of providing connectivity to the Internet). Because data traffic is inherently

---

5 Odlyzko, Andrew (2001): Talk, talk, talk: So who needs streaming video on a phone? The killer app for 3G may turn out to be – surprise – voice calls, in: Forbes, August 20, 2001, p. 28.

bursty and many end-users have dedicated facilities for which they pay a flat rate to connect to the Internet, and because they have already incurred the cost of the wireless access equipment for their own needs, FreeNet proponents argue that the incremental cost of supporting access is zero, and hence the price ought to be so also. While this may be true on lightly-loaded networks, it will not be the case as FreeNets become more congested and it will not be the case for traffic-variable costs upstream from the FreeNet. Moreover, if migration of consumers from paid access services to FreeNet access is significant, this will cannibalise the access revenues earned by service providers offering wireline or wireless access services. These issues raise questions about the long-term viability of the FreeNet movement. In any case, this movement is playing an important role in raising awareness and helping to develop end-user experience with using wireless broadband access services.

In addition to the FreeNet movement, there are a number of service providers now looking at using WiFi as the basis for wireless access over broad geographic areas. Most recently, the chairman and founder of Earth-link (one of the largest ISPs in the USA), Sky Dayton, formed a new wireless ISP called Boingo.[6] Boingo's business model will be to act as a clearing-house and backbone-infrastructure provider for local service providers interested in deploying WiFi access networks. Boingo will sell end-users a monthly subscription service that Boingo would then share with the WiFi network owners to compensate them for deploying and providing the service. Boingo would handle the customer billing and marketing, building out its footprint organically, as more and more WiFi local service providers join the Boingo family of networks. Partners may include smaller ISPs, hotels, airport lounges, and other retail establishments where potential customers are likely to be interested in getting wireless access.

Development of wireless ISP business models

With respect to deployment, 3G will require substantial investment in new infrastructure to upgrade existing 2G networks. However, when deployed by an existing mobile provider, much of the 2G infrastructure (e.g. towers and backhaul network) will remain useable. For WiFi, it is hoped that deployment can piggyback on the large existing base of WLAN equipment already in the field. In both cases, end-users will need to buy (or be subsidised) to acquire suitable interface devices (e.g. PC cards for 3G or WiFi access).

Differences in investment levels for 3G and WLAN

In contrast to 3G, WiFi wireless access can emerge in a decentralised, bottom-up fashion (although it is also possible for this to be centrally co-ordinated and driven by a wireline or mobile service provider). While the prevailing business model for 3G services and infrastructure is vertically integrated, this need not be the case for WiFi. This opens up the possibility of a

Decentralised coordination of WLAN access permits heterogeneous value chains

---

6 See Charny 2001

Payment preferences of
customers as an impediment
to development

more heterogeneous and complex industry value chain. One impediment to
the growth of paid but decentralised WiFi service offerings is consumer preference for one-stop shopping/single monthly billing. Boingo's model offers
one approach to overcoming this resistance. Alternative approaches that are
under research consideration (i.e. not commercially viable today) include
using some form of micro-payments (e.g. e-cash or credit card billing). It
is also well known that consumers have a demonstrated preference for flat-
rate billing, which may cause problems in a decentralised WiFi provisioning
model. If backhaul costs are traffic-variable (e.g. suppose the rate for Internet connection from base station to cloud varies with traffic), then offering
flat-rate service may be perceived as too risky for the base station owner.
Once again, Boingo's approach suggests how an intermediary willing to aggregate customers and take advantage of the scale economies associated with
serving a larger customer base (e.g. with respect to retail costs and backhaul traffic-management costs) can play an important role in facilitating the
emergence of decentralised networking infrastructure.

Spectrum policy and management

One of the key distinctions between 3G and WiFi that we have only touched
upon lightly thus far is that 3G and other mobile technologies use licensed
spectrum, while WiFi uses unlicensed shared spectrum. This has important implications for (1) cost of service; (2) Quality of Service (QoS) and
congestion management; and (3) industry structure.

First, the upfront cost of acquiring a spectrum licence represents a substantial share of the capital costs of deploying 3G services. This cost is
not faced by WiFi, which uses the shared 2.4 GHz unlicensed, shared spectrum. The cost of a spectrum licence represents a substantial entry barrier
that makes it less likely that 3G services (or other services requiring licensed
spectrum) could emerge in a decentralised fashion. Of course, with increased
flexibility in spectrum licensing rules and with the emergence of secondary
markets that are being facilitated by these rules, it is possible that the upfront

Secondary markets make a
more efficient use of
spectrum possible

costs of obtaining a spectrum licence could be shared to allow decentralised
infrastructure deployment to proceed. Under the traditional licensing approach, the licensing of the spectrum, the construction of the network infrastructure, and the management/operation of the service were all undertaken
by a single firm. Moreover, rigid licensing rules (motivated in part by interference concerns, but also, in part, by interest group politics[7]) limited the
ability of spectrum-licence holders to flexibly innovate with respect to the
technologies used, the services offered, or their mode of operation. In the
face of rapid technical progress and changing supply and demand dynamics,

---

7 See Hazlett 2001

this lack of flexibility increased the costs and reduced the efficiency of spectrum utilisation. High-value spectrum trapped in low-value uses could not be readily redeployed. With the emergence of secondary markets, it would be possible for spectrum brokers to emerge or service integrators that could help distribute the spectrum cost to enable decentralised infrastructure investment for licensed spectrum.

> Whose spectrum is it anyway? Electronic speech is protected by the First Amendment's Free Speech Clause. A licensing scheme, however the license is given out, is a serious restriction on speech. Until now, government licensing could be justified due to the basic assumption that spectrum is a scarce resource whose uses collided with each other. But suppose that the underlying assumption becomes invalid. Would not the entire licensing scheme then be subject to question? If electronic communications are an aspect of our fundamental free-speech rights, on what ground can these rights be sold to the highest bidder?
>
> *Eli Noam* (1998)[8]

Who does spectrum belong to?

Second, while licensed spectrum is expensive, it does have the advantage of facilitating QoS management. With licensed spectrum, the licensee is protected from interference from other service providers. This means that the licensee can enforce centralised allocation of scarce frequencies to adopt the congestion management strategy that is most appropriate. In contrast, the unlicensed spectrum used by WiFi imposes strict power limits on users (i.e. responsibility not to interfere with other users) and forces users to accept interference from others. This makes it easier for a 3G provider to market a service with a predictable level of service and to support delay-sensitive services such as real-time telephony. In contrast, while a WiFi network can address the problem of congestion associated with users on the WiFi network, it cannot control potential interference from other WiFi service providers or other RF sources that are sharing the unlicensed spectrum (both of which will appear as elevated background noise). This represents a serious challenge to supporting delay-sensitive services and to scaling service in the face of increasing competition from multiple and overlapping multiple service providers. A number of researchers have started thinking about how to facilitate more efficient resource allocation of unlicensed spectrum, including research on possible protocols that would enable QoS to be managed more effectively.[9]

Danger of interference for unlicensed spectrum

---

8 Noam, Eli (1998): Spectrum auctions: Yesterday's heresy, today's orthodoxy, tomorrow's anachronism. Taking the next step to open spectrum access, in: Journal of Law and Economics, Vol. XLI (October 1998), p. 770.

9 See Peha/Satapathy 1997

Third, the different spectrum regimes have direct implications for industry structure. For example, the FreeNet movement is not easily conceivable in the 3G world of licensed spectrum. Alternatively, it seems that the current licensing regime favours incumbency and, because it raises entry barriers, may make wireless-facilities-based competition less feasible. The flip side of this is that a licensing regime that creates entry barriers may make the benefits of deploying wireless infrastructure more appropriable, which would encourage investment in these services. This, in turn, may increase the likelihood that wireless will offer effective competition to wireline services.

2.2.3
Some Implications for Industry Structure and Public Policy

WiFi is good for competition

One implication that emerges from the above analysis is that success of WiFi wireless local access alternatives is likely to be good for local competition. First, if only 3G survives, then it is less likely that we will see non-vertically-integrated, decentralised service-provisioning. And the higher entry costs associated with acquiring licensed spectrum and the need to construct a geographically larger network to begin offering service will limit the number of firms that compete in the market. Of course, this does not mean that wireless access services would not be competitive – there may be more than enough competition among existing mobile providers to preclude the exercise of market power. However, there is also the possibility that the few 3G providers will become fewer still through mergers, and when coupled to the market power of wireline local exchange carriers, this could provide a powerful nexus for the continuation of monopoly power in last-mile facilities. Obviously, the firms that have a potential opportunity to establish such market power – the mobile providers and the local exchange carriers (which own a significant share of the mobile operators) – have a powerful incentive to collude to establish monopoly control over mixed wireless and wireline services.

Second, if both 3G and WiFi survive, then the diversity of viable networking infrastructure strategies will be conducive to greater facilities-based competition.

Third, success of the WiFi service model could help unlock the substantial investment in private networking infrastructure that could be used as the basis for constructing an alternative infrastructure to the PSTN and cable wireline networks. As noted above, this will require adding the necessary

Margin notes:

Spectrum regimes have an influence on industry structure

Competition in the last mile

Danger of monopolistic market control

Making WiFi investments pay their way

business functionality and technical support to enable base station owners to bill for WiFi service. Once this is developed, the opportunity to create novel ways to leverage the existing infrastructure investment will be increased.

Fourth, if only the WiFi service model survives, then we would expect this to be inherently more competitive because of the lower entry barriers for setting up local access services. The use of unlicensed spectrum means that property rights over the spectrum cannot be used to exclude potential entrants, although congestion – if not appropriately managed – could be just as effective in limiting competition. However, at the margin, the threat of competitive entry would limit the ability of any single or small group of providers to establish bottleneck control over the last-mile wireless access infrastructure.

Of course, since the WiFi model does depend on wireline infrastructure to connect to the Internet backbone, it is possible that wireline carriers could effectively leverage their control over wireline access facilities to adversely affect wireless access competition. Since many of the largest mobile service providers are affiliated with wireline providers, there is likely to be an incentive to discriminate against WiFi carriers if these are seen as competitors to either 3G or wireline services.

Control possibilities of Internet backbone providers

Fifth, the more flexible nature of the WiFi model means that it can seed a more complex array of potential business models that could fuel competition both at the retail level in services and at the wholesale level in alternative infrastructure. For example, WiFi could emerge as an extension of FreeNets, transmogrified into user-subsidised community networks, or via third-party aggregators such as Boingo. These networks could be in direct competition to 3G services.

WiFi visions

Another alternative might be for WiFi to be used as the last-few-hundred-feet access technology for alternative local loop facilities (e.g. a municipally-owned fibre network). In this mode, WiFi could reduce the deployment costs of overbuilders. A more generalised version of this scenario is any form of subsidised deployment, where the entity subsidising creation of the WiFi net might be a university (campus net), a government entity (municipal net), or a business (enterprise net). The lower costs of deploying wireless as compared to installing new wireline cabling plant may reduce the adoption costs of such a strategy, thereby increasingly the likelihood of their adoption.

Subsidised networks

" **WLANs will be integrated into future 3G networks.** *"*

WiFi and 3G can complement each other for a mobile provider

Integration of hot spots and 3G

Yet another alternative might be for WiFi to be integrated into 3G type networks. Actually, this seems the most likely scenario since there are compelling reasons why these two technologies may be used together. Indeed, a number of carriers have explored integrating WiFi hot-spot technologies into their networks, and a growing number of analysts believe that WLANs will be critical components for future 3G networks.[10]

Each of the technologies has distinct advantages over the other that would allow each to offer higher quality services under disparate conditions. Putting the two together would allow a service provider to offer a wider set of more valuable services.

Profitable at any speed?

The success of i-Mode in Japan, Blackberry in the US and SMS (Short Message Services) in Europe has aroused interest among investors worldwide. If even such slow-speed services are in such demand what about increasing the speed and capacity in order to provide even richer content, thereby potentially uncapping new demand and new revenues to be shared among operators, content providers and other vendors?

The outlook for mobile operators geared to provide "3G" services looks far less straightforward. Providing higher speeds implies not only higher costs, but also less revenue per MHz compared to using the available and scarce spectrum for less "capacity-hungry" applications such as voice, SMS (Short Message Services) and email.

Bertil Thorngren (2003)[11]

Mobile phone firms can implement such integration

The obvious adopter of such a strategy would be a mobile firm since it is easier for 3G to adopt WiFi and incorporate it into its networking strategy than for a WiFi facilities provider to go the other way. The reasons for this are several. First, there is the asymmetry in entry costs discussed earlier. Second, the natural ability of the 3G to implement bundled service offerings will make them more likely to be able to take advantage of a more complex infrastructure platform that will allow them to offer bundled services.

10 See anon. 2001
11 Thorngren, Bertil (2003): Profitability at any speed? In: Groebel, Jo/ Noam, Eli M./Feldmann, Valerie (editors): Mobile Media. Content and services for wireless communications, Lawrence Erlbaum Associates: New Jersey (in press)

Integrating 3G and WiFi networks provides the opportunity to offer both ubiquitous coverage with good voice telephony support (still the killer app for interactive communication networks) while providing local "hot spot" connectivity in high demand areas (airports, hotels, coffee shops) or in areas where existing WiFi facilities may be opportunistically taken advantage of (malls, multi-tenant office campuses). The hot spot connectivity would be attractive to offset the capacity limitations of 3G. The 3G mobile billing and wide-area network management capabilities (e.g. homing, hand-off control, authentication, resource allocation/management, etc.) could address some of the shortfalls that are limiting the capability of WiFi to evolve into a platform for mass wireless access.

Ubiquitous coverage through integration

Adopting such a strategy would offer the mobile provider the opportunity to tap new service markets: for example, allowing scheduled high-speed file transfers (e.g. queuing email with big attachments for downloading when opportunistically near a WiFi hot spot); or allowing more adaptive power management strategies (e.g. switching from WiFi to 3G service to conserve battery power with more graceful performance degradation, or vice-versa if external power becomes available). These and other services could increase the revenue opportunities available to the wireless service provider.

Win-win situation for mobile providers and customers

Additionally, adopting such a strategy would be defensive. Co-opting the competition is a well-known strategy. If WiFi succeeds, then 3G networks that fail to implement WiFi-like functionality will lose service revenues to WiFi-enabled competitors.

On the other hand, integrating WiFi into a 3G network may increase deployment costs. The business/service model will be more complex, and many adjustments will be required within mobile firms. When set against the potential revenue benefits, however, these higher coordination/adjustment costs do not seem likely to be overly substantial.

Increased complexity of business model

Spectrum policy is key

Obviously, spectrum policy has already had and will continue to have a critical role to play in how our wireless future evolves. One of the key distinguishing features between 3G and WiFi is the use of licensed versus unlicensed spectrum.

Continued progress towards creating secondary spectrum markets will benefit both 3G and WiFi models. For 3G, secondary markets would allow more flexible management of property rights. Secondary markets would allow spectrum to be reallocated more flexibly to higher value uses and could improve dynamic efficiency, for example, to balance localised supply and demand mismatches.

The role of spectrum markets

For WiFi, the emergence of spectrum markets may make it possible to adopt a suitable mechanism for addressing congestion issues. Of course, if implemented in the unlicensed band where WiFi currently operates, this would require additional policy changes to implement a market-based resource allocation process. The appropriate protocols and institutional framework for supporting such a market is an interesting topic for research. It may be easier to implement such a mechanism in a WLAN technology that could operate in a licensed band where there are clear property rights.

Success of WiFi is potentially good for multimedia content

Multimedia content benefits from higher bandwidth services, so the ability to support higher-speed wireless access may help encourage the development of broadband multimedia content.

The next challenge is digital rights management for mobile broadband content

On the other hand, the lack of a clear business model for deploying broadband services over a WiFi network may raise concerns over how content would be paid for and/or digital rights management issues. The digital rights management issues are perhaps more difficult to control (from a content provider's perspective) in a more decentralised, end-user-centric environment than in a centralised service-provider network (i.e. contrast Napster to AOL). The vertical integration model of 3G may offer greater control, which might actually encourage more content production.

This is a complex question that merits additional thought. It is premature to posit which of the two effects is likely to be larger.

Technical progress favours a heterogeneous future

Technical progress in wireless services favours a heterogeneous wireless future. There are several reasons for this.

Competition through heterogeneity

First, with each technology, the rapid pace of innovation means that multiple generations of each technology coexist in the network at the same time. Coupled to this heterogeneity, there is the ongoing competition among alternative wireless technologies. All of these share common benefits, so to a certain extent all benefit from advances in basic elements such as modulation techniques, smart antenna design, power management and battery technology, and signal processing technology. However, because the different technologies have asymmetric problems, basic advances affect them differently. This means that in the ongoing horse race different technologies are boosted at different times.

Once the world accepts the need to coordinate heterogeneous technologies, the capabilities to manage these environments evolve. For example, the success of the IP suite of protocols rests in large part on their ability to support interoperable communications across heterogeneous physical and network infrastructures. Analogously, developments in wireless technology will favour the coexistence of heterogeneous wireless access technologies.

One of the more important developments will be Software Defined Radio (SDR). SDR does a number of important things. First, it makes it easier to support multiple wireless technologies on a common hardware platform. Second, it makes upgrades easier and more flexible to implement since it substitutes software for hardware upgrades. Third, it facilitates new and more complex interference management techniques. These are useful for increasing the utilisation of spectrum.

The implication of all this for WiFi-like strategies appears clear. It improves the likelihood that WiFi will emerge as a viable model. This is further enhanced because the success of WiFi will, perforce, require additional technical progress to resolve some of the issues already discussed (e.g. security, QoS management, service billing). The implications for 3G are perhaps somewhat less clear. The 3G approach is similar to other telecommunication standards approaches (e.g. ISDN, ATM, etc.): it is most successful when it is monolithic. The centralised, top-down approach to network deployment is more vulnerable and less adaptive to decentralised and independent innovations.

2.2.4
Conclusions

This article offers a qualitative comparison of two wireless technologies that could be viewed simultaneously as substitute and/or complementary paths for evolving to broadband wireless access.

The goal of the analysis is to explore two divergent world views for the future of wireless access and to speculate on the likely success and possible interactions between the two technologies in the future.

While the analysis raises more questions than it answers, several preliminary conclusions appear warranted. First, both technologies are likely to succeed in the marketplace. This means that the wireless future will include heterogeneous access technologies, so equipment manufacturers, service providers, end-users, and policy makers should not expect to see a simple wireless future.

Coordination of heterogeneous technologies

SDR substitutes software for hardware upgrades

Diverging visions

The wireless future will provide parallel heterogeneous access technologies

Second, we expect 3G mobile providers to integrate WiFi technology into their networks. Thus, we expect these technologies to be complementary in their most successful mass market deployments.

Third, we also expect WiFi to offer competition to 3G providers because of the lower entry costs associated with establishing WiFi networks. This may take the form of new types of service providers (e.g. Boingo), end-user-organised networks (e.g. FreeNet aggregation or municipal networking), or a low-cost strategy for a wireline carrier to add wireless services. The threat of such WiFi competition is beneficial to prospects for the future of last-mile competition, and will also encourage the adoption of WiFi technology by 3G providers as a defensive response.

Our analysis also suggested a number of areas where further thought and research would be beneficial. These include the obvious questions of how to integrate 3G and WiFi networks or how to add the appropriate billing/resource negotiation infrastructure to WiFi to allow it to become a wide-area service provider platform. These also include several more remote questions such as which style of technology/business approach is favoured by the rapid pace of wireless technology innovation, or which is more likely to favour the development of complementary assets such as broadband content.

Chapter 2.3

That's What Friends Are For – Ambient Intelligence (AmI) and the Information Society in 2010

K. Ducatel, M. Bogdanowicz, F. Scapolo, J. Leijten and J-C. Burgelman

Ambient Intelligence (AmI) stems from the convergence of three key technologies: ubiquitous computing,[1] ubiquitous communication and intelligent user-friendly interfaces. In the AmI vision, humans will be surrounded by intelligent interfaces supported by computing and networking technology which is everywhere, embedded in everyday objects such as furniture, clothes, vehicles, roads and smart materials, even in particles of decorative substances like paint. AmI implies a seamless environment of computing, advanced networking technology and specific interfaces. It is aware of the specific characteristics of human presence and personalities, takes care of needs and is capable of responding intelligently to spoken or gestured indications of desire, and can even engage in intelligent dialogue. "Ambient Intelligence" should also be unobtrusive, often invisible: everywhere, and yet – in our consciousness – nowhere unless we need it. Interaction should be relaxing and enjoyable for the citizen, and not involve a steep learning curve.

Definition, functions and features of Ambient Intelligence

2.3.1
Four Scenarios of Life in the Future Information Society

Scenario 1: Maria – Road Warrior

After a tiring long-haul flight Maria passes through the arrivals hall of an airport in a Far Eastern country. She is travelling light, hand baggage only. When she comes to this particular country she knows that she can travel much lighter than less than a decade ago, when she had to carry a collection of different so-called personal computing devices (laptop PC, mobile phone, electronic organisers and sometimes beamers and printers). Her computing system for this trip is reduced to one highly personalised communications

AmI as a way of connecting people and a means of expressing identity

---

1 On "ubiquitous computing," see also the article by Mattern in this report.

device, her "P–Com," which she wears on her wrist. A particular feature of this trip is that the country that Maria is visiting has since the previous year embarked on an ambitious ambient intelligence infrastructure programme. Thus her visa for the trip was self-arranged, and she is able to stroll through immigration without stopping because her P–Com is dealing with the ID checks as she walks.

A rented car has been reserved for her and is waiting in an earmarked bay. The car opens as she approaches. It starts at the press of a button: she doesn't need a key. She still has to drive the car, but she is supported in her journey downtown to the conference centre-hotel by the traffic guidance system that had been launched by the city government as part of the "AmI-Nation" initiative two years earlier. Downtown traffic has been a legendary nightmare in this city for many years, and draconian steps were taken to limit access to the city centre. But Maria has priority access rights into the central cordon because she has a reservation in the car park of the hotel. Central access however comes at a premium price. In Maria's case it is embedded in a deal negotiated between her personal agent and the transaction agents of the car-rental and hotel chains. Her firm operates centralised billing for these expenses and uses its purchasing power to gain access at attractive rates. Such preferential treatment for affluent foreigners was highly contentious at the time of the introduction of the route pricing system, and the government was forced to hypothecate funds from the tolling system to the public transport infrastructure in return. In the car, Maria's teenage daughter comes through on the audio system. Amanda has detected from the "En Casa" system at home that her mother is in a place that supports direct voice contact. However, even with all the route guidance support Maria wants to concentrate on her driving and says that she will call back from the hotel.

Maria is directed to a parking slot in the underground garage of the newly constructed building of the Smar-tel Chain. She is met in the garage by the porter – the first contact with a real human in our story so far! He helps her with her luggage to her room. Her room adopts her "personality" as she enters. The room temperature, default lighting and a range of video and music choices are displayed on the video wall. She needs to make some changes to her presentation – a sales pitch that will be used as the basis for a negotiation later in the day. Using voice commands she adjusts the light levels and commands a bath. Then she calls up her daughter on the video wall. While talking, she uses a traditional remote control system to browse through a set of webcast local news bulletins from back home that her daughter tells her about. They watch them together.

Later on she "localises" her presentation with the help of an agent that is specialised in advising on local preferences (colour schemes, the use of language). She stores the presentation on the secure server at headquarters

Automation and machine-to-machine communication promote efficient time-management

Smart spaces support the personalisation of surroundings

Graded communication barriers filter communication partners

back in Europe. In the hotel's seminar room, where the sales pitch is to take place, she will be able to call down an encrypted version of the presentation and give it a post-presentation decrypt life of 1.5 minutes. She goes downstairs to make her presentation... This for her is a high stress event. Not only is she performing alone for the first time, but the clients concerned are well known to be tough players. Still, she doesn't actually have to close the deal this time. As she enters the meeting she raises communications access thresholds to block out anything but red-level "emergency" messages. The meeting is rough, but she feels it was a success. Coming out of the meeting she lowers the communication barriers again and picks up a number of amber level communications including one from her cardio-monitor warning her to take some rest now. The day has been long and stressing. She needs to chill out with a little meditation and medication. For Maria the meditation is a concert on the video wall and the medication....a large gin and tonic from her room's mini-bar.

Scenario 2: Dimitrios and the "Digital Me" (D-Me)

It is four o'clock in the afternoon. Dimitrios, a 32-year-old employee of a major food-multinational, is taking a coffee at his office's cafeteria, together with his boss and some colleagues. He doesn't want to be excessively bothered during this pause. Nevertheless, all the time he is receiving and dealing with incoming calls and mails.

AmI as a personal information and communication assistant

He is proud of "being in communication with mankind," as are many of his friends and some colleagues. Dimitrios is wearing, embedded in his clothes (or in his own body), a voice-activated "gateway" or digital avatar of himself, familiarly known as a "D-Me" or "Digital Me." A D-Me is both a learning device, learning about Dimitrios from his interactions with his environment, and an acting device offering communication, processing and decision-making functionality. Dimitrios has partly "programmed" it himself, at a very initial stage. At the time, he thought he would "upgrade" this initial data periodically. But he didn't. He feels quite confident with his D-Me and relies upon its "intelligent" reactions.

At 4.10 p.m., following many other calls of secondary importance – answered formally but smoothly in corresponding languages by Dimitrios' D-Me with a nice reproduction of Dimitrios' voice and typical accent, a call from his wife is further analysed by his D-Me. In a first attempt, Dimitrios' "avatar-like" voice runs a brief conversation with his wife, with the intention of negotiating a delay while explaining his current environment. Simultaneously, Dimitrios' D-Me has caught a message from an older person's D-Me, located in the nearby metro station. This senior has left his home without his medicine and would feel at ease knowing where and how to access similar

Calls are answered automatically

drugs in an easy way. He has addressed his query in natural speech to his D-Me. Dimitrios happens to suffer from similar heart problems and uses the same drugs. Dimitrios' D-Me processes the available data so as to offer information to the senior. It "decides" neither to reveal Dimitrios' identity (privacy level), nor to offer Dimitrios' direct help (lack of availability), but to list the closest drug shops, the alternative drugs, and offer a potential contact with the self-help group. This information is shared with the senior's D-Me, not with the senior himself, so as to avoid useless information overload.

Meanwhile, his wife's call is now interpreted by his D-Me as sufficiently pressing to mobilise Dimitrios. It "rings" him using a pre-arranged call tone. Dimitrios takes up the call with one of the available Displayphones of the cafeteria. Since the growing penetration of D-Me, few people still bother to run around with mobile terminals: these functions are sufficiently available in most public and private spaces, and your D-Me can always point at the closest... functioning one! The "emergency" is about their child's homework. For his homework, their 9-year-old son is meant to offer some insights on everyday life in Egypt. In a brief 3-way telephone conference, Dimitrios offers to pass over the query to the D-Me to search for an available direct contact with a child in Egypt. Ten minutes later, his son is videoconferencing at home with a girl of his own age, and recording this real-time translated conversation as part of his homework. All communicating facilities have been managed by Dimitrios' D-Me, even while it is still registering new data and managing other queries. The Egyptian correspondent is the daughter of a local businessman, well off and quite keen on technologies. Some luck (and income...) were needed to participate in what might become a longer-lasting new relation.

Scenario 3: Carmen – Traffic, Sustainability and Commerce

It is a normal weekday morning. Carmen wakes and plans her travel for the day. She wants to leave for work in half an hour and asks AmI, by means of a voice command, to find a vehicle to share with somebody on her route to work. AmI starts searching the trip database and, after checking the willingness of the driver, finds someone that will pass by in 40 minutes. The in-vehicle biosensor has recognised that this driver is a non-smoker – one of Carmen's requirements for trip sharing. From that moment on, Carmen and her driver are in permanent contact if wanted (e.g. to allow the driver to alert Carmen if he/she will be late). Both wear their personal area networks (PAN), allowing seamless and intuitive contacts.

While taking her breakfast coffee, Carmen lists her shopping since she will have guests for dinner tonight. She would also like to cook a cake, and the e-fridge flashes the recipe. It highlights the ingredients that are missing – milk

Margin notes:

Protection from information overload

Personal agents locate publicly accessible communications devices

AmI as a means of optimising mobility and everyday efficiency

and eggs. She completes the shopping on the e-fridge screen and asks for it to be delivered to the closest distribution point in her neighbourhood. This can be a shop, the post office or a franchised nodal point for the neighbourhood where Carmen lives. All goods are smart tagged, so that Carmen can check the progress of her virtual shopping expedition from any enabled device at home, the office or from a kiosk in the street. She can be informed during the day on her shopping, agree with what has been found, ask for alternatives, and find out where they are and when they will be delivered.

Forty minutes later Carmen goes downstairs onto the street, as her driver arrives. When Carmen gets into the car, the VAN system (Vehicle Area Network) registers her, and in this way Carmen sanctions the payment system to start counting. A micro-payment system will automatically transfer the amount into the e-purse of the driver when she gets out of the car.

In the car, the dynamic route guidance system warns the driver of long traffic jams up ahead due to an accident. The system dynamically calculates alternatives together with trip times. One suggestion is to leave the car at a nearby "park and ride" metro stop. Carmen and her driver park the car and continue the journey by metro. On leaving the car, Carmen's payment is deducted according to duration and distance.

Out of the metro station and whilst walking a few minutes to her job, Carmen is alerted by her PAN that a Chardonnay wine that she has previously identified as a preferred choice is on promotion. She adds it to her shopping order and also sets up her homeward journey with her wearable. Carmen arrives at her job on time.

On the way home the shared car system senses a bike on a dedicated lane approaching an intersection on their route. The driver is alerted and the system anyway gives preference to bikes, so a potential accident is avoided. A persistent high-pressure belt above the city for the last ten days has given fine weather but rising atmospheric pollutants. It is rush hour, and the traffic density has caused pollution levels to rise above a control threshold. The city-wide engine control systems automatically lower the maximum speeds (for all motorised vehicles) and when the car enters a specific urban ring, toll will be deducted via the Automatic Debiting System (ADS).

Carmen arrives at the local distribution node (actually her neighbourhood corner shop), where she picks up her goods. The shop has already closed, but the goods await Carmen in a smart delivery box. By getting them out, the system registers payment and deletes the items from her shopping list. The list is complete. At home, her smart fridge screen will be blank.

Back home, AmI welcomes Carmen and suggests that she should tele-work the next day: a big demonstration is announced downtown.

Real-time information from the environment

Scenario 4: Annette and Solomon in the Ambient for Social Learning

Collaborative learning and working

It is the plenary meeting of an environmental studies group in a local "Ambient for Social Learning." The group ranges from 10 to 75 years old. They share a common desire to understand the environment and environmental management. It is led by a mentor whose role it is to guide and facilitate the group's operation, but who is not necessarily very knowledgeable about environmental management. The plenary takes place in a room looking much like a hotel foyer with comfortable furniture pleasantly arranged. The meeting is open from 7.00 a.m. to 11.00 p.m. Most participants are there for four to six hours. A large group arrives around 9.30 a.m. Some are scheduled to work together in real time and space and were thus requested to be present together (the ambient accesses their agendas to do the scheduling).

A member is arriving: as she enters the room and finds herself a place to work, she hears a familiar voice asking "Hello Annette, I got the assignment you did last night from home: are you satisfied with the results?" Annette answers that she was happy with her strategy for managing forests provided that she had got the climatic model right: she was less sure of this. Annette is an active and advanced student, so the ambient says it might be useful if Annette spends some time today trying to pin down the problem with the model using enhanced interactive simulation and projection facilities. It then asks if Annette would give a brief presentation to the group. The ambient goes briefly through its understanding of Annette's availability and preferences for the day's work. Finally, Annette agrees on her work programme for the day.

One particularly long conversation takes place with Solomon who has just moved to the area and joined the group. The ambient establishes Solomon's identity, asks Solomon for the name of an ambient that "knows" Solomon, and gets permission from Solomon to acquire information about Solomon's background and experience in Environmental Studies. The ambient then suggests that Solomon join the meeting and introduce himself to the group.

Synchronisation and cooperation transcend space and time

In these private conversations, the mental states of the group members are synchronised with the ambient, and individual and collective work plans are agreed and in most cases checked with the mentor through the ambient. In some cases the assistance of the mentor is requested. A scheduled plenary meeting begins with those who are present. Solomon introduces himself. Annette gives a 3-D presentation of her assignment. A group member asks questions about one of Annette's decisions, and alternative visualisations are projected. During the presentation the mentor is feeding observations and questions to the ambient, together with William, an expert who was asked to join the meeting. William, although several thousand miles away, joins to make a comment and answer some questions. The session ends with a discussion of how Annette's work contributes to that of the others and the proposal of schedules for the remainder of the day. The ambient suggests a schedule involving both shared and individual sessions.

During the day individuals and subgroups locate in appropriate spaces in the ambient to pursue appropriate learning experiences at a pace that suits them. The ambient negotiates its degree of participation in these experiences with the aid of the mentor. During the day the mentor and ambient converse frequently, establishing where the mentor might most usefully spend his time, and in some cases altering the schedule. The ambient and the mentor will spend some time negotiating shared experiences with other ambients, for example mounting a single musical concert with players from two or more distant sites. They will also deal with requests for references / profiles of individuals. Time spent in the ambient ends by negotiating a homework assignment with each individual, but only after they have been informed about what the ambient expects to happen for the rest of the day and after making appointments for next day or next time.

2.3.2
Critical factors in building AmI in Europe

The four scenarios make it possible to identify key technological, socio-economic and political "drivers," baselines, uncertainties, constraints, opportunities and potential points of bifurcation or convergence surrounding AmI in Europe.

Critical socio-political factors

To be acceptable AmI needs to be driven by humanistic concerns, not technologically determined ones. Indeed, the very real risk of the technological scenario driving our lives provides an implicit black lining for Maria in her scenario characterised by a high-pressure lifestyle. As Dimitrios indicates, AmI could act as a facilitator of human interaction, especially with friends, family and colleagues. It will be important for AmI to build on its community-enhancing potential, though offering opportunities for interest groups to develop their own applications (Annette and Solomon).

The focus must be on the human being, not on technology

Second, AmI also has an important potential to enhance education and learning as an enabler of higher levels of consumer choice. Everyday-life skills will rise because of the rising opportunities and means of personal expression and interaction. At work too, there are likely to be rising demands for skills. Some will be higher requirements for technological expertise, but

Information management and social know-how gain in importance if the AmI manifesto is to be achieved the main increases in skills will be in social know-how and information management. The expert group advised that the responsiveness of existing educational institutions and appropriate policies will determine whether there is a weakening of education as a separate, identifiable activity or a strengthening of educational institutions.

Three dimensions of sustainability

Three main dimensions of sustainability seemed to be at stake.

– Personal physical and psychological sustainability: can AmI reduce (mental) health risks from information stress, virtual identities and information overload? What precautionary evaluation is needed to avoid new health impacts of pervasive electronic radiation?

– Socio-economic sustainability: digital divides emerging from unequal developments in access to the AmI infrastructure could be related to income, education and skills, age or work.

– Environmental sustainability: there are pressures created by new growth and the material wealth associated with AmI technologies. The scenarios draw a picture of a hyper-mobile society. The embedding of computers implies considerable extension of recycling and reclamation of electronic waste – perhaps based on smart tagging. The Carmen scenario implies new efficiency gains in transport to combat congestion.

A consistently strong response to AmI is the need to build trust and confidence. A key aspect is the management of privacy: more open systems tend to lower privacy levels. Technological developments are outpacing regulatory adjustments. To what extent can people be protected in the AmI landscape? What belief can we have that there will be effective norms of trust (in business, government, interpersonal relations) that prevent the invasive/intrusive usage of AmI technologies?

Protection of the private realm

Related to this, but important enough to merit a separate point, AmI should also be controllable by ordinary people. There was a consistent demand for some kind of volume control or on/off switch that would allow people to decide what level of access they have on what issue and when. But such technologies also raise concerns about a reduction of free will and choice. In essence, as with other key emerging technologies, AmI offers many potential advantages, but precautionary research and provisions will be necessary to make sure that it has the maximum positive effect on personal life and society.

Business and industrial models

Who will determine the course of AmI?

Economic questions abound. Who will make AmI work? Who will produce it? Who will live and consume in a world like that? Who will make money?

In terms of social processes and labour conditions, what problems are we going to meet? How will AmI change the way people work, think, learn and communicate, and how will it change the settings in which they do this? What are the main uncertainties? When will they occur? How do they translate into issues for research? The sheer diversity of possible factors defeats the establishment of a common economic baseline related to major certainties and uncertainties. These questions are difficult. However, a number of elements emerged from the scenario work as important for inclusion in the ten-year timeframe. Five main drivers of demand for AmI were rated as important:

Drivers of demand for AmI

– Improvements in the quality of life (including satisfying intangible needs, such as better community life and health, as well as rising material demands);

– Enhancements in the productivity and the quality of products and services, and applications in process innovations;

– New and emerging AmI firms will themselves be a key source of demand for AmI because of secondary demands for new products and services;

– Applications of AmI in industrial innovation and new products (e.g. household and office equipment, clothes, furniture);

– Applications in public services, e.g. in hospitals, schools, police or the military.

In the scenarios, demand for AmI is based on consumer added value and builds upon several revenue models. First, stand-alone models build upon the processes of miniaturisation and embedding of intelligence into personal devices. They offer glimpses of extended versions of today's PDAs and mobiles into secure ID authentication, transmission (i.e. with embedded agents for traffic management), voice and language recognition, and maybe sensors/actuators for behavioural and biological pattern-recognition. Embedding intelligence into devices may provide scope for innovative SMEs as start-ups, subcontractors or spinouts of existing leading multinationals. Product design will emerge for new intersectoral collaborations or strategic alliances due to the multidisciplinary, multisectoral competences required and the need to spread the risk when recovering investment. For this reason, and because most devices in the scenarios are networked, it is unlikely that pure stand-alone business models will be dominant even for consumer electronics in the AmI landscape.

Second, access models are currently a main way of building usage above critical mass and getting the strong multiplier effect known as Metcalfe's Law, which dictates that the value of a network expands as the square of the number of its users. This is a major mass consumption model and is a

Metcalfe's Law

strong driver for the Dimitrios and Carmen scenarios. Access models will be one essential means of providing widely distributed device networks and systems while offering low prices for communication. The profitability of future communication service provision remains a major question that will have to be resolved in the short-term.

A complementary approach to building market size through access is to look for higher yields from offering premium service levels. This is illustrated through the example of Maria, where high-spending corporate users access a package of services and demand high service quality in the form of reliable physical and service platforms in different countries. This points towards cooperation and the cross-financing of development among a wide range of very different players: credit card agencies, retailers and telecommunication operators.

In a fully developed AmI landscape, the tangible and physical interface that divides humans from ICTs will be blurred. By definition, the effort required to use such computer systems should tend towards the imperceptible. Use should be as imperceptible as using our own body and brain. Workable business models for this new AmI landscape are not easy to define, but one line of development that is already visible (see the roots of Dimitrios) is towards increased self-customisation of content. Further, as Annette and Solomon illustrate, media industries such as editorial, publishing or broadcasting firms may merge with other informational services such as training, education or business consultancy.

Key features of the new business landscape that emerges, therefore, are emphases on:

– Initial premium value niche markets in industrial, commercial or public applications where enhanced interfaces are needed to support human performance in fast-moving or highly delicate situations (e.g. for Maria in her harsh business negotiations).

– Start-up and spin-off opportunities from identifying potential service requirements and putting the services together that meet these new needs.

– High access/low entry cost, based on a loss leadership model in order to create economies of scale (mass customisation).

– Self-provision models, based upon the network economies of very large user communities providing information as a gift or at near zero cost.

Overall, most of these developments can be expected to come through in the form of partnerships. First, the development of the necessary communications systems requires expectations of substantial returns on investments in

Cooperation and cross-financing among market players

Key features of AmI business models

Business webs for AmI investment

generation after generation of new infrastructures.[2] The large sums involved point towards partnership models. We might also expect leasing and franchising models to be important in achieving a fast turnover of technological investment. Also, the development of many of the AmI applications requires cross-disciplinary and cross-sectoral capabilities.

Technological requirements

The underpinning technologies required to construct the AmI landscape cover a broad range of ICT and smart material technologies. In the course of the scenario-building work, a wide range of different technologies were identified as key enablers of AmI. From the scenarios it is possible to develop a set of common technological requirement areas. The sheer diversity of technologies involved means that neither the list nor the terminology can be definitive, but it does provide hints about the sets of technologies that will be essential for AmI and the technological trajectories that they imply.

No single key technology, but a whole range of technologies

Technological Requirement 1: Very unobtrusive hardware

Miniaturisation is assumed to follow its historic pattern to permit the necessary enabling developments in micro and optical electronics. Molecular and atomic manipulation techniques will also be increasingly required to provide advanced materials, smart materials and nanotechnologies. In addition there will have to be:

Molecular and atomic manipulation techniques will be necessary

- Self-generating power and micro-power usage in objects, for example very low-power radio frequency chips, in order to make feasible the interoperation of chips embedded in almost anything.

- Breakthroughs in input/output, including new displays, smart surfaces, paints and films that have smart properties. This is fundamental to the seamless interfaces that invisibly permit Maria, Dimitrios and so on to interact with their intelligent environment.

- Active devices such as sensors and actuators integrated with interface systems in order to respond to user senses, posture and environment or smart materials that can change their characteristics and/or performance by stand-alone intelligence or by networked interaction (e.g. smart clothing).

2 Some experts suggested that new policy requirements might stem from the simultaneous need to stimulate infrastructural investment while encouraging competition in these new cross-sectoral markets.

– Nanoelectronics and other nanotechnologies that permit miniaturisation trends to extend beyond the limits of micro-devices through hybrid nano-micro devices. Nanodevices would yield lower power consumption, higher operation speeds and high ubiquity.

– A design emphasis on human factors so that the widespread embedding of computers produces a coherent AmI landscape rather than just a proliferation of electronic devices with IP addresses.

Technological Requirement 2: A seamless mobile/fixed web-based communications infrastructure

Full network integration

Complex heterogeneous networks need to function and to communicate in a seamless and interoperable way. This implies a complete integration (from the point of view of the user or network device) of mobile and fixed and radio and wired networks. Probably all the networks would be operating with some equivalent of IP technology. Core and access broadband networks are likely to converge.

To deliver the full AmI vision (e.g. the 3-D real-time holographic rendering in Annette and Solomon), there will eventually be a need to move towards ultra-fast optical processing in the fixed network, for routing first and then full optical networks. These networks will have to be seamless and dynamically reconfigurable. They will require more advanced techniques for dynamic network management (see requirement three).

Technological Requirement 3: Dynamic and massively distributed device networks

Ad hoc configurations of networks and end devices

The AmI landscape is a world in which there are almost uncountable inter-operating devices. Some will be wired, some wireless; many will be mobile; many more will be fixed. The requirement will be that the networks should be configurable on an ad hoc basis according to a specific, perhaps short-lived task with variable actors and components. Databases, whether centralised or distributed, should be accessible on demand from anywhere in the system.

Plug and Play

This complexity extends well beyond the current capabilities of systems software and middleware, and calls for wireless "Plug and Play" solutions as well as dynamic, multi-domain networking. In turn, these have implications for the development of new ontologies and protocols, as well as the setting of new standards. The way to construct these networks is a major research challenge for the coming years, and the implications are numerous: new computer and communications architectures, new systems software that can adapt to changing hardware configurations, the development of networked embedded intelligence and distributed data-management and storage systems. Key to this will be the development of middleware and agent technologies (requirement 4).

Technological Requirement 4: A natural-feeling human interface

A central challenge of AmI is to create systems that are intuitive in use – almost like normal human functions such as breathing, talking or walking. On the one hand, "artificial intelligence" techniques will have to be employed for this, especially dialogue-based and goal-orientated negotiation systems as the basis for intelligent agents and real-time middleware. The key issue will be to move from relatively narrow domain-by-domain and highly structured databases to families of systems that can operate across domains to very general levels. These kinds of artificial intelligence techniques will be equally important for developing intuitive machine-to-machine interaction.

Artificial intelligence as the basis for interaction...

There are also demands for supportive and technologically cognate developments in user-interface design that is multimodal (multi-user, multilingual, multi-channel and multipurpose) for speech, gesture and pattern recognition. It should also be adaptive to user requirements, providing context-sensitive interfaces, information filtering and presentation, and cross-media content.

... and pattern recognition

Pattern recognition (including speech and gesture) is a key area of artificial intelligence that is already evolving rapidly. Speech recognition will have a big impact on the miniaturisation of devices and augmentation of objects, allowing hands free operation of personal ambient devices. In the scenarios, the use of voice, gesture and automatic identification and localisation are implicitly used to synchronise systems, so that services are available on tap when people want them. According to some of the scenario experts, speech instruction is likely to become more important than voice synthesis (i.e. displays will be very important as well).

Technological Requirement 5: Dependability and security

A consistent theme of the scenario work is the requirement for a safe, dependable and secure AmI-world. The technologies should be tested to make sure they are safe for use. On the one hand, this refers to physical and psychological threats that the technologies might imply. On the other hand, the creation of a landscape of interoperating AmI devices focuses even greater emphasis on the requirement for robust and dependable software systems.

Generic AmI Techno line

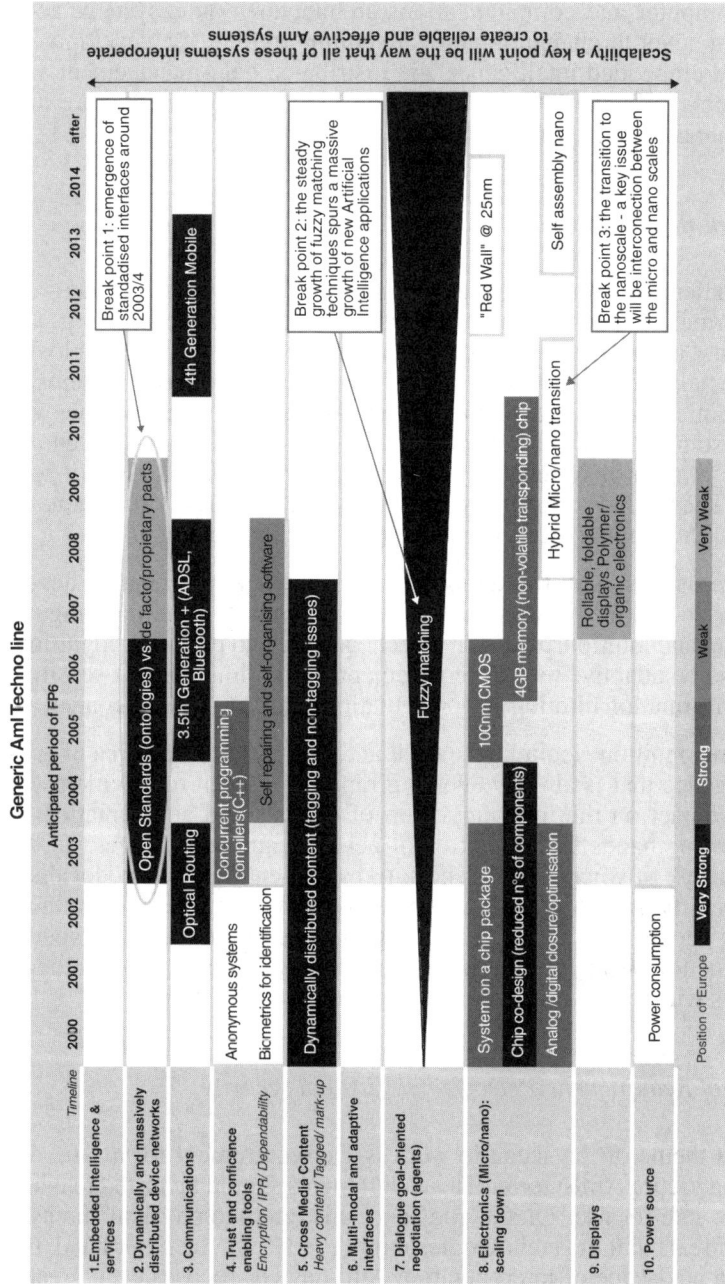

Abb. 2.3-1. Technological development towards AmI

For this reason there is likely to be an emerging emphasis on self-testing and self-organising software and techniques based upon software components.

It will also be important to have AmI systems that are secure against deliberate misuse. The scenarios assume techniques for secure ID authentication, micropayment systems and biometrics. These sorts of "trust technologies" and advanced encryption techniques are strong requirements for both the dependability and the likely acceptance of nearly all of the processes, products and services described in the scenarios. Practical and widespread use of micropayment is necessary for AmI according to some scenarios, in which the AmI features are accessed and used on an ad hoc basis (maybe with the aid of personal negotiating intelligent agents). But there is also the possibility that many of these transactions will be bought on a subscription basis. In computer security, biometrics will be important as a means of authentication based on measurable physical characteristics that can easily be checked (fingerprints, iris scanning or speech).

Protection against misuse – biometrics

In relation to all these requirements, the scenario construction group pointed to a number of break points that will be very important in determining the form that AmI takes.

First, under the condition that AmI calls for a very flexible and seamless interoperation of many different devices on many different networks, it is a key requirement that there be a set of common platforms or de facto standards to permit this interoperation to take place. The group of experts felt that this would have to happen around 2003/4 and would either be achieved through a deliberate effort to develop such open platforms or would arise from proprietary pacts between industrial suppliers. The group suggested that the former approach has been most successful in Europe, whilst proprietary dominance has tended to be more successfully deployed by U.S.-led consortia.

De facto standards and compatibility as paving the way

A second break point could occur from a step-up in the scale of know-how in the use of dialogue or goal-orientated negotiation techniques. These techniques were regarded as pivotal to AmI technologies and services such as ad hoc and sentient networking, dynamic and distributed database management, middleware, material-resource flow planning and cross-media content production. This is a particularly important dimension of AmI, given the relatively good position of European technology developers in this domain of competence.

Dialogue and goal-orientated negotiation techniques

The third main break point concerned developments in hardware. Towards the end of the decade in 2008-9, it was suggested that production techniques would be fully engaged in a transition from micro to hybrid nano-micro devices. This would affect the techniques used to produce all sorts of solid-state and optical devices. The key technical challenges of the transition would be to achieve interconnection between these two scales. The full

Potentials for development through nanotechnology

effect of any potential full nano-paradigm will probably have to await commercialisation of self-assembling nanotechnologies from around 2015. At the moment, Europe has as good a chance of benefiting from the nanotechnology break point as any other leading technology region, not least because of the strengths in many of the systems-on-a-chip, special application circuits and embedded systems that will provide the hardware technology pathways towards AmI.

Main Research Implications and Opportunities

The final step in the scenario construction procedure was to identify some large-scale research efforts that could support the emergence of a balanced pathway towards AmI. This covers socio-economic and political as well as technological aspects and aims at offering some challenging clusters of research issues.

Will optical fibre networks be enough?

AmI-compatible enabling hardware. The fully optical network is an important milestone, even though the experts had divergent opinions as to whether present and expectable network bandwidths would be sufficient for the streams of data (cf. Carmen) and quality video (cf. Salomon) important for AmI. Additionally, they reported that optics in access networks needed consolidated business plans to justify investments. The expert group also underlined the importance of research efforts on near-zero-cost embedded technologies, ambient power sources and compatible hardware enablers (nano-micro, sensors, power, displays), addressing social and political design and engineering factors (such as safety and health), as well as technological and economic challenges.

Service control platforms

AmI open platforms – for interoperating embedded devices, for wireless and fixed ad hoc networking, and for self-organising and self-repairing software/middleware systems. The centrepiece would be an integrated set of "service control planes" or "platforms" for each major application area: e.g. in the home, mobile and vehicle, e-commerce, security. The success of such a service control platform relies on advances in information processing (agents, data-mining and filtering, distributed processing).

MtM and OtO communication to prevent information overload

Intuitive technologies – involving efforts to create human interfaces with variable emotional bandwidth. Dialogue-based techniques and tangible user interfaces are needed in order to permit seamless human interactions. For example, this might involve the creation of interactive surfaces, the coupling

Key Enabling Technology	Position of Europe		
	strong	medium	weak
(1) Embedded intelligence		■	
Virtual & interactive reality		■	
Intelligent identifiers, autonomously	■		
Real-time transmission of multimedia contents		■	
Software engineering & components		■	
Intelligent homes		■	
(2) Middleware & distributed systems		■	
Big server networks		■	
Integration of appliances XML & others	■		
(3) IP mobile & wireless	■		
Portable digital assistants	■		
(4) Multi-domain network management		■	
Quality of IP service		■	
(5) Converging core and access networks	■		
High transit backcome networks	■		
(6) Micro- and opto-electronics		■	
Silicon micro-electronics	■		
Optic-electronic & photo-components	■		
Search engines & intelligent indexing		■	
Micro-electronics III V		■	
Batteries, micro-energy		■	
Mass memories			■
Flat screens			■

Fig. 2.3-2 European position in primary enabling technologies (Ministère de l'économie et de l'industrie. Paris (2000))

of objects and digital info that pertains to them, and the enhancing of ambient media such as airflow or light. Nevertheless, significant advances in machine-to-machine (MtM) and object-to-object (OtO) communication and understanding will have to complete this humanised interfacing, so as to reduce thresholds of information overload for human beings.

AmI vision is based upon humanistic principles

AmI support for individual and community development – including social and psychological aspects such as human factors in design, the application of socio-technical systems approaches to developing the AmI landscape, and initiatives towards community and societal-orientated AmI. The scenario experts unanimously stressed how important it is that the AmI vision should be built upon humanistic foundations. This implies a serious attention to socio-technical design factors, especially in user-interface design. There is also a need for AmI to provide tools to support human interaction, such as building community memories for the social sharing of knowledge.

Community memory

Metacontent services. The emphasis in the scenarios on access to information that is pre-filtered to support human dialogues and actions is predicated on considerable advances in information handling. This is necessary to support new forms of organisation based upon learning environments and community memory. An example could be an Information Factory Initiative that addresses the need for highly flexible and intelligent systems for information handling, such as smart tagging systems, semantic web technologies, and search technologies.

Security and trust. AmI technologies should support the rights to anonymity/privacy/identity of people and organisations, offering, for example, relevant combinations of biometrics, digital signature or genetics-based methods. Also of fundamental importance is research towards safe and dependable large-scale and complex systems (self-testing, self-repairing, fault-tolerant) to underpin the increasing reliance on ICTs implicit in the AmI landscape.

Matching this list with existing EU strengths and weaknesses offers an initial view on what might be research opportunities in the development path of AmI.

The French Key Technologies Programme, for example, rates both Europe's scientific and technological position and its industrial and commercial position. Encouragingly, the study suggests that, contrary to some conventional wisdom, in many cases the EU is neither leading nor lagging in relevant capabilities and that the technical and commercial positions of Europe are fairly evenly matched. The table reproduced below extracts those areas of technology that are regarded as most relevant for the AmI vision, indicating the rating of the European position for both of these factors.

2.3.3
Conclusions

The current pace of the ICT industry and the scenarios for future trends indicate a high sense of urgency of a global character in the business of ICT. This implies that whatever measures are taken in the Framework Programmes to support Europe's ICT-development, they should support fast responses, flexibility and worldwide scientific and technological cooperation, as well as entrepreneurship.

Major opportunities to create an integrated Ambient Intelligence landscape can be built upon European technological strengths in areas such as mobile communications, portable devices, systems integration, embedded computing, multi-platform content provision and intelligent systems design.

The strengths in European technology

A host of new business models will emerge, irrespective of the response by Europe. These new business models will be test-bedded by industry and entrepreneurs operating in the areas that provide the most fertile conditions for experimentation. The vision of Ambient Intelligence points at how to create these fertile conditions, in the technological domain and in the business environment.

But all the scenarios and all the experts involved emphasised the social dimension of innovation, the ability as well as the willingness of society to use, absorb or adapt to technological opportunities. Issues such as environmental and social sustainability, privacy, social robustness and fault-tolerance will determine the take-up of AmI. Thus, although technological feasibility is fundamental and an essential precondition, our work on AmI underlines the requirement that policies for the information society should not be driven by enthusiasm for technologies per se, but by the usefulness and relevance of its applications for citizens and consumers. In a certain sense, creating AmI is more a humanistic endeavour than a technological one. It requires a great deal of trust from the users' point of view. And having trust is exactly what distinguishes a friend from a foreigner.

Social dimension of the technological vision

Chapter 2.4

Evolutionary Perspectives[1]

Klaus Schrape

2.4.1
Introduction

The following story is considered worldwide to be a metaphor for what Paul Virilio has termed the dromological revolution, but also for the implications of digital, global capitalism.

"Every morning a gazelle wakes up in Africa. It knows it must run faster than the fastest lion in order not to be eaten. Every morning a lion also wakes up in Africa. It knows it must be faster than the slowest gazelle, otherwise it will starve. Actually, it's all the same whether you're a lion or a gazelle: when the sun rises – you must run!"

If one applies this metaphor to the current relation of scientific-technical progress and the change in social institutions, then the casting and the result of the race are apparently obvious. The gazelle of information and communication technology quickly picks up speed, multiplies and spreads fast (in the form of new applications), and increases its intelligence. The institution-lions of society with their outdated structures and slow learning processes have little to offer in reply.

The two fathers of evolutionary theory – Charles Darwin and Herbert Spencer – are dead. The theory of evolution, however, is more alive than ever before, although it too has been declared outdated several times in the last 100 years. Where does this present relevancy come from? Presumably it is from the paradoxical insight, bound up with scientific-technical progress, that humanity is itself a product of natural evolution, but also the only species able to control its own destiny. What is this specific characteristic based on? Darwin had already realised the answer: on the human ability to communicate with symbols (language). This is the decisive prerequisite

The gazelles of information and communication technology versus the institutional lions of society

Language as a basis for socio-cultural structures

1 This article first appeared in the volume of articles from the congress of the Münchner Kreis, "Leben in der E-Society – Computerintelligenz für den Alltag" (Living in the e-society: computer intelligence for everyday life).

for the construction, the conveying and the transformation of socio-cultural structures that become more and more complex.

Today we have apparently gone beyond a threshold value in social and scientific-technical development, a threshold value that on the one hand has made us (to a large degree) independent of natural (biological) evolution, but on the other hand also forces us to do the selecting ourselves in future, to take responsibility for this and stabilise (safeguard) it socially and culturally. This at least was made clear by the sensational debate last year between Ray Kurzweil and Bill Joy. At issue was the rapid merging of bio-, nano- and information technologies and the fear that man is making himself superfluous and will no longer be required for further evolution once thinking computers obtain the capabilities of the human brain.

Doing the selecting independently of natural evolution (and guiding this process)

The theme "living in the e-society" deals with the preliminary stage of this evolutionary threshold, with "embedded systems." The potential use of this new generation of networked and "intelligent" technical systems is considered to be almost infinite, but so far it has been fully realised only in its initial stages. Technological visionaries naturally assume that such systems will gain acceptance in almost all areas of life and all situations. I would like to make clear, however, that the successful realisation of such visions is anything but a sure success. It is dependent on diverse social and cultural preconditions which must still develop. To substantiate this thesis I proceed as follows:

Life in the e-society

– First, some theoretical and historical aspects of the co-evolution of communication media and society will be looked at.

– This will be followed by a current vision of life in the information society that was recently presented by the IST Advisory Group (ISTAG) of the European Commission.

– Finally, the focus will be on the institutional prerequisites that must be met in order for a trusting coexistence of machine/technical and human intelligence to succeed.

2.4.2
Co-Evolution of Communication Media and Society

Since the industrial revolution at the latest (with Condorcet and Saint-Simon), the tension between "technical progress" and "social development" has become the main theme of theories of social evolution. All theories drawn up since then – be they trusting or critical with respect to technology – have a common central problem: the question of the discontinuity (the imbalance and non-simultaneity) of scientific-technical progress on the one hand and socio-cultural change on the other hand, as well as the search for possibilities for controlling the undesired consequences of this cultural lag. Which of these consequences are seen as undesired varies with the perspective of the observer.

The question of discontinuity and "cultural lag"

Looking back on the history of theories of evolution, modernisation and transformation, it is conspicuous that the central role and importance of the communication media for social evolution has usually only been discussed marginally as a theme. This is also true for the theories of modernisation predominant between 1950 and 1980. In these dichotomous comparisons of traditional and modern societies, the dimension of communication is only one among many others. Exceptions confirm the rule. Thus, Marshall McLuhan[2] for example in the 1960s drew up his phase model of combined media / societal development (Figure 2.4-1). McLuhan assumes that the historical development of society was decisively shaped by the progress of communication technology and by the institutionalisation of the socio-technical media systems based on this technology. Depending on the media culture dominant at the time, the human perception and experience of reality also changes in the course of evolution. Since the 1970s Niklas Luhmann has also repeatedly stressed the central importance of the development of communication media for the evolution of society. Both are inseparably connected with one another.

The development of communication media and the evolution of society

To elucidate this correlation, here is a somewhat longer quotation from Luhmann:

> "Without communication no social systems are constructed. The improbabilities of the communication process [reaching, understanding, success] and the way they are overcome therefore regulate the construction of social systems. Thus, one can conceive of the process of socio-cultural evolution as a reshaping and broadening of the chances of propitious communication around which society constructs its social systems, and it is obvious that this is not simply a growing process, but rather a selective process that determines what kind of social systems are becoming possible and what (...) will be excluded."[3]

This is the system-theoretical version of McLuhan's well-known statement "The medium is the message." In other words, the information and communication systems that we construct, implement and use have a selective message or effect for further social evolution and for every human being.

Media innovations and social evolution

2 See McLuhan 1962
3 Luhmann 1981, p. 27

Era	dominant Media	dominant sense organ
1. Oral tribal culture	language	ear (acoustic perception)
2. Literal manuscript-culture	writing	synaesthesia & tactility
3. Gutenberggalaxy (national states)	book (print)	eye (sepatation of emotion reason)
4. Electronic age (Global village)	electricity (electronic network)	all senses

Fig. 2.4-1 McLuhan's phase model of (media-) history

Luhmann did not himself work out a phase model of the co-evolution of communication media and society up to now. According to Klaus Merten,[4] such a model could look as follows (fig. 2.4-2). As with McLuhan, central importance for societal evolution is here assigned to media innovations. Furthermore, it becomes evident that the communication system is becoming ever more complex in the wake of evolution.

En route to an information, knowledge or media society

Today we are no longer at the beginning but in the middle of a transition to a new stage of social evolution. This stage is alternatively termed an information/knowledge or media society. Yet it still remains rather unclear how this new social form, which is also called the second modernism (Ulrich Beck) or postmodernism (Lyotard, Flusser, etc.), differs from the first modernism (bourgeois society or industrial society).

Forms of modernism

Modernism generally refers to the bourgeois society developing from the end of the middle ages, in which public life is determined less by reference to supernatural authorities and norms, and more by rational forms of organisation and ways of life in all parts of society that have gradually been differentiated from one another (politics, economy, administration, science, etc.). A second determining criterion is the extensive and progress-oriented use of technology as science converted into action for organising public and private life, and above all as a motor of economic progress.

---

4 See Merten 1999, p. 201

Evolutionary prerequisites	Communication types	Types of society
Language	Interactive communication	Archaic tribal societies
Language Writing	Interactive and non-interactive communication	High cultures
Language Writing Mass Media	Interactive, non-interactive communication, mass communication	Industrial society
Language Writing Media Technology	Interactive, non-interactive non-organised communication, media communication, organised interactive communication	World society (Information -/ knowledge society)

Fig. 2.4-2 Communication types and stages in the evolution of society

Rational forms of organisation and technological and economic development had to, and still must, rely on a constant improvement in information and communication systems for securing their further progress in the face of the increasing division of labour, the growing complexity of tasks and processes, and rising transaction costs. In this respect, the development of modernism is synonymous with the development of information and communication resources, which it needs for its further evolution.

In this context, the emerging "information society" is just the continuation of the well-known process of modernisation/rationalisation and economisation, though with new technological means that allow the substitution not just of physical human labour and simple routines of human information-processing and communication, but also much more complex applications of human intelligence. As a final consequence, the information and communication systems that originally served to secure the further development of modernism are thus becoming the distinguishing feature of its future.

From a macroeconomic point of view, it is to be assumed that the fifth Kondratieff Cycle, which is borne by the basis innovations of the ICT cluster, will last for a long time yet (Moore's Law).

Information and communication systems as a defining feature of the future of society

The transition from the first to
the second modernism

From a social perspective, there are various assessments of the consequences associated with this self-transformation of the first modernism into the second modernism (Beck) and the institutional prerequisites or safeguards to be met or provided so that this transition succeeds, facilitating a coexistence of machine/technical and human intelligence without a crisis of confidence and without any loss of informational autonomy or powers of judgement.

Before I come back to these prerequisites I would like to quickly introduce a couple of scenarios which were presented by the IST Advisory Group (ISTAG) of the European Commission and elaborated by the Institute for Prospective Technological Studies (IPTS, Seville) for the DG Information Society.[5]

2.4.3
Current Visions of "Ambient Intelligence"

Embedding human action
within
communication-technical
intelligence

The goal of the study is to describe what the life of normal people might look like when their actions take place in an environment in which information and communication technical intelligence is embedded just about everywhere. For this, the term "Ambient Intelligence" (AmI) has been coined. A vision of the information society is presented in four scenarios in which intelligent technology offers a high level of user-friendliness, efficient services, user-empowerment, and support for human interactions. People are surrounded everywhere by intelligent intuitive interfaces that can be embedded in any object from their environment. These interfaces are networked among each other and with background systems and are capable of perceiving the presence of various individuals and reacting to them in different ways, inconspicuously, without causing disruption, and often without being seen.

Four scenarios of "Ambient
Intelligence"

The four scenarios worked out describe distinct but complementary directions and paths forming the way that leads to "Ambient Intelligence" (Figure 2.4-3). These can be diametrically distinguished on two dimensions: first, according to whether on the side of the provider priority is given more to personal, economic efficiency or to the social, human orientation; secondly, whether on the side of the user community or individualistic motives are the decisive factor.

---

5 "AmI and the Information Society in 2010": see the article by Ducatel et al. in this volume.

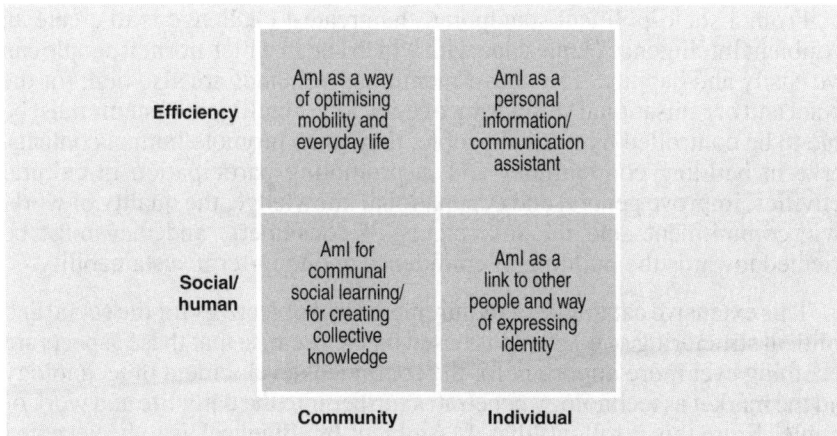

Fig. 2.4-3 Complementary target options for "Ambient Intelligence" (AmI)

The four scenarios describe how "Ambient Intelligence" can be used in the future:

– as a means of optimising mobility and everyday life

– as a personal information and communication assistant

– as a means towards social learning and for participating in collective knowledge

– as means for the expression of one's own identity in connection with other people.

In addition, the study also dealt with the future technologies that must still be developed for the realisation of these visionary scenarios and with the economic, social and political implications that result from the vision of "Ambient Intelligence."

The demands of technological performance are high and can only be met with a great deal of R&D. What is called for is highly unobtrusive, almost invisible hardware, seamless interoperability in the communication infrastructure (esp. fixed-line and mobile telephony), ubiquitous decentralised access to data bases, intuitively useful "human" interfaces, the identification and authentication of communication partners, and security in transactions.

Chapter 2.4
Schrape

" Technological maturity is not market maturity, market maturity is not market diffusion, market diffusion is not equal to use diffusion. *"*

Socio-political factors must drive technological AmI developments

From a socio-political standpoint, the greatest challenge is to create an "Ambient Intelligence" landscape with which and in which normal people can live easily and happily. The above-mentioned demands are also high for the social and organisational structuring of e-society. Intelligent systems must be able to be controlled by normal people; they must promote human contacts, serve in building communities and in promoting participation in cultural activities, improve general and occupational knowledge, the quality of work, civic commitment, and the sovereignty of consumers; and they must be oriented towards the building of confidence and long-term sustainability.

This extensive catalogue of requirements and objectives for the social and political structuring of e-society is based on the premise that these aspects are becoming ever more important for the continued development of technology and the market as technology penetrates further into the daily life and work of people. From this it follows that if "Ambient Intelligence" is to be accepted as a future path for technological development, then this vision must be considered and shaped as a positive force for the future social and political development of Europe. Only then will "Ambient Intelligence," as a new paradigm for ICT applications, open the door for creative enterprises and new, lucrative areas of business.

2.4.4
Institutional Preconditions for Further Socio-technical Evolution

Coexistence of human and artificial intelligence

After this excursion into a current vision of "life in the e-society," I now return to my central question. What institutional preconditions or safeguards are required to ensure a frictionless coexistence of machine/technical intelligence and human intelligence?

Three evolutionary mechanisms: variation, selection, retention

Why is this question so central? First, it must be remembered that evolutionary processes can be successful only when three evolutionary mechanisms act in combination: variation/innovation, selection, and retention/stabilisation. Scientific-technical progress makes sure that innovations are constantly forthcoming, the market mechanism decides which of them can be carried through, and politics and the law create the institutional conditions that guarantee planning and expectations and make innovations compatible with existing structures and acceptable for people.

It is by no means self-evident that this evolutionary triad will proceed harmoniously, but instead rather improbable. Technologically oriented visions and prognoses alone frequently go beyond what is economically and

"Face-to-face" situation	New Media
■ Said	■ Technological maturity
≠	≠
■ Heard	■ Market maturity
≠	≠
■ Understood	■ Market diffusion
≠	≠
■ Done	■ Media use

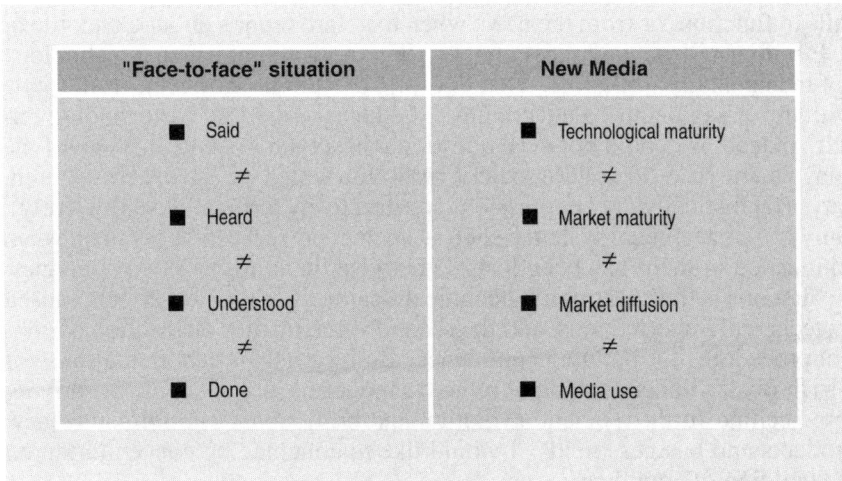

Fig. 2.4-4 Stages in the Diffusions of Innovations

socially "feasible." They easily lead to false estimates and considerable entrepreneurial and political risks, which cannot be overcome with just supply-side instruments. This practical knowledge is willingly suppressed. Yet the recent history of media technology is littered with product innovations that have been highly praised but have turned out as flops in the market (video disc players, Video 2000/Datamax, Btx, D2-Mac, DRS, Iridium) or developments that could be forced onto the market only with immense subventions or involuntary investments (16:9 TV sets, DAB, D-Box).

Konrad Lorenz, the well-known behaviour researcher, has developed a concise formula for face-to-face situations to show the stages that changes in behaviour go through. This states: "Said is not heard, heard is not understood, understood is not done." Its application for the introduction of media-technical innovations in society could run: "Technological maturity is not market maturity, market maturity is not market diffusion, market diffusion is not equal to use diffusion." None of these transitions is trivial, and each one requires time for learning curves to be passed through on the supply side as on the demand side.

Market maturity is no guarantee of success

A further factor is that intelligent information and communication systems result in new uncertainties that must be addressed institutionally. It is expected of a technical system that it should function, and should function in all conceivable situations in which it is used. Even today, each one of us constantly experiences that this expectation is occasionally not met: in everyday life when the car does not start, the computer or the navigation system

Everyday technology as "manufactured uncertainty"

fails to function, or from the news when there are reports about Concorde or ICE train accidents and virus attacks. We know, therefore, that technology is fundamentally imperfect. That does not prevent us, however, from living with this "manufactured uncertainty" (Giddens) produced by technology itself. Indeed, we could not even question it as a total system: it is one of the unavoidable risks of modern society, risks with which we can deal in different ways (fatalistically, by suppression, constructively, critically/destructively). Only certain technical systems (such as nuclear power) can be given up when confidence in them has been lost. Otherwise there are just two strategies: the first one is the constructive-technical treatment of the side-effects caused by technical imperfections, and the second is the institutionalisation of control procedures for building confidence. Both strategies can, in the sense of Ulrich Beck's understanding of reflexive modernisation, become the driving force behind further societal evolution and bring about a multitude of new products and business fields. I would like to conclude by concentrating on the building of confidence.

Even today there are innumerable indications of uncertainty and even mistrust as regards the use of information and communication systems. Examples range from the inexplicable system crashes while using the Windows operating system to the fear of looming information pollution, and from the frustration of conducting specific searches in the Internet to mistrust of the capability of software agents. The list goes on.

This uncertainty felt by the individual in the face of technology is really nothing new. To compensate for it, for a long time it was enough to refer to the consensus of the democratic public and to the rightness of scientific knowledge. Both forms of legitimisation no longer function directly. The increasing complexity and non-transparency of society are driving horizons of understanding apart. The public world is fragmented and transformed into a range of worlds delegated to the media. And even control of what is right in the sciences and the reliability of technology is delegated to experts. We deal with abstract and technical systems, therefore, in a state of general uncertainty with respect to information, uncertainty for which we try to compensate by delegating to and trusting others.

Confidence in technical systems is based only to a minor extent on explicit knowledge, and much more on a multitude of soft factors, which one can summarise in the concept of experience. Confidence-building is both a complex and sensitive process. Its success does not depend unambiguously on any single factor but on a mixture of many social, technical and psychological-emotional factors. Confidence is not easy to win and keep, but it is easy to lose. And for this reason too, confidence is a sensitive resource, because it can be easily misused without this being noticed right away. However, when disappointments of confidence do arise, a momentum

Confronting side-effects and institutionalising control procedures

Fragmentation of forms of legitimisation

Confidence as a sensitive resource – a form of moral credit

can quickly develop. Confidence is fundamentally not an intellectual, but rather an emotional quality, a kind of moral credit.

Confidence-building in dealing with abstract socio-technical systems like "Ambient Intelligence" depends on a multitude of social factors. I can list only a few here, factors that were not mentioned above with the uncertainty indicators. This list of factors that might influence successful confidence-building at the same time circumscribes the scope of the catalogue of tasks we face and the challenges we must overcome if the entire life-world that man can experience is to be enriched with electronic prostheses.

What sort of visions do we have for such heightened, technology-induced evolution in our society? Is man, as a god of prostheses, like Hephaestus the blacksmith in Greek mythology, technically creative but ostracised by the other gods of Olympus? Or is man a deficient being who compensates for the anthropological deficiencies that have become more evident in the wake of evolution through ever-new technological problem-solving and eventually makes even himself superfluous? Or are there other visions: for example, the artistically creative man who is always capable of transcending the potential of technical problem-solving in unforeseeable ways for aesthetic (cultural) and social values?

To ensure a frictionless co-evolution between man, as a bearer of consciousness, intelligent information and communication systems, and social institutions, two things in my opinion are required: human (co-) existence in the future first, a holistic conception of man that also considers the non-cognitive and non-rational dimensions, and secondly, an extensive, broad and permanent social discussion about what form good, information-knowledge-communication and media society can and should take. Let us not forget: we are still the ones who shape our future, and not technology.

Electronic prostheses

The co-evolution of man and technology

Chapter 3   Changing Society

Individual and Collective Life Options

Social networks are changing; virtual communities are emerging; the Internet is building bridges between locally rooted groups and individuals dispersed in space. Information and communication technologies and Internet use are decisively influencing the social life of users, reinforcing existing links and allowing new social relationships to be built up. People are moving towards one another, closer together, and the concentration generated by new communication technologies may even lead to the emergence of an "economy of opportunities," the aim being the active management of life options.

The following chapter focuses on some of the social implications of new information and communication technologies and converging media. The analysis will include, for example, the social logic implied by the spatio-temporal fabric and changes in the structure of social interaction. Are the new information and communication technologies really as socially significant as is generally assumed? How can social participation and access to information be made possible for all citizens? In other words, what measures must be introduced in order to overcome the digital divide?

In the chapter's opening contribution, *Ilkka Tuomi* investigates the significance of space for social relationships and communities, as well as the interdependence that exists between spatial organisation and the formation of knowledge. He shows how certain spatial configurations, such as traditional village structures, can serve as a basis for models of self-regulation. Social networks become important social capital, providing social support for the construction of individual identities. Specialised person-to-person networks are also becoming more and more important. In networks of this sort people play a variety of different roles. By taking part in these role-to-role networks, they gain a broad portfolio of necessary resources.

Hans Geser analyses the innovative potential of mobile phone technology from an evolutionary perspective and looks at how cell phone usage can facilitate or inhibit certain modes of social behaviour, interactions and relationships. Individual consequences include emancipation from local settings and the support it gives to segregated, self-controlled social networks. Further, the mobile phone endows individuals with the capacity to accumulate diverse roles simultaneously as well as to maintain "pervasive roles." Cell phone usage allows for a simultaneous increase of individual empowerment, personal responsibility and social control. *Geser* then discusses the

Ilkka Tuomi

Hans Geser

microsocial, mesosocial and macrosocial consequences of mobile phone usage, such as the deregulation of agendas and the ability of people on the move to stay connected (microsocial), the decentralisation and bilateralisation of intrasystemic communication (mesosocial) and the deregulation of intersystemic boundary controls (macrosocial).

Jean-Claude Burgelman and Martin Weber

One of the main tasks of the future will be to bring the advantages generated by the revolutionary development of information and communication technologies into line with heterogeneous cultures, values, political targets, and ways of work and life. In their article, "Mobile Europe: Balancing a Fast-changing Society and Europe's Socio-economic Objectives," *Jean-Claude Burgelman* and *Martin Weber* propose the notion of a "Mobile Europe" as one that might help reconcile the drivers of change in the new e-conomy with the values and goals of a united Europe. A Mobile Europe must approach these challenges on a number of levels, including infrastructure, the underlying legal and institutional framework, and ways of life, work and production.

Valerie Frissen

In her article on "The Myth of the Digital Divide," *Valerie Frissen* looks at the dichotomy in information society between information "haves" and have-nots." *Frissen* points out that the discussion about access and exclusion in the information society is in fact based on mistaken assumptions. Universal access to information and communication is a matter of market development and does not constitute the right starting-point for an analysis of non-use. A reconstruction of the process of acceptance in Internet non-users shows instead that the costs of information and communication technologies are only a decisive factor when the added value from the use of the technologies is considered to be very limited. It is the qualities of the information and communication technologies that are the real threshold value, and exclusion from technologies is more a cultural than a cognitive or financial question.

Benjamin Compaine

In his contribution on "The Vanishing Digital Divide," *Benjamin Compaine* confirms the great relevance of information access. Yet the importance of access to information and communication technologies should be looked at more closely in the context of the overall prosperity of U.S. society. Determinants of the broad acceptance of the Internet are falling costs, natural acculturation and the increasing availability of Internet access.

Chapter 3.1

Virtual Communities, Space and Mobility

Ilkka Tuomi

The advent of telecommunication has resulted in the uncoupling of space and time. Before electronic communication, simultaneity implied locality, and spatial distance implied temporal distance. With the uncoupling of space and time, the experience of simultaneity has been detached from the spatial condition of locality. Both time and space have become symbolically mediated. According to Thompson:

The symbolic mediation of time and space

> "By altering their sense of place and of the past, the development of communication media also has some bearing on individuals' sense of belonging— that is, on their sense of the groups and communities to which they feel they belong. The sense of belonging derives, to some extent, from a feeling of sharing a common history and a common locale, a common trajectory in time and space. But as our sense of the past becomes increasingly dependent on symbolic forms, and as our sense of the world and our place within it becomes increasingly nourished by media products, so too our sense of the groups and communities with which we share a common path through time and space, a common origin and a common fate, is altered; we feel ourselves to belong to groups and communities which are constituted in part through the media."[1]

Sense of belonging independent of place

As long as we have been reading newspapers and listening to the radio, therefore, our communities have been "virtual". In the 20th century the "virtualisation" was to a large extent produced by mass communication, which brought remote places and times together.[2] In the 21st century, the communication media bring together people. Instead of viewing the world, we are interacting with it.

---

1 Thompson 1995, p. 35
2 Harvey (1990) has called the shrinking time horizons of private and public decision-making "time-space compression." Time and space organisation also plays a central role in Giddens' theory of structuration (1984) and in Castells' analysis of network society (1996).

"Virtual communities" have been extensively discussed in the literature and popular press.[3] Often virtual communities have been described as a new type of community. This is partly true. Social networks are changing. Yet, as Wellman and Gulia note, sociologists have been wondering for over a century about how technological changes affect community. Much of the analysis of online communities has been parochial:

"It almost always treats the Internet as an isolated social phenomenon without taking into account how interactions of the Net fit together with other aspects of people's lives. The Net is only one of many ways in which the same people may interact. It is not a separate reality. People bring to their online interactions such baggage as their gender, stage in their life cycle, cultural milieu, socio-economic status, and offline connections with others."[4]

3.1.1
Geography and the Economy of Life Opportunities

Space continues to have crucial importance for communities in the age of Internet too. This is also true for individual social relations and for economic activity. For example, Matthew Zook has shown in his studies on Internet geography that Internet content production is spatially very concentrated.[5] In 1998 there were about three times more dot-com Internet domains per business firm in San Francisco than in the USA on average. Moreover, the registration locations of these domain names were highly concentrated in the financial district of San Francisco as well as the Multimedia Gulch in the South of Market district. If the theory was that the Internet makes spatiality irrelevant, and that Internet workers can live anywhere, this theory has empirically been shown to be wrong.

One reason for the high spatial concentration of Internet content producers is that content creators need access to information and knowledge that is difficult to express in digital and textual forms. The classic study that illustrates this problem is Collins' study of the transfer of scientific knowledge. Collins showed that it is often impossible to replicate scientific experiments simply by reading textual descriptions of them.[6] Often the

---

3 Influential contributions include Rheingold (1993), Turkle (1995), and Sproull/Kiesler (1991). Identity, social order, community structure and collective action in online communities are discussed in Smith/Kollock (1999) and Wellman (1999a).

4 Wellmann/Gulia 1999, p. 170

5 See Zook 1999

6 See Collins 1975; 1987

transfer of knowledge requires physical proximity and situational knowledge.[7] Moreover, innovation is often based on a serendipitous combination of ideas and perspectives. Innovative milieus and regions of innovative production, therefore, are places where space is organised to facilitate such a combination of cultural resources.

A number of authors have highlighted the importance of the social infrastructure that is the precondition for creative and innovative regions in their studies.[8] Landry, in particular, has emphasised that cultural creativity has often been associated with rapid social transformation, slack resources, old regional centres, and "third spaces" where people can meet and talk, whereas technological innovation has historically often occurred in more peripheral regions. Castells and Hall have analysed the attempts intentionally to create innovative regions, showing that such attempts often failed because of inadequate consideration of the social infrastructure of creativity. Saxenian, in turn, has highlighted the point that organisational culture, the institutional structure, and social networks have a major influence on the types of innovativeness that a region supports.[9]

The interdependencies between spatial organisation and the knowledge-creation capability of regions is one of the important research topics in knowledge society. As we already know, the ongoing transformation is closely associated with rapid concentration – not only of Internet content producers, but also of people in general. As was noted above, it has often been assumed that advanced telecommunication makes telework common and that access to services becomes location-independent. This has been expected to facilitate balanced regional development. As Castells has noted, the opposite often seems to be the case. New communication technologies make it possible for people to move close to each other. As knowledge-based work and people locate close to regional hubs, the centres can develop an "economy of opportunities" which increases the attractiveness of such hubs. This creates positive feedback between the concentration of work and life opportunities on the one hand, and economic activity and people on the other.

I have used the term "economy of opportunities" on purpose. The ongoing transformation is today associated with the idea that life consists of making informed decisions and choices. In other words, individual freedom is informationalised and associated with the active management of life options. As the requirement for "informing" oneself creates cognitive

The social infrastructure of creativity

"Economy of opportunities"

---

7 See Latour/Woolgar 1986; Suchman 1987; Salomon 1993; Hutchins 1995; Nonaka/Takeuchi 1995; Cole 1996; Engeström/Middleton 1996; Nardi 1997; Polanyi 1998; Bowker/Star 1999; Knorr-Cetina 1999

8 See Landry 2000; Hall 1998; Castells 1989; Saxenian 1994

9 See Castells/Hall 1994. The institutional structure of Silicon Valley, studied by Saxenian, has further been described and discussed in Kenney (2000).

" Individual freedom is associated with the active management of life options. "

overflow, a practical strategy is to go to places where collective processing and filtering is done, and where more options are available without an expensive search. Young people, for example, move to cities partly because the larger concentration of people in cities makes it easier to meet interesting new people, to find interesting new jobs through them, and to follow the crowd to the newest mental or physical "hot spot." Today we do not yet know how this economy of opportunities operates. For example, during the explosion of the new economy in Silicon Valley, economic growth was closely related to the capability of young people to "drop everything" and grasp emerging opportunities. This made young independent and technically competent people a key resource for economic growth. At the same time, it made social commitments, for example children and marriages, economically expensive.

Social costs of life-option management

In theory, this logic could lead to a "Hollywood economy," in which restaurants and streets are filled with independent people who are waiting for the real opportunity to materialise. Some forms of opportunity economy, therefore, might lead to a knowledge society where winners take all and where opportunity-seekers are ready to hang on at great individual and social expense just to be close to where the action is. One could also assume that people often acquire options which they do not cash and also combinations of options that are impossible to realise. Empirical research on the economy of opportunities could help us to develop policies that reduce the social costs of life-option management, for example by making important social options available independent of geographical location, and by creating "insurance" systems that manage the risks of "uninformed" choices.

3.1.2
The Social Logic of Time and Space

The relation between social interaction and the structure of time-space

To understand the ongoing transformation and its implications for the development of regional centres and social networks and communities it is necessary to study the ways social interaction and time-space are related. The cognitive and social aspects of space, or more accurately time-space, therefore, are key research areas when we try to understand knowledge society and social transformations associated with new communication technologies. Although time-space has in many ways been an important area of study in social theory, in the context of the Internet its importance becomes obvious. As Slevin notes, such a study highlights in an elemental way that:

"... individuals and organizations do not just use media 'in' time-space; they use it to organize time-space. By examining the internet in this light, we can begin to make an effort at grasping its impact on the volume of time-space available to individuals and organizations in the pursuance of their projects. We can study, for example, how the internet is affecting individuals and organizations in their ability to mobilize space and, by using the internet to facilitate the routinized specification and allocation of tasks, to coordinate the time-space trajectories of their projects."[10]

Space, however, is also a very difficult concept. It is used in many very different ways by different authors. It has been interpreted semiotically as a process, as concrete cities, as exteriority to body, as a foundation of metaphorical thinking, as an ever-compressing informational event horizon, as the context of situated action, and in many other ways. Today it seems that space is everything but the Cartesian coordinate system where the location of objects can universally be defined. As Crang and Thrift note: "Space is the everywhere of modern thought. It is the flesh that flatters the bones of theory. It is an all-purpose nostrum to be applied whenever things look sticky. It is an invocation, which suggests that the writer is right on without her having to give too much away. It is flexibility as explanation: a term ready and waiting in the wings to perform that song-and-dance act one more time."[11]

Concepts of space – between context and constraint

Virtuality, of course, is the more sophisticated cousin of space, tip-toeing pas de deux with her muddy mirror image in a space where gravity does not matter anymore. Yet the great interest in space does not emerge from a vacuum. It highlights the fact that context and its constraints are important. When we try to understand the ongoing changes in social interaction and community formation, it is necessary to understand how the contexts of interaction and their constraints change.

According to the traditional view, community was associated with locality and structures of kinship. Historical communities were understood to be bound to local neighbourhoods. According to Wellman, such communities had *door-to-door* connectivity. The traditional view on community saw it as a village, town and neighbourhood. Such communities were understood to be spatially compact and dense networks where many links existed between the community members. In such a community, it was a safe guess that everyone knew each other. As Wellman puts it: "Whether travelling with yurts or huddling in stone cottages the important point is that people went through villages and neighbourhoods to communicate. Most people in a settlement knew each other, were limited by their feetpower in whom they could contact, and when they visited someone, most neighbours knew who was going to see whom and what their interaction was about. The contact was essentially

Community as spatially compact networks

---

10 Slevin 2000, p. 70
11 Crang/Thrift 2000, p. 1

between households, with the sanction – or at least the awareness – of the settlement."[12]

In traditional communities, spatial organisation encoded important knowledge about social practice and interaction. The architecture of buildings, the layout of villages and towns, and transportation networks reflect accumulated logics of social interaction. As Hillier and Hanson note: "By giving shape and form to our material world, architecture structures the system of space in which we live and move. In that it does so, it has a direct relation – rather than a merely symbolic one – to social life, since it provides the material preconditions for the patterns of movement, encounter and avoidance which are the material realization – as well as sometimes the generator – of social relations."[13]

Hillier and his colleagues developed a "syntax of space" to analyse settlements, buildings and social encounters. In contrast to some other approaches to spatial analysis, which have used elementary shapes or distance and location as their starting points, Hillier's "social logic of space" described spatial structures in a way that focused on social interaction. This approach has relevance also when we try to understand communities and social interactions in cyberspace.

In Hillier's spatial syntax, the starting point was an "elementary cell," which divided space into interior and exterior space. Hillier and his colleagues used such elementary cells to analyse the arrangements of rooms in houses and the different forms of villages and towns. By analysing accessibility and constraints in the placement of elementary cells, they were able to find simple generative rules that produced settlement forms that structurally resemble historically existing forms. Moreover, by developing graphical representation methods for analysing space accessibility, they were able to show that many settlements and architectures were produced by a relatively simple set of constraints.

In Hillier's theory, Durkheim's distinction between "organic" and "mechanical" solidarity plays an important role. According to Durkheim, *organic solidarity* is based on interdependence that is produced by differences, for example by the division of labour. *Mechanical solidarity*, in turn, is produced by similarities, for example by group membership or shared beliefs.

According to Hillier and Hanson, the inhabitants of a house or village relate to each other spatially as neighbours. In addition, however, they also relate to each other conceptually, or transpatially, by sharing similar views, including views on how space is and should be organised. The exterior structure of a settlement, therefore, reflects organic solidarity, whereas the

Spatial configurations reflect social interaction

Elementary cells as starting points for a "syntax of space"

Organic versus mechanical solidarity

---

12 Wellmann 2000
13 Hillier/Hanson 1984, p. ix

interior structure of houses reflects mechanical, or transpatial, solidarities:[14] "We might even say, without too much exaggeration, that interiors tend to define more of an ideological space, in the sense of a fixed system of categories and relations that is continually re-affirmed by use, whereas exteriors define a transactional or even a political space, in that it constructs a more fluid system of encounters and avoidances which is constantly renegotiated by use."[15]

One central point in Hillier's theory was the distinction between "outsiders" and "insiders." The structure of a village, for example, could be analysed from the point of a view of a stranger who enters the village from the outside world and tries to access the different areas of the village. Hillier and Hanson showed that in many traditional villages and towns outsiders had very easy access to the main open areas of the settlement, but that it was much more difficult for them to access the interior parts of the settlement. The access routes were also very easy for the inhabitants to control. Similarly, the structure of accessibility of different rooms in English houses is independent of the actual layout. The analysis of "permeabilities" and accessibilities, therefore, provides a description of space which in some sense reflects the social meaning of spatial organisation. As Hillier and Hanson show by comparing houses from different time periods and sectors of the market,[16] the access logic of English houses is stable and also survives major conversions. The room with the best furniture, which is located next to the front door, is systematically the most isolated room. The kitchen is the next most isolated room, and the living room is the room with easy access to all the other rooms, making it the control centre of the house. Visitors, of course, are invited to the parlour room the least used and most isolated room, with the best furniture and effects. The isolation of the front parlour makes it possible to live everyday life in the house, and still maintain a place where transpatial interactions and solidarities can be organised and expressed.

To analyse the interaction structures of existing spaces, Hillier and his colleagues developed several techniques to represent and quantify spatial organisation. An example of one type of connectivity map is shown below in Figure 3.1-2. Figure 3.1-1, in turn, shows a conventional map of the same area of London, part of Somerstown, in the 19th century, as it is represented in the ordnance survey map. Using the map it is possible to find a set of maximal convex regions, in other words the "open spaces" of the area. It is

Relations in ideological and in political space

The logic of access and the permeability of space

The living room becomes the control centre of the house

Analysis of the interaction structures of existing spaces

---

14 Strictly speaking, there are of course complex interrelations between organic and transpatial solidarities that organise the structure of houses. This is partly because the family itself reflects specific understandings of the division of labour. Hillier and Hanson focus here on traditional forms of settlements, in which communication and space were not uncoupled. This is, however, a useful starting point precisely because it allows us to see how the new communication technologies change these more traditional structures.

15 Hillier/Hanson 1984, p. 20

16 See Hillier/Hanson 1984, pp. 155–163

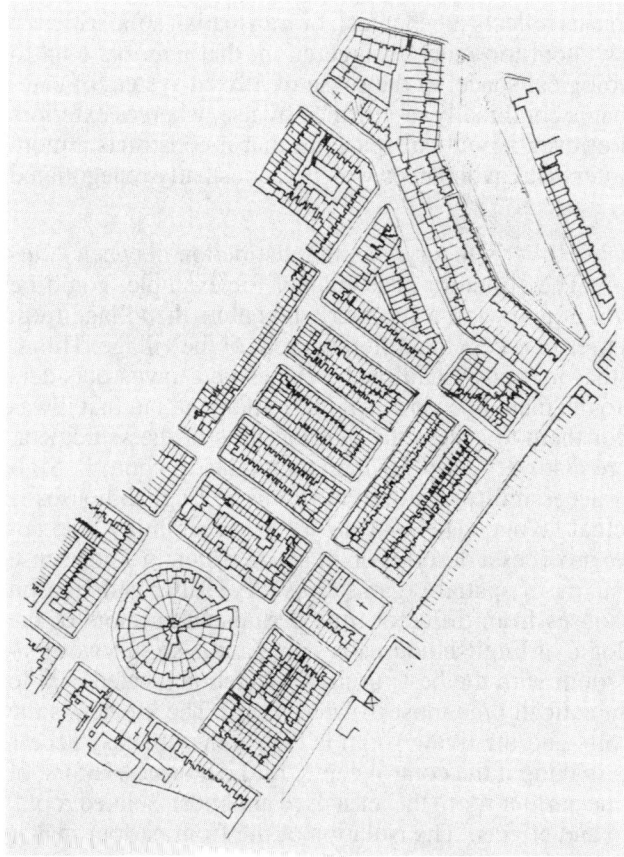

Fig. 3.1-1 Somerstown in the 19th century (Hillier & Hanson 1984, p. 134)

also possible to find entrances of buildings. By linking the buildings to those open areas that are directly accessible from the entrance, we get an "interface map" of the area. This interface map of 19th-century Somerstown is shown in Figure 3.1-2.

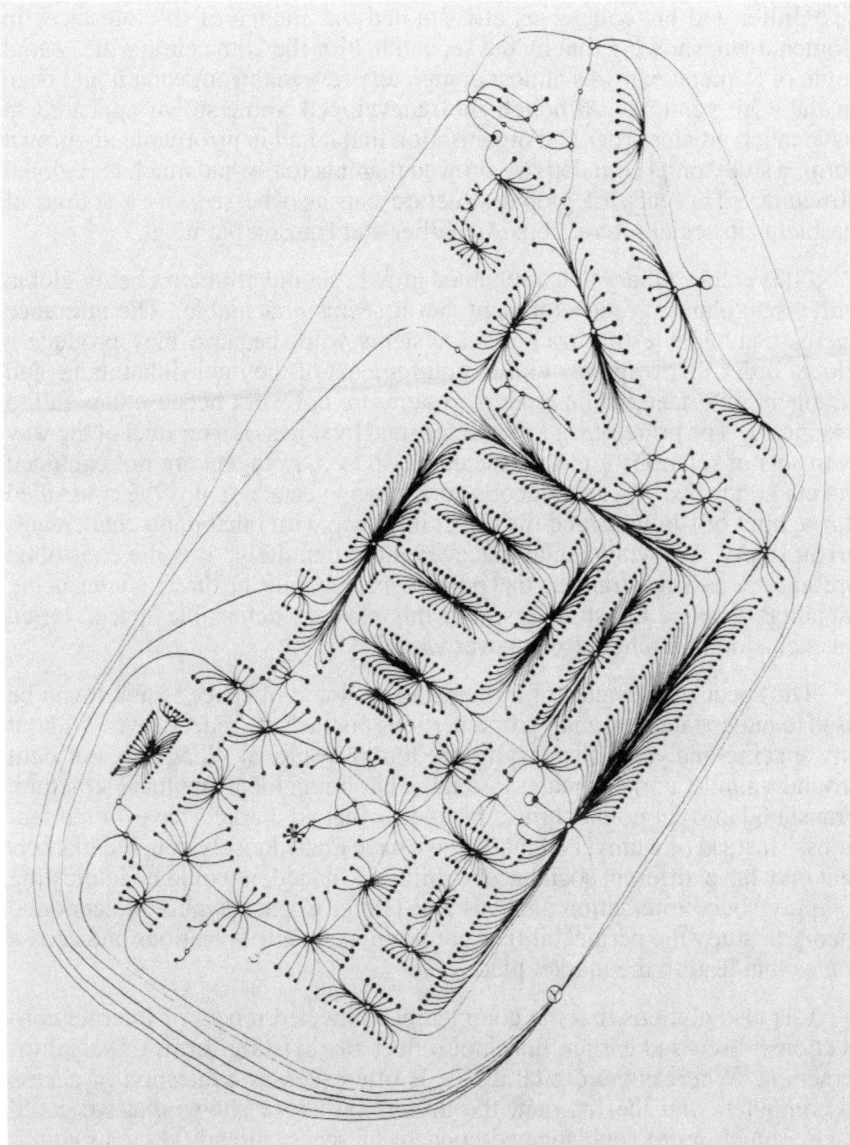

Fig. 3.1-2 Interface map of 19th-century Somerstown (Hillier & Hanson 1984, p. 135)

" Social interaction analysis should be applied
in economic theory. "

Hillier and his colleagues also studied the change of the interfaces in Somerstown, showing that by the second half of the 20th century the spatial logic of Somerstown was almost completely reversed from what it had been in the 19th century. Although the redeveloped Somerstown appeared to have much greater order and organisation that it had in its organically grown form, a study of its connectivity showed that it actually had much less global structure. This lack of global structure can also be seen as a source of problems in social interaction. As Hillier and Hanson put it:

"It is extraordinary that unplanned growth should produce a better global order than planned redevelopment, but it seems undeniable. The inference seems unavoidable that traditional systems work because they produce a global order that responds to the requirements of the dual (inhabitants and strangers) interface, while modern systems do not work because they fail to produce it. The principle of urban safety and liveliness is a product of the way both sets of relations are constructed by space. Strangers are not excluded but are controlled. As Jane Jacobs noted many years ago, it is the controlled throughput of strangers and the direct interface with inhabitants that creates urban safety. We would state this even more definitely: it is the controlled presence of passing strangers that polices space; while the directly interfacing inhabitants police the strangers. For this reason, 'defensible space,' based on exclusion of strangers, can never work."[17]

Strangers are not excluded but controlled

The specific relevance of Hillier's social logic of space is that it can be used to understand and analyse interactions on the Net. Indeed, even without any specific analysis, it is easy to see that the "global village" is not built around a single market square; instead, it has both global and local structure. Translated into economic terms, this means that all markets have "imperfections." Instead of a universal market, we have many loosely coupled markets that may have different social accessibilities. Indeed, it would be interesting to apply social interaction analysis and Hillier's space syntax in economic theory to study the permeabilities, entry points, control positions and access routes that lead to the market place.

Different social access opportunities to the Internet

It is also obvious that the completely connected model of Internet connections, discussed earlier, does not reflect any existing forms of social interaction. Whereas the digital divide is often seen as a question of access to computers and the Internet, the discussion above shows that we could have a much more sophisticated concept of access already on a structural level of analysis. Questions related to regulation and privacy also emerge in a new light when they are put in the context of boundaries, entrances and the policing of space. For example, it is possible to see that some Internet self-regulation models could be built using traditional village structures as starting points.

Village structures as the basis for Internet self-regulation models

17 Hillier/Hanson 1984, p. 140

An analysis of social interaction structure is also interesting as it can link characteristics of traditional community structure with characteristics of social interaction on the Net. Methods for interaction design, of course, have been developed and used in human-computer interaction studies and usability research. These, however, have focused on the individual as a user of a particular system. Technology-mediated interaction and especially technology-mediated social interaction are important research areas in the future.[18] In other words, it could be possible to describe physical space and cyberspace using the same analytic tools. This would mean that Wellman's request that virtual communities be studied as something that relates to the rest of reality could perhaps be addressed. A particularly interesting area of study could be research on the complementarities of spatial and communicative organisation. Analytical tools similar to those developed by Hillier and his colleagues could also make it easier for content providers to understand the interaction characteristics of specific Web sites.

3.1.3
Transpatial Solidarity

In modern cities, strangers do not have easy access to organic city life, and also the inhabitants have to cross a lot of empty space and boundaries before they meet their neighbours. In a way, organic life does not exist in modern cities. Indeed, one could speculate with the idea that modern cities have this characteristic simply because they are designed for strangers. Economic transactions and transpatial solidarities have to a large extent replaced organic solidarities. By creating structures where it is easy to add foreigners without the cultural control of the inhabitants, cities can absorb the flux of people moving from the periphery to the centre. Places that integrate people from different cultures, such as Silicon Valley, need to treat most of their inhabitants as strangers; or, more exactly, trivialise the distinction between inhabitants and strangers until it does not make a difference.

Economic transactions and transpatial solidarities

The forms of solidarity and social networks have been changing, but they also depend on culture. This is visible especially in countries and regions that have strong homogenous cultures, in other words where transpatial solidarities are commonly shared. The complex tensions created by evolving communication technologies, social networks and physical space are illustrated in very concrete terms in Figure 3.1-3. This shows the Nakagin Capsule Mansion, located in Ginza, Tokyo. By looking through a window

Changes in forms of solidarity and social networks

---

18 See Ducatel et al. in this volume. Both tools for modelling such interactions and analytical approaches will be important.

of the first prototype capsule, built in 1971 and exhibited on the street level, one can see a very compact theory of human life.

Next to the entrance of each capsule there is a small closed space for toilet and shower. Under the window there is a bed. Integrated with the end of the bed there is a control panel with an embedded reel-to-reel tape recorder, radio and telephone. Embedded in the wall, close to the roof, there is a television. Next to the communication machines there is a small space, a table, carved between storage lockers, where you can boil rice. Everything is immovable and nicely integrated within the capsule structure. Private life in a modern city, according to this theory, seems to be about mood control (by listening to music from the tape), transpatial solidarity (tuning in to the same hip-hop channel your friends listen to), seeing the world outside (watching television), and communicating with it (by phone). The rest of life, perhaps, is about work.

Communication media as an integrated part of everyday life

The Nakagin Capsule Mansion is, literally, a concrete example of the fact that "door-to-door" connectivity has acquired new meaning in modern cities. Without complex logistic and communication systems such a building would make no sense. In the Nakagin capsule, access to mass media, interpersonal communication, and technologies for symbolically mediated transpatial solidarity materialise in a mass-produced form, as an integrated part of everyday life.

Place-to-place connectivity

When one defines community by social interactions, and not spatially, it becomes obvious that communities also exist beyond spatial neighbourhoods. In the modern world, people obtain support, sociability, information and a sense of belonging from those who do not live within the same neighbourhood.[19] People maintain these community ties through phoning, writing, driving, railroading, transiting and flying.[20] According to Wellman, this has led to the emergence of communities that rely on *place-to-place* connectivity.

Historically, the *place* where community interactions occur has been closely associated with a household. In a typical English house this place was further defined as the parlour. Due to the centrality of the household in the community structure, marriage has been an important institution in linking individuals with social networks. As Wellman notes, married couples often see their friends in common, interact with each other's families, and get support from in-laws as easily as they get support from their own kin. The front parlour has to be close to the front door simply because it has to be easy to access from the outside world. Without a system of streets, however, the parlour would not make sense.

---

19 See Wellmann 1999a; 1999b
20 See Wellmann 2000

Fig. 3.1-3 The Nakagin Capsule Mansion, Tokyo

Place-to-place connectivity creates a fluid system for accessing material, cognitive and interpersonal resources. But although the social networks themselves may be fluid in modern society, they rely on infrastructure

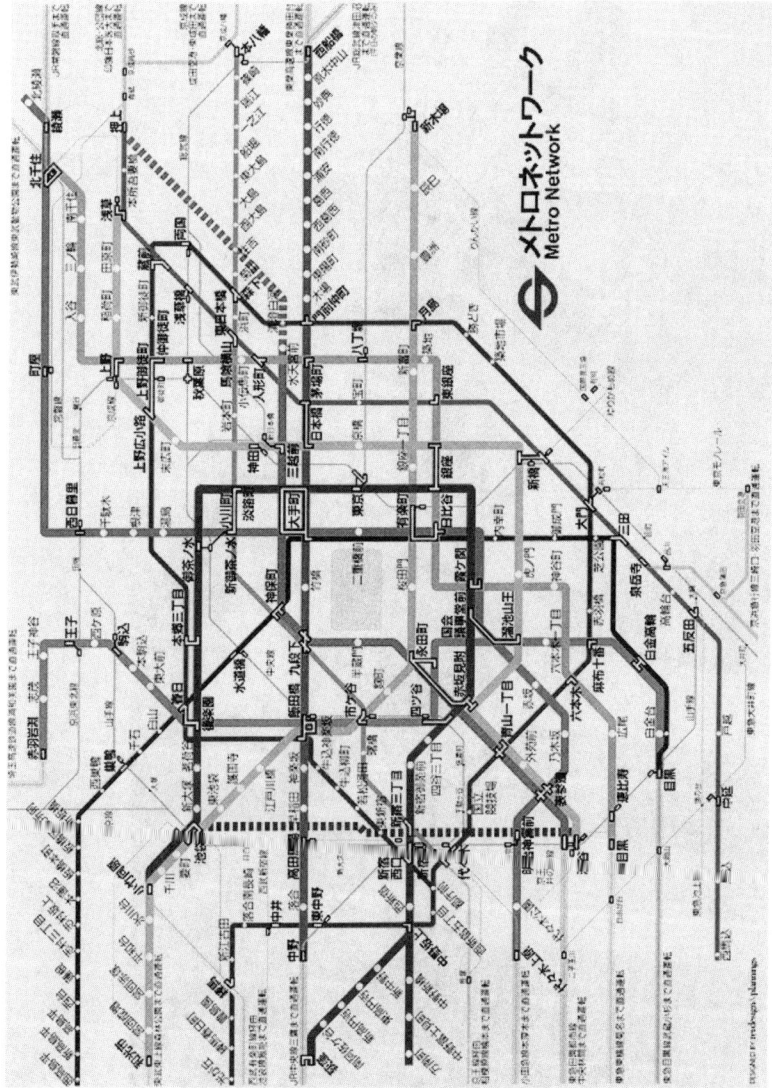

Fig. 3.1-4 Place-to-place connectivity: a graphic representation of the Tokyo subway network.

" Households are no longer the nodes of social networks. "

Chapter 3.1
Space and Mobility

networks that may be more rigid and inflexible. Indeed, one theory might
be that social interactions concentrate spatially in regions where the tensions
between changing infrastructure networks, i.e. communication and transportation networks, and changing social networks are being successfully
played out. The existing infrastructure networks always reflect the history
and logic of the old world. The requirements of the current social interaction structure generate developmental needs and in those places where new
infrastructure can fill the need, the growth is fastest. On a macro-level this
would be similar to Schumpeter's "swarming" hypothesis that was part of
his idea of creative destruction. Silicon Valley, for example, could then be
seen as a region where a relatively weak infrastructure, implying weak institutionalisation, and strong flows of people have collided and erupted into a
hot spot of new technology.

New versus old infrastructure

An example of a place-to-place infrastructure network, a representation
of the Tokyo subway network, is shown in Figure 3.1-4.

To control access to resources, members of place-to-place communities
have to simultaneously control both space and communication. As Wellman
notes: "On the one hand, the security of the household base and its surroundings are important, and neighbours are scarcely known and not knit into a
strong network. This makes a household's local politics one of securing
the property and area with guarded gates, getting people as neighbours with
the 'right' demographics and lifestyle, and encouraging a strong, responsive
police presence. On the other hand, residents want high-speed, unfettered
access to the Internet, expressways and airports to facilitate their links with
people in other places. (...) Their security concerns start turning to anti-
virus checkers, spam and obscenity filters, disk backups, and firewall-like
protection against hacker intrusion."[21]

Changing forms of security

In such place-to-place connected systems, control of resources therefore
becomes a mixture of control of property and control of network resources.
Networking skills and competencies become increasingly important, and
accumulated social networks become important social capital that can be
mobilised to get things done. In addition, networks provide social support
and a foundation on which individual identity can be built.

Control of property and of
network resources

According to Wellman, the increasing importance of place-to-place communities has profound implications. For example, it has become possible
to connect to several multiple social milieus, at the same time reducing the
control that each milieu can have. The increasing fragmentation, however,
also means that people must actively maintain their network ties. Communities are increasingly "voluntary" and based on achieved characteristics

Relations in multiple social
networks

21 Ibid.

*" Men's communities could become smaller
than women's communities."*

that people have acquired throughout their life course, such as lifestyles and interests, and less dependent on "ascriptive" characteristics such as age, gender, race and social class. Place-to-place connectivity has also reduced the value of group membership as such while increasing the value of connecting and brokering between multiple networks.

3.1.4
Role-to-role networks

Person-to-person connectivity

Both the Internet and mobile communications have radically changed the connectivity of social networks in a few years. As the social interaction structure and its constraints are deeply affected by this change, one might predict that the diffusion of these technologies will have more profound effects than we today realise. Whereas traditional telephone calls were made to specific places, today email and calls to cellular phones are personal and increasingly independent of time and location. *Person-to-person* connectivity also means that households lose some of their importance as nodes of social networks:

"As community moves out of the household and onto the mobile phone and the modem, there is scope for yet another renegotiation of marital relations. Women had set the rules of the community game in place-to-place relationships and borne the burden of community keeping. If person-to-person community means that it is every person for him/herself, then we might expect to see a gendered re-segregation of community (as in Elizabeth Bott's England, 1957) with the possibility that men's communities will be smaller than communities of networking-savvy women."[22]

Economic rationalisation of the family

Perhaps in the future Internet entrepreneurs will indeed live in capsules, especially if the capsules are piled up South of Market. Such South of Market capsules would remind us of Schumpeter's prediction that economic rationality will increasingly penetrate family relations and the home. Schumpeter[23] argued that the capitalistic system will die of its own success when the centre of capitalistic accumulation, the family home, becomes just a place to sleep. The transformation of home and family has been discussed by Carnoy.[24]

Person-to-person networks as role-to-role networks

Person-to-person networks are often based on specialised roles that people play in the network. As Wellman notes, this means that people must maintain differentiated portfolios of ties to obtain a variety of needed and

---

22 Ibid.
23 See Schumpeter 1975, p. 157
24 See Carnoy 2000

wanted resources. Such *role-to-role* networks, indeed, seem to be becoming increasingly important.[25]

Yet the emergence of individualised connectivity also reveals fundamental problems in our current conceptions of knowledge society. First, individualised connectivity, strictly speaking, is an oxymoron. Communication is interpersonal, and identity is constructed using social resources and expressed in social contexts. Theoretically, therefore, we need to develop concepts that enable us to talk about individuality as a social phenomenon. This leads, for example, to research on ecologies of different types of networks and communities. We do not know, for example, what strategies people apply in their everyday life to switch between the various networks, or, more generally, between communicative, cognitive, and material resources. This is important as it is possible that social inequality will in the future be closely related to an insufficient capability to switch between networks that provide complementary resources.[26] Indeed, one socially important question in the future may be where the loci of control of such "social switching" are and how people develop and lose the competencies required for network mobility during their life careers.

Second, role-to-role networks are closely associated with the organisation of production, and with the transformation to increasingly knowledge-intensive forms of economy. As Wellman notes, the value of individuals depends on their structural position in the network and their capability to link disjoint networks. On the other hand, as Brown and Duguid and Wenger[27] have emphasised, the competence and knowledge that is required for specific work tasks is often developed through socialisation in communities. The increasing importance of role-to-role networks is therefore closely linked with new forms of innovation-based competition and knowledge-based work. If access to work and competence-development opportunities require active management of role-to-role networks, maintaining the traditional household-based connectivity may, however, become difficult. In a simplified way, one might envision a world where the rapid growth in wireless communication is closely associated with a rapidly growing number of single-adult households. This, of course, would have important implications for many industrialised countries. It would be important to know whether such visions are actually realised.

Third, individualised connectivity may in important ways alter the public sphere of communication. Public discourse is obviously becoming increas-

What are the strategies used for switching between networks?

Network mobility vital for personal development

Management of role-to-role networks

---

25 See Nardi/Whittaker/Schwartz 2000

26 Software-related innovations and the "new economy" rely on a combinatory mode of innovation. When the combinatory mode becomes more important economically than specialisation, the competitive advantage of business firms increasingly depends on the capability to mobilise social networks.

27 See Brown/Duguid 2000; Wenger 1998

ingly location-independent, and many political themes are developed and discussed across national borders. It may be difficult to set common goals or argue different opinions if there is no shared domain where the various material and mental interests meet. Castells[28] has argued that a related transformation underlies the crisis in legitimacy of the old political institutions, as they increasingly link to transnational interests, losing their sources of legitimisation in the process. This problem may become particularly acute if political institutions and citizens link to different transnational or transpatial networks. An example here might be, once again, the social movements against the WTO and globalisation.

Fourth, one potential development prompted by the diffusion of technologies for role-to-role connectivity is that people with multiple role-to-role networks may become clustered in areas where such networks can be efficiently maintained. People flock to regions where they perceive rich selections of life opportunities, but they may also flock to places that act as spatial hubs in many relevant networks. One way to solve the "information overload" problem generated by multiple simultaneous role-to-role networks is to cluster around people who share similar portfolios of roles. If role-to-role networks are particularly important for work opportunities, this may also mean that economic differences could grow rapidly between different geographic regions. Silicon Valley and the City of London might be examples of such emergent social order. For example, if you are a high-tech entrepreneur, in Silicon Valley you may be able to physically locate yourself in a restaurant where most of the people you need to meet you will meet during one evening. Today, we know very little of the formation and dynamics of such "role clusters," or the ways ICT can be used to maintain or de-spatialise them.

Fifth, when role-to-role connectivity becomes ubiquitous, it becomes obvious that role-based networks are psychologically fragmented. Individuals connected through role-to-role networks need to use an increasing amount of their resources to maintain their identities. One could argue that much of the growth in the economy happens today in businesses that support identity management and construction. In their popular book, Pine and Gilmore[29] argued that we are moving towards an "experience economy." Perhaps a better term, however, would be "existential economy." Social network management, communication, and identity construction are key activities in such post-scarcity world. In such a world, people are not passive consumers, but they actively construct their social and psychological position using material and mental products. The term "existential" could be taken quite literally here. In a way, people are fighting for their life, trying to make a difference

28 See Castells 1997, p. 200
29 See Pine/Gilmore 1999

between "being nothing" and "being something." Communication technologies provide the opportunity to become interpersonally existent and thus they hit the core of this existential economy.

As there may be no spatially or culturally institutionalised "home bases" available for grounding one's identity in a role-to-role connected system, one has to actively reproduce one's self as a coherent identity. With the exception perhaps of the Queen of England and few others, roles are acquired and not inherited. In role-based networks the position is rarely defined by where one sits. Position, therefore, is not occupied but constantly produced. Without constant reproduction, positions are also easily lost. Paradoxically, this may mean that the importance of location increases, as people try to build coherent identities by grounding them on physical space. Alternatively, the grounding can also be based on one's body, which is more or less guaranteed to follow wherever one goes.

Communication technologies create and shape interpersonal existence

The increasing significance of space for a coherent identity

Towards a Sociological Theory of the Mobile Phone

Hans Geser

3.2.1
The Innovative Potential of Cell Phone Technology in an Evolutionary Perspective

Since its inception billions of years ago, the evolution of life on earth has been shaped by two highly consistent physical constraints:

1) *Physical proximity* was always a precondition for organisms to initiate and maintain interactive relations. On the human level, this is reflected in racial, ethnic-linguistic and many other differences along geographical lines – as well as in the high salience of face-to-face gatherings for the maintenance of social collectivities and institutions, and for the satisfaction of (physiological and psychological) individual needs.

2) *Stable dwelling places* were necessary for the development of more complex forms of communication and cooperation. Evidently, the increasing stability of settlement made possible by horticulture in the Neolithic period created favourable conditions for the emergence of more complex organisational structures and differentiated occupational roles, and the evolution of sedentary farming patterns in irrigated valleys (Egypt, Mesopotamia, India) was certainly a precondition for the emergence of higher-level civilisations.[1] In more recent times, the importance of tightly organised factories and densely populated urban areas for the emergence of industrialised societies has again demonstrated that the achievement of higher levels of societal complexity is still based on the physical proximity of many human individuals in very stable locations.

Rather than vanishing, the restraining effects of these physical factors seem to increase in the course of socio-cultural evolution, because they collide more and more with other outcomes of this same evolution: the increase

Physical proximity and stable dwelling places as physical constraints

---

1 See Lenski/Nolan/Lenski 1995; Coulborn 1959

of spatial mobility on the one hand and the rising capacities for communication on the other.

Thus, while the increase in population density has certainly facilitated primary interpersonal communications (by furthering spatial proximities), increments in locomotion have again reduced it, because whenever individuals are walking on streets, driving on roads, cruising on ships or flying in planes, their communicative capacities are sharply reduced.

Seen in this very broad evolutionary perspective, the significance of the mobile phone lies in empowering people to engage in communications which are at the same time free from the constraints of physical proximity and spatial immobility.

As it responds to such deeply ingrained and universal social needs, it is no surprise to see the mobile phone expanding worldwide at breathtaking speed.

One of its major impacts stems from its capacity to include mass populations in poor southern countries who are partly illiterate, who will never have the means to buy a computer, and who hitherto were not even connected to the traditional networks of landline phones.[2] A recent empirical study by the International Telecommunication Union provides striking evidence of how the cell phone has contributed to narrowing the century-old gap in telephone usage between highly developed and less developed countries. It shows that in 2001, about 100 nations (among them many African) had more mobile than landline phones in service, and that cell phone technology is far more potent than computer technology in connecting poorer populations to the sphere of digitalised information.[3]

There is wide agreement that handheld phone sets can substitute stationary PCs or mobile laptops to a considerable degree, because they are in the course of becoming multimedia devices able to transport voice, text messages, pictures, musical sound, software programmes and anything else coded in digital format.[4] More than that, these multimedia functionalities are combined with significantly reduced size, weight, energy needs and buying prices, as well as a much simpler, more user-friendly interface, which makes it possible for them to be used by smaller children, the illiterate, handicapped people and many other rather marginal population segments not able to come to terms with MS Office and W2K.

About 100 nations have more mobile than landline phones in service

---

2 See Townsend 2000

3 See World Telecommunication Development Report 2002

4 On the other hand, empirical studies show that email and phone are considered as media with completely different functions. Even intensive email contact does not lead to a reduction of aural communication. One reason is that voice contacts have more capacity to articulate personal emotions – which explains the high relevance of phone contacts with absent family members (Sawhney/Gomez 2000).

Nevertheless, while the *possession* of cell phones may become ubiquitous (so that their value as status symbols disappears), they may still accentuate social inequalities insofar as their *factual usage* patterns are tightly correlated with the various purposes of social actions, as well as with different situations, social relationships and social roles.

On the theoretical level, this situation calls for the development of highly elaborated analytical concepts and typologies suited to grasping the major differences in usage patterns, as well as the various symbolic meanings attributed to mobile phones sets, messages and users; on the methodological level, it implies the need for survey studies for assessing such variables empirically in quantitative as well as qualitative ways.

There is a need for the development of analytical concepts

As the empirical evidence hitherto gathered by systematic quantitative study is rather limited and of questionable relevance for the (even short-term) future, theory-building at the moment has to rely heavily on the much more numerous studies based on qualitative (e.g. ethnographic) methods, and even more on impressionistic essays which provide plausible hypotheses often anchored in suggestive anecdotal illustrations.

Nevertheless, a preliminary synthesis of this amorphous material seems fruitful in order to develop more generalised theoretical argumentations and hypotheses to be tested in future empirical research.

As in the case of other current technologies which widen rather than constrain the range of alternatives options, the cell phone cannot be seen primarily as a factor of causal determination, but rather as a tool providing a set of specific functional capacities which may be more, less or not at all exploited under various socio-cultural or psychological conditions.

Cell phone cannot be seen as a factor of causal determination

Thus, theory-building has to focus not primarily on "causal impacts" or "determinate consequences" of cell phone usage, but more generally on its "implications": i.e. its specific functional capacities to facilitate or inhibit various modes of social behaviour, interactions and relationships, and to create new environmental conditions under which conventional social systems have to operate.

In the following, a few of these implications on the subsequent levels are addressed:

1) On the individual as a self-guided actor

2) On inter-individual fields of interaction

3) On face-to-face gatherings

4) On groups and organisations

5) On inter-organisational systems and societal institutions

" Mobile phones extend the capacities of mental emigration
to real interpersonal communication. "

3.2.2
Individual Consequences

The emancipation from local settings

Long before the invention of mobile phones, books, radios, TV sets, VCRs, computers and other gadgets opened the way for individuals to free themselves functionally, as well as psychologically, from their immediate social surroundings, by empowering them to fulfil many needs without relating to anyone else in their vicinity.

Reading a book, for instance, implies that one is absorbed by thoughts and feelings normally not shared by other individuals currently present in the environment, thus reducing the capacity to relate to the others by living through common experiences or by finding common topics of discussion.

Consequently, such devices help people in urban settings to evade unwelcome interactions with surrounding strangers. Reading a newspaper, using a walkman with a headset and also engaging in telephone calls are all visible activities which can be used to communicate to bystanders: "I'm not currently available for any approach or talk."[5]

The special significance of the telephone has always been its function to extend these capacities for "mental emigration" to the sphere of real interpersonal communication, in contrast to books, radios or TV sets, which only open opportunities for receptive experiences inconsequential for "real social life." This functionality is especially crucial for individuals disposed to cultivating dense networks of social interaction systematically incongruent with their current spatial locations, e.g. adolescents in the course of cultivating social networks which transcend the family within which they have been born and raised.[6]

On a methodological level, it has to be concluded that the cell phone lowers the degree to which causal relationships between spatial allocation and social relationships can be expected. For instance, to see 3,000 scientists participating in a big congress may not tell us anything about the probability and prevalence of mutual interaction among them, because most of them may be absorbed by phone calls most of the time. Or observing five million people migrating to a huge city may not allow any conclusions about the likely emergence of any kind of "urban mentality" and "urban culture," when it is known that most of these new inhabitants remain firmly embedded in their

5 Haddon 2000; Cooper 2000
6 See Ling/Yttri 1999

original ethnic setting by daily phone contact with their relatives left behind in rural regions.

Opportunities for complexity avoidance and regressive social insulation

A main function of face-to-face gatherings is to expose oneself to making new acquaintances and to unforeseen social interaction. Cell phones can easily be used to shield oneself from such unpredictable contingencies by escaping into the narrower realm of highly familiar, predictable and self-controlled social relationships (with close kin or friends), so that the chances of making new acquaintances are reduced.[7]

Given their capacity to maintain primary social relationships over distance, the use of cell phones can well go along with regressive psychological tendencies, e.g. with the need to cushion the traumatic experiences in foreign environments by remaining tightly connected to one's loved ones at home. Thus, the mobile can function as a "pacifier for adults," which reduces feelings of loneliness and unprotectedness at any place and any time.[8] Another, similar metaphor conceptualises the cell phone as an "umbilical cord," making processes of social emancipation more gradual and less traumatic by allowing parents and children to retain a permanent channel of communication in times of spatial distance.[9] Such tendencies of social closure are additionally supported by the fact that in contrast to fixed phone numbers, which are usually publicised in phone books, cell phone numbers are usually only communicated to a narrow circle of self-chosen friends and acquaintances, so that no calls from unpredictable new sources have to be expected.

> Use of cell phone can go along with regressive psychological tendencies

Thus, when growing children increase their range of independent locomotion and increase their times of absence from home, the cell phone can help to cushion these emancipative processes by keeping children connected to their parents by a communicative link – however sporadically it may be used.[10]

As a consequence, individuals may well become less prone to develop certain "social competencies": e.g. to react adaptively to unpredictable encounters, to participate in conversations on unforeseen topics, to form a

> Individuals may well become less prone to develop certain "social competencies"

---

7 See Fortunati 2000
8 See Maira Kalman, the president of M&Co (a Manhattan product and graphic design group) in: Louis 1999
9 See Palen/Salzman/Youngs 2001
10 This is another illustration for the capacity of cell phones to transform dichotomous role switches into more gradual changes (the "greying of the social world").

quick impression and judgement about newly met people, or to learn quickly how to behave conformably in new collocal gatherings and groups.

> *"In reality, we are in a situation of communicative stalemate, as we continually lose the capacity for social negotiation."*[11]

They can catalyse the emergence of sub-cultural segregations

Considering the high potential of cell phones to support rather segregated, self-controlled social networks, it is not astonishing that they can catalyse the emergence of sub-cultural segregations. Contrary to the highly public fixed phone, which promoted the establishment of highly generalised linguistic forms (e.g. answering formats like "Hallo", "Pronto" etc.), the cell phone may well facilitate the emergence of linguistic habits peculiar to single families or friendship circles.

Role-integrative functions

In two highly different ways, cell phones help individuals to reduce role strains and role fragmentation, typically generated by highly complex social environments and societal conditions.

1) By increasing the capacity to accumulate and coordinate diverse (simultaneous) roles

According to Georg Simmel,[12] modern societies give rise to individuals who combine a multitude of different roles, and individualisation grows to the degree that each person realises his own idiosyncratic set of roles and his specific trajectory of role shifts over time. Insofar as each role demands one's physical presence at a specific place (workplace, private apartment, church, school, etc.), reconciling different roles usually implies sequencing role involvements diachronically and taking the burden of frequent and stressful locomotion. By providing the opportunity for swift role-switching without changing location, cell phones facilitate the harmonisation of different role duties, because diachronic role change can be substituted by (almost) synchronous role involvements.[13] Thus, women can engage in "remote mothering" when at work, or "remote work" when doing housework at home.[14]

Cell phones facilitate the harmonisation of different role duties

It is important to note that this capacity to play different roles simultaneously is paradoxically based on certain limitations of cell phone technology. First of all, the neat separation of local and remote role-playing is much facilitated when only the recipient (not the bystanders) can hear the voice

11 Fortunati 2000
12 See Simmel 1908, pp. 305
13 See Gillard 1996
14 See Rakow and Navarro 1993, p. 153

of the caller. And secondly, the capacity to perpetuate local offline roles would be seriously hampered if cell phone calls became multimedia events involving visual channels of communication as well.[15] Thus, insofar as such role-compatibilisation effects are the main rationale for cell phone adoption, it might be concluded that customer demands for broadband phone transmission are much lower than many optimistic telecommunication strategists (who invest large sums in UMTS) are currently assuming.

2) By increasing the capacity to maintain "pervasive roles" (which demand unlimited involvement)

Cell phones can be instrumentalised for preserving diffuse, pervasive roles which demand that the incumbent is available almost all the time, because such encompassing availability can be upheld even when individuals are highly mobile and involved in other social or private activities.

Thus, mothers can use mobile phones for perpetuating contact with their children even when they are at work or on travels, and traditional family doctors can be available to their patients whenever needed, even if they are at a dinner party or some other private location.

Staying in contact during absence

Similarly, managers can preserve a traditional patriarchal leadership role which demands their availability around the clock. They can thus inhibit processes of organisational differentiation by remaining remain themselves "on duty" all the time instead of delegating responsibility to subordinates.

The simultaneous increase of individual empowerment, personal responsibility and social controls

Many recently emerging technologies are "empowering" in the sense that they increase the range of alternative actions available to individuals or social groups. But in all cases, such gains in freedom and autonomy go along with countervailing increases in social responsibility and social control, because individuals face greater social expectations to make active use of these new options, and greater demands to legitimise and justify what they do or omit.

Thus, one significant downside of cell phones is that they expose individuals to additional attributions of personal responsibility, and thus increase the need for explanations, justifications and excuses of the sort: "*I wanted to call you, but I was not able to because I couldn't find a public phone.*"

---

15 See Ling 1997

> *"* The freedom of anytime anyplace connectivity is counteracted by the increasing duty of immediate answer. *"*

Such apologies are largely ruled out in the age of cellular phones, because calling nowadays is always a ready option – except in meetings, during flights or church services, or in other circumstances that rule out phone calls because of physical inhibitions or strict formal rules. In fact, "one higher order consequence of wireless communication is that it makes us more responsible, for both our own actions and those of people for whom we have assumed responsibility. In effect, we become more subject to social control."[16]

Thus, the freedoms gained by being able to connect to anybody from anywhere at any time are at least partially counteracted by the increasing duties to answer incoming calls and to "keep in touch" with kin and friends who expect to be contacted.[17]

3.2.3
Microsocial Consequences: Towards More Flexible Forms of Interpersonal Coordination

The deregulation of agendas

Continuous campfire sites established up to 500,000 years ago[18] testify to the capacity of emerging hominids to reach agreement about convening at the same place at a specific hour (or day). Such a capacity for planning the future is not known in subhuman species, because animals typically lack the conventional symbols for communicating about the future, as well as the concept of objective time.[19] Today, people typically manage written agendas where they note future dates, so that they know in advance when they have duties, when they have to travel and to what places, and when they are "really free." Thus, planning is crucial to organising personal life as well as to managing collective forms of behaviour, e.g. to preparing a meeting known to take place within two hours from now, or for cooking a meal knowing that exactly seven guests will appear at one's home at around 7 p.m. On the other hand, planning can be cumbersome because I have to submit rigidly to the fixed dates even if I have fixed them myself, and disappointments are inevitable when definite dates are missed because of traffic jams or other unpredictable events.

By looking at these handicaps, it becomes clear that under conventional technological conditions, preplanning was inevitable because people had no

16 Katz 1999, p. 17
17 See Bachen 2001
18 See for instance Mustafayev 1996
19 See Kummer 1971, passim

means of communicating at later points in time. Especially when participants were already on the move, no opportunities existed for changing dates. From this perspective, it is evident that cell phones reduce the need for temporal preplanning, insofar as rearrangements can be made at any moment, even very shortly before the agreed time. Thus, a new, more fluid culture of informal social interaction can emerge which is less based on ex-ante agreements, but more on current ad hoc coordination that allows people to adapt to unpredictable short-term changes in circumstances, opportunities, or subjective preferences and moods.

"With the use of mobile communication systems, one need not take an agreement to meet at a specific time and place as immutable. Rather, those meeting have the ability to adjust the agreement as the need arises. In addition, mobile communication systems allow for the redirection of transportation to meet the needs of social groups."[20]

Cell phones increase personal flexibility

When fully used within a social collectivity the cell phone effects a transformation of social systems from the "solid" state of rigid scheduling to a "liquid" state of permanently ongoing processes of dynamic coordination and renegotiations. Such social settings are "real-time systems" where everything happening is conditioned by *current* situations, while the impact of the past (effected through rules and schedules) and of the future (impinging in the form of planning activities) declines.[21]

In Sadie Plant's worldwide qualitative study, for instance, "some people said they often found themselves caught in what seemed to be eternal states of preparation, arrangement and rearrangement, with nights out characterized by endless deferrals and reshufflings of meetings and events which might never occur."[22] Consequently, hosts occupied with precooking party meals are well advised to focus on food that can be prepared (or enlarged in quantity) very quickly because they do not know exactly how many people will arrive or at what time. And many boring parties will face mass emigration by frustrated participants who have meanwhile checked by phone where something more exciting is going on....

As a result, it may prove more demanding to stabilise collocal social gatherings, because other alternatives are available to participants in case of dissatisfaction.

---

20 Ling/Yttri 1999
21 See Townsend 2000
22 Plant 2000, p. 64

*The evolutionary rise of "nomadic intimacy"
and "nomadic social participation"*

Compared with people walking the streets or riding on public buses, who are physically unprotected from intrusions by others, automobile drivers enjoy a kind of "ambulant privacy" by carrying with them a closed moving box which allows them to listen to personalised music or engage in private conversations with close family members riding in the same car. The cell phone can be seen as a device which amplifies this trend by empowering moving individuals to connect to distant partners at any point in time, regardless of location and speed. Thus, a "nomadic intimacy"[23] can be realised by empowering people on the move to remain embedded in their personal social networks.

First of all, higher communicative contacts *between moving and unmoving individuals (or social aggregates)* can be established. In the era of fixed phones, moving people could use public phones to connect with stationary individuals, but they themselves could not be contacted. Consequently, moving people were very isolated from new incoming information (e.g. about unforeseen developments or events) and could not participate in social actions which demanded very rapid communication (e.g. vertical communication between stable organisational centres and moving peripheral employees). By using cell phones and other devices of mobile translocal communications, there is a greater degree of freedom for combining stationary and moving cooperation units without losses in transmission speed and reaction time.

Secondly, higher communicative connectivity *among various moving actors* can be achieved. As a consequence, mobile phones can be expected to promote revolutionary changes in traffic systems, because they allow for more coordinative communication between moving vehicles.

"It was not until the rise of mobile telephony that transportation and communication were again linked together. Previous to this one who was in transit was also incommunicado. Now mobile telephony allows for nearly continuous and ubiquitous communication under transport. This barrier has fallen and those who are in motion or away from a known "fixed" terminal are also available telephonically."[24]

First, moving drivers can be called to redirect their vehicles to other places, thus adapting to quickly changing circumstances and needs. Consequently, taxi drivers in cities seem to reach their destination more efficiently. Secondly, the "softening of time schedules" becomes more tolerable, as a driver who is too late for a meeting can easily reassure the other participants that he is at least on the way, and may arrive only 10 minutes late. And

Moving people were isolated
from incoming information

---

23 Fortunati 2000
24 Ling/Yttri 1999

thirdly, there is more capacity to substitute rigid time scheduling altogether by processes of "gradual approaches," so that the time and place of gatherings are fixed only just before they occur.

"A third variation is the progressively exact arrangement of a meeting. Two parties might, for example, generally agree to meet somewhere at an approximate time. As the two are in transit they might call each other to confirm the timing and the location. Finally, if the two can not locate each other at the agreed upon place at the agreed upon time we can have a third round of calls for the final location of each other. Thus mobile communication allows for the structuring and rationalization of interaction, particularly in the face of distributed participants."[25]

It is also possible to keep the composition of participants open to change, e.g. by phoning around to additional individuals who may be ready to participate because they happen to be in the region.

On a most general level, it can be argued that the cell phone eliminates at least some of the advantages of sedentary life styles which are responsible for the constant decline of nomadism since the inception and expansion of higher human civilisation. In fact, modern mobile technologies may facilitate the emergence and social mobility of new segments of "high-tech nomads" (e.g. venture capitalists, global traders, business consultants, itinerant journalists, etc.), who feel sufficiently integrated into society without possessing fixed addresses and stationary resources.[26] Similarly, cell phones can reduce the marginality of many traditional ethnic groupings (like Bedouins, gypsies etc.) characterised by constant movement through geographical space.

Cell phone eliminates some of the favours of sedentary life-style

Such developments may also help equilibrate the communicative social integration of the two genders. The fixed phone undoubtedly privileged women – at least in all those social settings where females are still expected to stay at home while males are more likely to be on the move. Even in the United States, where most women have employment outside their home, this gender difference is still manifested in the statistical regularity showing that women use home phones about fifty percent more than men. The cell phone has weakened (or even reversed) this gender gap because the same statistics show that men make more extensive use of it than women.[27]

The fixed phone privileged women

---

25 Ibid.
26 See Garreau 2000
27 See "Men Talk More on Cellular Telephones, Survey Shows" (Reuters, 14 June 2001).

3.2.4
Mesosocial Consequences

*The decentralisation and bilateralisation
of intrasystemic communication*

As fixed telephones belong to specific locations rather than to specific individuals, they support depersonalised and collectivised communication structures, as found mainly in bureaucratic organisations as well as in many less formalised settings (e.g. dormitories or traditional family households).

Bureaucratic organisations in particular have become highly sophisticated in using landline phone systems for designing communication channels in accordance with their formal structure. For instance, traditional police communication is characterised by radial communication flows: itinerant policemen phoning in to a central radio dispatcher, who then automatically has an overview of what is going on. Nowadays, when all peripheral policemen can contact each other directly by cell phone, they can easily circumvent this centralised relay station, substituting it by direct horizontal communication and coordination. On the one hand, such short-circuiting is functional for abridging unproductive red tape and for accelerating the speed of reaction, but, on the other hand, it can challenge the structures and processes of formal organisation in three ways:

1. Communication channels are no longer predefined. Instead, they are chosen by the subordinate members themselves, so that management has no overview about who contacts whom, who is cooperating with whom....

2. Less information about peripheral events, activities and developments flows into the organisational centre: this means that superiors have less knowledge which would enable them to react and to intervene.

3. All these covert horizontal exchanges are potential breeding grounds for autonomous subgroups and informal organisation as well as for various kinds of deviant behaviour, because the participants can easily agree to circumvent certain prescribed rulings.[28]

"The specific effects of the mobile telephone are that it allows back channel communications between officers, between officers and other agencies and also between officers and various private individuals. Thus, it provides a back channel through which they can agree upon various irregular covert activities. This means that the mobile telephone can change the specific routines associated with police work. Where one relied on a central dispatcher

Communication channels are no longer predefined

---

28 See Manning 1996

to communicate messages to other agencies and organizations, the police officer is able to do this by himself. In some cases this may lead to more efficient work. On the other hand, there is a reduction in the pool of general knowledge provided by the traditional radio communication. This may mean that the information, and perhaps the activities of the agency are more disjointed."[29]

Similar changes occur in households where the singular fixed phone has become a supportive element of a collectivised communication structure with the function of mediating between incoming phone calls and individual recipients. Thus, the ethnographic study by Sawhney and Gomez of the communicative interaction pattern of recent immigrants to the USA has shown that wives acted as real "information hubs," by maintaining two-way relationships to all other family members.[30] By contrast, cell phones promote segregated bilateral relationships which usually cannot be overheard by third parties.

At this point, it seems rewarding to reflect on the "latent functions" of "unsuccessful calls" which do not reach the targeted person. Such unintended recipients may be a nuisance to callers who want to deliver their message directly to a specific person – especially when this message is highly confidential, or when others should not even know that the contact has taken place.

"Latent functions" of "unsuccessful calls"

In many other circumstances, however, unplanned recipients have a positive function:

Unplanned recipients have a positive function

a) they are accepted as "secondary partners" with whom an unplanned talk unfolds;

b) they can be used as go-betweens who will deliver the message to the targeted individual;

c) they are relevant third parties who can provide useful additional information and advice (for instance: "How is mother really doing, please, father, tell me the truth. . . ");

d) they can enlarge the bilateral phone call into a multilateral conversation, thus transforming it from a private talk to a community conversation.

By eliminating the "risk" of unintended answerers, cell phones reduce the degree to which experiences and social contacts are shared among family members. Specifically, we may find that each family member has many acquaintances and ongoing interactions unknown to the others.

---

29 Ling 2000b
30 See Sawhney / Gomez 2000

In Simmel's terms, the family is under increasing strain as it becomes a system characterised by "crossing circles" (*Kreuzung sozialer Kreise*): a social system which has to preserve its cohesion against especially powerful forces of centrifugal fragmentation stemming from the divergence of personalised communication spheres, which mirror the different motivations, needs, capabilities and preferences of its different members.

Given these strong bilateralising impacts, the conclusion seems unavoidable that mobile phones cannot be potent instruments for quick and large-scale social collectivisation – except under highly specific circumstances, when many group members assume the role of active propagators. Such conditions hold, for instance, in "pyramidal structures" in which every recipient acts as a multiplier.[31] Only when such broad, active participation is ensured can a snowball-effect take place which leads to a rapidly growing base of activated members or sympathisers. In addition, oral communication demands that messages are extremely simple, so that they do not get distorted in this process of multi-stage diffusion. With text-based messages like SMS, distortions are minimised because they can be reproduced and distributed in identical form. Thus, the chances of quick and extensive collective activation accrue to groups with a high absolute number of activists functioning as transmission relays in such network systems.[32]

Speeding up and intensifying system-environment interactions

Many institutions such as the police, fire departments, ambulance services, etc. are designed to be externally activated in emergencies that can happen anywhere, anytime and anyhow. Thus, their functionality depends critically on factors they cannot control: e.g. that there are external informants who call the service without delay and who provide the precise information necessary for deploying adequate resources. Cell phones can be extremely useful for interconnecting emergency agencies with their environment, because they increase the chances that somebody watching an emergency event has a phone and is disposed to make a call.[33] This implies that emergency services are (a) activated very quickly and (b) are often contacted by different callers, so that they are able to gather more precise information and ensure that they are not the victims of mere hoaxes.

Emergency services benefit from cell phones

Of course, the more ubiquitous cell phones become, the more important it is that certain "civic duties" are instilled in all citizens alike: e.g. the duty to know the emergency numbers by heart, to take time for such calls even

Civic duties need to be instilled in citizen

---

31 See Ling 2000b
32 See Ibid.
33 See Ling 1998

when in a hurry, and to provide well-elaborated information based on precise empirical observation (or on the testimony of other informants). Evidently, such civic duties are especially relevant in sparsely populated rural areas, where it is to be expected that I may be the only bystander able to call for help. This may at least partially explain the very high use of the cell phone in the Nordic countries (Finland, Norway, Sweden) with their extensive system of herding, fishing and agriculture.

Shrinking spheres of autonomous individual responsibility and individual decisions

Within organisations, much of the need for the delegation of responsibility and for taking individual decisions arises from lack of communication. For instance, when a service worker sent to a customer (or a social worker sent to a client) meets an unexpected or new kind of problem situation, he has to decide on the spot how to proceed, thus also carrying the responsibility for possible failures. Similarly, paramedics called to an emergency patient have to take measures on the spot, without consultation with a doctor.

In many cases, such delegation of autonomy leads to strain because these peripheral agents have rather low qualifications. This problem is vividly illustrated in the case of policemen who have to exercise very high discretion when confronted with cases of group violence, civil disobedience or public unrest, despite the fact that they occupy very inferior hierarchical positions.

Delegation of autonomy

For many organisations, this usually means that their ambulant members have to be equipped with detailed instructions and specific rules, so that they know exactly what to do in most (probable and improbable) circumstances. For instance, life insurance companies have to fix rigid conditions for contracts, so that their agents are not able to adapt the conditions to each specific customer. The cell phone can ease such discrepancies between low formal and high factual discretion by providing the inferior employees with a means to contact their superiors as well as colleagues or specialised experts in order to get information and advice, but, especially, to legitimise their decision by reaching consensus and mobilise support. This may be particularly functional for novices who are not yet very experienced. Even beginners with rather low knowledge can be sent to do peripheral service tasks because whenever an unfamiliar problem arises, they can contact more experienced collaborators who tell them what to do.

"Just in time" consultations
can substitute forms of
supervision and instruction

Such "just-in-time"-consultations can substitute traditional forms of supervision and instruction which usually rely on preplanned meetings and instructional courses.[34]

Given the constant availability of external communication partners (as sources of opinion and advice), individuals may easily unlearn to rely upon their own judgement, memory and reflection, thus regressing to a state of infantile dependency upon always the same narrow circle of "significant others" – even in cases where they are 10,000 miles away.

"In Chicago, a group of young intellectuals expressed the concern that such connectivity might even undermine people's self-reliance, making them unable to operate alone, and leaving them dependent on the mobile as a source of assistance and advice. Rarely stranded incommunicado, the person with a mobile is less exposed to the vagaries of chance, unlikely to be thrown onto resources of their own, or to encounter adventure, surprise, or the happiest of accidents. Some people interviewed in Tokyo felt that there was now less chance that time would be spent standing and staring at, for example, the cherry blossom, and more excuses to avoid being alone with one's thoughts and one's own inner resources."[35]

Facilitation of resource sharing and increase in transactional efficiency by decentralised processes of just-in-time coordination

All increases in communication capacities facilitate the efficient usage of resources. For instance, firms do not have to buy and store rarely-used raw materials or technologies (which may become obsolescent without being used) when they have the opportunity of procuring them "just-in-time" from other corporations in case of urgent need; two or three individuals are better able to share a single car when they can coordinate its usage by phone; and housewives can easily call their husbands to stop on their way home to buy some items in the store, so that extra trips can be spared.

"Just in time" adoptions to
unpredictable changes in
need

The cell phone is especially functional for making short-term just-in-time adaptations to unpredictable changes in needs. Generally, it facilitates processes of permanent allocation, so that given resources are more intensely and more productively used. Thus, the "metabolism rate" of markets, cities and other decentralised social systems will be increased.[36]

34 See Ling/Yttri 1999
35 Plant 2000, p. 62
36 See Townsend 2000

Of course, such functionalities can be better exploited by text-based SMS messages than by audio-calls, because SMS makes it possible to send identical messages simultaneously to a potentially unlimited number of receivers. In the future, this feature is very likely to be exploited for the purpose of influencing local and regional populations, e.g. by distributing information about sales outlets for cheap umbrellas in regions where it is currently raining, or inviting all the people in a city to participate in a specific public demonstration.

Locally oriented political campaigns may become more vigorous because parties use cell phone systems to target electoral propaganda at the populations of precincts or counties; local churches may inform neighbourhoods about their services; and regional drugstores, hospitals, schools or welfare institutions may provide the relevant public with information (e.g. about new services, prices, changes in opening hours etc.).

Thus, SMS may become a major tool for creating or reinforcing social integration on a territorial basis, e.g. providing information about or reinforcing solidarity with local or regional institutions.

Similarly, large festivals with different simultaneous stage productions can be organised in a more flexible fashion because visitors can be notified very rapidly when new performances are going to start in specific places.[37] For highly mobile individuals unacquainted with the environment in which they are currently located, such SMS services are especially useful for finding out where the nearest pizzeria, dentist, police station or flower shop is located. For them, the cell phone is another "urban navigational tool" substituting or complementing street maps, city guides, public information offices, etc.[38]

By lowering the costs of acquiring information even in highly complex urban environments, individuals are better able to make efficient use of everything a big city has to offer, so that the attractiveness and competitiveness of big cities (and the sprawling agglomerations surrounding them) may be considerably increased. Through such chains of causality, the cell phone may well contribute to a vigorous increase in urban concentration.[39]

SMS may become a mayor tool for social integration

37 See Nilsson et al. 2001
38 See Townsend 2000
39 See Ibid.

3.2.5
Macrosocial Consequences

The deregulation of intersystemic boundary controls and
the shift from location-based to person-based social systems

By building factories, churches, opera houses, schools or psychiatric institutions and by organising congresses or meetings, social systems with rather stable and neatly defined boundaries are created, because these boundaries are anchored in physical space. Especially under traditional conditions where primary no-tech communications prevail, such anchoring has the double function of:

a) providing accessibility for the participants of the social system;

b) setting clearly marked boundaries between the system and its environment.

The linkage between architecture and social institutions is a primary basis for social power

According to Foucault, this linkage between architecture and social institutions is a primary basis of social power, because by constructing buildings and designing physical technologies, societal elites have powerful media at hand for implementing their (class-specific) values and norms.[40]

Usually, the power to define and maintain system boundaries accrues to the elites who found and manage these organisations and arrangements, e.g. by controlling gates so that only members have access to the buildings or gatherings, or so that employees do not leave their workplace at any self-chosen time. In the course of societal evolution, such processes of "authoritative segregation" have been crucial, because by insulating social systems from their general social environment, the preconditions have been created for subjecting them to processes of systematic (e.g. technological and organisational) development and specialisation.

Thus, modern economic systems are heavily based on industrial organisations that have separated work processes from their traditional embedment in family households or other (e.g. religious) institutional affiliations, and modern medicine would be unthinkable without the hospital where patients are spatially concentrated for systematic diagnosis and treatment. Conventional theories of modernisation usually give much weight to such achievements of interinstitutional segregation, like the physical segregation of workplace and family households as well as the separation between private and public spheres.[41]

---

40 See Foucault 1984
41 Among many other examples, consult Parsons & Smelser 1956

By articulating differences in location, fixed landline phones have even contributed to more pronounced segregation between different social spheres. For example, the widespread traditional habit of juxtaposing private numbers and office numbers (e.g. on personal cards) has certainly reinforced the structural segregation between work and family, e.g. by facilitating the establishment of different normative expectations about when (and for what purposes) the one or the other of these phone lines should be used.[42]

Evidently, fixed phones are adapted to a society primarily structured in terms of stable location-based social systems, like households, offices and firms. They are most functional when the purpose is to reach such locational units, irrespective of the people who are present there at that moment. This premise is certainly fulfilled in the case of stable families inhabiting the same apartment, or among employees of the same firm.[43] However, the use of place-specific communication technologies is rather dysfunctional when the individuals inhabiting the same place have quite loose connections or no relationships at all (e.g. in the case of student dormitories where phones are located on each floor, or in hospital rooms where several patients are sharing the same phone). In such cases, cell phones are more useful, because they help to reach specific individuals directly, thus circumventing any need for intermediary messengers located at the same place.[44]

> Fixed phones are adapted to stable location based social systems

This functionality is particularly crucial in the case of divorced parents, providing the absent father with the potential to reach his kids directly, without interference from the divorced mother.[45] A similar emancipative effect is found in the case of prostitutes, for whom cell phones open the way for individual arrangements with their customers, thus promoting their independence from hierarchical controls and organised exploitation.[46]

Seen in a more generalised perspective, various electronic means of communication have the capacity to undermine such segregation by increasing the permeability between hitherto strictly separated contexts of social life.

> Electronic means of communication can undermine segregations

At many workplaces, for instance, PC users are free to switch back and forth between private and professional computer usage at any moment of time, and work may extend into private life when office calls are received during evenings, weekends or vacations. Under such new circumstances, centralised institutional control of system boundaries is more difficult to maintain, because it is no longer achieved as a simple correlate of physical

---

42 See Laurier 2000

43 As a consequence, traditional white-collar workers working permanently in the same offices at the same desks show a rather low need for mobile communication (Palen/Salzman/Youngs 2001).

44 See Wellman 2001

45 See Ling/Helmersen 2000

46 See Plant 2000, p. 59

walls or spatial distances but has to be actively upheld by constant controlling procedures (e.g. by preventing employees from using PCs and mobile phones for private purposes).

Control of formal institutions is weakened

Cell phones tend to weaken the control of all formal institutions over their members' behaviour, because they open up the opportunity for all members to reduce or interrupt their formal role involvements by engaging in alternative role behaviour and completely private interactions anywhere and anytime, e.g. during office hours, school lessons or military duties, and when driving a car or piloting a plane.

Thus, schools come under pressure to allow kids to use cell phones, because their parents are eager to keep in touch at any time whenever needed.[47] While in the past communicative isolation during school hours was easy to maintain because technology made external calls difficult anyway, such isolation now has to be actively produced and legitimated by providing convincing reasons, by exercising authority and by implementing (potentially disputed) measures of social control. While audio calls may readily be repressed because they can be easily observed, it is much harder to prevent kids from receiving SMS messages during school hours.[48] In fact, Norwegian researchers have reached the conclusion that cell phone technology "has become part of the classroom context."[49]

Institutions lacking sufficient authority and controls will easily be destabilised by such waves of role diversion and informalisation, so that their members can no longer be assumed to be focusing their full attention on formal role duties during the whole time of their physical presence in the institution. On the other hand, institutions may draw on inputs from members not currently on duty, e.g. by reaching them during evening hours, at weekends or on vacation. This implies that it will be less and less viable to measure individual work inputs by simply verifying the time of physical presence; rather, companies must ensure that employees do not use working time for private online activities and personal calls.

In a very general way, cell phones introduce an element of entropy into all socio-locational orders, because they permeate them with communicative relationships that transcend system boundaries in highly heterogeneous and unpredictable ways. Thus, the cell phone "can connect a theatre-goer to anyone at all: an employer, a reporter, a dental office administrator, or a fellow club member, among many others."[50]

---

47 See Mathews 2001
48 See Ling 2000a
49 Ling 2000
50 See Agre 2001

In other words, locational systems are eroding under the intrusion of many uncoordinated "person-based systems": mostly bilateral, microsocial relationships, which produce "chaos" mainly because they occur independently of each other and are opaque insofar as they cannot be observed (or even controlled) by any centralised agency.[51]

Mostly bilateral, microsocial relationships

Of course, family homes, churches or school buildings will continue to symbolise the unity of families, parishes or schools as organisations and institutions, but they will lose much determinative influence on what is "really going on" on the level of social communication and cooperation. In particular, their physical immovability can no longer be taken as a valid indicator of stability on the level of institutional norms or social practices. In fact, they may become "empty shells," losing their cultural meaning, as old memorials of forgotten "great men" in public parks do.

As a consequence, the highly salient question arises: how can the stability of social institutions become guaranteed when it can no longer be anchored on the secure basis of physical structures? It seems evident that the vanishing impact of hardware factors has to be substituted by much softer media which allow for more fluid definitions and redefinitions of social resources, status distinctions, cooperation practices and normative structures.

It is reasonable to assume that these developments will have an increasing impact on future architectural designs. First of all, architecture will become freed from many institutional constraints, so that buildings can be designed to satisfy non-institutional (e.g. aesthetic or psychological) values and needs. Secondly, rooms will have to be designed to meet the needs of cell phone users (e.g. by creating many small niches where individuals can phone undisturbed). Thirdly, architects will have to provide for individual activities related to other roles and institutions (e.g. for work activities in private apartments). In short: "Physical places and things will become more plastic, and thus more capable of playing roles in a wide variety of institutionally organized activities."[52] And fourthly, buildings as well as settlements and whole urban structures will increasingly be designed to fulfil those "residual functions" which still demand spatial proximity and technically unmediated primary communication.

Physical places will become more plastic

"As a result, world cities such as New York increasingly consist of financial people, together with those support services, such as restaurants and cultural activities that still require physical proximity."[53]

To summarise, the mobile phone empowers individuals to decide on their own about the modalities of segregation or permeability between different

51 See Ibid.
52 Ibid.
53 Ibid.

institutional settings, social systems, interindividual relationships and individual roles. As a consequence, such boundaries are likely to become much more fluid, modifiable and unpredictable than in the past and, especially, much more a matter of intentional decisions, which risk being controversial (and therefore have to be justified and legitimated) among the different individual actors.

Borders between institutional spheres change

Analytically, the borders between institutional spheres (e.g. work and home) are likely to change in three ways by becoming (1) *more permeable*, insofar as components of one sphere can more easily enter the other; (2) *more flexible* to the degree that the extension of different spheres can be varied according to current situations and needs; and (3) *more interpenetrating* (or "*blending*"), insofar as role activities may expand and belong to different domains at the same time.[54]

Of course, it might be hypothesised that such an "anomic" state of individualism is a transitory phenomenon, characteristic of these first stages of "cell phone society," in which transindividual (or institutional) norms for phone usage have not yet been established. But we might equally well assume that such "normlessness" is likely to perpetuate itself in the future, because each individual is eager to preserve autonomy in managing his or her own idiosyncratic set of roles.

3.2.6
Some Preliminary Conclusions

The most general function of cell phones is to lessen the degree to which social relationships and social systems are anchored in space, and they increase the degree to which they are anchored in particular persons.

From the point of view of individual users, the cell phone provides opportunities:

1) to enlarge the number of potential communication partners available at any specific place and moment;

2) to distance oneself from current collocal interaction fields by directing attention to remote partners;

3) to expand the peripheral layers of social relationships by cultivating weak ties to partners one is not ready to meet;

---

54 See Geisler et al. 2001

4) to shield oneself from new and unpredictable contacts by signalling un-availability and by maintaining more frequent interaction with familiar partners (e.g. friends and kin);

5) to maintain contact with any other individuals (or organisations) irrespective of movement and changing spatial locations;

Maintain contact with any individual

6) to combine divergent roles which would otherwise necessitate one's presence at different places at the same time;

7) to switch rapidly between highly different (and usually segregated) roles and situational contexts, so that there is more discretion as to how they should be separated or combined;

8) to take over "boundary roles" in any social system, e.g. in order to get information about the external environment or to participate in processes of external interaction and adaptation;

Take over "boundary roles"

9) to fill empty waiting periods with vicarious remote interactions;

10) to reduce the reliance on one's own inner judgment by asking others for advice;

11) to occupy highly diffuse roles which demand involvement at any hour of the day (e.g. care-giving functions etc.), or "standby" roles which demand permanent readiness (e.g. in emergencies);

12) to live more "spontaneously," without strictly scheduled agendas, because meeting hours can easily be rearranged.

"Live more spontaneously"

From the point of view of *social systems* the cell phone has the capacity

1) to decrease the positive impact of spatial proximity on social interaction and integration;

2) to decrease the negative impact of spatial mobility on social interaction and integration;

3) to increase the functional viability of very small groups and single individuals, because they have increased opportunities to mobilise additional resources from outside actors, or to include additional remote members on an ad hoc basis when needed;

4) to ease the penetration of bilateral interpersonal microsystems into multilateral groupings, formalised social collectivities, as well as public spheres;

5) to increase the capacity of organisations to fully integrate spatially remote and moving subunits and to relate to customers whose location is changing and not known;

Functional capacity of organisations on the move increases

6) to increase the functional capacity of collectivities and organisations on the move, e.g. military or police units, ambulances, refugee groups, etc.;

7) to privilege collectivities constituted on the basis of particular members rather than particular places or territories (e.g. families and ethnic groupings rather than cities, parishes or schools);

8) to encourage emphasis on highly segregated bilateral relationships – while larger multilateral allegiances are losing ground;

9) to facilitate swiftly constituted, ad hoc gatherings with highly variable composition, so that social system structures can be flexibly adapted to rapidly changing situational conditions;

10) to lessen the need for central "communication hubs" within groups and organisations because each member can directly receive (and send out) his/her own calls;

11) to minimise the "spillover" from communications to unintended third parties because messages can be precisely targeted at intended individual receivers;

12) to increase intersystemic permeabilities, blendings and interpenetrations, while lowering the capacities to keep such contacts under centralised and regularised control.

Undermining of traditional mechanisms

In a very general way, mobile phones undermine traditional mechanisms that have secured the segregation of social system levels from the level of individual members, as well as the segregation between different social systems. Instead each individual now is burdened with the task of maintaining a difference between personal behaviour and social roles, and with regulating the boundaries between different social relationships, groupings, organisations or institutions.

The demand for social control will rise

Therefore, the demand for social control will rise because, in a world where social differentiations can no longer be based on spatial segregation, they have to be increasingly secured by controlling individual behaviour.

Such control can be realised in three forms:

1) *intraindividual self-controls*: e.g. in the case of users avoiding or shortening incoming calls in order to concentrate on ongoing collocal interactions;

2) *informal interindividual group controls*: e.g. in the case of collocal partners showing impatience when cell phone calls go on for longer than expected;

3) *formal institutional controls*: e.g. in the form of regulations prohibiting cell phone calls during school or working hours. For instance, the institutional differentiation between school and family is no longer guaranteed by physically segregated school buildings and closed classroom doors, but by actively preventing pupils from receiving and answering mobile phone calls and SMS during the courses.

Will the mobile phone change society?

On the one hand, it will certainly spread explosively because it fulfils so many needs which have remained unfulfilled, not only during the most recent periods of human history, but during the whole of biological evolution.

On the other hand, its functionality to complement or even substitute traditional no-tech communications will be limited by the basic fact that this same evolution has created deeply anchored needs for basing social interaction on spatial proximity at stable locations (e.g. physiological needs to have sex with "zero-distance" partners, or psychological needs to socialise with others at informal face-to-face gatherings).

Thirdly, it has to be borne in mind that mobile phones are only capable of supporting highly decentralised network-like interactions, especially on the simple level of bilateral communications. Thus, older space-dependent interactions are still essential for supporting multilateral interaction fields, as well as more tightly integrated collectivities like communities and organisations.

Finally, the formulation of determinative causal propositions (or even precise forecasts) is severely hampered by the fact that, in sharp contrast to industrial machinery, cell phones (like personal computers, PDAs, etc.) belong to the class of empowering technologies that are likely to amplify (instead of to reduce) psychological, social and cultural divergences, because of their capacity to be used for different purposes in any sphere of life.

This versatility has the implication that mere hardware possession is not a very informative indicator, because it does not tell us anything about the extent and the ways these instruments are in fact used. Instead, much extensive and sophisticated research is necessary in order to assess how they are actually used, how they affect various kinds of social relationships, and how they become embedded in the evermore complex sphere of all other communication media.

Will the cellular phone change society?

Of course, these indeterminacies increase to the degree that cellular phones assimilate more and more different functions, e.g. the capacity to send alphanumeric messages, to hook up to the WWW or to use the GPS for determining geographical locations. Another implication is that as individuals have a broader range of behavioural options at hand, the impact of psychological, social and cultural factors on such behaviour is likely to be increased.[55] In other words, while behaviour in low-tech environments is predominantly shaped by "hard" physical factors (e.g. apartment walls, loudness of voice, spatial proximities and distances, physical means of transportation), behaviour in high-tech settings will be more determined by "soft" factors like subjective preferences and motivations, informal or formalised role expectations, cultural customs and habits or purely functional needs.

---

55 See Davied et al. 1999

Chapter 3.3

Mobile Europe: Balancing
a Fast-changing Society
and Europe's Socio-economic Objectives

Martin Weber and Jean-Claude Burgelman

The IST revolution (revolution in Information Society Technologies) is emerging as a new paradigm (the "e"-paradigm) that is about to transform our patterns of living, working and producing,[1] even if there may be differences between sectors in terms of the magnitude and timing of this transformation. Production systems are becoming more flexible, globalised and real-time; patterns of work are increasingly shaped by the use of computers; digital devices are entering all layers of society; and the emergence of "ambient intelligence" or "ubiquitous computing" is about to change our daily lives fundamentally.[2] The speed of change is regarded by many as unprecedented in the history of mankind.

3.3.1
The E-Paradigm as a Key Driver of Change

But not only does the e-paradigm have a technological dimension (mobile communications, the Internet and pervasive computing), it also has its origin in developments that are social (e.g. mosaic society), economic (e.g. electronic business, the e-conomy) and political (e.g. enlargement, regionalism).

Dimensions of the e-paradigm

Especially in the European context, the pressure for change is further augmented by other drivers such as the enlargement of the EU, the process of economic integration, demographic transformations and migration. Some of these forces are an expression of political will others reflect wider social and economic developments.[3]

1 We prefer the term Information Society Technologies to Information and Communication Technologies, as it marks a more citizen-centred approach to technology.
2 See IPTS, Futures Report Series 03.
3 See in more detail www.futures.jrc.es

Social objectives versus
economic opportunities

In view of these fundamental ongoing transformations, Europe faces at least two major challenges. First of all, the e-paradigm could put in question several of the societal goals, values and principles that Europe stands for. On the other hand, it promises tremendous economic and social opportunities, but the balance between opportunities and risks still depends on actions to be taken now and in the near future. For example, social cohesion could be affected by the widespread uptake – or lack of uptake, as the digital divide suggests – of IST. Indeed, these technologies offer opportunities for better connecting less favoured regions to the main economic centres in Europe, and IST and related service activities offer potential "economies of scope" that favour their clustering around the main existing centres. Similarly, major European cities are increasingly integrated in the global business networks, but at the same time the gap between their centres and their peripheries is tending to grow. There is also little doubt that we are moving away from the traditional 9-to-5 society, towards a 24-hour society, at least in the major cities. This brings many advantages, e.g. in terms of access to services around the clock, but it also challenges the institutions and frameworks needed to run a stable working and family life.

Europeanisation as a
challenge to institutional
boundaries

The second major challenge that these drivers bring about concerns many of the traditional spatial and institutional boundaries framing economic and social life. This affects especially the political and legal frameworks, and the organisation of (public) services, which still tend to be defined at national or regional level. The level at which framing actions need to take place is shifting increasingly either to the European and global level, or to the local level. Both globalisation and localisation are facilitated and enabled in many ways by IST. While the efforts to build a European or global institutional framework to match the global and European scale of many of the drivers of social and economic change are confronted with many concerns, there is a desire, as expressed in the Commission's position on modern governance, to bring decision-making closer to the grassroots level.[4] The role of flexible markets in dealing with the challenges of the new economy is also emphasised. In any case, a growing divergence becomes apparent between the emerging requirements of the new economic and social space on the one hand, and the existing institutional and policy context on the other.

Mobile Europe as a guiding
framework for future
developments

The key future task for Europe is thus how to reconcile the new techno-economic paradigm on the one hand with the main European values and policy goals on the other. To achieve this, new organisational and institutional principles of governance will be required. What is needed is a guiding framework that helps policy make the necessary choices to steer future developments in a desirable direction.

---

4 See Prodi 2000

The notion of a "Mobile Europe" is suggested as a basis for formulating a roadmap that helps to reconcile these forces for change with the characteristics and goals of the growing European Union and its society. It stands for a European approach that is able to exploit the potential benefits of the e-paradigm in an open market under the current circumstances of fast change, but at the same time respects Europe's societal values.

Mobility, as used here, has a wider scope than just the two fields of transport and labour to which the term has traditionally been applied. It covers a wide range of areas of social and economic concern. Obviously, infrastructure systems such as transport or telecommunications have an important role to play, as have mobile labour markets. But also less obvious areas can be captured by the concept of Mobile Europe: social security systems that need to enable the easy transfer of social rights; research systems that favour the exchange and mobility of qualified researchers as well as the creation of European research networks; flexible production systems and public services; and a culture of tolerance that is open to change. Finally, perhaps the most important element to be considered is the ways of life of Europe's citizens, especially in the major cities, where the pace of change is fastest.

Mobility – from infrastructures to systems of social security and research

A Mobile Europe thus represents a new, emerging way of living, working and producing in Europe that acknowledges the challenge of the e-paradigm (in terms of speed and flexibility) and reconciles it with the main principles and goals of European society (i.e. social cohesion, welfare and cultural diversity). From that perspective, a Mobile Europe is subject to the principles of modern and good governance that the EU has set out for itself: accountability, visibility, transparency, coherence and effectiveness.

3.3.2
Governing Mobile Europe:
What Requirements must be met?

Such a mobile society raises a number of new requirements that need to be met in the future. These requirements not only apply to social and economic life, but equally to governance in Europe. The abovementioned principles of accountability, visibility, transparency, coherence and effectiveness can indeed be interpreted as elements of governance that are compatible with a Mobile Europe. More specifically, the new requirements can be summarised by the following five principles:

Five principles for a Mobile Europe

– *Accessibility of networks.* Mobility means that every citizen, worker or consumer, wherever he/she is from, should be able to tap into the physical or non-physical networks he/she needs for working and living. This should be achieved at the lowest possible social and financial cost, considering both skills and price elements. This argument can be applied to information networks like the Internet, but also to energy or seamless transport networks. A Mobile Europe therefore guarantees maximum access to the networks of Europe, so as to allow maximum participation by its citizens.

– *Compatibility and feasibility of transfers.* While accessibility is a one-way interaction, the possibility to exchange work, immaterial goods and communication between regions and countries requires the compatibility of the units of exchange. Products need to meet certain specifications, e.g. for safety or environmental reasons, and services need to guarantee predefined quality standards to be widely accepted. Most obviously, electronic exchange needs to rely on a set of well-defined standards to work at all. But also social rights should be compatible irrespective of the initial location of their bearer. A Mobile Europe therefore fosters compatibility between the different networks and applications of Europe, so as to allow seamless operability.

– *Tradability and economic exchange.* Once economic value is assigned to the exchange of goods and services, a Mobile Europe needs to guarantee that these exchanges can be performed smoothly, and under conditions of equal opportunities for working and doing business from wherever in Europe. A Mobile Europe therefore requires the lowering of the thresholds for e-commerce as much as possible, regardless of the nature or the location of the business, so as to create a thriving and "universal" e-market.

Respect for regional
structures

– *Cohesiveness and coherence with culture.* A Mobile Europe can only work if the compatibility of patterns of working, living and producing with local and regional cultures is respected. Imposing an e-logic alien to the diversity of local cultures in Europe would most likely not be sustainable. On the contrary, it would create protest and social tension, as expressed, for example, in the recent movements against globalisation. A Mobile Europe therefore needs to operate bottom up, by exploiting the diversity of its cultures rather than imposing a unified approach.

Policies to promote flexibility

– *Adjustability and ability to adapt.* The ability to react flexibly to changing circumstances will become a key feature of successful regions, cities and individuals. A mobile Europe should therefore develop the rights, tools and policies to stimulate innovation-mindedness at every level.

Meeting these five requirements will be essential to keeping Europe globally competitive in the new networked e-conomy, but they also reflect Europe's social goals. There are different possible ways of addressing the challenge of coping with and shaping the emerging e-paradigm. Technology, and especially ICT, may be very much at the origin of the e-paradigm and of the risks it brings about, but technology also has a great potential to help address these risks. It can help to create the innovations that are necessary for realising the social and policy goals.

3.3.3
Realising a Mobile Europe on Different Levels

The challenge of realising a Mobile Europe can be tackled on three different levels. While the trans-European networks initiative looked at the transport, energy and telecommunications problems in Europe mainly from the point of view of *infrastructure*, mobility, as understood here, also addresses two additional dimensions: the *legal and institutional contextual conditions* and the actual *patterns of living, working and producing*. All three together (infrastructure, contextual conditions, and patterns of living, working and producing) constitute a Mobile Europe, and in all three dimensions there are still many problems to be solved in order to meet the requirements of a Mobile Europe, though with major differences from area to area.

Three dimensions of a Mobile Europe

Regarding the first level, the *creation of flexible infrastructures* is one of the overarching issues for guaranteeing not only accessibility, but also equal access for the entire population. In both transport and telecommunications, the infrastructure part is quite well developed or continuously improving, though most of the highways of Europe seem to have reached their saturation point. Not only are there capacity bottlenecks (as in air traffic), but also the physical limits to handling traffic seem to have been reached. The increasing traffic jams, virtually permanent delays, etc. in most European countries speak for themselves here. In IST, the issue of accessibility is more one of a deficit in the skills that are required to ensure equal access than in the network itself. Due to competition, Europe is getting wired at a very fast pace, and a potential digital divide is therefore more likely due to the lack of net literacy. A typical problem of infrastructures used to be their inflexibility. Once established, they are hard to change. Here too, newly emerging IST infrastructures and devices (e.g. mobile telephony, personal digital assistants, etc.) and applications in the field of ambient intelligence offer new solutions.

Open access to infrastructures

Enhancing mobile ways of living, working and producing is the second level on which the issue of a Mobile Europe needs to be addressed. As we move from a 9-to-5 industrial logic towards a 24-hour economy and society, global production systems remain in operation all day long, based on the shift of key data from Europe to America, and then further on to Asia. A contradiction is emerging between on the one hand the way of organising working and living we inherited from industrial society and on the other the needs for a 24-hour competitive society.

In particular within the enlarged Europe, the creation of such integrated and coordinated production systems is likely to become a crucial issue for competitiveness.

The 24-hour society still lacks social support systems

The way life in cities has changed is perhaps the most striking example of mobility and its implications. The major cities have turned into the hubs of the global production system, and operate around the clock. Shops

Expansion of the EU offers potential for synergies

Implementation of the Single Market programme

E-business as support for enterprise networks

Mobile Production and Distribution Systems in Europe

One of the economic opportunities for Europe in the coming years will be to exploit the potential synergies between the economies of the pre-accession countries and the EU15. One of the ways to achieve this is through highly integrated production systems that are coordinated by means of advanced IST and logistics technology.

For such systems to operate smoothly, excellent *infrastructures* for both high-speed telecommunications and for the physical transportation of goods and intermediate products are required. The *legal frameworks* to make this coordinated production operate smoothly are about to be addressed by the implementation of the Single Market programme, both within the EU15 and in the pre-accession countries. This involves recognition of standards and norms, environmental regulations, etc. The actual *setting up* and *operation of such highly integrated production systems* is first of all a task for the private sector, even if similarly advanced forms of networking are likely to become imperative for public administrations too in the future. The automotive industry has been at the forefront of integrated production across Europe. In fact, research and development is increasingly carried out in cooperation between different sites, with each of them drawing on its specific strengths and competencies. Hungary, for example, has not only attracted major production sites for key components, but has also turned into an important location where automotive R&D is carried out.

In many cases, the co-operation in such networks no longer operates within a single company, but is outsourced to a multitude of firms that are interconnected by means of e-business portals. The recent initiatives of car manufacturers to set up B2B portals for dealing with their suppliers are just the latest element of a longer-term strategy of reorganising business relationships. Again, this applies not only for standard operations, but also for certain R&D tasks that are carried out jointly with first-tier suppliers or entirely outsourced to contract research organisations.

Similarly, relationships with the final customers are changing. Products and services are increasingly available on the web, even if the potential to sell complex products and services online is assessed rather cautiously. Moreover, the influence of the final customer on the design and definition of the final result is changing rapidly. Customisation is increasingly required by the end-user, implying either local presence strategies (e.g. in car manufacturing or in many services) or an excellent customer service through the Internet (the Dell model). For Europe to gain a competitive advantage from enlargement, it will be necessary to introduce such practices on a large and broad scale.

---

and supermarkets are open 24 hours a day. What is striking is that the social support systems that have stabilised the industrial logic of producing, working and living have not yet developed new modes of supporting a 24-hour society. The main deficits in this respect are to be looked for in areas such as childcare, education and access to public services.

Other areas where we are still far from achieving a Mobile Europe are the labour markets. Not only are there language and cultural barriers to labour mobility, but also the social security systems (e.g. transfer of pension rights,

---

Living and Working in a Post-Industrial Society
After World War II, a number of global shifts occurred in the way life was organised in Western Europe. First, labour distanced itself completely from the private and entered the public domain, where it was organised according to standardised and usually highly formal procedures (nine-to-five, etc.). Freelance and wage work at home, living next to the factory, and so on, became things of the past. Thanks to the rise of the unions, collectively negotiated labour agreements, etc., labour and related activities became completely part of the public domain. Moreover, the twentieth century's increased mobility rendered any link between the place where one works and the place where one lives obsolete.

It is precisely the return of labour into the private domain that is made possible by new technologies. The appeal of teleworking, for example, can be partially explained by the need to render labour more personal. But in the meantime the private sphere has also changed. Many tasks from the private domain – like education and training – have become public. This was not least due to the growth of female labour participation, which was a result of the need for a greater labour force in the fifties as well as of a change in female identity in the course of the rise of feminism.

In short, two trends are dominant in post-World-War-II Europe.

– First, the transformation from an industrial organisation of work to a post-industrial organisation of work and hence the demands for change in its related institutions (labour unions, schooling system, and so on).

– Second, the transformation from the "extended family" type of living to a more individual type.

The convergence of both trends, the individualisation of living and working, is underpinning what is being called the "mosaic" way of living and constitutes the nucleus for the problems of the future.

Indeed, the outcome of the shifts in the organisation of work was a very sequential and differentiated way of organising time. Working, living, learning, etc. were clearly separated in a logical, well limited (9-to-5), sequential order – school, student, learning, work, kids, etc. The continuing pressure on the organisation of work, stemming from the 24-hour economy, requires the permanent availability and flexibility of services, labour force, etc. The big conflict in this field is therefore to be expected in the friction between the industrial way of organising life and the demands of the "informational," service-based way of working and living.

Teleworking, or the return of labour to the private domain

"Mosaic" way of life as nucleus of the problems of the future

health insurance) are very inflexible. The research systems in the European member states are a good example of institutional barriers to mobility as well. In many countries, universities are effectively closed to foreign candidates, underlining the urgency of the recent EU initiative regarding the creation of a European Research Area.

The third level on which a Mobile Europe needs to be addressed is that of the *legal, institutional and contextual conditions* that govern economic and social life. The aforementioned issue of the transferability of pension rights or of unemployment benefits is a problem of legal frameworks. The barriers to accessing the educational systems are institutional in nature and are only beginning to be broken down at university level. At lower levels of education, however, large barriers still exist. But mobility also applies to the fact that our organisation of education should be adapted in terms of time. Nowadays, school starts in many countries at 9 a.m. and finishes at 4 p.m. In a 24-hour e-conomy, work is no longer organised along these time lines, and therefore a rethinking of the educational, childcare and work system is inevitably on the agenda.

In other areas, such as electronic commerce, standards are crucial for uptake to be achieved. The Single Market regulations, based on the principle of mutual recognition, show how national regulation standards and the need for a free flow of goods on the European market could be reconciled within an overarching framework.

3.3.4
Anticipating and Preparing a Mobile Europe: A Key Task for Policy

The overall challenge outlined is of a magnitude that will require a major joint European effort if it is to be met. In fact, the creation of a Mobile Europe could be understood as the next step, after the creation of the Single Market and the Monetary Union, towards building a competitive Europe and maintaining a high quality of life.

Mobile Europe refers to two sets of ambitions. On the one hand, it refers to the need for people, capital, goods and services to move freely and seamlessly in Europe in order to respond to the economic, social and technological challenges that a unified market, enlargement and a globalised world impose on the EU. On the other hand, a Mobile Europe also refers to the distinctive ambitions of European societies to maintain their identities and qualities of life. A Mobile Europe, therefore, is a Europe-specific paradigm for creating a more attractive location to produce, but also a better place to live and work in.

Mobility calls for adaptation on the part of the legal and institutional framework

Freedom of movement and a frictionless flow of goods and capital

In order to develop a strategy for moving towards a Mobile Europe, two important preparatory steps should be taken as soon as possible. First, we need a better diagnosis and analysis of what areas are likely to be most affected by the new paradigm, and secondly we need a debate about how Europe wants to look and how it does not want to look in the future (i.e. a debate about a future vision for the era of the e-paradigm).

Regarding the first point, we need to deepen the research into and understanding of mobility requirements and how a Mobile Europe could be achieved. There are a number of candidate areas that seem to be particularly affected by the changes described. There is a need for a better understanding of the changes, opportunities and risks emerging. Due to their Europe-wide relevance, they would lend themselves to deeper consideration in future European research activities:

An analysis of areas affected

- *Transport and mobility visions for an enlarged Europe*, which would have to look beyond the construction of new infrastructures, but aim to explore new forms of e-mobility and organisational solutions to satisfy mobility needs with less transport. This would encompass the development of critical paths and policies to achieve a decoupling of transport and economic growth by a wider use of IST-based solutions.

The need for European research projects

- *B2B-commerce and its impact on production structures*, which should focus on changes in the structure of production systems, but also look at the critical role of payment systems and web-based interfaces to enable and facilitate the introduction of new production and distribution systems in Europe.

- *Community services in the health sector*, which would look at one of the service areas that entails a very high and growing cost to society. The focus should be on the impact of new distance services and medical data exchange on economic efficiency and patterns of organisation in the health sectors in Europe. There is a potential for improving the efficiency of the health sector by networking specialised health centres by means of IST. Making the health sector more mobile would also imply strengthening such patterns of cooperation (but also of competition), which at the moment are still underdeveloped, across national borders.

- *Mobile media services and patterns of living in future cities*, which would look at the transformation of space and time in and around cities, as well as between cities and their hinterland. New "good" practices concerning how life and work are organised and facilitated by local policies need to be continuously monitored and exchanged, as does collaboration in global city networks.

– *Open labour markets in Europe and cross-border communities*, i.e. the barriers to an effective single labour market, and the means to overcome them. For example, the lack of mobility of social protection across national borders has been identified as a critical impediment to mobility.[5] But this research issue also links up with the current debates on future education systems and the creation of European cross-border research networks.

Competing visions of a Mobile Europe

Regarding the second point, we need to shape a mobile society that is compatible with Europe's values and goals. For the moment, it does not seem to be very clear what Europe wants to look like in ten or twenty years' time. At least there seem to be competing visions.[6] A wider societal dialogue about the objectives of a Mobile Europe project would thus be important, similar to the intense debates seen during the preparation of the Single Market and Monetary Union projects. This would even be a requirement in terms of the principles of governance for which a Mobile Europe stands.

Bridging the gap between science and technology and socio-economic issues

As part of this debate, research policy will have to make sure that the implications, consequences and mechanisms underlying Europe's move towards a mobile society are better understood in order to inform decision-makers about the options and risks involved, and the orienting choices possible. This could possibly already be taken into account in the Sixth Framework Programme, with Mobile Europe being a model issue that bridges the gap between traditional S&T issues and socio-economic concerns. Moreover, the European Research Area initiative seems to be very much in line with the notion of a Mobile Europe.

---

5 See the new Social Policy Agenda until 2005, adopted by the Commission on 28th June 2000.

6 Bertrand/Michalski/Pench 1999

Chapter 3.4

The Myth of the Digital Divide

Valerie Frissen

After an initially somewhat one-sided emphasis on the technological and economic dimensions of the information revolution, the *social* implications of ICT developments have in recent years become more central in discussions about the information society. The fact is that obtaining an integral vision of the information society requires us to make a certain effort to examine the social imbedding of ICT and the potential social consequences of ICT developments. This stronger accent on social questions has also highlighted the importance of gaining an insight into the *user* side of ICT. Conquering the user is in fact the "last frontier" on the path towards an information society, a path on which economic interests – disguised as social questions – certainly play a far from unimportant role.[1]

ICT and its social consequences

To me, information is all about openness, accessibility, connectivity, networking, democratisation, decentralization, and as a result social transformation. Information is power; at times people don't like to share it. Information is not about telecom, telephones and communications. It is about empowering people.

Information gives people power

Sam Pitroda (2001)[2]

---

1 Good examples of this are the participation of the Media Plaza corporate platform in an action to stimulate electronic voting or the *Mission Statement* of The Internet Society: "To assure the open development, evolution and use of the Internet for the benefit of all people throughout the world." See www.mediaplaza.nl and www.isoc.nl

2 Pitroda, Sam (2001): Telecommunication and development in India: Speech to the Alcatel Foundation, Berlin, November 7th 2001.

> **❝ A whiff of political correctness hangs over the dichotomy discussion. ❞**

Social dichotomy and exclusion

A prominent place in the debate on the social implications of ICT developments is taken by the topic of "social dichotomy and exclusion." A whiff of political correctness hangs over the dichotomy discussion. Visibly, no party interested in ensuring its place in the forward march of the nations can escape, sooner or later, the need to pay lip service to the importance of avoiding the menacing dichotomy between information "haves" and "have-nots."

"Digibetism"

Having made the necessary obeisance, one quickly moves on to the other items on the agenda. A number of things stand out here. First of all, there is no disputing that there is indeed a very real threat of a dichotomy. Worst still, this dichotomy is not just a new form of social inequality ("digibetism"), but rather reinforces existing social inequalities in society by manifesting itself to the detriment of those groups which already only too often get the short end of the stick: persons on low incomes, the unemployed, older persons, women, foreigners, in short the well-known social victim groups. Noticeable also is that this discussion continues to turn in a circle without anything much happening, without structural solutions being suggested or developed, quite apart from any well-intentioned experiments. Now and then, yes, we discuss new forms of universal access or philosophise about an ICT basic package for every citizen,[3] but in practice we scarcely find any policy that is directed at realising equal access for everyone. With a pinch of ill will one could even demonstrate that, in those social areas, like education, where access to good ICT provision is an absolute must, policy is so poor that the ICT infrastructure approaches that of a developing country. What does appear to have had an unexpected but significant impact on the accessibility of information provision are recent market developments, such as the sudden very strong growth in the number of mobile telephones and Internet connections among Dutch consumers or the stiff competition between those offering free Internet access.[4]

Unexpected market developments

In short, whilst public discussion on ICT accessibility remains at the stage of fretting and a certain paternalistic head-shaking, market developments are again making this discussion hopelessly outdated. The penetration rates for mobile telephones, the Internet and personal computers have now reached a high general level in Europe. According to Bert Mulder, adviser to the Second Chamber of Dutch Parliament on ICT developments, the average Dutch citizen himself invests more in advanced ICT equipment than the average company, not to mention the government.[5] Inequalities in access to ICT appear to be disappearing on their own.

---

3 See Van Dijk 1998

4 These observations refer to developments in the Netherlands.

5 In a column in the newsletter of the Instituut voor Publiek en Politiek (www.publiek-politiek.nl/nmbb/5/inhoudi.htm).

The question that is central to this article is not, however, whether the discussion about dichotomy and exclusion is still on the agenda, but whether it is being carried out from the right *starting points*. ICT developments and the resulting virtual world need also to reflect the basic democratic values in society – such as freedom of information, equality of opportunity to take part in society, and the provision of high-quality information in a variety of media formats. In this sense a discussion on ICT access for citizens is a very relevant issue and obviously a public task. In order to be able to fulfil this task, it is meaningful, however, to take a closer look at a number of assumptions that underlie the discussion about dichotomy and exclusion/inclusion.

The right starting points for the discussion?

1998 saw the publication in the Netherlands of the book "From Forum to Supermarket? Citizens and consumers in the information society." The book established that, even today, little detailed policy-relevant information exists on users in their role as consumers and citizens, even though there is certainly no shortage of normative assumptions about consumers. A frequently heard position, for example, is that the blessings of the information revolution will not automatically accrue to everyone, and that socially weaker citizens in particular are in danger of becoming the pariahs of the modern information society. Their lack of financial resources, knowledge, skills or "cultural capital" is said to prevent them from plucking the fruits of ICT developments, so reinforcing their disadvantage and existing forms of inequality. This can produce a divide between information-poor and information-rich, with the threat, in a certain sense, of a new form of social injustice. In a society in which ever greater importance is being accorded to information and communication and thus to ICT, the social participation of these groups comes under pressure, thereby in essence endangering democracy.

Assumptions about the origins of the digital divide

How far are these assumptions supported by actual knowledge of what is happening among ICT (non)users? To answer this we need not only data on the number of Internet connections or on PC ownership, but above everything else answers to questions like: what factors determine acceptance or non-acceptance of innovations among users? What do specific user groups actually do with ICT in their daily lives, and why do they do it? How do users react to the unlimited possibilities that ICT offers them according to the generally bloated rhetoric of technological discourse? This means asking questions like: is it legitimate to interpret information "poverty" more or less self-evidently in terms of *social injustice*? Can information poverty also represent a conscious user choice or the expression of a certain diversity in the use of ICT? What do differences in the handling of ICT signify for *social participation*?

"Information poverty" – a free choice or social injustice?

The debate on dichotomy in the information society is in fact full of assumptions about specific (non-)user groups on the one hand and social participation and citizenship on the other. In this discussion I shall be subjecting these two types of assumption to critical analysis. This article will therefore:

– analyse assumptions about potentially *excluded groups* in the information society and about the *use* (and non-use) of ICT and related factors;

– analyse assumptions about citizens' *social and political participation* and the significance of ICT for this.

3.4.1
The Divide between Information Haves and Have-nots

Drowning in the digital delta

Clear differences can be established between citizens when it comes, for example, to the ownership of hardware, the number of Internet connections, or access to networks. The report "Drowning in the Digital Delta" from 1999, based on various research data, observes that foreigners, older people, the less educated, lower income groups, unemployed persons and women (in particular single women and single-parent families) do indeed trail behind on the electronic highway. The front runners are young people, the highly educated, those in work, high income groups and families with children. Leaving aside minor differences, this picture is confirmed in various investigations. Looking for explanations for these differences, the report concludes that, apart from personal features such as gender, level of education and ethnic background, this inferiority can be explained by financial, practical, psychological and social elements. The differences established in access between users are interpreted in this study, and in general also in other discussions, with little further reflection, as a *divide*. Here we are talking not only about *differences* but also about *inequality* of access, with an implicit, but unmistakable normative colouring being given to the empirical facts. This calls for some further analysis and remarks.

Analytic differences and normative inequalities

"Divide" as a static concept, the diffusion of the Internet as a dynamic process

First of all, a number of remarks about the assumed victims: The term "divide" suggests that the observed differences are static in nature. In fact, sufficient empirical indications exist that this is not the case. Certain groups of citizens are, it is true, not in the vanguard, but they are quickly catching up, as is occurring with women and senior citizens. History also shows us that "early adopters" of innovations are always young, white, male and well educated, and that other user groups are reached in the course of time, with only a very small portion being "left behind." This is referred to as the S-curve for the diffusion of technological innovations.[6] The recent development of the market is showing that we are right now at a turning point in this curve,

6 See Rogers 1996

marked in general by the attainment of a "critical mass." This curve means – at least according to Rogers – that the large majority of users will finally be reached. If not, we cannot speak of successful innovation.

This S-curve, which suggests that these differences in access are part of a natural, ongoing process, does not mean that this development is therefore without its problems. The one-sided composition of the early adopter category points to a more fundamental problem, the problem that in the design and development phase of innovation a one-sided user image is being used with all design and marketing strategies directed initially in an economic-technological direction. This means that exclusion begins at a very early stage, and is more or less part and parcel of technological development itself. In most discussions about dichotomy, the development process of technology itself remains untouched, and the problem is seen to lie unilaterally with victims, who are required to make a "catching-up effort." That this generally works only when the market is substantially expanding and that account has to be taken of a wider diversity of consumer needs, is self-evident. Attempts in the past to get socially fragile groups in front of computers have thus also, unfortunately, proved unsuccessful because their starting point was unsound. People should not have to adapt to technology, but technology to people.

Based on this thought, policy that wishes to prevent exclusions will have to direct itself more at *culture policy* objectives, that is, stimulating and protecting diversity and pluriformity of design and use, rather than new forms of universal access. Universal service provision as a policy issue is no longer relevant. We may also reasonably assume that this access is regulated via the market. In the longer term we shall probably see not only free Internet access, but also free decoders and perhaps even PCs, in the same way that we see free mobile phone sets for mobile phone subscribers. On the market it is no longer a question of selling items of equipment or network connections, but of what people will be doing with this technology. In short, "content is the message." Policy will also have to be increasingly directed at this.

A second comment relating to figures on "victims" is the large variations in ICT ownership and access within these categories of purported victims, variations which we are in danger of missing in these quantitative generalisations. Although this is to a certain extent an unavoidable problem of this type of – in itself valuable – research, it is nonetheless good to maintain a certain caution, since socially weak groups are repeatedly in danger of being stigmatised in this way. Information about what people in socially disadvantaged groups do with ICT may well provide starting points as interesting for policy as a one-sided focus on those who do nothing with it. Seniorweb and Webgrrls[7] are well-known and good examples of this, as is the intensive use

Marketing strategies directed at early adopters

Market expansion by taking account of a broader range of consumer needs

Not hardware but functionality is decisive

Heterogeneity of "victims"

---

7 www.seniorweb.nl, www.webgrrls.nl

of Internet by young people from the Antilles and Surinam.[8] More detailed information about those people who are *not* connected or have nothing to do with ICT may well provide surprising insights: in essence we still know very little about the reasons for "exclusion." In many cases it is assumed, just like that, that this is due to structural factors, such as a lack of financial resources, knowledge or skills. A number of comments can also be made about these assumptions.

Good reasons for non-use

Research in this area is often based on a circular argument. Because certain groups, such as the less well educated, older people, the unemployed and low income groups are less frequently connected, the explanation for this is sought more or less self-evidently in a lack of knowledge or experience with computers or in a lack of financial resources. In very few cases have these groups been closely questioned about their reasons for being without computers or Internet connections. The fact is that non-users often have very good reasons for this. More about this later. According to Breemen and Terstroot,[9] the following factors influence the adoption and use of computers and Internet:

Six factors determining
acceptance and use of
Internet

1. *Financial factors:* this relates to the ability to pay for new media and the Internet. Higher-income individuals/households more often own ICT equipment such as computers, modems and Internet connections and also replace them more frequently and acquire more expensive and newer products.

2. *Knowledge and skills:* the skills required in order to use computers and computer applications break down into the ability to read and write ("literacy"), the ability to use quantitative information ("numeracy"), and skill in and knowledge of the use of ICT, including earlier experience of and acquaintance with new technology ("informacy"). Education/training is an important indicator for knowledge and skills. The lower people's education/training, the less their ICT ownership and access.

3. *Psychological factors:* fear and "stage-fright" about using computers. Stage-fright can arise because people think that computers are difficult to use or because of negative first experiences. This seems to apply in particular to older persons and, to a lesser extent, to women. They often continue to see technology as something outside their daily lives.

This is connected to the following two reasons, which concern more the qualities of the ICT itself that can explain this non-usage:

8 See Bureau Veldkamp 1998
9 See van Breemen/Terstroot 1999

4. *Perceived usefulness/functionality of ICT:* users need to have the feeling that a new medium represents a certain added value, usefulness or function in their daily lives. An experience of lack of functionality can be found, for example, more often among older people who have not actively grown up with computers: they can feel that computers and related skills are not (no longer) necessary for their purposes in life.

5. *User-friendliness:* one important, but undervalued reason for the non-acceptance or non-use of ICT remains the lack of user-friendliness. One factor for older people, for example, is that ICT takes insufficient account of hand-eye coordination among older people, of the problems of people with poor sight, and of the longer period of practice that they need.

6. *Social factors:* social networks of friends, colleagues or family play an important role in awakening awareness in the computer area, in providing the necessary knowledge and skills in using computers, and in calling for help in the case of problems, etc.[10]

This list of possible explanations underlines the fact that differences in ICT access can be ascribed to a whole series of factors, with the *position* of (non-)users playing a role, and where the *qualities of ICT* can be a major threshold factor. Most discussions about dichotomy fail to start from such a series of related factors, reducing various dimensions of difference to a crude and simple divide between the information-poor and the information-rich. Qualitative research into ICT acceptance and use in daily life also shows not only that non-users often have good reasons for shying away from ICT, but also that people outside the "excluded" category are under little pressure to adopt these technological innovations.[11] There follow a few more specific comments based on this type of research.

Multidimensionality of differences

Reconstructing acceptance processes shows that people weigh up different factors and that the *costs of ICT* are decisive only when the added value of ICT is seen as very limited. This is healthy, critical consumer behaviour. Moreover, it is not per se true that lower income groups spend little money on communication facilities: comparatively speaking, a relatively large portion of a household budget can be spent on ICT, albeit in certain cases on a games computer, broadband TV or a satellite dish rather than on a multi-media PC.

Distribution of the ICT budget

– Older people are often in fact particularly interested in new developments such as Internet, but feel that "they are not for them," because ICT marketing is directed exclusively at fast-moving young people,[12] or at the

---

10 See ibid.
11 See, among others, Silverstone/Hirsch 1992; Silverstone/Haddon 1996; Silverstone-/Hartmann 1996-1998; Frissen 1998; Haddon 1998
12 See NPOE 1998/1999; Weijers/van Rijsselt 1998

Focusing on the surprising,
amusing, trivial and everyday
possibilities of ICT

Pragmatic use in the case of
women

Availability of time is an
essential factor in use

technologically experienced, and is not presented as a collection of new services that can be of interest precisely to older people. Their resistance or stage-fright is directed in these cases not so much against the innovations as such, but against the language in which this innovation is couched and with which it gains social significance. Exclusion in such cases is much more a *cultural* than a cognitive question (of knowledge and skills) or a financial question. Trailers on the digital highway would probably be better served by making them acquainted, in a manner tailored to their situation, with the surprising, amusing, trivial and everyday possibilities of ICT than by providing them with deadly serious catching-up and refresher courses under the banner of "lifelong learning."

– Research also shows that an interpretation in terms of *lagging behind,* for example in the way women react to ICT, has its problems. Gender differences certainly appear to exist in patterns of use: women generally tend to be pretty functional and pragmatic in their use of ICT (and therefore to use it less) and also more often take a repudiatory attitude towards ICT. Many women are less interested in endless playing with computers or surfing on the Net, which is seen rather as a waste of time or associated with unhealthy nerd-like behaviour, which they wish not to be associated with. This results in certain cultural values and norms about masculinity and femininity being "embedded" in the technology, notions that also bring with them a certain degree of inclusion and exclusion. This again points to the need for more *culture policy* concepts in ICT policy, which can stimulate a certain diversity of "content" and use.

– One factor which until now has been entirely absent from the discussion about dichotomy is that of *time*. The qualitative research mentioned earlier clearly shows time availability to be a major factor in ICT (non-)acceptance and use.[13] For certain types of households (double-earners with children, "urban professionals," etc.), time is becoming an increasingly scarce commodity. In this light one is not surprised, for example, at the conclusion of IT trend studies by KPMG on status and development in the field of information and communication technology.[14] These show that people between 30 and 55 are seriously lacking in knowledge about the possibilities of ICT. The under-30s group scores "reasonably well" to "well" when it comes to ICT knowledge and the 55+ group "reasonably well" (sic!). Cause for concern is precisely the knowledge of the group in between, even though these people are in good social positions and traditionally are expected to embrace things new. Research shows also that people who have extensive experience with and knowledge of ICT in the framework of their work often make limited use of the possibilities that

13 See, for example, Silverstone 1998; Frissen 1999a; Frissen/Punie 1998
14 See KPMG 1999

ICT offers them, among other things owing to a lack of time, or because of the feeling that the innovations demand too much time, even of them (sic!).[15]

– Finally, on the basis of qualitative research into the acceptance and use of ICT we can conclude that users are not only to a large extent *conservative* (it is those ICTs which can adapt to the processes and routines of daily life that are successful), but also *irrational* besides: emotions, lifestyles, everyday trivia and apparently pointless rituals are often more decisive for acceptance than the functional properties of ICT.

Users show "irrational" acceptance behaviour

The above-mentioned "alternative" research results show clearly that discussion of the accessibility of the information society requires more insight into complex and differentiated user practices before one can even start to identify the relevant social problems.

In this way we can conclude that there are certainly differences in access to ICT, but that these differences do not necessarily justify all kinds of conclusions about exclusion and dichotomy. Discussions about dichotomy are not, in essence, so much about differences in access *per se*, but about something else, i.e. the question: *access to what?* This brings me to a number of fundamental comments of another sort. Why are differences in ICT ownership or access such a serious *social* problem at all? The implicit assumption is that people who are excluded from ICT are also poorly informed and therefore unable to participate as full citizens in a democratic society.

Many conclusions about exclusion and dichotomy are not justified

3.4.2
ICT and Social Participation

The dichotomy discussion suggests in essence a self-evident link between ICT access and social participation. We are threatened with a serious social problem, the more so because information poverty affects the socially weak, whose involvement in society is none too large (so one assumes). ICT reinforces the existing dichotomy between those with ample opportunities and those with few, adding a new dimension: a divide between the information-poor and information-rich. Information, or knowledge, is here seen as the path to social participation. The question that we can ask here is whether these connections are so easy to make.

Questioning the implicit assumption that information access equals social participation

In the discussion about social dichotomy, worried noises about people's weakened involvement in society are the order of the day. Citizens' purported low social participation gnaws at the roots of democracy. Symptomatic of

15 See Frissen 1998

this are a growing individualisation and fragmentation of interests, a lack of social cohesion, and a lack of political interest, as expressed, for example, in low turnouts in elections, etc. However, in the "Social and Cultural Report" of 1998, a comprehensive study of social and cultural life in the Netherlands, which is at the same time an overview of 25 years of social change, we hear very different noises. A chapter in this report is devoted to participation. Starting from a broad definition of social participation as the involvement of citizens in voluntary social relationships, also included under the denominator of "civil society" or "the social midfield," the SCR comes to the conclusion that participation has never been higher in the Netherlands than in the past 25 years. We find a clear trend precisely towards "active citizenship," expressed for example in increased affinity with extra-parliamentary forms of action, "cheque-book activism"[16] and a blossoming of the social midfield. One comment here is that voluntary work is growing less, a fact that the SCR ascribes to the lack of time amongst "that part of the nation that is better equipped for political and social action."[17] This again focuses attention on the "time" factor as a possible explanation for differences in participation, as well as indicating that low social participation is not only specific to disadvantaged groups (quite the contrary). We also observe that the nature of the commitment has become more fleeting, with a greater concentration on informal associations, with a strong trend toward "single issues" and less emphasis on direct meeting. These new socio-political connections are often loosely organised and are easily combined with membership of other social organisations, making participants' involvement more fragmentary and non-committal. The SCR concludes that there is no question of a steep fall in social and political participation in the past decades. Such a conclusion is only justified, to a certain extent, when it comes to political behaviour in the narrow sense of the term, such a voting behaviour and activity in political parties. On the contrary, citizenship and social commitment appear to have received new impulses, and many new faces.

This links into what Giddens defines as a shift from "emancipatory politics" to "life politics."[18] People's political and social involvement in "late-modern" society takes the form not so much of membership of large political emancipation movements, but of involvement in moral issues and social associations that are directed strongly at self-fulfilment in emancipated social conditions and at "single issues" of major relevance in everyday life. Here the question is not so much that of fighting for equality between citizens, but much more the desire to give expression to diversity and pluriformity.

Socio-political engagement becomes more fragmented, but does not diminish

"Life politics" in the late-modern era is oriented towards self-fulfilment

16 SCR 1998, p. 772
17 Ibid., p. 771
18 See Giddens 1991

> *"* Attempts to use technology to inhale new life into traditional democracy point to an optimism that is pitiful in its desperation. *"*

"(...) because of the 'openness' of social life today, the plural-isation of contexts of action and the diversity of 'authorities,' life style choice is increasingly important in the constitution of self iden-tity and daily activity. (...) It becomes more and more apparent that life-style choices (...) raise moral issues which cannot be sim-ply pushed to one side. (...) Life politics – concerned with hu-man self-actualisation, both on the level of the individual and col-lectively – emerges from the shadow which 'emancipatory' politics has cast." [19]

The SCR's findings justify the conclusion that the assumed lack of social involvement and participation by citizens, which plays such a prominent role in discussions of dichotomy, is in fact largely unfounded. The question that we then have to ask is about the relationship between ICT use and social participation. Here we must note first of all that establishing a self-evident effect of ICT use on social participation is somewhat problematic. Until now, for example, we have no empirical indication that non-connection to the Internet leads to people being seriously ill-informed or to citizens being marginalised in terms of social involvement and participation. Such assumptions testify to a severe over-rating of ICT and of its social significance at the present moment. Nor can the Internet or other ICT formats be expected to be able to substantially influence social problems such as social inequalities or political disinterest, which are the outcome of all kinds of complex social processes. In this respect, attempts to use technology to inhale new life into traditional democracy, for example in the form of electronic discussion platforms or chats with those in power, point to an optimism that is pitiful in its desperation.

No direct connection between social participation and the Internet

Although we must not overestimate the social significance of ICT at the present time, this significance will certainly increase. ICT will gradually play a more important role in all kinds of social processes and will to a certain degree also become a reality per se, in which democratic values such as equality, diversity and quality, tolerance and the like will remain important, but probably also take other forms. The shape of future ICT developments will reflect society at that time with all its positive and less positive sides. Starting, for example, from the current blossoming of social participation, as described by the SCR, we can already observe that the Internet fits well into this pattern: Internet is one of those new platforms where the individualised commitment that marks late-modern society is taking shape.

For example, the *network character* of Internet both implies and sup-ports new forms of connectedness, community-forming and cultural iden-tity, based, for example, on shared interests.[20] This is reinforced by the fact

The changing relationship between information suppliers and users

---

19 Ibid., pp. 5
20 See Jones 1995; 1997

Role swapping

Dealing with intimacy and
anonymity

New patterns of inclusion
and exclusion

Internet's power of
mobilisation

that *time and space* form less of a barrier to connection with other people than before. Another contributory feature is that Internet appears to break through traditional hierarchical relationships, making possible *a different relationship between information suppliers and users.* Increasing user choice, coupled with limited time availability, make it more and more difficult for suppliers or governments to create an "audience" or "market." At the same time, the technology makes it easier for users to supply and disseminate information themselves, turning upside down the traditional division of roles between transmitter and receiver. In terms of participation, this reversal of roles can support and stimulate new forms of citizenship and participation, as the SCR observes. Already, new cultural practices, forms of expression and relationships are developing on the Internet, pointing to other forms of social participation. "Internet language" reflects another way of handling formal relationships and intimacy/anonymity, which would appear to facilitate entering into and being involved in new associations. At the same time, however, we can also observe new patterns of inclusion and exclusion on the Internet, for example in the behavioural codes and "netiquette" which streamline participation based on "new" normative frameworks.[21] And finally, we are witnessing the development of more and more *hybrid* information and communication platforms, in which the traditional dividing lines between amusement and serious information, debate and personal discussion, image and text and between social issues and personal interests are becoming less sharply drawn.[22]

As more and more people make use of these platforms, ICT will also increasingly reflect the capricious and unpredictable manifestations of real life. One example of how ICT can be used to support and give form to political and social participation can be seen in the pupil strike organised over the Internet in the Netherlands. In this case the Internet made it possible to mobilise fellow-militants very rapidly and create an issue with a strong political impact. An even better example – because it shows that social participation, in part due to ICT, can more easily take shape in grass-roots mode outside the existing legal order and can develop into a very particular and uncomfortable reality – is that of the paedophile "neighbourhood watch." This platform uses Internet, among other things, in order to keep paedophiles out of local neighbourhoods. Nothing human is foreign to the Internet.

---

21 See Frissen 1999b
22 See Frissen 1998

3.4.3
Conclusion

In this discussion, two types of assumptions controlling the discussion about exclusion and dichotomy in the information society have been subjected to closer analysis: assumptions about the users and non-users of ICT on the one hand, and assumptions about the relationship between ICT and social participation on the other. When it comes to the divide between the information-poor and information-rich that is purportedly in danger of arising as a result of differences in ICT access, this analysis and alternative data about ICT acceptance and use can raise a number of questions. We have shown the discussion about access and exclusion to be in fact based on incorrect starting points. In terms of policy implications this signifies that the discussion has, until now, not gone much further than a few ideas about new forms of universal access, and can now be regarded as having been overtaken by market developments.

The discussion about access has been overtaken by developments

In essence the dichotomy discussion involves something more fundamental, i.e. ICT as access to the *information and communication* deemed necessary in order to be able to take part as fully-fledged citizens in a democratic society. The more implicit idea here is that ICT represents a means of solving the "democratic deficit." This "deficit," as read from decreasing political-social participation by citizens and the exclusion from information, is seen as potentially further reinforcing this process. Given that it is precisely the "socially weak" who have less access to ICT, it is precisely the involvement of these already marginal groups whose involvement in society will be impaired. The present article again places question marks in front of these assumptions. An initial criticism is that the somewhat limited definition of citizen participation used as a starting point fails to take account of a number of social changes in later-modern or post-modern society which have given a totally different outward form to participation. Starting from a broad definition of participation as used by the SCR, what we see is precisely a huge blossoming of citizen participation. ICT can play an interesting role in this process (for example Internet as a new platform) as it comes to be used by more people. However, its role must not be overestimated. The fact that citizens lack access to ICT does not signify in itself that they are also poorly informed or that their opportunities to take part in society are limited.

Closing the democratic deficit?

Increases in citizen participation

The policy implications of this analysis could well be that public tasks lie less in the area of equal access, but more in the field of the provision of information itself. More important is protecting citizen choice (which is not guaranteed per se by the market). It is important to secure varied, multimedia information provision and a wide range of communication platforms, which reflect and give shape to a diversity of forms of citizen participation.

Provision of information, not access, is decisive

This signifies a fundamental shift from a discussion in terms of equality and universal access to a discussion in terms of diversity and the concepts of cultural policy. This means, among other things, that the accent is more on content and user practices, with the balance shifting from traditional suppliers of public information and communication to new ones, to new social participation platforms and to users. The upshot of this is that we are perhaps talking of a new public domain.

Chapter 3.5

The Vanishing Digital Divide

Benjamin Compaine

Disraeli (1804–1881) observed that "as a general rule the most successful man in life is he who has the best information." In an information-intensive economy not having access to this information may be considered to be a handicap. According to some versions of the scenario, those who have access will further their distance from those who do not.

Competitive edge through information

The digital divide popularly refers to the perceived gap between those who have access to the latest information technologies and those who do not. It has been applied to differences within a society, such as the United States. It may also be applied to differences between developed and developing or under-developed countries. Although there is some commonality between the two applications of the term, there are significant differences in policy responses as well as players and stakeholders. The specifics in this article refer to differences within the United States, though some of the general analysis should be pertinent to policy within most developed economies.

Social divide in terms of access to IC technologies

The topic of what should be public and private responses to the digital divide has taken precedence over what is or should be measured in determining a divide. But only by first addressing the latter can policy-makers substantively debate whether there is indeed a chronic divide or simply a short-term gap which, as with television or VCRs, will quickly disappear through natural forces.

Notions of government being responsible for providing digital access to all U.S. citizens are therefore derived as an extension of the "telephone gap" of the 1930s. This ultimately led to the phenomenon of a nationwide averaging of telephone rates. That is, residential phone users paid roughly the same for a given level of local telephone service regardless of the cost of providing that service. Thus, residential users in communities that were relatively inexpensive to serve, such as high density urban areas where there might be hundreds or even thousands of subscribers in a square mile, were generally charged more by the phone companies – with the urging and blessing of the state regulators – than the cost of providing the service. This excessive "profit" helped subsidise subscribers in low density areas such as suburban

Telephone as a model of a universal right to use

The right to Internet access

and rural areas. Here there might be dozens or fewer subscribers in a square mile.

3.5.1
The Evolution and Boundaries of the Digital Divide

In 1999, about 6% of U.S. households did not have wired telephone service. But the reason for not having basic services is not always purely economic. With various subsidies that make it possible to have phone service for as low as $4 or $5 monthly, one would reason that there is little excuse not to be at 100% penetration. Two researchers interviewed households without telephone service in a low income neighbourhood of Camden, N.J. They found that at least some proportion of these non-subscribers chose not to be connected. In some cases it was because they preferred to spend their money on the high entertainment value of a more expensive cable subscription than a telephone connection. In other cases it was because they feared they would run up sizeable monthly long distance bills if the phone were too convenient. The researchers concluded that it was often the use of the telephone beyond basic local service that caused concern, not the cost of access itself. Thus, some gaps may be self-imposed.

ITU World Telecommunication Development Report 2002

Redefining the concept of telecommunication

The idea that access to information opens the door to wider economic and social development is not new. In 1984, the Commission for World-wide Telecommunications Development, headed by Sir Donald Mait-land, published the Missing Link Report. While the Report pointed to the fact that the lack of telecommunication infrastructure in developing countries impedes economic growth, its scope was limited in that it was mainly concerned with teledensity, that is, access to telephones, as opposed to today's understanding of ICT.

We found the missing link: mobile communications

Mobile has raised access to communications to new levels. With just short of one billion subscribers at the end of 2001, mobile is poised to take over from fixed lines in the early part of 2002 as the network with the most users (see Figure 1).

Telecommunications as a foundation for economic development

The missing link: mobile communication

Telephone subscribers, world (millions)

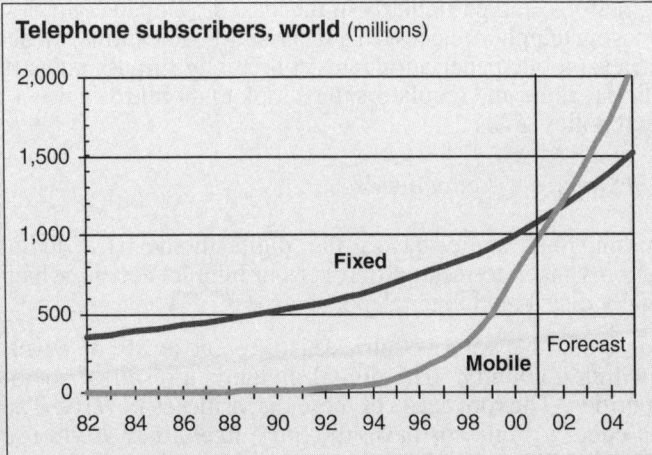

Fig 1. Mobile and fixed telephone subscribers worldwide, 1982–2005

It may be hard to believe, but less than one per cent of the world's inhabitants had access to a mobile phone in 1991 and only one third of countries had a cellular network. By the end of 2001, over 90% of countries had a mobile network, almost one in every six of the world's inhabitants had a mobile phone and almost 100 countries had more mobile than fixed telephone subscribers (see Figure 2).

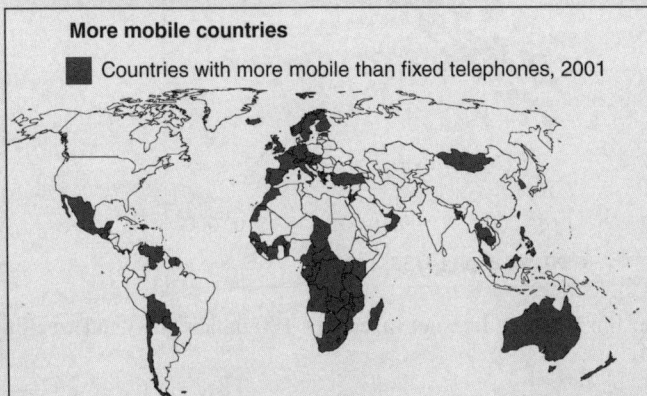

Fig. 2. Countries with more mobile than fixed telephone subscribers, 2001

Mobile telephony has already overtaken landline telephony

Surprising common ground between countries

Mobile communication as a
way of realising
socio-political aims

In developing nations, and particularly in the least developed countries, mobile is increasing telephone access in a surprisingly quick time. In developed countries, mobile penetration rates continually surpass industry forecasts. Policy-makers and regulators must look to mobile as a way of achieving social policy goals.

The new missing link: the digital divide

Today, the "missing link" is referred to as the "digital divide." The digital divide is commonly taken to mean differences in Internet access, which is more unequally distributed than telephone access.

This divide exists between countries at different levels of development, and within a country. The digital divide is a result of socio-economic disparities. The root cause of these disparities is poverty. The more money a country's citizens have, the more likely they are to use ICTs (see Figure 3).

Effective solutions will require a triumvirate pact between governments, development agencies and the private sector.

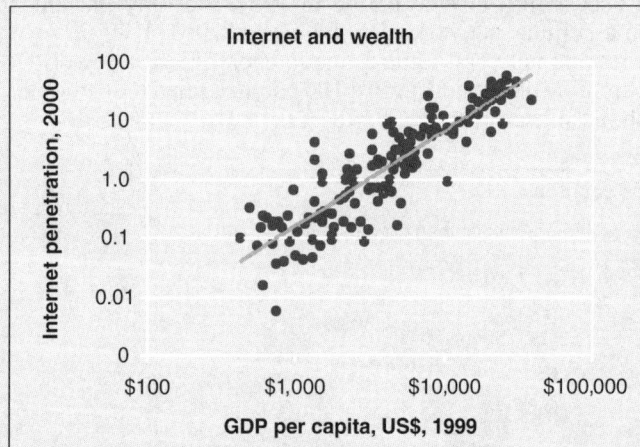

Fig. 3. Relationship between Internet (users per 100 inhabitants) and wealth (GDP per capita)

Lack of complete penetration
in the USA

In 1999, about 6% of U.S. households did not have wired telephone service. But the reason for not having basic services is not always purely economic. With various subsidies that make it possible to have phone service for as low as $4 or $5 monthly, one would reason that there is little excuse not to be at 100% penetration. Two researchers interviewed households without telephone service in a low income neighbourhood of Camden, N.J. They found that at least some proportion of these non-subscribers chose not to be connected. In some cases it was because they preferred to spend their money on the high entertainment value of a more expensive cable subscription than a telephone connection. In other cases it was because they feared they would run up sizeable monthly long distance bills if the phone were too convenient. The researchers concluded that it was often the use of the telephone beyond basic local service that caused concern, not the cost of access itself. Thus, some gaps may be self-imposed.

Although the goal of universal service was to make access to a dial tone affordable to all, it was never extended to incorporate subsidies for the actual *use* of the telephone. That is, long-distance calls were, until well after the break-up of AT&T in 1984, priced well above cost to help subsidise local basic service. Information that could be accessed by phone – from time and weather to pay-per-call services such as 900 exchange calls – was not part of the universal service contract. But the digital divide debate has included some component of the cost of information that could be available online.

Internet access as part of the universal service?

Thus there is the question of whether the cost of *information* should be part of the policy debate of the digital divide. If in fact there is a disadvantaged population on the short end of the divide, is providing hardware and access enough? Or should there be a provision, in effect, to subsidise the digital equivalent of newspapers, magazines and books? If so, where would one draw the line between information and entertainment? Much of what is available on cable and DBS, on newsstands and online, is reasonably characterised as content for entertainment. If public policy-makers wanted to make content available to some disadvantaged groups, should they or could they differentiate between public affairs that might be useful to the body politic and the digital equivalent of situation-comedy reruns?

Does the price of information play a part in the digital divide?

In the debate over what should be included in the expanded concept of universal service, it is also useful to differentiate between access to an infrastructure and access to content. For example, while cross subsidies helped make basic residential dial-tone service lower-priced than the actual cost, there have been no serious proposals to subsidise 900 services that charge for horoscopes or sports scores. Though public funds have made books available in libraries and for many decades subsidised postal rates for magazines, U.S. policy has not provided newspaper or magazine subscriptions nor book purchases for the less well-off economically. So in the debate on online access, what, if anything, might be subject to some sort of need-based subsidy: the hardware needed for access; the ability to connect to the Internet; or the cost of services available online?

Subsidies for contents or hardware?

The sum of the historical context of the recent surveys documenting a digital divide is often unclear about what services or substance are involved

Where are the limits of the divide?

in determining any "divide." Nor is it always clear what the fault line is for a divide: income, ethnicity or race, gender, all of these, any of these? Even the oft-cited NTIA reports included data that showed that the groups that had the largest gaps were catching up, based on the rate of change of users with Internet access.

Technologies in general and information technologies in particular are being developed and implemented at historically unprecedented levels. Those who are motivated to learn about the impact of information technology quickly discover the mantra: smaller, faster, cheaper, better. That is, anything touched by the development of the microprocessor has been impacted by Moore's Law.

3.5.2
The Economics of Online Access: In Brief

The economics of online access involve the consumer's capital cost – equipment and its upkeep – and the operating costs – subscription and connection fees. Socio-cultural factors address the McLuhanesque nature of screens versus paper, keyboards or dictation versus pens and pencils. The two have some relationship: if wireless connections and paper-like reading devices are economical (we know they are technologically feasible), then some of the socio-cultural nuances could be diminished.

Expenditure by private households on media is on the rise

Consumer spending on media in the USA was estimated to be an average of more than $49 per month per person in 1999, not including online access. The average household had 2.4 television sets and 5.6 radios in 1996. More than 84% of households had videocassette players, four times the penetration of 10 years earlier. Overall, consumers increased the proportion of their personal consumption expenditures on media from 2.5% in 1980 to 2.9% in 1996.

New technologies constantly call for new or updated end devices

Just as consumers had to buy radios, phonographs, televisions and VCRs to make use of previous waves of new media technologies, to make use of online media they must have access to other devices. Initially these were personal computers, but supplemented by less expensive options such as dedicated TV set-top boxes. From home, consumers must have telecommunications access to the Internet via a telephone line, cable wire or wireless.

The spread of television sets bears some significance for the spread of Internet devices. TVs in 1950 were expensive: equal to 3.6 weeks of average earnings. By the late 1990s, the cost had declined to under four days of work. Meanwhile the quality improved as well. From nine inch black and white screens with high maintenance tubes to 27" and larger solid-state colour and remote control, the cost by any measure fell continuously and substantially throughout the decades.

The cost of the hardware associated with online information has followed an even more steeply declining curve. Consistent with Moore's Law, the number of transistors on a chip has increased more than 23,900 times, from 2,300 on the Intel 4004 in 1971 to 7.5 million on the Intel Pentium II processor that was the standard in 1999 to 55 million on the Pentium 4 in 2002. Meanwhile, other components also decreased in cost while increasing in capacity: mass storage, modems, CD-ROM drives, even monitors. This brought the retail price of Web-ready full-featured (for that date) personal computers to about $550 or about 1.3 weeks of average weekly earnings. This was a level not reached for colour television sets until the mid-1980s.

Internet PCs became affordable more quickly than television

Based on historical trends, the capital cost of hardware is likely to continue to decrease in both current and real dollar terms, as is the cost of access fees. Online access, which typically cost about $2.00 per hour in 1996, is now widely available from multiple vendors in the USA for $22 for unlimited dial-up access and $35 to $50 for unlimited broadband access.

The rate of adoption for the Internet and PCs is historically unprecedented compared to radio, television, VCRs, cell phones, automobiles or microwave ovens.

3.5.3
Factors in Internet and PC Adoption Rate

The rate of adoption of personal computers and the Internet has been stimulated by at least five trends: rapidly declining costs and increasing power of the hardware; improving ease of use; increasing availability of points of presence (POPs) for local Internet service provider access; decreasing cost of Internet access; and network externalities associated with email and chat.

Factors involved in the rate of adoption

– Rapidly declining costs and increasing power of the hardware. The difficulty in directly graphing the decline in computer cost alone is that capabilities and features have been increasing while absolute prices have declined.

For example, an Apple II+ personal computer with an 8-bit central processing unit (CPU), running at 1 MHz, with 64 KB of memory, two floppy drives that each stored about 160,000 bits and a crude monochrome monitor sold in 1981 for about $3,000. A 300-baud modem added later cost $300. Word processing and the VisiCalc spreadsheet were the two useful applications. In 2002, $549 bought a Dell personal computer running a 32-bit Intel

Hardware costs: falling costs and rising power

Celeron CPU at 1.2 GHz, with 128 MB (that's 2,000 times more memory), 20 GB of hard disk storage, a 15" high resolution colour monitor, a 56 Kbps modem and a host of other features that did not even exist for PCs in 1981: sound and speakers, CD drive, and so on. There is every reason to expect the declining cost curve to continue in hardware.

– Improved ease of use, via Apple Macintosh and Microsoft Windows "point and click" operating systems.

Ease of use improved by graphical user interface

Before the graphical user interface (GUI), operating a PC took a certain determination and level of learning that most casual users found to be on the losing end of the cost-benefit equation. The breakthrough of point-and-click, first developed by Xerox, then implemented in the Apple Macintosh and later Microsoft Windows, greatly lowered the technical barriers to entry. Similarly, the original Internet and first iteration of the World Wide Web were character-based, meaning they required lots of typing of commands to make things happen. It was not until the Mosaic browser was popularised by Netscape in 1994 that the Web and with it the Internet became transparent enough to interest a mass, non-technical audience. The next breakthrough in ease of use, reliable voice recognition, will further lower the skill level required to access information, create documents and otherwise perform functions that have heretofore required some modicum of skill in operating a keyboard and mouse.

– Increasing availability of points of presence (POPs) for local Internet service provider access.

Increasing number of local ISPs

At the end of 1999, there were 5,078 Internet service providers in the United States, up 233 from a year earlier. These were the "on and off ramps" for the Internet. Among these, 184 were considered "national" ISPs by virtue of having a presence in more than 25 area codes. By the spring of 1998, barely four years after Netscape introduced the Web to the mass audience, 92% of the U.S. population had access by a local phone call to seven or more ISPs. Fewer than 5% had no access other than by a toll call. As might be expected, the few areas that were underserved tended to be in lower population – primarily rural – counties.

– Decreasing cost of Internet access.

Decreasing cost of access owing to high competition

Only 2.55% of the U.S. population lived in counties with three or fewer ISPs, while more than 85% of the population lived in or adjacent to counties with 21 or more competitors. Greater competition is generally associated with lower prices and higher quality of services. Meanwhile, some services have developed business models that offer no charge to consumers. In 2002, this included the ISP Juno.com, which claims that it offers access by a local call to 96% of the USA. Prior to 1996, most services, such as America Online, charged about $9.95 for only five hours of use, then a per-hour rate, typically $2.50. In that year AT&T Worldnet offered the first flat rate, unlimited ISP service. Most others followed.

– Network externalities associated with email utility.

Network externalities refer to the increase in value to all users of a network as more users join the network. When only a few businesses and households had telephones, they were of limited value. The postal network, by contrast, was of great value because anyone could reach anyone else. In the early days of email, systems in large companies had internal email not connected to the outside world. Online services, such as Prodigy and America Online, had email systems that only allowed exchange with other members of that service. Thus, email had not been an application that drove many people online. As the Internet's reach accelerated, consumer demand and commercial practicality quickly forced – or encouraged – the various networks to open their systems to sending and receiving email over the Internet, using standard protocols. Whereas in the early 1990s there were roughly 15 million email accounts worldwide, by the end of 1999 there were 569 million. An estimated 110 million U.S. Americans were using email, or 52% of Americans more than 14 years old. This compared to about 7% six or seven years earlier.

Positive network effects caused by rising numbers of users

3.5.4
Special Concerns

From a policy perspective, there are other reasons that the digital divide is less a crisis than a temporary and normal process. There remain some of the specific subsets of the digital divide concerns.

Rural Users

Surveys implicitly link "poor" and "rural" together. There remain assumptions that rural dwellers need economic help with networks because they live in low-density territories that are more expensive to wire. There are, to be sure, poor rural families. But the subsidies in the past also went to middle-class farmers and wealthy ranchers who, when unable to get cable, routinely installed $15,000 satellite dishes. Meanwhile, single working mothers in the cities and mom-and-pop store owners paid telephone rates that helped subsidise the rural subscribers.

"Poor" and "rural" are not mutually dependent

Although most attention has focused on the higher cost of serving rural areas and the "burden" of charging full cost recovery in the pricing to rural users, often overlooked are countervailing economies associated with rural living. These savings, when compared to urban and suburban dwellers, may be ripe for consideration when determining whether continued subsidies for telecommunications are justified and fair.

Summary of Forces and Trends

Data presented here or in the research cited in this paper support the following conclusions:

– Compared to other technology innovations, there has been unprecedented rapid adoption of the Internet and email between 1994 and 2000 among all strata of the population.

– Many other similar technology-inspired products achieved near universal adoption without massive government or even private programmes: radio, television sets and VCRs among them.

– Prices for computers and similar devices have been falling constantly and substantially, to levels equal to a decent colour television set.

– Though services such as telephony and cable have tended to lag behind in adoption rates due to ongoing fees, free Internet access is available using a broadcast TV and radio model in areas that include most of the population.

– Rates of adoption for those groups variously included on the unwired side of the early divide are greater than for the population as a whole.

– Some gaps have already disappeared. For example, from 1994 to 1997 there was high visibility of the gender gap: initially more than two thirds of Internet users were male. By 2000, that gap all but disappeared, as 50.4% of Internet users were women. This simply reflected that early users came from computer science and engineering disciplines that were more heavily male.

– Among those who do have access to computers and the Internet, patterns of use are similar across income, gender and ethnic lines.

The cost of living in town vs. country

Phone Service vs. Auto Insurance

It is beyond the scope of this article to compare fully income and the cost of living in urban and rural areas. There are significant differences however.

While the cost of providing telecommunications services in lower-density areas is higher per user than in urban areas, pricing of such services has been quite close to equal on account of various cross subsidies. On the other hand, some substantially lower-cost services in rural areas have not been averaged to account for higher costs in urban areas: for example, automobile ownership, in particular the cost of automobile insurance. Assuming that there is general agreement that access to an automobile is at least as important as access to a computer and the Internet, it is meaningful to realise that there are huge real gaps in costs for auto insurance. For example, a resident of a low-income neighbourhood in Philadelphia would pay $3,940 to insure a car for which the same driver in rural Atchison, Kansas, would pay only $617: a difference of $3,323.

This calls into question policy responses for subsidising Internet access in rural areas because their costs are higher there than in urban areas. Similar gaps may exist in other large-ticket and important items, such as the cost of urban housing compared to rural areas. As a percentage of total household budgets, telecommunications, including cable or DBS fees, is substantially less than items such as housing and auto insurance. Similar reasoning would apply to schools in rural versus urban communities. Expanding this type of analysis would seem appropriate to provide a more realistic context for deliberating the need – or even direction – for future cross subsidiaries across gaps.

The Case of Voluntary Nonusers

In the statistics on non-subscribers to telephone, cable service, PC ownership or Internet connectivity, there has been scant attention paid to voluntary nonusers – those who could afford it but choose not to. A study of Hispanic households found that the second most voiced reason for not owning a computer, at nearly 40%, was "Don't need." Another 6% had similar reasons – "Too old" or "Not interested." This is generally consistent with a survey conducted by National Public Radio, the Kaiser Foundation and Harvard's Kennedy School of Government. Of those characterising themselves as being "left behind" in computers, barely 20% blamed cost. A third was just not interested. This is consistent with interviews of low-income non-telephone subscribers, which found households that were willing to pay $20 or more per month for cable but not $6 for a dial tone.

There is both anecdotal evidence and increasing statistical verification that large numbers of individuals are voluntary non-participants, for whom no manner of programmes of financing will change matters until they see the personal value. Further research is needed to help determine an accurate number of those who *want* PCs and Internet access but who do not have it

A divide in housing costs too

Voluntary nonusers are part of the divide

because of cost. It is likely to be somewhat smaller than the absolute nonuser number.

Wiring Schools and Libraries

The use of tax revenue...

The policy of helping schools and libraries with their education and information missions in the light of changing technologies is on more solid historical and policy footing than policies directed at individuals and households. Still, there remain caveats that seem to have been given little attention in the digital divide debate.

Foremost among them is the type of aid that schools should be given and the conditions, if any, that should be attached. Currently, the Universal Service Fund tax on telephone bills is providing billions of dollars earmarked for wiring institutions to the Internet and providing related equipment. With the money available, schools are spending sums for construction and hard wiring far in excess of what it might take to install an improving breed of wireless technologies.

... in the absence of a technical ...

A study from the Benton Foundation raises questions about how these "E-rate" funds are being used. There is often not a clear sense of what they will do with their wired buildings. In Cleveland, for example, though the Educational Technology Office has programmes to train teachers on computers, it is not coordinated with the Curriculum and Instruction Department, which would be responsible for bringing technology uses into the classroom. And where there is the semblance of a plan, it is often in the absence of a sound pedagogical footing.

... or pedagogical programme

Hardly any social differences in Internet access in the education system

Having computers available in the schools is an unassailable necessity, just as is having a school library. That there are differences between the libraries in wealthier school districts and poorer ones has long been a reality as well. However, those differences in Internet connectivity were small and narrowing, at least along minority and income lines. In 1999, schools with high minority enrolments (50% or greater) had one computer per 6.5 students. This compared to one computer per 5.0 students in schools with under 5% minority enrolment. Results were slightly better when comparing poor students with wealthier ones. In schools where over 50% of students qualified for the federal free lunch programme, there was one computer per 6.2 students compared to one per 4.9 students in schools with no such students. Thus, a "wealthy" school with 1,000 students might have 204 PCs, while the poorest schools of similar size had 161 PCs. That would translate to a potential of about six hours of computer time per student per week available in the wealthiest schools to almost five hours per student in the very poorest.

Overall, in 1999 84% of the schools with the most poverty-level students had Internet access, compared to 94% of the wealthiest. However, the poorer schools are closing the gap rapidly. Between 1997 and 1999, the poorer schools had a 42% improvement in access, compared to half that rate for the wealthiest schools. Moreover, most if not all these improvements came prior to significant expenditures from the E-rate programmes of the Universal Service Fund, indicating they are the result of local budget commitments.

There is also reason to conclude that the poorer schools, having been later to the game, are benefiting from lower costs for equipment and the improved performance of PCs compared to those that would have been purchased by the "cutting edge" schools at higher prices a few years earlier.

3.5.5
Policy Issue: Democracy or Entertainment?

The digital divide debate has been characterised as a "lively, dynamic and enlightening" process that is one of the joys of democracy. Politicians in particular are prone to wrap their rhetoric on the digital divide in terms of furthering democracy. And in many respects this is a political issue as much as a social one. Typical was the former Chairman of the Federal Communications Commission, William Kennard: "Our society is not represented by a chat among a homogeneous few, but rather a democratic chorus of many different voices and divergent views." However, it may be more tenuous to equate access to the Internet or to cable as an issue on which the Republic depends.

Internet as a foundation for democracy?

Much of this is "déjà vu all over again." Television had raised the expectations of many social theorists for education and the political process. The Kennedy-Nixon presidential debates of 1960 seemed to lend some hope for these expectations. But despite television's important roles in forming public opinion during the Vietnam War and creating shared experiences during events such as the O.J. Simpson trial in 1996, for most viewers most of the time it is a source of simple entertainment. Ratings for national network news shows, never high, have been moving steadily down. The all-news cable networks get ratings of 0.5%, while special interest networks such as C-SPAN – all-public-service-all-the-time – have even lower viewership. Home shopping shows have higher viewership than public affairs. The old commercial broadcast networks, though way down from their pre-cable peaks, still get 15% or so of households each during prime time. The issue for policy-makers: is it a national policy priority to keep basic cable rates low to provide U.S. citizens with "Rug Rats" (a popular children's show in 2000)?

Entertainment has the greatest market share

Internet as a foundation for
social and economic takeoff

Telecommunication and Development in India

Sam Pitroda

"Create a unique model of telephone accessibility. Worry about access to telephone, don't worry about giving everybody a telephone, because you can't do it. This gave a lot of access to telephone to rural people. We installed 750,000 of these phones, gave jobs to 750,000 people.

Telecom, especially the Internet, to me is a major tool for development of human issues. In India we had four million water pumps to repair. How do you print booklets in fifteen different languages to show people how to repair a water pump? And then the logistics of distributing them? By the time you are done, you find that people have books in wrong languages, because the logistic is very bad. If it was on the Internet in fifteen different languages where you can access information where you want, when you want it, in the format you want it, with three-dimensional pictures, there it becomes very simple. We had to train two million nurses for immunization. How do you train two million people on something? This is the power of information, that connection between human resource development and IT, that connection between water and IT, that connection between agriculture and IT. It is something people don't appreciate. In the water project we had geohydrological service, satellite imaging, and then we could drill with much better scientific data as opposed to take a stick which was conventional technology. So high tech has direct connections with lots of these developments."

Sam Pitroda[1]

The Internet is similarly a mixed bag. Undoubtedly, being connected has its value. But surveys have found that services such as chat rooms (sex is popular), sports, and game-playing top the list of activities. It is wonderful having access to news and finance and diverse opinions from providers who would never have had a worldwide audience pre-Internet. But as research repeatedly confirms, once digitally enabled, all groups – by income, ethnicity, gender and education – fall into almost identical patterns of usage. News and public affairs is way down the list of uses. Connecting those not yet connected will likely result in a continuation of this pattern.

---

1 Pitroda, Sam (2001): Telecommunication and development in India: Speech to the Alcatel Foundation, Berlin, November 7th 2001.

3.5.6
Conclusion

The overwhelming weight of the data points in a direction that is historically consistent and socially positive. New and expensive technologies have to start somewhere, and almost invariably that means with two groups: those who find it undeniably useful – often commercial entities – and those who can simply afford it. Similarly, where infrastructure must be built, the providers will start their build-outs aimed at audiences who are most likely to understand the value and be amenable to their service. Again, that typically means a focus on commercial ventures and wealthier residential areas.

The economic advantage of this market-driven self-interest is that it creates an invisible cross subsidy for those who follow. The early adopters pay higher per-unit costs that reflect lower production volumes of manufactured products – such as PCs – or start-up costs of services, such as Internet access via the cable system. But as production builds, unit costs decline, product costs decline, and manufacturers are able to lower prices. In the case of personal computer devices, that process is compounded by advances in component technologies such as hard disk drives, as "box" manufacturers increase their own output.

The builders of networks – traditional and new telephone, wireless, cable and even electric distribution players – similarly know that the marginal cost of adding users to a network is low and thus highly profitable. Once the fixed cost of the network has been made, additional users not only cost them little to add, but network externalities actually make their service of greater value to current and new customers. Thus they have an incentive to lower price and increase utilisation.

Does cost create a barrier? The simple answer is, of course. Any cost is a barrier. The real question is whether it is a fatal or unfair barrier given the standard of living (referring here to the United States, but applicable to societies of similar wealth)? It is, perhaps, a huge testimony to the overall prosperity and well-being of U.S. society at this point in history that an issue such as the digital divide can marshal the attention and commitments it has.

The data is clear that there are households and institutions that are disadvantaged, in information access as in other arenas. It is endemic to the democratic capitalist system and to any other system that has been tried. By the same token, programmes and policies historically have taken the hardest edge off those gaps. But in the past, where goods or services are truly important to people there has been great success in minimising differences among groups – automobiles, radio, television and cable are examples in this context.

Expensive technologies always begin with a divide

The early adopters pay a large part of the development costs

Costs as a barrier

Decisive divides have come and gone in the past

"I also think the term ["digital divide"] sometimes is dangerous in the sense that the minute a new and innovative technology is introduced in the market, there is a divide unless it is equitably distributed among every part of the society, and that is just an unreal understanding of an American capitalistic system. ... I think there's a Mercedes divide. I'd like one, but can't afford it.... I'm not meaning to be completely flip about this – I think it's an important social issue – but it shouldn't be used to justify the notion of, essentially, the socialization of deployment of the infrastructure."

Michael Powell (2001)[2]

How important is access to information?

Information access *is* important. But where does it sit among the schedule of other phenomena for which there has been little or no concern about gaps and few advocates who demand government programmes to remove them. Having access to an automobile and a licence to operate one was certainly more critical to one's livelihood in the second half of the 20th century than having access to email may be today. And undoubtedly there were gaps between those who could afford an automobile and its ongoing operating expenses and those who could not. Were there studies of income and ethnicity and gender to document the auto have-and-have-not gap? The policy question is not whether some group of citizens has more of something than another. It is abundantly obvious that that is true and will continue to be true.

The digital divide is on the wane

The forces and trends summarised in this article suggest that self-evident forces of declining cost, natural acculturation and growing availability are so far moving the Internet quickly in the direction of widespread adoption. At some point before the end of this decade, the declining cost curves and adoption curves will flatten. At that point, it will be time to take stock of whether a true divide remains, who is on each side, and then determine what policies can best address the resolution.

---

2 Powell, Michael (2001) cited by Ahrens, Frank (2001): The great Deregulator, in: *The Washington Post*, June 18, 2001, p. C01

Chapter 4   Changing Rules

Deregulation and reregulation

The changes in the interlinked systems of communication, law and democracy that have been produced by digitalisation call for an understanding of the new foundations of regulation and legislation. The perspectives presented in this chapter range from an analysis of the social assumptions of legislation, studies of problems in the implementation of intellectual property, competition policy and e-democracy, through to an appeal to the ethical dimension of media use and regulation.

For *Ilkka Tuomi* the new basis for regulation includes theoretical questions on the social foundation of legislation and the public sphere. *Tuomi* also argues that the regulation of technical media has to be bound to the technical architecture.

Ilkka Tuomi

A historical perspective on the realm of intellectual property as a social and cultural construction is provided by *Hannes Siegrist*. The discussion of intellectual property here moves between the poles of individual interests (the economic perspective) and the public good (the political perspective). *Siegrist* traces changes in the division of labour and hierarchies between former rights-owners that have been produced by digitalisation. The value of an author is now determined more by demand than by intellectual achievement. Moreover, the fluidity and mobility of intellectual works – heightened by digitalisation – make it more difficult to control protection outside nation-state territories. Copyright, which from a historical viewpoint emerges as the right of a national cultural cartel, is called into question by digitalisation.

Hannes Siegrist

The danger of copyright violations of digital contents is the topic of the contribution by *Stefan Bechtold*, which looks at innovative opportunities for protection in the form of Digital Rights Management. Such systems replace copyright as the primary mechanism of protection with a conglomeration of diverse interlocking mechanisms that are technical, legal or contractual in nature. Various user-identification or copy-management technologies are utilised in DRM systems, raising issues of system integration and standardisation. DRM systems are in a constant process of development, and the signs are that they will be increasingly important in the future.

Stefan Bechtold

In their paper, *Arnold Picot* and *Dominik K. Heger* raise the issue of the need for a new competition policy. They identify innovation as one of the key parameters for competition in the Internet economy. By analogy with

Arnold Picot and Dominik K. Heger

patent protection, which is limited in time, *Picot* and *Heger* propose that after a certain period of time knowledge – or in the case of network products access – might be declared to be common property, meaning that access could no longer be denied provided suitable prices were charged. In the context of the convergence of the media, telecommunications and IT sector, *Picot* and *Heger* analyse excessively strict market definitions as a further major problem of anti-trust legal practice. In the Internet economy with its highly-specialised players, this can lead to inappropriate notions of market domination and premature intervention.

Steve Coleman

By contrast with the viewpoint of the business enterprise, *Steve Coleman* in his paper adopts the perspective of the state and governments. *Coleman* makes the critical point that the use of the Internet as an instrument of government communication has little to do with democracy. It does, however, offer the opportunity to create closer and more interactive relationships between government and governed, representatives and represented. E-democracy is thus not only a technological challenge, but consists above all in creating an open political culture and a democratisation of democracy. From a European perspective *Coleman* recommends using the Internet as a basic arena of communication if Europe is to be perceived as a unified political space.

Roger Silverstone

Roger Silverstone too calls for a new starting point for reflections on regulation. The basis for this is the challenge posed by the new media in terms of what it means to be human and the meaning of humanity. *Silverstone* points out that many reflections on the Internet mistake connection for closeness, closeness for commitment, and reciprocity for responsibility. He extends the concept of regulation to cover private spaces. In private as in public, regulation is a struggle for the rights of and control over representation and as such it is part of a moral order. With mediation as a central component, citizenship demands the development of a moral responsibility and participation that should increasingly determine the process of regulation. *Silverstone* explains that time-space distantiation or time-space compression, as well as certain notions of the network society, are susceptible to a profound misconception of two sorts of distance: the spatial and the social. As a moral category, says *Silverstone*, distance requires what he terms "proper distance," which permits responsibility and care for others and thus opens up new scope for action.

Chapter 4.1

Regulation and Law

Ilkka Tuomi

One of the questions that has emerged as a major theme in policy discussions related to the knowledge society is the question of regulation. A simple approach to answer this question is to require new laws that address ICTs. A more detailed analysis, however, shows that the question is about a profound change in the interlinked systems of communication, law, power and democracy. One could argue that the Internet moves and erodes the foundations on which many of our current social institutions are erected. It is, therefore, important to understand where we could find new bases for social institutions that are viable in the knowledge society. One starting point is the realisation that our current political systems are to a large extent based on specific characteristics of traditional industrial forms of mass communication.

The Internet shakes up social institutions

4.1.1
Regulatory Forces

According to Thompson,[1] the exchange and circulation of symbolic content is constrained by the characteristics of technical media. In addition, however, an institutional apparatus of transmission defines *channels of selective diffusion* and *mechanisms of restricted implementation*. The channels of selective diffusion constitute the institutional framework for controlling access to a technical medium. Mechanisms of restricted implementation, in turn, enable and constrain specific types of circulation of information and other symbolic forms. Both enable and constrain media use, and encompass users in asymmetric relations of autonomy and dependence.

Selective diffusion and restricted implementation

As Slevin notes,[2] the channels of selective diffusion often lock into the characteristics of the storage. In other words, the architecture of the storage enables specific forms of control and plays an important role in the circulation of symbolic forms. As the "digital divide" fundamentally concerns exclusion from and inclusion in the flows of communication, the architecture of storage

The architecture of the storage is crucial

1 See Thompson 1995
2 See Slevin 2000, p. 67

could therefore be characterised as the "infrastructure of social exclusion." This means also that regulation of technical media, in other words policy, has to be linked to the technical architecture.

William Mitchell and Lawrence Lessig have made a similar point,[3] emphasising that technical architecture is one of the factors that regulate the use of technology. According to Lessig, software systems are increasingly being regulated by the architectures of software code, and the legal code has lost some of its importance. In addition to these two forms of "code," norms and markets also regulate the use of technological systems. Regulation, therefore, occurs in a field where these four forces interact.

Lessig argues that much of the regulatory power of law has disappeared and that legitimate democratic rule-making has to a large extent been substituted by non-transparent architectures of software code written by some unaccountable programmers working for profit-oriented companies. Mayer-Schönberger, however, shows that this view is based on the assumption that the conflict between the authority of law and the regulation of cyberspace has to have winners and losers. According to Mayer-Schönberger, there have been three common and different views about the relationship between law and the Internet. First, the Internet has been conceptualised as a technological frontier that needs to be civilised and cleaned up. Mayer-Schönberger notes that there have been two variations of this theme: cyberspace has been seen as a domain of criminal and indecent activity, prompting the need for new laws that can clean up all the dirt; alternatively, it has been argued that there is nothing particularly new in cyberspace and that existing laws well cover activity on the Net. In both variations of this view, the underlying assumption is that cyberspace has to be controlled by law.[4]

In Mayer-Schönberger's analysis, Mitchell and Lessig represent an alternative view. They argue that the authority of law cannot control cyberspace simply because so much of its regulation is already embedded in software architectures. In other words, the fight is already over, and cyberspace rules.

The third approach discussed by Mayer-Schönberger is the one where the Internet remains an independent domain of freedom, with its own rules. This view is promoted by cyber-anarchists and some techno-libertarians.[5] The most visible example of this view has been the famous Declaration of the

Codes, norms and markets regulate the use of technological systems

Must cyberspace be controlled by law?

Has cyberspace already defeated the authority of law?

Self-regulation as another approach

3 See Mitchell 1995; Lessig 1999
4 See Mayer-Schönberger 2001
5 For example, Rheingold (1993) and Raymond (1998; 1999) view the Internet as a frontier where the old rules are substituted by new freedoms. See also Winner 1997, Loader 1997, Borsook 2000

The Future of Ideas

Lawrence Lessig

Always and everywhere, free resources have been crucial to innovation and creativity. ... Thus, especially in the digital age, the central question becomes not whether government or the market should control a resource, but whether a resource should be controlled at all...

There is a benefit to resources held in common and ... the Internet is the best evidence of that benefit. ... The Internet forms an *innovation commons*. It forms this commons not just through norms, but also through a specific technical architecture. The Net of these norms and this architecture is a space where creativity can flourish. ... The tragedy of the commons ... is the tragedy of losing the innovation commons that the Internet is, through the changes that are being rendered on top.

(In *Code and Other Laws of Cyberspace*) I argued that the original architecture of cyberspace was changing, as governments and commerce increased the ability to control behaviour in cyberspace. Technologies were being deployed to better monitor and control behaviour, with the consequence, for better or worse, of limiting the liberty of the space. As the architecture changed, the freedom of the space would change, and change it did...

A similar change is occurring with respect to innovation. Here, too, the architecture of the space is changing, interfering with the features that made innovation so rich. And the consequence again will be a decrease in this value that we thought defined the original Net.

But here, the change in architecture is both a change in the architecture in a technical sense and a change in the legal architecture within which cyberspace exists. ... The emphasis here is on the interaction between changes in law and changes in code that together will undermine innovation. ...

Two companies – AOL Time Warner and Microsoft – will define the next five years of the Internet's life. Neither company has committed itself to a neutral and open platform. Hence, the next five years will be radically different from the past ten. Innovation in content and applications will be as these platform owners permit. ... We will have re-created the network of old AT&T, but now on the platform of the Internet. Content and access will once again be controlled; the innovation commons will have been carved up and sold.

This is the future of ideas.

Lawrence Lessig is Professor of Law at Stanford Law School. [6]

Regulation reduces the space for creativity

Increasing control of behaviour in cyberspace

Value paradox of the Internet

Platform owners will determine the future

" The architecture of cyberspace leads to conflicts. "

Independence of Cyberspace, by John Perry Barlow.[7] A less radical, but still closely related view is that in which the users of the Internet "self-regulate" the Net.[8] In this conception, traditional law and the rules that regulate the Net remain independent.

The concept of self-regulation as an euphemism?

As Mayer-Schönberger notes,[9] however, when the rules and mechanisms of "self-regulation" eventually emerge, they may well look like a copy of the real world. The idea of "self-regulation" is according to Mayer-Schönberger a euphemism, associating concepts of civic participation, Western democracy, and critical rational public sphere with the emerging new world of cyberspace. So far, however, empirical evidence on the different self-regulatory domains on the Net has not supported such utopian views.[10]

All these three conceptions of the relationship between law and cyberspace share the common assumption that the authority of law itself does not change. Mayer-Schönberger, however, argues that the Net reinforces existing structures of authority, at the same time fundamentally displacing them. For example, the Habermasian idyll of rational public discourse seems to be close at hand in the age of the Internet. In practice, however, public authorities are more or less unable to engage in bi-directional interaction and public discourse. For meaningful interaction, the authorities should be able to act on the basis of communication. This is increasingly impossible precisely because the volume of communication is becoming overwhelming. Mayer-Schönberger gives an illuminating example of this: the White House computer responds automatically with a polite boilerplate email, informing that the White House receives so many emails that they cannot be processed and will be automatically discarded. The bi-directional communication capability is therefore not necessarily creating a civic society and democratic involvement. Instead, bi-directionality has perhaps its main role in allowing businesses to deploy mass-customised production, connecting consumers and suppliers directly to systems of flexible production.

Internet displaces prior structures

From the perspective of theory of law, Lessig's position should therefore be extended to deal with situations where law and its processes themselves change as a result of informationalisation. This leads to theoretical questions concerning the social foundations of law and public sphere.

From a sociological perspective, Lessig's representation of regulative forces obviously lacks at least two important dimensions. One is the actual social practice. A more complete theoretical model of regulation would

6 Extract of Lessig (2001): The Future of Ideas.
7 See Barlow 1996
8 Price/Verhulst 2000
9 See Mayer-Schönberger 2001, p. 15
10 Studies on electronic communities (e.g. Reid 1999; DuVal/Smith 1999; Tuomi 2001) have shown that viable communities develop strong social control mechanisms.

include the use of technology as an important component. A theoretically robust analysis of regulation would require detailed study on the theory of social practice.[11]   Often there exist sophisticated forms of dynamic complementarity between the regulative forces of routinised action, i.e. "the way we do things here," and technical architectures.[12]   On the other hand, as de Certeau has described,[13] there are many different ways people turn constraints of design into resources in their everyday life. As regulation has been one of the important issues that have touched the social dimension of information society, theoretical developments of such ideas have clear practical implications. Furthermore, as social practices are deeply embedded in cultural contexts, comparative studies quickly reveal hidden assumptions. Regulative code may have quite different implementations even within national boundaries, for example, when we move from the U.S. East Coast to its West Coast. The different balances in the regulatory mix of markets, laws, norms, architectures and standardised practices could be characterised as "regulatory styles."

> Dynamic complementarity between regulative forces of routine action and technical architectures

> National differences in the implementation of regulative code

4.1.2
The Transformation of the Public Sphere

The second dimension lacking in Lessig is communication. Regulation occurs also through the continuous reproduction of meaning[14] and social categories[15] and through controlled access to the various arenas of circulation of information and symbolic forms.[16] This leads us to study the links between regulation and the structures and processes of communication. An important starting point here is Habermas' concept of the public sphere.

> Regulation versus structures of communication

Habermas based his concept of the public sphere on the idea of communicative ethics.[17] In the public sphere, the members of a society make their public views visible and available for critical reasoning on the part of others. If the access to this public sphere is open to all members of the society, and the participants adhere to a shared goal of finding common agreement, the public sphere provides a basis for legitimate democracy. At the same time,

> Public sphere as the basis of democracy

---

11 See also Bourdieu 1977; Giddens 1984; Latour and Woolgar 1986; de Certeau 1988; Engeström 1987. Organisational procedures have been discussed, for example, by March (see March/Olsen 1989).

12 See Tuomi 2001

13 See de Certeau 1998

14 See Berger/Luckmann 1966; Foucault 1979

15 See Bowker/Star 1999

16 See Bourdieu 1993

17 See Habermas 1989

the criteria for a politically legitimate public sphere can be used as norms to evaluate existing media and structures of communication.

A central distinction in Habermas' theory is the separation between public and private. This distinction has its roots in Kant's theory of public reason. Kant argued that the autonomy and freedom of individual subjects rests on the ability to think for oneself. Freedom of thought, according to Kant, is the foundation of civil society, as everyone has to be able to consider the opinions of others without having to accept them as dogma. This Kantian view, therefore, links politics and epistemology. As Garnham notes,[18] the crucial point is that it leads to a theory of the relation between communication and politics which assumes the prior existence of private, autonomous individual subjects. The democratic public sphere is expected to protect the rights of the individuals, whose autonomy, and therefore potential for freedom, is itself built on public discourse.

Public sphere should protect the rights of individuals

Kant solved the basic contradiction between individual freedom and social behaviour by translating the problem to an epistemological level. Hegel, however, criticised the Kantian vision by pointing out that individual identities are essentially socially constructed. The members of a community are never completely free to make up their minds. Indeed, the existence of a community of "free individuals" already implies that individuals have agreed on some shared values. A democratic public sphere, therefore, cannot only be about rational argumentation. It also needs to be a place where identities can be constructed and where individuals and their views can get recognition.

Public sphere as a place where identities are constructed

Several authors have proposed alternatives to the Habermasian public sphere. As Garnham notes, the communitarian critique of the public sphere has tried to make previously private interests and values part of public discourse. For example, the rights of women and gays and harassment at the workplace are topics that have not received much visibility in the public sphere until recently. On the other hand, the communitarian critique often rejects the idea that there could be a single universal rationality that could provide the foundation for the public sphere.

Is there one universal rationality?

In theoretical terms, we could, therefore, have three different ways to implement the public sphere. Benhabib calls the first one the integrationist strand in communitarianism.[19] In this model, everything is public, and the divide between public and private disappears. The norms and values that guide individual action do not change when the individual moves between public and private.[20] The foundation of the public sphere, i.e. rationality

The public sphere as independent of place

18 See Garnham 2000, p. 49
19 See Benhabib 1992
20 See MacIntyre 1981

and accepted values, is universal and independent of the place where one stands.

The participationist strand of communitarianism, on the other hand, accepts the point that in modern society many different systems of value exist; however, a legitimate public sphere needs to be based on a generic and universal system of communicative ethics. This implies a multitude of communally grounded perspectives and interests that are negotiated in a shared public sphere.

The universal value-system of communicative ethics as basis of the public sphere

The third alternative is adopted by people who see universal rationality and values as expressions of dominant social interests. This view would lead to a system of loosely coupled communities, each with its own public sphere. These spheres could have different forms of rationality, and they could provide different domains of visibility to the community members.

Juxtaposition of distinct public spheres

Although the public sphere has often been discussed in the context of mass media and political theory, on the Internet it is also an empirical question. Opinion-formation is a key aspect of any social action, and it seems that the Internet has facilitated the emergence of special interest groups and communities that support social movements. The revolutionary upheavals in Eastern Europe in 1989 have often been presented as an inevitable result of developments in communication technologies, and the Internet is often viewed as a technology that drives societies towards democracy. Theories of communicative ethics and rationality may provide the foundation for such views. In practice, however, the collapse of the Soviet Union may have been the last major revolution where the Internet did not play a crucial role. In the future, opinions may be formed within communities that operate outside a common public sphere. The Seattle anti-WTO demonstrations may be an interesting case of the new dynamics of public-opinion formation. Although the theoretical study of the public sphere may provide important starting points for understanding the political dimension of the ongoing transformation, empirical research on the actual forms and rationalities of current and emerging public spheres is a key area when we study knowledge society. Such study will have important consequences, for example, for e-Governance initiatives.

Internet as an instrument for political action

Chapter 4.2

The History and Current Problems of Intellectual Property (1600–2000)

Hannes Siegrist

The history of intellectual property asks how the conception of "property" has spread and manifest itself at different times in the sphere of symbolic forms, expression, ideas and intellectual activity.[1] History asks about lines of development, continuities and breaks. At first sight, current changes in the world of the media and intellectual property seem to be the expression of a deep historical break between the Gutenberg era and the digital age. Historians observing the present processes and problems from a long-term perspective are now able to make out certain continuities. From the 18th century until today, the development of intellectual property has been characterised by tensions between "private" and "public" interests as well as conflicts between professional and "status" groups.

The following article asks how, why, under what circumstances and with what interests and motives in mind combinations of signs, forms of expression, works, texts, images and stocks of knowledge have at various times been ascribed to an (individual or collective) social player and legal subject. "Intellectual property" (and related concepts such as "authors' rights," "copyright," etc.) is considered as an idea and a legal institution with which exclusive rights to act and relations between persons and social groups (authors, reproducers, distributors and users) are regulated with respect to dealings with symbols and artefacts. From a historical viewpoint, "intellectual property" appears as a historically variable bundle of rights and responsibilities determining the reworking, appropriation, accessibility, distribution, exploitation and use of symbols and knowledge (texts, images, brands and inventions).

Digital age changes the issue of intellectual property

Intellectual property as a variable bundle of rights and responsibilities

---

1 See Wadle 1996; Fisher III 1999

> " 'Authorship' and 'intellectual property' are social, cultural and legal constructs. "

4.2.1
Intellectual Property in the Modern Age

Dynamics of the modern era calls for constant renegotiation of rights

The history of intellectual property and copyright law in the modern age analyses the historical, cultural, political, social, economic, technical and legal conditions under which the disposal of ideas and forms of expression is assigned to an "owner" of intellectual property (the author). Given the dynamics of culture, communication technologies, the economy and politics, modern, sophisticated societies must constantly negotiate the criteria that regulate the rights and opportunities to act of authors, reproducers, distributors and users.

Assumptions, concepts and roles in dynamic societies

To whom does knowledge belong, and how is it to be distributed?

A characteristic feature of the history of culture, knowledge and intellectual property from the 18th century to today is that those involved (traditionalists and innovators alike) seek to interpret and influence developments using a bipolar set of assumptions typical of the "modern age." Perceptions, interpretations and actions have been guided by conceptual dichotomies such as private property / public property, private benefit / common good, creativity / routine, integration / disintegration, stagnation / progress, tradition / innovation, culture / commerce, national / ubiquitous, one's own / someone else's. This is how decisions are taken about such fundamental questions as "To whom does 'culture' belong?"; "Who is in charge of 'knowledge'?" and "How are culture and knowledge to be distributed?"

"Authorship" and "intellectual property" are social, cultural and legal constructs. The discipline of history inquires into the concrete, historical manifestations of such abstractions in concepts, roles, structures, practices and institutions. It reconstructs the meaning and function of intellectual property in its particular historical contexts by investigating the processes of negotiation through which producers, distributors and users have reached agreements about the criteria, norms and institutions that ground the intellectual property-owner's rights to act and that determine the characteristics of a work that can be protected. The tangible result of this conflict-ridden process of negotiation emerges in the concrete historical meaning and function of concepts and roles such as:

Keys to understanding intellectual property

– "Work," "original," "forgery" and "plagiarism";

– "Authors' rights" and "intellectual property";

- "Author," "scientist," and "artist," to each of whom social and cultural capabilities, skills, functions and rights to act are attributed;

- "Craftsman," "layperson" and "dilettante," from whom the "author" is set apart;

- "Performing artist," "reader," "art critic" and "applied art," which are ranked beneath the "author" and "art";

- "Printer," "reproducer," "publisher," "provider" and "producer," who are assigned to the trade and commercial realm;

- Non-commercial intermediary roles of culture and knowledge in education, science, libraries, museums and archives;

- The "public" and the "public sphere" (recipients, buyers, consumers and owners of cultural artefacts).

The distinction between the "author" on the one hand and the "other players" on the other hand is based in each case on a host of cultural conventions and social norms and practices. The author only becomes the "owner" of intellectual property and thus – in a legal sense – its "author" by being legally posited as such. Legislation, jurisprudence and legal doctrine define the figure of the "intellectual producer" and "owner of the control rights of reproduction and distribution" by establishing the concept of an "intellectual work," laying down the scope, quality and duration of protection for works, and regulating the conditions for reproduction and the contractual conferral of rights upon third parties.

Intellectual property defined by legal doctrine

The concept of intellectual property is determined by legislators who represent specific political, social, economic and cultural interests. It is developed and interpreted by professors of law, judges and lawyers, who reduce the complexity of bundles of social, cultural and economic functions and roles with the aid of interpretations and procedures peculiar to their profession. Accordingly, there is often a difference between the prevailing legal conception of the "author" and the "intellectual work" on the one hand and cultural, social and commercial notions of the author on the other.

Discrepancy between the legal conception and other notions of the author

In everyday life, the tension between the idea of the author determined by cultural and social values and the legal concepts of "authorship" and "intellectual property" is frequently ignored, glossed over with analogies, or made manageable by stereotypes (e.g. tales of the culturally productive but financially unsuccessful author). When the gap between the function and position of the author and his rights becomes too great or is perceived to be intolerable, however, authors use the concept of intellectual property as a battle cry or call for mobilisation. In so doing, they are articulating

Defending interests through the concept of intellectual property

individual and collective interests and giving voice to their social, cultural and economic demands.

Memory, historical awareness and historiography

Ahistorical concept of intellectual property

As the cultural ideas, social roles and legal norms formed in times of upheaval and radical change sooner or later become established and turn into new habits, awareness of the historicity of "intellectual property" and the interests and roles associated with it likewise fades. This also comes to light in those sciences that conceive of the author, the work and intellectual property in ahistorical terms (using atemporal functional, philosophical or moral categories) or consider them as timeless, quasi-natural phenomena. The reduction of the term's historical origin to a myth claiming timelessly valid didactic status draws a veil over historically real circumstances, interests, interpretations, conflicts and strategies of power. On account of the open nature of historical interpretation, certain historical accounts (e.g. jubilee histories of professional and employers' associations) now also contribute to the "naturalisation" of intellectual property by projecting present perspectives onto the past in order to justify the interests and strategies of a particular group using history and tradition. As in the past, this sort of de-historicisation and naturalisation of concepts, images of self and other, roles and practices, can be observed not only among authors but also among publishers and providers, state-owned cultural mediators and the "public" of consumers, users and citizens.

Different views of intellectual property. . .

The academic literature on the history of authorship, intellectual property and copyright is characterised by a high degree of scholarly specialisation: historians of literature and art concentrate on the conditions, features and procedures of cultural creativity and production, or reconstruct, for example, the birth, the crises, the end and the revival of the author.[2] Social, cultural and media historians focus on the literary and artistic market, the history of the media, and the development of the public, the buyer, citizen and recipient. Historians of education, knowledge and institutions enquire into the function and meaning of public, state-run and civil institutions (clubs and associations) in the production and conveyance of culture and knowledge. The history of the professions is concerned with the development of academic and artistic vocations. Legal history treats general and specific developments in literary, artistic or intellectual property from the perspective of law. Economic history looks at the history of intellectual property from the viewpoint of the enterprise, the market and the economy.

2 On the discussion of the author in literary theory, see Jannadis et al. 1999

Here as in the rare cross-discipline syntheses it becomes clear that each historical conceptualisation and institutionalisation of intellectual property is based upon the complex interaction of various players within the particular historical context. Authors, publishers, printers, reprinters, providers, customers, the public, lawyers and politicians each approach the common problem from their own specific angle and with their own particular interests in mind. Historical research shows that in the modern age intellectual property not only serves to reward the author or guarantee the viability, autonomy and security of the author or the commercial provider. Rather, its purpose is always also to secure the dynamic working of culture, society and the economy and mediate between tradition and innovation. Depending on the country and the era, the general tendency is to increase authors' rights, the publisher's rights to act, and the rights of the public. All in all, the development hovers between the poles of individual interests and the common good.

... as signs of the author's viability and as guaranteeing innovation

As academic authors too have their interests and do not always find it easy to distance themselves intellectually from their own prejudices and the prevailing trends of the time, assessments of the past in the literature on intellectual property vary considerably. In the second half of the 19th and 20th centuries in the West, an individualistic-liberal interpretation was dominant, emphasising the implementation of individual authors' rights.[3] Against the background of debates about (private) intellectual property "getting out of hand," a revision of this historical picture is now beginning to take shape.[4] It is now pointed out, for example, how even when the modern protection of intellectual property was first established around 1800 the legislature gave the common good primacy over private benefit, providing the author with rights of disposal only insofar as this seemed beneficial to progress and the common good.

Common good takes precedence over intellectual property

Current problems and concepts in a historical perspective

Current debates on the way (private) intellectual property is "getting out of hand," on the privatisation of the symbolic world through new "enclosures," and on the "end of the author" in the digital age refer to real and putative developments that are partly new and partly classic in nature. Frequently, the new phenomena are discussed using traditional assumptions and concepts.[5] Users criticise the fact that liberalisation and the commercialisation of rights of disposal have led to supplies of symbols and knowledge being put under the control of private enterprises and the mechanisms of the market instead

Demand for "semiotic democracy"

---

3 See Gieseke 1995; Barta/Markiewicz 2001
4 See Davies 1994
5 Grassmuck 2002

of the non-commercial, publicly coordinated sphere of civil society. What is being demanded is free or publicly subsidised access to "culture" ("socio-culture," education as a civil right) and, in the case of the Internet, what has been termed "semiotic democracy." The expansion of private copyrights, it is said, is calling into question the historically established equilibrium between private benefit and the common good, and between authors and providers: the privatisation of signs, symbolic forms and stocks of knowledge infringes the rights of persons, consumers and citizens, undermines the social and cultural integration of society, and ultimately jeopardises the dynamics of culture, its prosperity, and democracy.

Media enterprises extend their rights of disposal to the detriment of authors

Media enterprises and the authors of products that are in great demand on the market often use similar rhetoric of the "common good" to legitimise the opposite argument, i.e. that strong and reliable private copyrights are indeed necessary. In fact, major commercial providers are using the concentration and expansion of the markets and the new media to extend their rights of disposal at the expense of sizeable groups of authors. Whether the slogans coined to justify these strategies actually make sense remains to be seen.

The spectrum of authors who are today often brought together under the collective term of the "creative" ranges from highly-renowned artists, through salaried, civil-servant, freelance or entrepreneurial professionals, to freelancers working for newspapers or advertising agencies or casual intellectual workers. Authors are becoming increasingly aware that when they sign a contract the relative increase in the power of commercial providers is weakening their own rights. Accordingly, they are calling for a revision of copyright law, and in Germany specifically of the author's contract rights, to provide better protection for the author as the weaker party (as a rule) in the signing of contracts.

Revision of copyright law

Digitalisation fundamentally alters the division of labour

Those who belong to the classic authorial professions are realising, moreover, that the relations among intellectuals and authors are themselves changing. In the 19th century, writers and composers placed themselves above performing and applied artists in the division of labour when it came to the moral and financial rights of authors. In the course of the 20th century and to a greater extent in recent decades, this hierarchy has been called into question on account of changes in the division of labour in theatre production, film and television: producers, directors, actors and musicians are increasingly asserting the creativity of their work and the originality of what the performing artist does.[6] The digitalisation of image, text and sound is changing the divisions and hierarchies among the "creative professions," each of which is once again now seeking to extend its authors' rights and copyright protection in fundamental terms.

6 See Raschèr 1989

In the wake of the democratisation of culture and society and against the background of the competition between companies and whole economies, the 20th century saw a shift in the definition of "creativity" from something exceptional and rare to a general human attribute, a shift that has also blurred the 19th-century hierarchies and distinctions between artists and intellectual experts on the one hand and craftsmen, industrial designers, dilettantes and laypeople on the other. Since the late 19th century, the work of these groups is thus increasingly being accorded protection as intellectual property.[7] In certain spheres the courts may still demand that an intellectual work (a work of art) be distinguished by a certain formal quality or by standing out from the norm. Yet in the modern, commercialised, mass and popular culture of the 20th century more and more works of all sorts are in fact coming under copyright protection: even trivial and popular texts whose authors consciously eschew originality or demanding forms, formulaic songs, and electronically supported mixtures of sound and image sequences. As criteria such as novelty and demand have come to compete with the traditional conception of the creator and his work (though not only today and not only for this reason), there has been an erosion of the figure of the great author and man of genius to which constant reference has been made since the establishment and spread of authors' rights in the 18th century.

Since the 1980s, the cultural, social and legal classifications and hierarchies have again become more and more fluid. The previous assignment of knowledge, abilities, skills and works to traditional professions and owners is being increasingly questioned. At issue is not only intellectual property (including invention rights and trademark rights as well as authors' rights), but the social, economic and cultural order as a whole.[8] It is not just about symbols and knowledge forms as private and public property, but how professional groups, public institutions and private enterprises can position themselves within the information society and in the system of economic, social and cultural inequality. The intensity of the current debate is reminiscent of the profound transformation undergone by intellectual property around 1800. With a brief look back at the premodern age, this will be sketched below.

Property protection is increasingly independent of quality

7 See Bertrand 1999
8 See Rifkin 2000

4.2.2
Knowledge, Professions and Exclusive Rights of Disposal from the 16th to the 18th Century

It is not only with the modern society of private property-owners that control over intellectual works and exclusive rights of disposal over their reproduction and distribution have come upon humanity. Phenomena and rights that in Europe and progressively further afield have over the last 200 years been conceived as "intellectual property" already existed before 1800 too. Yet until well into the 18th century people generally used other terms and institutional models to make symbols, knowledge and their material carriers subject to an exclusive right of disposal, terms such as "control," "privilege," "monopoly," "profession" and "estate."

In premodern estate-based society, rights of control and disposal over symbols and forms of knowledge were assigned exclusively to secular and church authorities, estates, professions and corporations.[9] Exclusive rights of disposal and exclusion were legitimised by religion, tradition and common law, but also increasingly by legal privileges granted by emperors, popes, princes or free cities, primarily to trade and professional corporations. The clergy and church institutions controlled stocks of religious knowledge and symbolisations as well as their reproduction and distribution; the nobility controlled the knowledge used for the purpose of domination; the scholarly professions and the university as a scholars' corporation controlled, for example, medical and legal knowledge, guilds the technical knowledge of craftsmen and artisans, traders' corporations the commercial knowledge.

As knowledge and the media became differentiated, expanded and assumed new functions, it was not only the hierarchy and importance of symbols and forms of knowledge that changed, but also the hierarchy between secular and church authorities, estates and professions. Traditional relations of patronage waned as professions requiring new or more learning, such as law, came into competition with traditional ones, such as the clerical. As "court artists," sought-after artists could evade the control of municipal artists' guilds. With the emergence of societies based on territorial states, knowledge relevant for control came to be controlled increasingly by the state, which took on responsibility for higher education and turned civil servants and professors into a new informational and functional elite. For reasons of economics and power politics, the mercantilist state promoted the economy, science and art, granting trade and commercial privileges to publishers and printers, setting up academies and controlling universities. Theatres were supported by princes or run by powerful managers.

Intellectual property – no new concept

Control of knowledge by church and nobility

Secular knowledge overtakes clerical knowledge

---

9 See Burke 2001

When secular and ecclesiastical authorities granted rights of disposal and control over symbols and knowledge in the form of precisely worded and carefully specified privileges and monopolies or printing rights, their intention in so doing was either to protect tradition or foster innovations with a view both to boosting their own power and enhancing prosperity and culture. Often the privileges were not conferred upon the actual author or inventor, but the person in the circles of power who was first to spread or utilise the work or idea.

At this time, printing and publishing privileges were conferred either upon individual persons or, as in Paris and London, upon the printers' and publishers' guilds. Privileges for authors were awarded relatively infrequently: authors' rights as such did not yet exist.[10] The rights for a book's reproduction and distribution lay with the publisher or printer (publisher rights), whose task was also to help the ruler to control the reproduction and distribution of both acceptable and dangerous writings as part of censorship policy. A small group of publishers and printers that imposed its own discipline through professional conventions was privileged since it owned the technical and commercial means of reproduction and distribution.

Yet control of the reproduction and distribution of the symbols and knowledge tied to a particular publication had its limits, for the privilege was only legally binding within one's own territory, and even there it was constantly being infringed. Printers and publishers in the provinces and in neighbouring states produced "reprints," which were sold by traders who were exceedingly difficult to control. In England the reprints came from Scottish and Irish publishers, in France from the provinces as well as Belgium and Switzerland, and in the northern and central states of Germany from the southern states.

In the debates about "reprinters" and "pirates" (as they came to be termed in the seafaring nation of England), printers, publishers, lawyers and authors developed new conceptions of publishers' and authors' rights. To be able to protect the material form of a book more effectively, legislators and publishers have since the 18th century even been prepared to grant the author the right to the immaterial form of expression and the content of the work. The Statute of Anne, dating from 1710 in England, and the legal regulations elaborated by the Royal Court in France finally permitted court decisions recognising the writer as the legal author of the work, who by contract cedes his rights to the reproduction and distribution of the work to the publisher.

In the 18th century there were increasing signs of a growing awareness in authors that their work was a product of their own making and that they were thus entitled to copyright protection. There was a greater perception of the traditional right of authors and artists to put their name on their work.

10 See Gieseke 1995

Printing rights as a base for the distribution of knowledge

Geographical limits to intellectual property

Pirates influence the formation of copyright law

Authors increasingly break free from power structures

Analysis of the content of forewords and dedications shows that authors were freeing themselves from the patronage of rulers and printers. In test cases against publishers and printers in England and France, individual authors – with the help of lawyers – made it clear that they were claiming their work as their own property.

From copier to creator

The emergence of the modern profile of the author as a creative individual entitled to control over his own work was also influenced by the debates of philosophers and pamphleteers in the second half of the 18th century. In small but growing circles, writers, academics and artists discussed concepts such as "original," "imitation," "compilation," and "forgery," reconstructing the figure of the author using new moral, philosophical and aesthetic arguments: the artist and author did not merely copy nature or represent truth according to the traditional rules of rhetoric, it was said, but was a "creator," "discoverer" and "inventor," whose structuring and forming activity produced texts, forms of expression, thoughts and images that were "proper" to him. The author, now also increasingly conceived as a "genius," lent thought a specific and distinctive form in which his individuality and subjective creativity came to expression. The work he "animated" could unequivocally be distinguished as an original from other immaterial and material productions.[11] It might be technically reproduced, sold in material form (as a book), and appropriated as text and content by a reader, yet the form of the thought and its expression belonged inalienably to the author. The concept of property merged with the concept of being intellectually "proper" to the author.[12]

Property as what is "proper" to an author

A decisive issue was the redefinition of the relationship between the materiality and immateriality of the work. By subordinating the printed work – as a secondary material form – to the spiritual work, the intellectually active author was placed above the printer and publisher, whose activity was that of a skilled craftsman or merchant. This conception of the spiritual character of the author's labour and the work he produced went hand in hand with its separation from trade and commercial activities.

The grounding for this distinction between immaterial (spiritual) and material property was in certain respects new. Yet it also harked back to the traditional corporative distinction between socially "higher" spiritual work, "middle-ranking" commercial work and "lower" manual labour. Following the gains in status enjoyed by printers, publishers and traders from the 16th to the 18th century on the basis of their skilled and commercial work, authors now used the argument that theirs was individual, spiritual work to justify their social superiority over those who reproduced and commercially disseminated the work as a material artefact. In so doing, they were turning two previous hierarchies on their head, declaring themselves to be the patron

11 See Bosse 1981
12 See Plumpe 1979

of the publisher and also contesting the legitimacy of the traditional clerical and secular authority that stood above both the author *and* the publisher. For strategic and pragmatic reasons the publishers gradually came to accept their arguments. Given the expansion of the market for books and pamphlets from the late 18th century on, they had little to fear in economic terms. Experience told them that the owner of the material resources (capital, technology, material) would remain in a relatively strong position when it came to drafting the contract with the author. With the help of the author, they would be able to free themselves from the control of kings and princes with their traditional claims to feudalistic property rights in the world of material and immaterial goods alike.

The emergence of the modern figure of the "author" was supported by the spread of "possessive individualism" in agriculture, industry and commerce. This incorporated the notion that the creator of a product was entitled to that product as private "property," and that prosperity and the common good were better served by private property than traditional rights of dominion, professional rights, privileges, the arbitrary will of princes, and common property.

In legal reports and pamphlets on reprinting in the 18th century, lawyers and political commentators applied the conceptual and legal figure of private individual property to the author and his work. Using analogies drawn from commercial law, Roman law and natural law, the author was redefined as a "property-owner," who like any other commercial producer or owner should reap the benefits of his work – no less than the maker of furniture or the proprietor of a house and its land.[13]

In the second half of the 18th century the breakthrough to the modern concept of the author and intellectual property emerged more and more clearly. The step taken by the author from the patronage of estate-based and aristocratic society to the general bourgeois, "contractual" society was based on the notion of "property." The new co-protagonists of authors were also constructed at this point (the "public," the "rational individual," "society in general"), as well as key concepts and procedures that were to ground the new structure of bourgeois society as a whole, concepts such as "liberty," "property," "rights," "contracts," "constitution," "equality" and "progress."

---

13 See Rose 1993

4.2.3
The Author and the Work
in the Modern Regime of Property (1800–2000)

Legal institutionalisation of
intellectual property

The legal institutionalisation of intellectual property took place around 1800, as a consequence of political and institutional revolutions in the United States and France and in the wake of the gradual expansion of the liberal, contractual society in most European countries. It was at this time that the basic models were formulated, standardised and institutionalised, the effects of which can still be felt today.

The breakthrough and expansion of intellectual property rights

Exclusive rights for authors

In France the revolution did away with intermediary powers and put an end to professional corporations and privileges, including the privileges for theatre entrepreneurs, printers and individual works of authors. Freedom of trade was introduced. With the 1793 Decree, the legislature took one step backwards but two steps forwards in favour of authors. The Decree defined the professional groups that were to count as proprietors or owners of an exclusive right: "The authors of writings of all types, musical composers, painters and artists ... enjoy a lifelong, exclusive right to sell, to cause to be sold, or to transfer their works, wholly or partially, to third parties, within the territory of the Republic. Their heirs succeed them in this respect for a period of 10 years after the death of the author."[14] The North American Copyright Law of 1790 (An Act for the Encouragement of Learning), conceived on the English model, provided authors with the exclusive right of disposal over the printing, publishing and vending of their works (books, maps and charts) for a period of time stipulated as up to 28 years.[15] The Prussian "Law for the Protection of the Ownership of Works of Science and Art against Reprinting and Copying," dating from 1837, stated that the printing and mechanical reproduction of a text, sermon or lecture was the sole entitlement of "the author of the same or those authorised by him."[16] In this case, the right of ownership was established as lasting 30 years after the death of the author.

Extension of copyright
protection to other disciplines

In the 19th and 20th centuries, addenda and supplements, as well as new national laws, have extended copyright protection to countless further types of work and media forms, from sound carriers, photography and film through to computer programmes, data bases and web pages. Each case has been preceded by intense debate in which professional groups, entrepreneurs,

14 Quoted in Davies 1994, p. 186
15 See Samuels 2000, pp. 14
16 Quoted in Gieseke 1995, p. 238

politicians, customers and users have sought to come to an agreement on criteria and effects.

Legal, moral and social dimensions of intellectual property

Around 1800 the associations between copyright and property law were to the fore. Works of the intellect were considered as "property" by analogy with land and real estate. What were later to be conceived as the moral rights (droits moraux) or "personality rights" of the author were as yet of little interest to politicians and lawyers.

Moral and social dimension

The early legislation on intellectual property and copyright was liberal in spirit, but not liberalistic: intellectual property was regulated not only with a view to the private interests of the author, but ultimately targeted the public interest and economic and cultural progress. The sovereign reserved the right to make certain parts of knowledge and culture available free of charge to society in general and to the individual user in his institutions (education, science, the military). The limited duration of copyright was a matter of public interest and cultural and economic dynamics. The form of a thought or image was viewed as only passingly individual. As it was based on a reworking and appropriation of a general stock of cultural goods (defined with increasing frequency as a "national culture") and was destined sooner or later to become common property once again due to circulation and dissemination, intellectual property rights were initially limited to one or two decades. In the course of the 19th and 20th centuries, the duration of copyright protection was repeatedly lengthened to the benefit of the author and his heirs, today lasting 50 to 70 years after the death of the author.

After a certain term copyrights become common property once more

From the late 19th century onwards, intellectual property rights – initially a matter first and foremost of property law that stressed the author's rights over reproduction and income – gradually came to be extended to an explicitly "moral" ownership of texts, images and sound sequences. The "inalienable" moral and "personal" rights of the author protected the work from forgery, distortion and imitation by third parties. These were grounded on aesthetic and moral arguments as well as appeals to the personality rights of the author, and since the late 19th century have been approved first in case law, then statute law. This occurred in Germany earlier than in France,[17] and only recently in the USA, where copyright traditionally refers above all to the rights of reproduction and distribution.

Works are protected from forgery

17 See Wadle 1999

*Proponents and opponents of intellectual property:
discourses and interests*

In the 19th and 20th centuries, the development of copyright law was boosted by a variety of discourses seeking to convince a broader public of the significant and necessary role played by the author in cultural and social progress. The vindication of authors' rights was backed by the heroic status accorded (great) authors and artists in popular-science biographies and the media, as well as the canonisation of their works in histories of science, literature and art, where the activity of the creative individual was declared to be the foundation of ("national" or "human") culture in general. The author was made sacred by being set apart in cultural terms from the popular writer, the kitsch artist and the dilettante, and in legal terms from the plagiarist and the pirate.

Authors themselves contributed to such stylisation of their activity, work and role, and committed themselves increasingly to protecting their rights. At first just a few, but with time more and more writers, academics and artists became involved in polemics and politics, in public debate and legal action, not only to protect but even to extend the scope of intellectual property.

In the 19th century, the issue of intellectual property came to a head in the public debates on the (possibly even indefinite) extension of the term of copyright of an author and his heirs. The opponents of more extensive protection here cited the (potential) negative consequences such an extension would have on the media industry and the general public. Some stated bluntly that it would damage their own professional and commercial interests. Others referred to the fact that culture was a collective, national or human good. In the mid-19th century, the early socialist Proudhon thus opposed plans for extending the term of copyright in France with the argument that it would lead to the creation of "ancestral estates of the intellect" that would impede the dynamics of culture.[18] In the debate on reforming copyright law around 1840, English utilitarians spoke out against extension because, they said, it would lead to "monopolies" that would force prices up: culture was primarily a public domain and should remain accessible to all through cheap prices, public libraries and by allowing parts of works to be reprinted in school books.[19] Only thus, they said, would it fulfil its civilising and integrative function.

In the era of the nationalisation of culture and society, both the proponents of the social benefits of intellectual property and the champions of the public ownership of culture discovered and invented the author as a central figure

Heroic status given to artists and authors

Authors fight to extend their rights

Art as between commerce and the collective, national good

Author as a central figure of national culture and identity

---

18 See Götz von Olenhusen 1982
19 See Woodmansee 1998

of national culture and identity. In imperialistic states such as England, the achievements of the great poets on occasion even ranked alongside those of generals in the process of civilising the world. For this, it was argued, he and his family deserved not only honour, but also property (rights).

As such debates make clear, certain authors – together with their friends in the press, politics and law – tended to see the creator not merely as the owner of his work, but as a patron of the general public and culture at large. In this respect, the history of the author and the artist displays similar tendencies to that of the professionalisation of other fields of knowledge and expertise (such as academia, law and medicine).[20] Authors, frequently from the academic professions, base their claim to a privileged position with reference to the general significance of their knowledge.

Organisations: From authors' circles
to the World Intellectual Property Organisation

The 19th century saw the foundation of clubs, circles, societies and associations where writers, journalists, academics or artists discussed the role, function, importance and interests of their profession and elaborated strategies for improving their position and rights. This in turn led to the formation of regional and national professional associations, as well, from the late 19th century onwards, as collecting societies, which supervise and administer the authors' rights and collect duties from individuals and groups that utilise an author's work.

The development of
professional associations

In the second half of the 19th century, authors (of various professions) and lawyers met at a series of international congresses, which in 1887 finally led to the "Bern Convention," at which the signatory states promised foreign authors the same treatment as nationals.[21] International cooperation and author lobbying continued in the early 20th century with several revisions being made to the Bern Convention and with the international movement of "brainworkers." At the end of this development, which was characterised by an increasing combination of lobby and state strategies, there today stands the World Intellectual Property Organisation (WIPO).

---

20 See Siegrist 2001
21 See Püschel 1986

*From the internationalisation to the globalisation
of intellectual property*

Internet and digitalisation
reopen the debate

In today's era of globalisation and digitalisation, international agreements and supranational organisations are aiming at worldwide control of intellectual property. In so doing, they are confronting a problem that today arises in new form as a result of digitalisation and the Internet, but that had in principle already become virulent by the 19th century due to the mobility and fluidity of intellectual works. When authors and providers appropriated texts, ideas and images from foreign copyright-owners in the 19th century, they often

Problem of cross-border
rights

themselves received full copyright for this in their own country. Countries with a low level of intellectual production disregarded foreign legal titles, considered translations as originals (since they were not literal "copies"), and tolerated unauthorised versions and reprints of foreign works because this was an aid to economic vigour and cultural life. The USA at times cared just as little about the rights of English authors as Belgians and West-Swiss entrepreneurs did about those of French authors.

Gradually, however, states and nation states developed rules and procedures that protected the rights of foreign authors and providers as well. These were initially bilateral agreements, whereby France, for example, would

Need for bringing national
copyright regulations into line

promise a Prussian author whose work was printed in France the same legal treatment as a French author. The 1887 Bern Convention extended the principle of mutual "national treatment" to all authors from the signatory states. This in turn provided a substantial impulse for bringing the various national copyright laws into line with one another. Following the Second World War, further international copyright agreements sought to integrate post-colonial states into the international system of copyright protection.

Eventually even the socialist states joined the Bern Convention. After the Russian Revolution had initially declared the works of important authors to be the property of the people, the Soviet Union and the socialist states later fashioned a copyright law that formally laid considerable emphasis on the personal rights of the creator as well. In fact, however, the intention was that the author should serve socialism. The system of producing and transmitting art, science and culture under state socialism, as well as the lack of independent jurisdiction, led to the deformation of the personality right of the author.[22]

Agreements on copyright
implementation

In large parts of Europe, copyright law is today being unified by European Union guidelines. On a worldwide scale, the General Agreement on Trade and Tariffs (GATT) and bodies such as the World Trade Organisation (WTO) have sought to implement copyright protection through the

22 Levitsky 1964

TRIPS accord on Trade-Related Aspects of Intellectual Property Rights. A central role has here been assumed by the supranational WIPO, which globally champions the idea that the original creator of works that are protected against reproduction enjoys basic rights regarding revenue and moral rights: "Why protect copyright? Copyright and related rights are essential to human creativity, by giving creators incentives in the form of recognition and fair economic rewards. Under this system of rights, creators are assured that their work can be disseminated without fear of unauthorized copying or piracy. This in turn helps increase access to and enhances the enjoyment of culture, knowledge, and entertainment all over the world."[23] The WIPO programme uses traditional rhetoric and concepts that are as time-honoured as they are ambiguous. Given the current problems in the world of intellectual property, some people are thus asking whether the concept of "creators" refers more to the major providers and patent-owners than to the classically "creative," who are now even threatened with losing their grip on the very concept of creativity, as intellectual property seemingly becomes a matter primarily of trade interests. This is a criticism made by all those committed to an increase in authors' rights or the rights of users or the general public.

Intellectual property as a matter of trade interests

Worldwide, the WIPO represents those powers that seek to prolong existing conceptual and legal figures even in changed circumstances, extending them to as many symbols and forms of knowledge as possible. The aim is to reinforce the discursive hegemony in the public sphere, on the one hand defaming and criminalising unauthorised users as hackers and pirates, on the other utilising educational campaigns to instil the ethically and legally correct use of intellectual property in citizens, users and customers.[24] Countries that ignore this conception of intellectual property or are slow to put it into practice or implement it institutionally are sanctioned with credit restrictions, the denial of tariff advantages, and trade boycotts.

WIPO uses boycotts to impose rights

4.2.4
Conclusion

In the nation states of the 19th and 20th centuries, copyright law helped grant authors a certain degree of control over the authenticity, reproduction and commercialisation of their works, control which they are today threatened with losing. Current developments are calling into question traditional forms of the division of labour, the associated cultural, economic and legal hierarchies, and the arrangements between professional groups and interest groups.

Control being lost once again

---

23 WIPO homepage.
24 See Halbert 1999

" **The value of an author and what he produces is determined increasingly by commercial interests and less and less by intellectual achievement.** *""*

The "creators" lament vociferously that the established hierarchy between intellectual producers and commercial providers is being obliterated as concentration, globalisation and digitalisation permit the latter to extend their rights of disposal at the expense of the former. Much less clamorous, by contrast, is the debate about the changes in the established positions even amongst intellectuals and authors. The digitalisation of image, text and sound is changing the division of labour and the legal hierarchies between the classic categories of the author, giving rise to new, hybrid roles and professions.

Digitalisation reduces control over reproduction

The classic construction of the author was based upon the distinction between intellectual and technical or distributive-commercial work. In the late 19th and early 20th centuries, authors' organisations and collecting societies gave authors a certain share of the control over the commercial functions – collectively and often with the aid of the state. Today they face the prospect of losing this control, as digitalisation makes it substantially more difficult to supervise the integrity of the work, its reproduction and distribution. This transforms not only the relationship between the author and the commercial provider, but also that between the author and the recipient, user or public. The traditional forms of the division of labour, solidarity among professional groups, and social contracts among the players and interest groups are disintegrating. Digitalisation and the concentration of the media on the one hand, and the broadening of citizens' and consumers' demands for culture and entertainment on the other hand, are challenging the "creative" and undermining their formally guaranteed intellectual property rights. New forms of distribution, exploitation and commercialisation mean that the value of an author and what he produces is determined increasingly by commercial interests and demand and finds its legitimation less and less in "intellectual achievement."

Value of an author as dependent upon commercial potential

Multiculturalism through new media

Finally, the transformation of the nation state and relativisation of what has traditionally been termed national culture or identity is also having ambivalent consequences for the creative (as well, at times, as for providers and the public). The new developments in the media and in communication are creating and fostering new forms of interculturalism and multiculturalism. Hybridity is replacing homogeneity; internationalisation, Europeanisation and globalisation are leading to a de-territorialisation and de-juridification of the conception of "culture."

The classical nation state, which from the 19th century was the decisive authority for culture, authors, publishers and intellectual property rights, understood its task as promoting and shaping the national art and culture with a view to nurturing social integration. This was the major assumption underlying the ideas of copyright, intellectual property and the mediation of private and public interests. Knowledge, symbols and images might in a certain sense lie beyond boundaries, yet from the 19th century until into the 1960s each nation state organised and territorialised its culture in its own specific way: as a cultural and constitutional state it defined and fostered national art and culture, and with its institutions and laws it protected its artists within the framework of the market and the public cultural regime.

In the process of deregulation, Europeanisation and globalisation, the postmodern nation state is considerably reducing its claims to cultural homogenisation and hegemony and thus also its competence to shape and regulate copyright. The patronage of the cultural state, which has hitherto greatly benefited the author, is being called into question, for it is no longer simply taken for granted that the state should use its cultural, educational and legal policies to provide special care for its national authors when works of great cultural and academic value and marketable products of popular and mass culture are being offered in great abundance and diversity on an international market without boundaries – and especially when these seem to be accessible at any time and any place thanks to digitalisation. In this context it again emerges particularly clearly that traditional copyright law and intellectual property protection was the right of a national cultural cartel, allowing the relationship between producers, providers, the public and politics to be regulated in the national interest. This basic model is today being challenged by de-localising economic and cultural concepts and strategies of de-nationalisation, trans-nationalisation and globalisation, facilitated and supported in one way or another by the technical possibilities of digitalisation and the digital media.

Despite the obvious real breaks with the past, both discourse and practice still display great continuity. At times it seems as though the new phenomena are being interpreted with the classical concepts, metaphors and clichés – as ambiguous as they are abstruse – simply in order to bring the social, economic, political and cultural struggles of the 19th and 20th centuries back to life once more on the digitalised stage of the 21st century. The debate frequently moves among the discursive formations of the 19th and early 20th century, without fully realising it. Guided by an everyday political and practical orientation, it often lacks more fundamental historical and systematic reflection. Accordingly, the aim has here been to cast a glance at history to show how the idea of intellectual property and the intellectual property-owner has been constructed and constantly revised. Once this is realised, it will be easier to elaborate a new set of concepts more suited to the peculiarities of today's situation and to discuss the legal regulations, instruments and procedures that can mediate between the conflicting interests and between tradition and innovation.

Deregulation calls into question nation state borders

Historical reflection as a basis for contemporary discussion

Digital Rights Management: Between Author Protection and the Protection of Innovation

Stefan Bechtold

Napster, Gnutella, KaZaA, Morpheus, Grokster, Freenet, Madster, eDonkey, Overnet – the list of peer-to-peer systems that the sound carrier and film industries hold responsible for the sharp decline in their turnover goes on and on. While the danger of copyright infringement on the Internet goes soaring, the power of copyright to react provides food for thought. The media industry is increasingly reliant on protective measures that lie outside traditional copyright law. "Digital Rights Management" systems – or DRM systems – promise new and comprehensive opportunities for protection.

P2P systems throw the media industry into turmoil

DRM systems permit the safe distribution of digital contents – including copyrighted works of music, film and authorship – over the Internet and other channels of digital communication such as CDs, pay-TV decoders, digital video recorders, portable players and mobile telephones. They make it possible for rights-owners to sell their products safely to authorised users, facilitate effective and sophisticated rights administration, and thus open up new business models for digital contents.

Control over digital contents is regained

DRM-systems lie at the intersection of law, technology and economics. Alongside the many technical and economic problems, from a legal viewpoint its relationship with copyright law is of particular interest.[1] By comparison with traditional copyright law, DRM systems promise an undreamt-of degree of control over the distribution and use of digital contents.

---

1 DRM systems also raise problems in the field of data protection law, consumer law, contract law, monopolies law and patent law. See Möschel/Bechtold 1998, pp. 571

4.3.1
Protective Mechanisms in DRM Systems

DRM systems protect digital contents in many ways. The idea is that a variety of interrelated technical protective measures allow the provider to transmit its contents through secure channels to the authorised user, at the same time preventing unauthorised third parties from using these contents as well.[2] An important role is here played by encryption procedures and what are known as "digital containers." "Key revocation" procedures ensure that compromised terminals are excluded from further use of the DRM system, while "rights locker" architectures make it possible for users to use their contents at various points on all their terminals ("anytime, anywhere access to all my content").[3] Using copy-management systems[4] it is possible to control the number of copies a user can make of a particular digital content. With the aid of metadata, contents, rights-owners, conditions of use and users can be described in a formalised and machine-readable form.[5] This facilitates the automated sale of digital contents. By means of digital watermarks, metadata can be embedded directly into digital contents, making it at the very least more difficult to remove them.[6]

DRM systems employ various technologies to identify users and trace back illegal copies of digital contents. Digital fingerprints (a variant of digital watermarks), serial numbers and "traitor tracing" procedures can provide evidence for legal steps taken against unlawful users. Digital signatures, hash functions, fragile watermarks and challenge-response procedures are deployed to establish the authenticity and integrity of contents, metadata, system components and users. Tamper-proof hardware and software components are designed to make security attacks more difficult. Finally, DRM systems also utilise procedures intended to make it harder to produce analogue copies. DRM systems are frequently combined with payment systems or integrated in comprehensive e-commerce systems. To provide a universally high level of security and an efficient sales platform, the individual components of a DRM system must function and engage smoothly with one another. Questions of system integration and standardisation are thus of paramount importance.[7]

Copy-management systems and licences regulate reproduction

Types of DRM system

---

2 For an overview of the technical protection provided by DRM systems, see Bechtold 2002a, pp. 19–145; Rosenblatt/Trippe/Mooney 2002, pp. 57–137

3 Sander 2002, pp. 64, 66

4 Exemplary here are the "Serial Copy Management System" (SCMS) used in DAT players and the "Copy Generation Management System (CGMS) used in DVD players.

5 This may be done, for example, using the "Digital Object Identifier" (DOI) or the "eXtended rights Markup Language" (XrML).

6 For a comprehensive account of digital watermarks see Katzenbeisser/Petitcolas 2000; also Wayner 2002, pp. 291–302

7 Important standards in the sphere of DRM include the "Content Scramble System" (CSS),

The development of DRM systems is far from over. Nonetheless, there are clear signs that DRM systems will feature prominently in the field of future e-commerce. Even today DRM components are to be found in DVD players, pay-TV decoders, video recorders, portable players, mobile phones and many software applications. These include the Microsoft operating system Windows XP and the Windows Media Player, the Adobe PDF format, and a number of peer-to-peer systems.

The advance of DRM systems

Despite all these efforts of a technical order, no DRM system provides perfect protection. The aim of fully developed DRM systems is not normally to prevent professional attackers with large-scale resources from producing pirate copies. Rather, DRM systems are geared to the mass market with the intention of making this impossible for the normal user.[8]

Protection can only ever be partial

DRM systems are based not only upon technological but also legal protective mechanisms. In recent years legislators have been creating regulations worldwide that prohibit the circumvention of technical protection measures and certain preparatory operations. At the level of international law, the relevant directives can be found in two treaties passed by the "World Intellectual Property Organisation" (WIPO).[9] At a European level, the Directive on Copyright in the Information Society (2001)[10] and the Conditional Access Directive (1998)[11] provide for such legal protection of technical protection measures. While the Conditional Access Directive was transposed into German law in spring 2002, the corresponding law for the Directive on Copyright in the Information Society is still in the legislative process. In the United States, similar regulations are to be found in the "Digital Millennium Copyright Act," passed in 1998.[12]

Legal harmonisation on a global scale

> "It showed that, contrary to the assurances of the copyright industry when the law was enacted over the warnings of many critics, the DMCA is indeed being used for outrageous purposes – to slam down speech in ways that should be unconstitutional."
>
> *Dan Gillmor (2002)*[13]

---

the "Content Protection for Recordable and Prerecorded Media" (CPRM), the "Digital Transmission Content Protection" (DTCP) and the "High-bandwidth Digital Content Protection" (HDCP). See in greater detail Bechtold 2002b, pp. 101–127; Bechtold 2002a, pp. 213, 215

8 See Sander 2002, pp. 64, 67–72; Marks/Turnbull 2000, pp. 198, 208

9 The two treaties – the "WIPO Copyright Treaty" (WCT) and the "WIPO Performances and Phonograms Treaty" (WPPT) – were passed in 1996 and came into force in early 2002.

10 Directive 2001/29/EG, Official Journal EG Nr. L 167, 22 June 2001, p. 10

11 Directive 98/84/EG, Official Journal EG Nr. L 320, 28 November 1998, p. 54

12 For a detailed account of these directives, see Bechtold 2002b, pp. 196–248; Wand 2001

13 Gillmor, Dan (2002): HP backs off copyright threat against security researchers, posted in Silicon Valley, www.siliconvalley.com 2. August 2002.

Licence agreements as part
of DRM systems

Along with such legal anti-circumvention provisions, content providers in DRM systems can also protect their interests through contractual arrangements with individual users. Licence agreements of this sort may have a considerable range of application.[14] The user may be forbidden by contract, for example, to burn protected digital contents on CDs, copy them on portable players or play them more than ten times. With the aid of metadata, such conditions of use can be expressed in machine-readable form. In this way DRM systems can ensure by technical means that contractual conditions of use are adhered to. Should an attacker succeed in altering or removing these metadata, he is violating the aforementioned norms of legal anti-circumvention protection.[15]

Patent licensing agreements
as part of DRM systems

Finally, technology licensing agreements are used in DRM systems to protect authors and those entitled to copyright protection. Many DRM technologies are protected by patents or as business secrets. The appropriate licensing agreements, which manufacturers of consumer appliances in particular must enter into, contain a whole range of stipulations for the protection of digital contents.[16]

4.3.2
Implications

DRM systems are characterised by the interaction of diverse protective mechanisms: technology, legal anti-circumvention protection, licence agreements, technology licensing agreements and copyright (see figure 1).

Replacement of copyright by
DRM systems

DRM systems have little left in common with copyright in the classical sense. They provide a level of protection that can far exceed traditional copyright in terms of effectiveness and security. From an economic point of view DRM systems – like copyright – solve the "free rider" problem of information as a public good. In the digital realm, the interconnected protective mechanisms of DRM systems could increasingly come to replace copyright. In this context, copyright as a mechanism for protecting the author will lose in significance.

New business models
supported by DRM systems

In principle this development is to be welcomed. Compared to copyright, DRM systems provide a previously unheard-of measure of flexibility. They can be individually adjusted to the needs of the content provider and support innovative business models. Lower transaction costs and new opportunities for price discrimination also contribute to this.

---

14 See Bechtold 2002b, pp. 160–178; Bechtold 2002a, pp. 213, 217
15 On this interplay, see Bechtold 2002b, pp. 273–277; Bechtold 2002a, pp. 213, 217
16 See in detail Bechtold 2002b, pp. 178–196; Bechtold 2002a, pp. 213, 218

Protection through

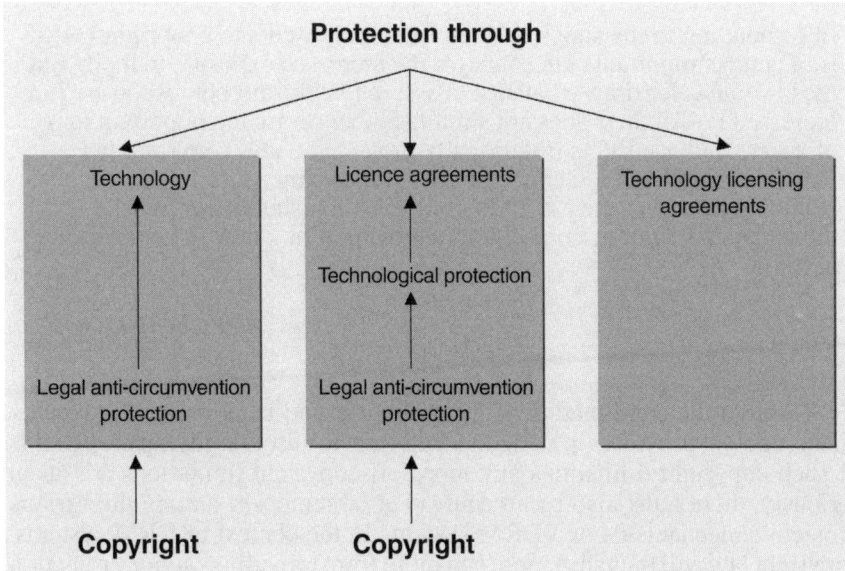

Fig. 4.3-1 Different protective mechanisms in DRM systems

Types of protective
mechanisms

Yet the development also has its problems. In their strongest form, DRM systems are akin to copyright cast in silicone, the scope and arrangement of which are determined by those who develop the systems and use them for the protection of digital contents. DRM systems can thus be applied to protect contents that are not covered by copyright protection. They are also capable of controlling the use of digital contents in highly subtle ways. Such control of use is foreign to traditional copyright.

DRM systems as overriding
copyright limitations

There is a danger, in particular, that DRM systems might override copyright limitations. From a legal viewpoint, copyright limitations, as contained in §§ 45 ff. of the German Copyright Law, serve to promote freedom of information, innovation, free competition, data protection and the interests of education and culture. In short, they serve the interests of the general public.[17] From an economic perspective, copyright limitations are meant to overcome shortcomings in the market, facilitate dynamic processes of innovation, and restrict the impairments to social welfare caused by under-use of the protected contents and to this extent near-monopolistic situations.[18]

17 See Guibault 2002, pp. 27–90
18 See Bechtold 2002b, pp. 313–317, 324–336; Bechtold 2002a, pp. 213, 223–225

Protection against theft must not restrict use rights

> In responding to the shock that the Internet presents to copyright law, it is of course important to account for the increased exposure to theft. But the law must also draw a balance to assure that this proper response to an increased risk of theft does not simultaneously erase the important range of access and use rights traditionally protected under copyright law. ... Now we should add a second concern to that same story: artists deserve compensation. But their right to compensation should not translate into the industry's right to control how innovation in a new industry should develop.
>
> *Lawrence Lessig (2001)*[19]

The shift from author protection to user protection

Through the combination of technological and legal protective mechanisms, content providers in DRM systems can stop users enjoying the benefits of such copyright limitations any more. If copyright limitations are taken seriously, there must also be an equivalent of some sort among the various protective mechanisms of a DRM system. In the context of DRM systems, copyright law will thus shift more and more from providing *author* protection to *user* protection.[20]

Lack of a consistent programme on the part of legislators

The legislation has in part responded to this challenge. On occasions it is not possible for copyright limitations to be contractually overridden.[21] Many regulations that prohibit the circumvention of technical protection measures are in turn provided with limitations. However, the existing limitations are characterised by a high degree of complexity and by logical inconsistencies. The copyright limitations in the U.S. American "Digital Millennium Copyright Act" are indecisive and lack an underlying legislative programme.[22] The relevant regulation in the European Directive on Copyright in the Information Society is a toothless tiger that can easily be circumvented using a suitable business model in the Internet.[23] A consistent conception of how DRM systems are to be brought into line with copyright limitations does not exist at present.

---

19 Lessig, Lawrence (2001): The future of ideas: the fate of the commons in a connected world, Random House: New York, p. 200.
20 See Bechtold 2002b, p. 382f.; Lessig 1999, p. 127
21 On the relation between copyright limitations and licence agreements see Guibault 2002.
22 See Samuelson 1999
23 See Bechtold 2002a, pp. 423–28

If copyright law must protect fair use – meaning the law cannot protect copyrighted material without leaving space for fair use – then laws protecting code protecting copyrighted material should also leave room for fair use. You can't do indirectly (protect fair-use-denying-code protecting copyright) what you can't do directly (protect copyright without protecting fair use).

Lawrence Lessig (2001)[24]

Protection for protection?

4.3.3
Conclusion

Developments in the realm of DRM are far from over. Technical procedures are still evolving. The underlying legal framework is slowly being adapted to the digital environment. Considerable economic analysis is still required both on a theoretical and an empirical plane.[25] Companies are trying out a variety of business models based upon DRM systems. There are no obvious patent solutions for all these problems.

Despite the uncertainties involved certain tendencies can be discerned in the developments. In DRM systems, copyright loses its status as the primary mechanism of protection. It is replaced by a conglomeration of interlocking mechanisms that can far exceed copyright in the level of protection and the effectiveness they offer. Such an excess of protection – or "hyperprotection" – is not unproblematic. It can prove detrimental to innovation[26] and produce a concentration and homogenisation of information production.[27]

DRM systems make copyright superfluous

There is an increasing tendency to use private or legal standardisation to anchor DRM components in as many terminals and system components as possible.[28] Although such developments may seem desirable in a market decisively influenced by network effects, the risks of perpetuating obsolescent

The danger of perpetuating obsolescent technologies

---

24 Lessig, Lawrence (2001): The future of ideas: the fate of the commons in a connected world, Random House: New York, p. 188.
25 See Bechtold 2002b, pp. 319–369; Cohen 1998
26 See Koelman/Herberger 2000, pp. 165, 221; in general Lessig 2001; see Elkin-Koren/Netanel 2002; Dreyfuss/Zimmerman/First 2001
27 See Benkler 2002
28 In the USA there now exist several relevant bills and initiatives on the part of the Federal Communications Commission. Microsoft's Palladium-Initiative and the "Trusted Computing Platform Alliance" (TCPA) could also go in this direction.

technologies, impairing the competition between technologies, and overemphasising particular interests should also be borne in mind. DRM systems are being used more and more for the purpose of providing hardware and software platforms with broad technical, contractual and legal protection. This allows control to be exercised over the development of the applications that run on these platforms. An increasingly crucial role is thus played by private-sector initiatives and legal limitations for keeping such information and technology platforms open, allowing the independent development of compatible and interoperable applications. DRM systems can also be used to seal markets off. From the point of view of data protection law, the creation of extensive use-profiles by DRM systems can prove problematic.[29]

The privatisation of legal protection through DRM systems

At the intersection of DRM systems with traditional copyright, what emerges is that Digital Rights Management permits content providers to cobble together their own copyright law, so to speak, themselves fixing its scope.[30] A privatisation of legal protection can be discerned. All over the world legislators are supporting this development by creating new anti-circumvention regulations to protect technical protective measures and by increasingly recognising licence agreements as effective. It is open to debate whether this privatising tendency is going too far. The question is whether the privatisation of legal protection should be restricted for the sake of the public interests that conflict with it.

Who should be allowed to control information?

These features – the increasing protection by technology and contract, the increasing privatisation of legal protection with the underlying support of the legislator, the restriction of this privatising tendency by legal regulations in defence of public interests, and the progressive transition to indirect regulation by the legislator – are not peculiar to DRM systems. They are tendencies that can be observed in Internet law in general.[31] The issue is who should be allowed to control the access and use of information and how far this control should go. At stake are questions of the legal design of technology and state-regulated self-regulation. Defining the basic conditions of information access and information use could prove to be the task of the information law of the future.

---

29 See Bygrave 2002, p. 51; Bygrave/Koelman 2000, p. 59
30 See Burk/Cohen 2001
31 See Bechtold 2002b, pp. 439–48

Chapter 4.4

Does the Internet Need a New Competition Policy? A Global Problem from a German Point of View

Arnold Picot and Dominik K. Heger

Many parallels can be drawn between the Internet and the Wild West. The gold rush can be likened to the share rush on the new markets and the euphoria about the development of the Internet, the burst Internet bubble to the end of the gold rush. In both cases, the manufacturers of tools in particular – tools for gold-prospecting on the one hand and the tools of hardware and software on the other – seem to have earned a lot of money. There are also parallels with respect to the rules. Either there are no rules at all, or if there are rules, there is not enough clout to enforce them. The economy itself creates practical rules, which might be regarded as the equivalent of the typical Wild West practice of enforcing the law of the jungle.

WWW and the Wild West

Against this background the question is whether it is really necessary to adapt competition policy to the changed circumstances of the Internet economy. This will be analysed with reference primarily to German competition policy.

4.4.1 Competition Policy

The Law against Restraints on Competition

The Law against Restraints on Competition (*Gesetz gegen Wettbewerbsbeschränkungen*, shortened to GWB) was created in 1957 as an independent German law for the regulation of competition policy.[1] This law broadly followed the neoclassical idea of free competition. The considerations at the heart of the Law against Restraints on Competition can be subdivided into three problems of competition theory that call for competition policy measures:[2]

Central considerations of competition law

---

1 See Neumann 2000, p. 45
2 See Schmidt 1999, pp. 166

– deterioration of the market structure (e.g. by mergers and cartels resulting in a non-competitive market structure)

– anti-competitive or competition-damaging behaviour (exclusionary practices, e.g. boycotts and refusals to supply)

– market results not in line with competition (e.g. excessive prices).

Market structure

Defending the ability of businesses to compete

The Law against Restraints on Competition in principle forbids agreements, resolutions and pre-arranged behaviour that are aimed at or result in the prevention, restriction or distortion of competition (§1 GWB).[3] Any collaborations are meant to foster the competitiveness of small and medium-sized businesses in order to compensate for their disadvantages compared with large businesses. Accordingly, cooperation agreements between small and medium-sized businesses are permitted as long as they promote the competitiveness of the cooperating businesses, but do not essentially restrict competition in the market (§ 4 GWB).

Exclusionary practices

The basis for ascertaining the exclusionary or exploitative abuse of a market is the purpose of the relevant market and the domination of that market by one business (§19 GWB).[4]

Preventing exclusionary practices

The exclusionary abuse of market power occurs when the business dominating the market substantially restricts the competitive chances of other businesses without objectively justified reasons. It also takes place when the business dominating the market refuses to grant other businesses access to their nets or other infrastructure facilities for a reasonable fee. This aspect in particular becomes increasingly important in the Internet economy, as will be shown later.

The exploitative abuse of market power comes about when the business dominating the market applies fees or terms of trade that in all likelihood could not be enforced if there were effective competition. It also refers to the situation when less favourable fees or terms of trade are demanded than the market-dominating firm itself demands in comparable markets.

---

3 Certain special forms of cartels are exempted from this law (cf. §§ 1-8 GWB). These are not dealt with in any more detail here.
4 See Schmidt 1999, pp. 168

Further possible elements of exclusionary abuse are boycotts and the refusal to supply, (price) discrimination, as well as exclusive dealing and tie-in agreements (cf. §§ 19 ff. GWB).

Market results not in line with competition

Originally the GWB did not automatically consider market power to be something bad; it was rather the fact that the business dominating the market took advantage of its position that was regarded as bad. This point of view was only revised in 1973 when the Merger Control Law was passed. Under this law large mergers are controlled (cf. §§ 35-37 GWB) whenever a dominant position in the market (cf. §19 GWB) is created or increased. If, however, the merging businesses can prove that the merger produces improvements in the conditions of competition in the market and that these improvements outweigh or compensate for the disadvantages, then the burden of proof can be reversed (§ 36 GWB).

Preventing businesses from taking advantage of market power

4.4.2
Politico-Economic Instruments
for Influencing Competition

The central idea of competition policy is to maintain competition. An important means of achieving this goal – apart from supervising the abuse of competition – is the possibility of prohibiting mergers. The conditions for prohibiting such mergers as set out in legal systems generally differ considerably from country to country. Nevertheless the criteria for prohibition can be divided into two groups: the principle of market domination on the one hand and the principle of the "substantial lessening of competition" (SLC) on the other.

Maintaining competition

When assessing mergers, almost all member states of the European Union as well as the European Union itself consider whether the merger in question creates or increases a dominant position in the market. This is estimated to consist, for example, in a market share of 35%. The USA, Canada, New Zealand and Australia, by contrast, are supporters of the SLC principle, which prohibits all mergers that would result in a substantial reduction in the level of competition.[5] A merger may here also be rejected even though there is no market domination provided a reduction in competition could nonetheless plausibly be adjudged to come about.

---

5 See Bundeskartellamt 2001, p. 1

In the context of the reform of the Merger Control Law, the European Union is thinking about introducing the SLC test.[6]   The following table provides a comparative overview of the respective concepts and criteria for prohibiting mergers:

Is the competition law still sufficient?

The object of the following discussion is not to determine whether a shift towards the SLC principle should take place. The focus is on whether the current Law against Restraints on Competition in Germany functions with regard to the Internet and the resulting changes in competition. To lay the foundations for these considerations, there follows a preliminary analysis of certain aspects of Internet use and the economic peculiarities of the Internet.

4.4.3
Features of the Internet Relevant to Competition

The burst Internet bubble as well as the continued rapid spread of the Internet raise the questions of which aspects of the phenomenon have impelled it in this way and what are the implications relevant for competition.

Dematerialisation and digitalisation

A shift of processes into virtual space

As a rule anything which can be broken down into data packages is suitable for transportation and distribution via the Internet, e.g. software, text, image, sound and video files. The Internet economy is thus understood in terms of a change from physical atoms to digital bits, rendering traditional strategies and rules – especially in the context of production and sales – increasingly ineffective. More and more processes can be transferred to virtual space, lessening the need for space, storage facilities and physical transportation. As a consequence, the factor of location, which used to be vital for businesses, is now less important. These developments, referred to as dematerialisation or, more commonly, digitalisation, have caused firms to concentrate increasingly on their core competencies. Such concentration not only implies the need for new forms of cooperation, but also means that these businesses become specialists in relatively small "markets" where they might soon become monopolists. This raises the question of defining the relevant market, since to a certain extent it does not make sense to speak of a "market" for a highly specialised service as this service can only be exchanged within a particular affiliated group rather than freely exchanged on the market.

Concentration on core competencies leads to small markets and new forms of cooperation

---

6 See Hoenig/Scheer 2001

	Germany	EU	USA	Australia
Criterion for prohibiting mergers	Mergers that are expected to create a monopoly.	Mergers that create or strengthen a monopoly, where this would considerably restrict effective competition.	Mergers where the effect may be substantially to lessen competition, or to tend to create a monopoly.	Mergers that would have the effect, or be likely to have the effect of substantially lessening competition in a market.
Actual or potential competition	Actual or potential competition by businesses located within or outside German jurisdiction (…)	Actual or potential competition by businesses located within or outside the EU.	Binding market entry (=new competition necessitating the payment of important "sunk costs" for market entry and market exit).	Actual or potential import competition in the market.
Choices and interests of the competitors	Possibility of the competitor to switch to other businesses.	Choices of the suppliers and customers. Interests of the intermediate and end users.	Degree of possible substitution with products/ areas outside the relevant market.	Actual of probable availability of substitutes. Probability that the customer will considerably and permanently increase prices or profit margins.

Fig. 4.4-1. Comparison of concepts and criteria for prohibiting mergers

Comparison of criteria for assessing competition

Reduction of transaction costs

Reduction in transaction costs as distances are more easily overcome

The level of transaction costs[7] decisively determines which forms of coopera-tion (e.g. business webs) are efficient and which institutions are instrumental in facilitating or stabilising cooperation. A major part of the transaction costs is formed by the costs for overcoming distances in collaborations where the individual parties do not have the same location. As explained above, the Internet allows digitalised information or files to be transferred more easily and at ever decreasing costs. It is hard to determine the exact extent of this reduction in transaction costs. It is a fact, however, that large distances are no longer an important barrier. Noteworthy is that these reduced transaction costs lead to a decrease in the costs of market coordination compared with other institutional arrangements.[8]

The formation of networks

Due to the high degree of dynamism and complexity of the markets, it be-comes increasingly difficult for businesses in the Internet economy single-handedly to put marketable products on the market. This makes it necessary to find an alternative to such exclusively self-sufficient development. One of the possibilities that is often chosen is to form the aforementioned business

Business webs

webs.[9] Business webs are groups of businesses that act independently in economic and legal terms, while at the same time efficiently complementing each other and cooperating to achieve maximum added value, with each busi-ness concentrating on the service it provides best.[10] The common goal is the

Added value of a complementary system product

added value of a complementary system product. Each business concentrates on its core competences, but they can only be successful if the value-added network is successful. In this context it is common to speak of the creation of "virtual businesses."[11]

Consequently business webs cause the lines between businesses to blur. From the point of view of competition policy, the question thus arises whether it would make more sense to concentrate on business webs rather than on individual businesses when assessing market shares. Since such networks tend to be instable in the long run, however, intervention for the sake of fair trading seems to be questionable in the case of business webs.

---

7 See Coase 1937, Macneil 1980, Picot 1982, Picot/Dietl 1990, Williamson 1981, 1983, 1985
8 See Picot/Reichwald/Wigand 2001, pp. 335 in greater detail
9 See Hagel III 1996, and ECC 2001, pp. 180
10 See Wirtz 2001, pp. 189
11 See Picot/Neuburger 2002 and Scholz 2000

On the Internet individual intermediaries can take over the organisation of markets and set general conditions in cyberspace by defining rules for concluding transactions. The auction house eBay is a good example of this. If several suppliers get together in order to organise a market as in the case of Covisint (a collaboration between the major car manufacturers Ford, GM and DaimlerChrysler), then even the line between cooperation and competition can become blurred. In the specialist literature this condition is referred to as "coopetition."[12] Such structures require special observation from the perspective of competition policy, as the boundaries between monopolies and additional services that foster efficiency may well become blurred.

Coopetition as difficult to regulate

The decreasing significance of spatial distance produced by the reduction in transaction costs – and the concomitant process of globalisation – means that competitiveness now depends on attributes other than spatial localisation. From the point of view of governmental regulation, the formation of global networks made possible by the Internet has also caused, for example, an accelerated internationalisation of money markets, which raises questions of stock exchange supervision, etc. It is now becoming ever more difficult to define a particular market in spatial terms. As a consequence, the need for coordination between the monopoly authorities of individual countries is increasing.

Globalisation and legal boundaries

Standards and network effects

Web-linking in an open and dynamic world calls for standards for the coordination and compatibility of system products. Standardisation in the form of the Internet Protocol TCP/IP was the most important prerequisite for the rapid development of the Internet.[13] The establishment or implementation of a standard[14] generally depends on the resulting benefit, also referred to as a technology effect. As a consequence, the advantages created by the introduction or change of a standard must at least offset the costs incurred on account of this change. Since standards affect a large number of users, network effects have to be assumed.

Overcoming the costs of changing to a standard

A network effect means that the individual benefit to the network participant depends on the number of users participating in this network.[15] In order to bring about an individual change, the technology effect and the network effect have to be commutated. Since a critical mass of users has to be achieved before a standard can function, the users wait until this is achieved.

Commutating the technology effect and the network effect

12 See Browning/Reiss 1998, p. 112 and Nalebuff/Brandenburger 1996
13 Beck/Prinz 1999, p. 38
14 See Erhardt 2001 for a fuller account
15 See ECC 2001, p. 214 and Shapiro/Varian 1999, p. 13

If the users wait, the suppliers also hold back due to predicted sales problems. With respect to networks such as the Internet, for example, this means that potential users do not decide to join the network unless a number of interesting use-possibilities is offered first. The Internet has achieved this critical mass.

One argument frequently cited in support of governmental intervention in competition policy is inferior standardisation.[16] Here it is assumed that even an inferior technology can be successful if there is a lock-in. In this sense, government intervention would be justified as a means of supporting superior technology. If a government determines a standard, however, a monopoly will be created since one supplier's system will have to be established as the standard, which in turn seems a questionable practice from the point of view of competition policy. If no standard is determined, there is a greater chance that a technically more advanced solution is developed, which then substitutes the current standard.[17] Often a kind of monopoly is necessary for realising network effects. The network effects in turn are vital for the proper functioning of the product and are therefore a prerequisite for entrepreneurial success. In the German Law against Restraints in Competition it is the exploitation of a monopoly rather than the monopoly per se that is regarded as negative. There is a possibility, however, that methods for creating network effects, such as giving products away for free, financed, for example, by cross-subsidisation, might be considered a distortion of competition.

Convergence of fields of trade

Digitalisation also leads to new possibilities for combining multimedia and interactive uses of media. This has its basis in the fusion between the media, telecommunications and IT sectors, creating a new convergence sector.[18] There has been a blurring of boundaries between the individual branches. Over the last few years the value chains of the media (print, music, film), telecommunications and IT sectors have become more and more interlinked. This becomes clear when observing demand in the IT sector. The increased demand in this sector was boosted primarily by the development of telecommunications applications such as data communication via the telephone line (e.g. email, www). However, the media contents available via these channels were also an important prerequisite for the use of IT devices. One can thus speak of a convergence of the three value chains.

16 See Arthur 1985, 1989, 1994, 1996
17 See Beck/Prinz 1999, pp. 38
18 See ECC 2001, pp. 140

Monopoly as a condition for the success of network products *(margin note)*

Boundaries between sectors grow blurred *(margin note)*

The process of convergence has several effects. On the one hand, the transmission of media contents, for instance, is no longer restricted to broadcasting (cable, satellite or terrestrial nets), but can also take place via computer or classical telecommunications networks. Due to the continuous development of new methods for compressing data such as HDSL, larger and larger quantities of data and more and more media contents can be transmitted via the existing telecommunications nets. As a consequence, two players that had previously acted independently of each other are now competitors, and the definition of the relevant market from the point of view of competition legislation becomes increasingly difficult. On the other hand, there is a trend towards fusion when it comes to devices, as exemplified by the cases of Internet telephony, Internet broadcasting, etc. This raises the issue of jurisdiction. In the case of Internet telephony, for example, is it the regulatory authority for telecommunication that has jurisdiction? Is a computer a device for which the user must pay a fee, as for television sets and radios?

> Broadcasting and telecommunication become competitors

Economies of scale and scope

In the digital, networked economy the first copy costs of certain products such as software systems and information products are very high. By contrast, each further copy or use incurs only minimal additional costs, which might even approach zero. This results in new economies of scale, which are even bigger and can be even more readily exploited due to the worldwide networked market access. These economies of scale can be readily exhausted by both organic and external growth. For this reason many of the current mergers and takeovers make very good sense as far as efficiency is concerned. Nonetheless, there will increasingly be many small businesses that concentrate on regional or local services such as consultancy, media services, personal services or health. These in turn are one of the important prerequisites for new economies of scope: if companies are networked as outlined above, new potentials for linking (system) products and services as well as "cross-selling" can be opened up.

> Economies of scale through worldwide networked market access

Economies of scale and economies of scope as such are no new concepts. They are well-known from business management literature and were already thoroughly discussed in the pre-Internet era. However, as the high first copy costs only pay for themselves if there is a sufficient sale of the product, there is a greater need for a high degree of market penetration or even a monopolistic position and thus the realisation of economies of scale.

> Monopoly as a condition for economies of scale

Such market penetration can be achieved by consciously giving the product away for free.[19] Companies such as Netscape, which have followed this

> "Follow the free"

19 See Scientific Advisory Board 2001, pp. 7

principle, have thus banked on financing the first copy costs of developing their browser indirectly and with a time delay. The aim here is to attain a critical mass of customers and in this way establish a de facto standard. As a result, on the one hand it makes sense to use the product, and on the other hand the development costs can be refinanced by selling follow-up or complementary products. In the case of the bundling and cross-subsidisation exemplified by Microsoft with its browser "Internet Explorer," it is also possible to speak of economies of scale in the broadest sense of the term. The browser was provided free of charge together with the operating system, thus achieving broad distribution. Microsoft thus finances the costs for its "Internet Explorer" with the sale of its operating system, which has a virtually monopolistic position in the market. In this context, therefore, the U.S. authorities have faced the question of whether cross-subsidisation of this order distorts competition and should accordingly be declared inadmissible.

Use of the Internet

Commercial versus non-commercial Internet use

The issue of Internet use also throws up a number of peculiar features. Here it is in general possible to distinguish between Internet use with mainly commercial aims and that with mainly non-commercial interests. Noteworthy here is that much non-commercial use of the Internet is having commercial effects and should thus also be taken into account in considerations of competition policy. Private file-sharing services such as "e-donkey" or "Napster" have caused traditional music or video sales to plummet dramatically.

In the case of commercial Internet use, the Internet forms the basis for profit-making activities: for example, the mail-order business – as a result of technical progress and changes in purchasing and use habits – is witnessing a slow change from physical to electronic transactions and goods. Electronic goods (such as software and music) can be copied any number of times and at very low costs without any loss of quality, which is on the one hand a strong incentive for suppliers to make the most of these economies of scale, while on the other hand the author of the content or the proprietor of a copyright must face the danger of pirate copies that might considerably decrease their turnover.

Boundary between buyers and sellers becomes blurred

The boundary between buyer and seller is becoming increasingly blurred. There are more and more intermediaries who organise markets where the buyers name products and prices while suppliers of usually quite expensive products make their offers. The line becomes completely blurred when the buyers of a product in turn develop this product even further and then make an improved version available to others. A good example of this is the Open Source Movement.

The special features of the Internet show that the boundaries between suppliers and consumers, between one business and another, as well as between previously separate industrial sectors are all blurring. From the perspective of competition law, this makes it increasingly difficult to define a particular market, in this case since the products that are further developed may possibly belong to a different market. It also becomes harder to catch and sanction the actors in the case of competition-damaging behaviour.

4.4.4
Internet and Competition Policy

It need not be assumed that the Internet calls for our current competition policy to be reconsidered in its entirety. The discussion will now focus, however, on how the peculiarities of the Internet economy can be adequately taken into consideration when applying competition law. The Internet sheds a different light on changes in the market structure and the concept of abuse. Even cooperation in research and development is becoming more problematic. The following argumentation is based on the aspects discussed above, *viz.* market structure, exclusionary practices, and market results not in line with competition.

Do the principles underlying competition law still work?

Market structure

In the case of the Internet economy, control of the market structure is also to the fore because this is easier to implement than the control of market behaviour. However, it is much harder to apply the rules for merger control in this context since on the one hand it can often not be proved beyond doubt that a merger has taken place (as with business webs) and on the other hand, as mentioned above, it is difficult to define the relevant market. Against this background it becomes very hard to determine whether a dominant position in the market is actually at issue.

Merger control is made much more difficult

Mergers in Germany have to be permitted by the Federal Cartel Office (*Bundeskartellamt*) or the EU Commission if the turnovers involved exceed the legal threshold values. If the businesses concerned had to go through this procedure for every joint project, then forms of cooperation such as virtual businesses would be effectively ruled out. Consequently, a sensible approach would be for merger control only to check those general agreements that result in a long-term business network. Whether a merger has actually taken place would depend on whether a fully functional community is created and whether this fully functional community will be a long-term one, as illustrated by the example of business webs. If this is not the case, the prohibition of

Heterogeneous business conglomerates do not restrict competition as much

restrictive agreements applies. This prohibition will not restrict cooperation too much, however, since companies from different lines of business will cooperate, and it can hardly be claimed that this results in a restriction on competition.

Whether a restriction on competition is judged to occur depends decisively on how the relevant market is defined. If the definition is broad in its scope, then market domination occurs only very rarely. The current view is that the EU Commission applies quite a strict definition to markets in the Internet economy. "The EU Commission thus refers to the digital distribution of music via the Internet as an individual market. Analogue and digital distribution via radio or cable networks does not belong to this market any more than the offline sale of the same contents through CDs."[20] It is to be doubted whether such strict differentiation makes sense in the Internet economy. Taking into account the high degree of dynamic innovation, which is one of the most marked features of the Internet economy, it is obvious that new markets that have to be determined and observed are being created all the time.

In such highly innovative markets with short product life cycles, the pressure of competition is not created so much by the current or potential competition in the same market. Instead, the manufacturers of music re-production appliances, for instance, are in competition with mobile phone producers as the latter increasingly integrate MP3 players into their cell phones. Producers of video consoles face similar problems.

The assumption underlying anti-trust law, which is that imitations and substitutes erode market power and thus create the pressure of competition, is refuted by reality since products or innovations from new or current markets not only drive the present market players from the market, but eliminate the whole market over the usual forecasting horizon of three to five years. This means that competition might not even have taken place in the particular market that has been defined.

If competition pressure is caused by innovations, it would be logical for merger control activity to check whether the merger causes the innovation pressure to rise. This would mean that a merger that resulted in increased innovation pressure would not be regarded as detrimental to the functioning of competition.

Furthermore, it has become increasingly difficult to distinguish between a product and its sale. This raises the question of what the customers of Internet music providers are looking for when they buy songs parts of which they have heard as samples: are they buying a radio service in the form of a sample, a

Strict basis for regulation *(margin note)*

Markets do not last long *(margin note)*

The separation of product and distribution has become unclear *(margin note)*

---

20 See Scientific Advisory Board 2001, p. 25

delivery service in the form of files for downloading, a music product in the form of an MP3 file, or everything rolled into one? When considering what the relevant market is, this question becomes really difficult to answer. Is the provider acting in the radio market, the market for downloading, etc.?

What emerges is that by strictly defining the relevant market the analysis of market structure loses its meaningfulness, since the businesses and their decisions are also influenced by businesses from other markets that produce substitutes. In the example discussed above, the CD market should certainly be considered part of the relevant market in order to be able to make more precise statements about competition.

Even when the relevant markets are broader in scope, it is still difficult to ascertain a dominant position in the Internet economy. Especially important are markets where network effects play a major role. In these cases, a prerequisite for the functioning of the market as a whole is that one product should prevail as a standard, which is tantamount having to a large market share. The consequence is low competition pressure in the market. What can be expected, however, is competition pressure due to innovations replacing the current network product.

If no such innovations take place, then businesses can grow in such a way that they effectively dominate the market. Unlike the German monopolies law, the U.S. anti-trust law permits such businesses to be broken up in order to stimulate competition.[21] Whether this break-up is actually carried out depends on the political agenda, as can be seen in the case of Microsoft. The Bush administration prevented the break-up of Microsoft into one business for operating systems and one business for software applications, which was one of the targets of the Clinton administration.

Exclusionary practices

Network effects are an important aspect of the Internet economy. If a private provider takes over the task of generating the critical mass for the functioning of a network good, this is advantageous for all users. In the context of measures taken to achieve critical mass, therefore, government intervention is not yet justified, even though these measures may include dominating the market for this network good. A good example is Microsoft's operating system, which can be considered a network good since hardware and software have to be adjusted to it. When the number of users increases, it also pays off to write compatible programmes since additional programmes increase the added value for all users. This means that market domination causes

Market domination can only be ascertained with difficulty

Market domination and innovation

Is government intervention justified on the way to critical mass?

Added value through market domination

---

21 Note that in case of network goods the question of technological progress and increasing economic welfare often plays a role in the decision.

added value to be created. If, however, this domination is used to deny suppliers of complementary goods access to the market, it is possibly no longer advantageous for all users. In this case government intervention should be considered.

From the point of view of anti-trust legislation, it seems difficult to assess the strategies of businesses that make use of their dominant position in one market in order to penetrate neighbouring markets. A good example of this, as already outlined above, is Microsoft's "Internet Explorer," which was sold together with the company's operating system. Using this strategy the dominant position in the market for operating systems was extended to the market for browsers. The combination of these two products, however, resulted in invigorated competition in the browser market, likewise a market for network goods that was dominated by one provider (Netscape).

The Microsoft .Net initiative, which is also trying to penetrate the market for operating systems and software, has similar goals, while competitors such as Palm are trying to prevent this from happening. It remains to be seen to what extent Microsoft will use its market dominance in other markets.

In the case of digital goods there is a very special cost structure. The first copy costs are quite high, whereas the costs for making further copies are almost zero. Although not to the same extent, this also applies to other products such as automobiles, for example, where the development costs for the first prototype are much greater than the costs of the serial product that is then put on the market. Yet one of the most prominent features of many digital goods, moreover, is that there is no rivalry with respect to consumption. This means that the service as such can be both passed on and retained at the same time. In the first stage, the aim of providing the digital product is to achieve rapid market penetration in order to attain the critical mass. Only in the second stage is the aim to generate turnover by price and product differentiation. Businesses that have already achieved the critical mass – referred to as an installed basis – can by this time realise economies of scale.[22] Such strategies are not necessarily improper since they may also augment welfare. Monopoly law should not intervene unless a supplier imposes prices that restrict competition. It is thus not permitted to lower the prices in a market segment in order to make it harder for a competitor to enter this segment.[23]

A critical view must be taken of the Internet economy when it comes to the practice of demanding network access for a suitable fee, even for other market participants. If the supplier of a network product were to grant other providers access to its network, then the competitors would be benefiting from the

The danger of extending market domination to other markets

Revenue generation in two stages

Critical mass makes it possible to deny access

22 See Coppel 2000, p. 16
23 See Scientific Advisory Board 2001, p. 35

supplier's entrepreneurial achievement without having taken the necessary entrepreneurial risk. From the point of view of anti-trust legislation, this objectively grounded reason is sufficient for competitors to be denied access to the network, or only granted it at a suitable price, which would include a share of the entrepreneurial risk.

If this access were granted with a view to preventing exclusionary practices, possibly even free of charge, however, the incentive for private industry to create standards – and thus the innovation pressure – would be relatively small. It is not in the interests of anti-trust authorities to decrease innovation pressure and ultimately also competition. If a monopoly turns out to be permanent due to the absence of innovations in the field in question, as in the case of voice telephony or the energy supply, it has to be decided whether the network product so established, as well as the access to it, still has to be protected. By analogy with the time limits on patent protection, it might be worth considering whether after a certain period of time knowledge – or in the case of network products access – should be declared to be common property, so access can no longer be denied provided suitable prices are charged.[24]

The argument that access is common property

Market results not in line with competition

As anti-trust practice has assumed that development and research collaborations operate in the run-up to competition, this aspect was never dealt with too strictly.[25] Yet since innovation, as already mentioned, is one of the most important parameters of competition in the Internet economy, this approach can no longer be justified. Given that this pressure to innovate reduces the problem from the point of view of anti-trust legislation, research and development collaborations (such as business webs) must be critically examined. From the point of view of anti-trust legislation, development collaborations appear to be questionable when businesses dominating the market in question participate in them and it can be assumed that their object is to strengthen or even to extend the scope of this market domination.

Critical analysis of R & D collaborations

Collaborations are justified if the idea of teaming up is realised, i.e. if one supplier is unable to raise the funds for developing a new product. In such cases collaborations do encourage the desired dynamic innovation.

24 In the case of voice telephony, for instance, large-scale deregulation has taken place in Europe.
25 See Scientific Advisory Board 2001, p. 36

4.4.5
Conclusion

The practice of anti-trust law must be adjusted

Even after the speculative bubble has burst, the Internet still generates drastic changes in the economy. Market participants will grasp the chances they are offered without an explicit revision of the rules of government intervention. In Germany this is possible because of the high level of abstraction of current monopoly law, which is in principle able to deal with the peculiarities of Internet economy. However, the daily practice of the monopolies authority and the anti-trust court has to be adjusted.[26]

Competitive pressure from neighbouring sectors

The value of the technical and organisational infrastructure of the Internet increases as the number of users increases. A network good can only prevail if a sufficient number of customers can be convinced of this good. The strategies necessary for achieving this goal can not be generally regarded as improper. Often there is no longer any discernible competition in the market. Pressure of competition is then created by innovation pressure, which comes from neighbouring lines of business. From the viewpoint of competition policy, it is thus vital to promote the development of forces capable of producing innovations as an alternative to existing markets in the Internet economy and to reduce any obstacles to such developments. In this context, research and development collaborations also need to be examined and analysed more closely.[27]

Problems of defining the relevant market

From now on, the problem of defining the relevant market in the context of the convergence of the media, telecommunications and IT sectors will be daily routine for anti-trust legislation. In the Internet economy with its highly specialised players, over-strict market definitions may result in inappropriate assessments of market domination and premature intervention.

International coordination of anti-trust authorities

It has to be emphasised that the Internet is a global phenomenon and that monopolistic processes are thus often outside the jurisdiction of German or European anti-trust laws. However, the "principle of effect" permits anti-trust authorities to act as soon as any effects are noticeable within their jurisdiction. If the effect occurs in the anti-trust law jurisdictions of various countries, the respective authorities usually coordinate their actions so there are rarely conflicts.[28] Given the global nature of the Internet and the realm of convergence as such, it is particularly important to pursue more intensive, institutionalised, worldwide cooperation between anti-trust authorities, which would ideally lead to a common anti-trust authority.

---

26 See ibid., p. 40
27 See ibid., p. 41
28 See ibid., p. 42

It can be concluded that the Internet does not need a new competition policy. However, the daily practice of anti-trust legislation and its international coordination need to be organised in a way that takes into account the peculiarities of the Internet economy.

Towards an E-Connected Europe

Stephen Coleman

4.5.1
Interactivity – The New Media Paradigm

In the age of the Internet it is harder than ever before to be elitist about political communication. The Internet transcends once intractable barriers of distance and time, lowers the cost of entry for message creation and dissemination and, most importantly, and uniquely, provides a two-way communication path which eliminates traditional distinctions between producers and receivers. The potential of the Internet as a technology of democratic diversity and participation is unmissable – although this is a vulnerable potential, shaped by political, economic and cultural trends and decisions no less than any previous new technology.

Internet is opening up new opportunities for democracy

The stimulus to e-democracy has been a growing sense that traditional politics has fallen into disrepute. For most people in most countries, the leading institutions and actors of democratic politics seem aloof, uninteresting and confusing. In most (but not all) liberal democracies there is a downward trend in voter turnout, with 18–25 year-olds conspicuously alienated and uninvolved. Non-participation extends to a fall in membership of political parties, a mass turn-off from broadcast political news and discussion, and a growth in public cynicism towards professional politicians of all kinds, as measured by opinion polls. There is no evidence that this turn-off from politics reflects disenchantment with democracy as such. People are still very much involved in trying to change the world that they live in, but such activities tend to ignore the conventional channels of governmental and party politics. Twenty-first-century political activists tend to be driven by single issues, operating locally, but thinking in increasingly global terms.

Political disenchantment does not mean disenchantment with democracy

To national governments, the e-governance agenda has offered two prospects. Firstly, the possibility of delivering services and engaging in transactions with citizens via the Internet (or even digital TV), as a way of reducing bureaucratic costs and enhancing public convenience. In itself, the use of the Internet as a government delivery mechanism has little to do with democracy; hence the

E-governance results in lower costs and a closer relationship to citizens

fact that Singapore is a leader in this field. Secondly, there is the prospect of using the Internet to build a closer, more interactive relationship between government and governed, representatives and represented. Governments have been committed to this ideal of e-democracy more in rhetorical than practical terms so far: there are only a few examples of e-democracy projects, and these have tended to be experimental.[1] The temptation for politicians to regard interactivity as a new form of public manipulation is a major problem; in most cases, e-campaigning during elections has amounted to little more than the adoption of dull and ineffective offline practices in an online environment.[2]

A civic commons in cyberspace

Having been onlooking outsiders with respect to political debate for too long, media interactivity offers citizens the possibility of a more participatory, inclusive form of democratic deliberation. Blumler and I have argued for the creation of a new public space – a civic commons in cyberspace – to be established:

"Electronic commons as part of the democratic furniture"

"(it) would be neither a talking shop in splendid isolation, nor a replacement of representative by direct democracy. It would be instead an open-ended, institutionally backed extension of people's opportunities to make contributions to public policy on those matters that specifically concern them – an extension which could grow in involvement and influence to the degree that those opportunities are taken up and used by all concerned. Ultimately, the electronic commons could become part of the democratic furniture; an integral component of the representative system (the Commons) and an open space for the represented to gather and talk (the civic commons.)"[3]

4.5.2
E-Democracy and EU-Democracy

Networking the players

The EU has every reason to look beyond traditional forms of governance as a way of relating to its citizens. The EU comprises a huge and diverse population spread across a vast continent. Its political institutions are new and insufficiently connected to the European public. E-democracy offers the prospect of building three specific kinds of connection: between European institutions and citizens; between European representatives and those they are elected to represent; and between citizen and citizen. If Europe is ever to be conceived as a unified political space, within which a collective European conversation takes place, the Internet is likely to be a principal arena in which this happens.

1 See Coleman/Gotze 2001.
2 See Coleman 2001.
3 Blumler/Coleman 2001, p. 5

There has sometimes been a degree of over-optimism about the capacity of the Internet to democratise the European polity. For example, in the first annual report of the EU's Information Society Forum (ISF) it was stated that

> *"the new technologies could have extraordinarily positive implications for our democracies and individual rights by strengthening pluralism and access to public information and enabling citizens to participate more in public decision making. The vitality of political debate could be reinvigorated through more use of direct democracy."*[4]

The ISF's 1999 report bordered on the utopian:

> *"The new information technologies may, for the first time in the history of industrial societies under liberal regimes, make it possible to recreate the perfect information arena, the agora of Ancient Greece, a meeting place where citizens could go to be fully informed and to participate directly, with no intermediary, in the government of the city, exercising all their political rights unconditionally and without restriction."*[5]

The EU's e-Europe initiative, adopted in 1999, has stimulated serious thinking about ways of using the Internet to integrate European society. Following the White Paper on European Governance, a series of working groups were set up to explore ways of broadening and enriching the public debate on European matters. On the basis of a number of expert hearings, the working group examining public participation concluded that "the interactivity and speed of the new ICTs make them essential tools for European institutions that are determined to listen and debate with the public"[6] and made a number of practical recommendations, including a call for the Europa web site to be redesigned, with an improved search engine; the setting up of more opportunities for online debate, with contributions published online, regular summaries of citizens' inputs, individualised responses to citizens' contributions, and opportunities for citizens to register for interest-based information groups; and the creation of an "online dialogue task force," comprising EU administrators who would be prepared to participate actively in a range of online discussion fora.[7]

These proposals were consistent with the Commission President's communication on the redesign of the Europa web portal, in which he stated that

Strengthening individual rights and participation in informed decision-making

Integration of European society through Internet

Active participation by citizens

---

4 Information Society Forum 1998
5 Information Society Forum 1999
6 Coleman/Gotze 2001, p. 15
7 See the Report of the Working Group on Broadening and Enriching the Public Debate on European Matters 2001, p. 15

" **E-democracy does not offer a panacea for twenty-first-century democracy.** "

"exploiting Internet interactivity to offer better communication services means to open real-time, on-line, multilingual, two-way dialogue with the Commission's target audiences for the shaping of policies and activities."[8]

This is an ambitious objective which, if implemented as more than a token gesture towards e-communication, could have a transformative effect upon EU governance, making it potentially more accessible, meaningful and inclusive. A key move in this direction was the Communication on Interactive Policy Making designed to systematically and continuously collect feedback on policy proposals.[9] It is too early to evaluate this project, but it is manifestly original and theoretically well constructed. At the same time, efforts are being made to redesign the Europa web portal so that it follows a more transparent logic and is more user-friendly. On a more experimental level, the Commission has provided funding for the development of a number of new e-democracy tools; the key here will be to evaluate them critically and honestly and to ensure that they are applied usefully and in a joined-up fashion.[10]

Governance becomes more accessible to citizens

Many governments are currently experimenting with e-democracy and some are developing strategic policies in this area. The extent to which any of these are serious attempts to democratise governance, rather than concessions to fashion – or, worse still, acquiescence to the seductive rhetoric of dot-com vendors – remains to be seen. E-democracy does not offer a panacea for twenty-first-century democracy. Indeed, making ineffective institutions and bad governance practices more interactively transparent and accessible would simply result in greater public disenchantment with the EU. So, the adoption of e-democracy must be embedded in a wider process of institutional and cultural re-invention. Specifically, a successful EU e-democracy policy needs to embrace three objectives:

Passing fad or genuine opportunity?

– promoting access and accessibility for all EU citizens;

– facilitating a meaningful, inclusive, deliberative dialogue, both between citizens and institutions, and citizens and citizens;

Tasks of e-democracy

– linking the process to the principle of representation.

---

8 Ibid., p. 21

9 See Towards the e-Commission – Europe second generation, Communication by the President to the Commission, 05.04.01, Brussels 2000

10 See Communication on Interactive Policy Making, SEC/522 (2001)

4.5.3
Access and Accessibility

According to Eurobarometer,[11] 26% of European citizens use email or the Internet.[10] Whereas this number might be encouraging from the perspective of e-commerce, insofar as it constitutes a significant market of potential online buyers, it is not acceptable from a democratic perspective. Any form of political communication that fails to connect with 73% of citizens is doomed to marginality. In fact, the situation is even worse than that, because the one in four email/Internet users are concentrated into certain demographic groups.

Firstly, men are more likely to be online than women. Secondly, younger users are much more online than older ones. Thirdly, while most managers used email and the Internet, only one in five European manual workers are users and fewer than one in twenty retired Europeans. As well as demographic inequalities in online usage, there are significant national differences.

These figures cast serious doubt upon the present capacity of the Internet to facilitate an EU-wide, inclusive and representative online dialogue. This is not a reason to abandon e-democracy. Firstly, all of the evidence suggests that these figures will increase, perhaps quite rapidly, and the EU needs to have an online communication framework in place for when that happens. Secondly, there is evidence to suggest that specific groups of European citizens are using the Internet as a key information resource. Interestingly, young Europeans predominate within this group; it would make sense, therefore, to target young Europeans as seed participants in European e-democracy initiatives.

Beyond basic access, which is an essentially economic matter, there are other, cultural barriers to accessibility which must be overcome if e-democracy is to become a reality. Firstly, there is the challenge of European multilingualism. Only 15% of Europe's population speak English as a first language, and only 28% speak English at all.[12] Under one third of European web users visit English sites. Yet over 70% of the two billion web pages available on the Internet are in English; 60% of host computers in the world are in the USA; and there are few non-English search engines. A twin-track approach needs to be adopted, both promoting multilingual web content and developing effective online speech and text translation tools. Beyond that, the development of a sustainable European sector of the web, supported by its own domain identities, search engines and content services, would do much to encourage a distinct sense of European web space.

> Distinguishing e-commerce and e-democracy

> The disparities will lessen

> Dominance of English-language web sites

---

11 Eurobarometer, 54, April 2001
12 See Global Reach

Secondly, online information needs to be made more user-friendly. The Europa web portal, like most current government portals, is a useful resource for those who already know their way around the European Union, but is rather forbidding and labyrinthine for those who are unsure how the EU works or what they are looking for. Most government web sites are excessively wordy, dull and confusing to navigate. Making such sites accessible calls for more than expensive design plans: site producers must analyse user needs, simplify information paths, ensure that interactive connections exist between information providers and users, and develop online tools for users rather than simply present people with web sites to look at.

E-democracy is not attractively packaged

4.5.4
Creating a Dialogue

A recent "Friends of Europe" report suggested that

"The EU uses a negative and unfriendly body language that works against dialogue. Information, particularly on web sites, has a tendency to be officialese designed for a small group of stakeholders."[13]

E-democracy must produce visible results

Time as a key factor

If the EU is to invite citizens into an online dialogue with it, this must lead somewhere. People will not devote their precious time and good ideas to a process that amounts to little more than a virtual suggestion box or an opportunity to rant freely. Connecting dialogue to the policy process requires a serious investment of time by politicians and officials, who must participate in the dialogue with a view to learning from it, and a degree of institutional restructuring so that hitherto closed bureaucratic processes can absorb and respect public inputs. Political commitment to two-way communication needs to be in place before interactive dialogues are set up or publicised.

New skills are required

Online dialogues need to be managed professionally. They require a designed environment, where deliberation can be encouraged, structured, moderated and summarised. These are new skills which democratic communicators must acquire and develop, just as journalists in the past had to adapt to the requirements of first radio and then television. There are currently few examples of successful online deliberation in the context of policy formation; these must be evaluated critically and used as a basis for developing meaningful online dialogue within the EU.

Online dialogue should not only be encouraged between citizens and politicians, but also between citizens and citizens. Across Europe there are thousands of voluntary organisations, interest groups and communities; these

13 Friends of Europe 2001, p. 8

should be talking to one another and helping to set the EU agenda. Despite the rhetoric of "one Europe," it is still rare for Danish farmers to exchange experiences and views with Italian farmers, German nurses with Greek nurses, Irish students with Portuguese students. Establishing communication channels that strengthen European civil society, regardless of national borders, is in itself a democratising act.

Communication channels as a first step towards e-democracy

4.5.5
E-Representation

Italian MEP, Marco Cappato, has called for

"audio-video broadcasting via the Internet and filing in archives of Parliament's plenary sessions and committee meetings. The plenary session of Parliament in January 2002, on the occasion of the election of the President of the European Parliament, was broadcast on the Internet, and there is apparently nothing preventing this practice from being extended to all public sessions of Parliament. It would suffice for all the internal organs of the Parliament to decide, even independently of the other institutions or of the reform of the Treaties, to broadcast their own proceedings fully online. This decision could be accompanied by the decision to set up an internal system of identification (e.g. a digital signature for all members of parliament) which would also make it possible to place the activities of individual members online, beginning with the tabling of documents."[14]

Transparency through public webcasting

This would be an important step in the direction of transparency. Several national parliaments, and even local authorities, currently webcast their proceedings. Given the absence of an easily accessible pan-European TV network, webcasting is the best available way of ensuring that everything that goes on in the EU's representative chamber can be seen and heard by the millions of citizens who are represented there.

But transparency does not guarantee accountability. The web is more than merely television for small screens and small audiences; it is an interactive medium and offers an opportunity to support interactive institutions of governance.

The web is no guarantee of accountability

The European Parliament has an opportunity to become an innovative model of a two-way institution, interacting directly with the citizens it represents. As an e-Parliament, its proceedings and papers would not only be totally transparent online, but would take evidence for committee inquiries and legislative debates via online consultation fora; besides an e-Parliament

---

14 Cappato 2002

Creating online communities
of interests

could provide direct channels through which citizens can raise problems and suggestions with their MEPs, create a network of online communities of interest which would feed into various policy areas, hold regular online seminars, linking experts in various countries to parliamentary debates and offer interactive civic education about the Parliament and its work, especially for school and college students.

The EU as a pioneer?

For this to be a strategic commitment and not a token gesture or gimmick, the Parliament needs to think in terms of re-inventing itself for the age of interactive communication. It would involve much training for MEPs, their staff and officials, as well as a well-resourced publicity campaign explaining the advantages of interactive representation. In implementing such a policy, the European Parliament would stand a chance of being seen as a relevant, cutting-edge institution, with a real interest in strengthening representation. Other parliaments will go down this path in the coming years, but the European Parliament's lack of popular legitimacy or relevance make it an ideal candidate to become a pioneer in this field.

4.5.6
Beyond the Nation State:
the New Geo-Politics of Cyberspace

Mass communication helps
to give political spaces
greater significance

Political spaces have never emerged spontaneously. They are cultivated, nurtured and communicated. There has always been an intimate relationship, rooted in more than etymology, between notions of community and processes of communication. Aided by technologies of mass communication and dissemination, political spaces are given significance and publics come to feel (or imagine) a sense of communal, national or supranational identity.

Pre-national solidarities were driven by the emergence of print and vernacular languages. As Anderson has sagely observed,

"Speakers of the huge variety of Frenches, Englishes, or Spanishes, who might find it difficult or even impossible to understand one another in conversation, became capable of comprehending one another via print and paper. In the process, they gradually became aware of the hundreds of thousands, even millions, of people in their particular language-field, and at the same time that only those hundreds of thousands, or millions, so belonged. These fellow readers, to whom they were connected through print, formed, in their secular, particular, visible invisibility, the embryo of the nationally-imagined community."[15]

15 Anderson 1983, p. 47

If print was the technology of emergent nationalism, radio and television have been the quintessential media of nation states. The broadcast media have been organised in terms of national airwaves, reach and service. News broadcasts on radio and television are, for most people, the nearest thing to a daily revised text-book of national history and identity.

In an essentially deferential democracy, the citizen is a spectator of mediated politics. As spectators of the staged debates and interviews produced by the electronic media, most citizens come as close as they ever will to the political deliberations that determine the policies and laws by which they live. For much of the twentieth century this culture of "weak democracy" seemed to suffice: the media were trusted as communicators of what the people needed to know, and political institutions were trusted by most people to get on with their job. Politicians were recipients of the popular vote, despite the disengagement of citizens from the heart of deliberation. Indeed, defenders of deferential democracy rather celebrated the inertia of citizens, agreeing with Lippmann that it was their job to protect "the hopelessly inept, bewildered, biased, frivolous and incurious citizens from the duty and rigour of decision making."[16]

But deferential democracy has fallen into disrepute, as citizens have become better educated, more consumerist and politically volatile. The idea of the media as a window through which the passive, gawping public can look on from a safe distance at the deliberations of the political elite is becoming obsolete. The age of democratic deference is passing and twenty-first-century politics must change or become increasingly marginal to civic life.

At the same time, the idea of politics based upon national sovereignty appears increasingly outdated. There are fewer than ever conversations that British people need to have only with other British people. Cyberspace is, in this sense, the quintessential communication environment of globalism. It respects no borders, is accountable to no single nation state and is open to all, regardless of origin. From the perspective of nationhood, cyberspace is unmanageable and anarchic; only international institutions of governance can hope to establish rules for the online environment. The US-led attempt to regulate Internet domain names and addresses via the unwieldy and unaccountable ICANN structure has been a spectacular failure, demonstrating the impossibility of managing global channels on the basis of national agendas.

So, e-democracy presents a challenge to democratic governance that is more than merely technological. It is about how to transcend a culture of political deference and design a more inclusive, open and accountable

16 Lippmann 1922

Side notes:

Media hitherto organized in geographical terms

Democracy as a spectator-event

Political isolation of citizens from the heart of the decision-making process

The end of the political elite

Cyberspace is politically unmanageable

E-democracy as a challenge for the future

political environment. It is about how to share the common knowledge of citizens within a space that is bigger than the nation, but close enough to people's lives to make sense of local and personal experiences. It is about "democratising democracy" for the twenty-first century (to use a phrase from Giddens), and that will involve more than technocratic high hopes.

Chapter 4.6

Regulation, Media Literacy and Media Civics

Roger Silverstone

The locus of our regulatory concerns needs to shift. In the new media world, a world that still includes old media and old yet resistant values driving institutional processes of mediation, the concern with markets, competition and content needs to be rethought. This is not only because of the decline of spectrum scarcity or the incapacity of national governments to control international flows of information and communication, but because new media are challenging what it means to be human, through their increasing salience as both information and communication resources, and as such as crucial components of our relational infrastructure and our social life.

I want to suggest, in this short essay, that an understanding of what it is to be human is, or certainly should be, the central question underlying, and in the final analysis regulating, the development of the mediated world in which more and more of us live, and by which almost all of us are affected. I intend to argue that existing forms of media regulation, at best operationalisations of what can be called applied ethics,[1] at worst mindless enforcements of vested political or commercial interests, are not sufficient as guarantors of humanity or culture. Regulatory reform is still mostly a matter *for* governments and media industries and a matter *of* establishing professional and commercial guidelines for practice (variously enforced) without conscious attention to first principles of social action or media representation, and without addressing other ways of enabling not just responsible and accountable media, but a responsible and accountable media culture. Responsible and accountable media can be encouraged and regulated, however imperfectly and however vulnerably. A responsible and accountable media culture is another matter entirely, for it depends on a critical and literate citizenry, and a citizenry, above all, which is critical with respect to, and literate in the ways of, mass mediation and media representation.

And I wish to suggest that at the core of such media literacy should be a moral agenda, always debated, never fixed, but permanently inscribed in public discourse and private practice, a moral discourse which recognises

New media call into question what it means to be human

Media regulation as an attempt at applied ethics

A responsible media culture calls for critical citizenry

---

1 See Christians 2000

Moral discourse as a criterion
for media competence

our responsibility for the other person in a world of great conflict, tragedy, intolerance and indifference, and critically engages with our media's incapacity (as well as their occasional capacity) to engage with the reality of that difference, responsibly and humanely. For it is in our understanding of the world, and our willingness and capability to act in it, that our humanity or inhumanity is defined.

4.6.1
Media as Environment

As Cees Hamelink has recently pointed out, the media are central in this increasingly urgent project of identifying what constitutes our humanity precisely because they are at the forefront in representing, through endless sequences of narratives and images, the "historical reality of dehumanisation on a grand scale."[2]

And the media are indeed quite central to our capacity to be and to act in the world, as Marshall McLuhan once upon a time noted. It was he who most forcefully suggested that media, all media, are extensions of ourselves. They create and sustain an encompassing cultural environment which we all share. As we enter a digital age, one in which both the speed and range of communication seem to have been so intensified; as we shift from, at best, an active engagement with our singular media to an increasingly interactive engagement with our converging media, media which give us the world, access to the world and information about the world, we are confronted with this McLuhanistic vision even more insistently.

Media as extensions of
ourselves

Of course McLuhan profoundly misrepresented the totality and homogeneity of media as providing a kind of cultural blanket over all peoples of the world. He persistently disregarded the significance of geography and society as in turn mediating power and access to material and symbolic resources.[3]

Nevertheless, and despite its political innocence, this mediated cultural environment is as significant, it might be said, for the human condition as the natural environment is. Though it is rarely so remarked upon. Indeed both have holes in their ozone layers, chemical and moral in turn. Both are subject to the depredations and exploitations of the insensitive, the malicious and the self-interested. So although this environmental perspective makes, perhaps, more sense now than it ever did, it leaves untouched the thorny questions of who and what we are, and of how what we are in turn affects the ways in which media emerge and develop. And it still fails to register mediation

Both mediated and natural
environment are significant
for human beings

(In)humanity: key
components in the question
of mediation

2 Hamelick 2000, p. 400
3 See McLuhan 1964

as both a social and a political process. In other words, the humanity and inhumanity at the heart of the dynamics of mediation are left unexamined; they are presumed to be unproblematic.

Similarly, regulatory discourse rarely examines why regulation should take place in the first place. When it comes to public interest, freedom of expression, rights to privacy, competition policy, intellectual property and the like, it assumes an ordered or at least an orderable world, and indeed a world that would benefit from deliberative, and presumably accountable, regulation. Yet regulatory procedures, focusing on producers but addressing consumers, are at best based on an acknowledgement and an acceptance of what I have already called applied ethics: sets of morally informed but rarely interrogated prescriptions for, or proscriptions of, practice. The main beneficiary of such regulatory impulses and practices is the putative citizen, in his or her public and private life. In such present regulatory discourse and practice such citizens need to be protected against the depredations of untrammelled vested interests, be they commercial or imperial. They need to be given freedoms to speak and to be heard; they need to be given freedoms of choice. They need to be consulted on how regulatory policies are formed and implemented.[4]

Regulatory processes are based on applied ethics

But who is the citizen these days? And how has his or her status as citizen been affected by the media, both old and new, both broadcast and interactive? In what ways do our media enable or disable our capacity to relate to each other as citizens, but also as human beings? In what ways do they enable or disable us as ethical beings in our relationship to the world? In what ways do the media both address us as, and enable us to be, global citizens, participants and actors in natural, commercial and cultural environments all of which extend beyond both the immediacy of neighbourhood and nation?

Do the media make citizens passive and uncritical?

Home ...

In an earlier essay,[5] I argued that almost all our regulatory impulses, those that engage with the ownership of media industries on the one hand and those that concern the welfare of the family on the other, are between them concerned with the protection of home. What links them is a preoccupation with *content*: with the images, sounds, narratives and meanings which are transmitted and communicated daily, and over which regulators increasingly feel they have little control. What appears on the page or on the screen, what is represented, especially in its consistency or inconsistency, its decency or indecency, its intrusiveness, is deemed to be important precisely because it

Regulation – from the public media to the individual bedroom

---

4 See Collins and Murroni 1996
5 Silverstone 1999

has been allowed to cross this principal threshold, seeping into private spaces and private lives. This was, of course, the impetus for the earliest attempts at content regulation, in the Hays Code, for the cinema. But these anxieties and the regulatory attempts to manage them have become more insistent as twentieth-century media migrated away from public to private screens, and from shared sitting rooms to solitary bedrooms.

Banal though it may seem, the media are seen to be important because of the power they are presumed to exercise over us, *at home*, a power that no amount of audience research can quite completely deny, and of course which most of us believe, one way or the other, naturally to be the case. Home, of course, needs to be understood in both literal and metaphorical senses. The defence of home is a defence of both the private spaces of intimate social relations and domestic security, i.e. the household; as well as of the larger symbolic spaces of neighbourhood and nation, i.e. the collective and the community. The two are complex in their interrelationship and do not always share common interests. Yet both are threatened by the media extension of cultural boundaries: both laterally, as it were, through the globalisation of symbolic space, and vertically through the extension of accessible culture into the forbidden or the threatening. In both cases home has to be defended against material breaches of symbolic security.

The liberalisation of mainstream media and telecommunications in the 1980s and 1990s by a neo-liberal Conservative government brought with it an unexpected and unwelcome reduction in the capacity to control the flow of media content into the UK. Self-induced deregulation in one context and for one set of dominating economic reasons produced, as it was bound to, a moral panic in another context, that of culture. The Broadcasting Standards Council was, as a consequence, created to protect both the vulnerable child at home and the vulnerable homeland as if it were a child. Current debates on the future of public service broadcasting in the UK rehearse the same dilemmas, for once again what is at stake is the moral integrity both of the home and the nation, in its citizen's capacity to exercise, both privately and publicly, meaningful choices (a precondition for a moral life) as well as a perceived need to protect that same citizen from the immorality of meaningless or threatening choices that unregulated commerce might be expected to bring in its train.

For every deregulation there is a re-regulation, but not always in the same domain, and rarely for clearly defined or well-examined reasons.

Competition policy is, therefore, as much about, and with consequences for, such breaches of personal security and domestic integrity – of the rights of the person and the personal – as it is about cross-media ownership and the future of public-service broadcasting and the public sphere. Indeed it is precisely the private which is at stake in the discussions and deliberations on the latter.

And yet while regulators struggle to control and direct, to label and to license content (as well as competition), parents and families struggle over a personal and private culture, shaping and protecting the domestic spaces where public and private moralities are supposed to coincide. This is a struggle for control, a struggle which propagandists, advertisers, television schedulers and portal designers well understand. And it is a struggle which parents understand too, as they argue with their children over time spent online. It is a struggle which at least in part defines, across lines of age and gender, the particular politics of individual households.

Regulation is, then, a private as well as a public matter. It takes place in front rooms as well as in debating chambers, in the cut and thrust of discussions over viewing habits, as well as in international debates over v-chips[6] and trans-border media flows. In both these environments what is being fought over are the rights of, and control over, representation: the availability of, and access to, the continuities and consistencies of both the immediacy, and the flow, of images and narratives. And in those representations what is at stake are the rights to define a relationship: between what is known and not known, between what is valued and not valued, between what one believes to be the truth and what one suspects as falsehood, and between what one lays claim to and what one can discard in one's relationship to the rest of the world. What is at stake in these moments and mechanisms of regulation is, essentially, a moral order.

... And away

As we become increasingly dependent on the mediated word and image for our understanding of what takes place beyond our front door; as everyday life, in its taken-for-granted ordinariness, becomes inseparable from the mediations that guide us through it and connect or disconnect us from the everyday lives of others, how the media position us, or enable us to position ourselves, becomes crucial.

As citizens we are expected to take responsibility for, and to act responsibly in relation to, ourselves, our neighbours and also the strangers amongst us. Such expectations have been, arguably, undermined by (among other things) a century of electronic mediation, which has led to increasing privatisation and individualisation. The dominant trope in the analysis of twentieth-century public life has been its erosion: the palpable lack of care,

The clash of public and private morality

The pursuit of a moral order

How the media position us or let us position ourselves

Mediation as leading to reduced responsibility for fellow human beings

---

6 Editors' note: v-chips (violence chips) make it possible to filter out television programmes containing violence or pornography.

the paradoxical lack of communication, have been revealed in increasing alienation from the formal processes of politics and engagement in public life, perhaps not for all, but for many, especially in the wealthy and highly mediated democracies of industrial society.

These societies, it equally goes without saying, are becoming increasingly connected to each other. What imperialism once enforced, globalisation now enables, or indeed requires: a mutuality of increasingly highly stratified economic and financial structures and processes; a shared but still massively and unevenly discomforting physical environment; a political space that no longer knows, nor much cares about, national boundaries and territorial sovereignty; networks of information and communication that shrink social and cultural space and time to the size of a handset.

Regulation as a question of global governance

In this context, and taking the broadest sweep, problems of regulation become problems of governance, in which order and accountability are dreamed about on a global scale and at the level of states and trans-national non-governmental organisations. Foreign and domestic policy converges. Somehow even these dreams depend on a notion of citizenship, though a transcendent one, but they still require an engagement with the human – and they challenge it too. However, they leave untouched and unexamined, for the most part, the individual in his or her humanity, in his or her sensibility. In what ways, if at all, can or should this humanity be affected by our regulatory impulses and institutions? In what ways should this humanity (or its lack) inform and affect our attempts at regulation and governance?

Media both connect and separate

Early commentators, both utopian and dystopian, on the emerging late-nineteenth-century wireless and telegraphic space recognised the implications of what has subsequently come to be known as the double life of media and communication: that they separate as well as connect. This paradox inevitably gives the lie to any contemporary notion of the media's role in what is called the death of distance. It raises the question of isolation and not just privatisation – and isolation of both the individual and of the group. It also raises the question of the illusion of connection: that in our mediated innocence, in our mediated naïveté, we are unable to recognise how imprisoned we are, how easily blinded we are, by the mediations that apparently link us together. And it is somewhat ironic to observe that the supposed revolution in media culture occasioned by the arrival of digital and online technologies should be seen to be so singular and radical, above all in their capacity to transcend the limits of electronic communication, limits perfectly well recognised (and feared) throughout the analogue twentieth century.[7]

---

7 See de Sola Pool 1977; Marvin 1988

As I have argued elsewhere,[8] there is often quite a fundamental confusion in much of the writing on the sociology and geography of new media. Time-space distantiation, or time-space compression, even ideas of the network society, suggest a profound and misleading elision between two kinds of distance: the spatial and the social. It is presumed in these discussions that the electronic mediation of physical or material connection provides at the same time social, cultural or psychological connection. The technologically enabled transformation of time and space which marked the entry into the modern world certainly provided new conditions and possibilities for communication, communication that provided connection despite physical separation. Yet the contradictions at the heart of such communication become even more profound the more we insist that electronic mediation brings no penalty when it comes to understanding and caring for the other. Indeed when we insist, on the contrary, that our world view is now global in its reach. That there is no escape. That nothing can be hidden, nothing can be, or is, ignored. But of course it can.

The use of media to overcome spatial and social distance

My point is that distance is not just a material, a geographical or even a social category, but it is, by virtue of all of these and as a product of their interrelation, a moral category. The overcoming of distance requires more than technology and indeed more than the creation of a public sphere. It requires what I have called proper distance.[9] Proper distance is the critical notion that implies and involves a search for enough knowledge and understanding of the other person or the other culture to enable responsibility and care, as well as to enable the kind of action that, informed by that understanding, is in turn enabling. We need to be close, but not too close, distant, but not too distant.

Distance as a moral category

Proper Distance

The media have always fulfilled the function of creating some sense of proper distance, or at least they have tried, or claimed to be able, to do so. In the reporting of world events, the production of news, the fictional representation of the past, the critical interrogation of the private lives of public figures, the exploration of the ordinariness of everyday life, what is involved, in one way or another, is a negotiation between the familiar and the strange, as the media try, though always imperfectly, to resolve the essential ambiguities and ambivalences of contemporary life.

Media between the familiar and the strange …

Yet such mediations have tended to produce, in practice, a kind of polarisation in the determinations of such distance. The unfamiliar is either

… between proximity and distance

---

8 Silverstone 2003
9 Ibid.

pushed to a point beyond strangeness, beyond humanity, or it is drawn so close as to become indistinguishable from ourselves. And, it should be said, there is also very little sense that we are the objects of the others' gaze, that how *we* are seen and understood by those far removed from us also matters; we need to see and understand that too. Perhaps this has never been more the case than now.

On the one hand, we find ourselves being positioned by media representation as so remote from the lives and worlds of other people that they seem beyond the pale, beyond reach of care or compassion, and certainly beyond reach of any meaningful or productive action. Technology has a habit of creating such distance, and the bureaucracies that have been built around technologies have in the past, and with cataclysmic effects, reinforced this sense of separation and alienation, this immorality of distance.[10] This is certainly and obviously the case in times of conflict, but it is rarely far away even in peace.

The immorality of distance

Per contra, the representation, just as frequent and just as familiar, of the other as being just like us, as recoupable without disturbance into our own world and values, has, though perhaps more benignly, the same consequence. We refuse to recognise not only that others are not like us, but that they can be made to be like us. What they have we share. What they are we know. They are as they appear in our documentaries and in our advertisements. Such cultural neo-imperialism represents the other side of the immorality of distance, in its refusal to accept difference, in its resistance to recognising and to valuing the stranger. Perhaps this could be called the immorality of identity.

The immorality of identity

In both cases we lose a sense of the commonality and difference that should inform the ethics of how we live in the world. Either way, we lose the capacity effectively to grasp both what we share and what we do not share as human beings. The irony of the electronically mediated century just passed, in which we have come to believe that the immediate and the visible is both necessary and sufficient to guarantee connection, is that this apparent closeness is only screen-deep.

The impropriety of distance

Distance can, therefore, be proper (correct, distinctive and ethically appropriate) or it can be improper. If improper distance can be, and is, created, *inter alia*, through the mediations that electronic technologies provide for us, then it follows that we can use the notion of *proper* distance as a tool to measure and to repair the failures in our communication with and about other people and other cultures and in our reporting of the world, in such a way that our capacity to act in it is enabled and preserved.[11] And it follows

---

10 See Bauman 1993
11 See Boltanski 1999; Silverstone 2003

too that we can use the notion of proper distance as a way of interrogating those arguments, most recently in the analysis of the supposedly miraculous capacity of the Internet, that mistake connection for closeness, and closeness for commitment, and which confuse reciprocity with responsibility.

It is with the convergence between the public and the private, the personal and the social, that the notion of proper distance seeks to engage. And it is at this interface, perhaps increasingly confused and confusing, that social beings, citizens real or manqué, need to confront a moral agenda that is appropriate both to the conditions of the mediation of the world and to the resulting mediated world, the world in which the other person appears to us – as through a glass darkly.

The notion of proper distance

4.6.2
Media Literacy and Media Civics

Regulation has always been a technical activity. To suggest that it should also be a moral one has its dangers. Yet these dangers need to be confronted. What is missing so often in the regulatory discourse is the question: regulation for what, and for whom?

The focus on content, on media as representational technologies, is in many ways atavistic. It brings back concerns that many had thought long since buried in the analysis of mediation: concerns with ideology, effects, with false consciousness even. On the other hand, our regulatory concern is still implicitly (and sometime explicitly) based on such assumptions as these: a political economy in which ownership determines content, and where content in turn determines meanings and effects.

Yet even if we can acknowledge, with recent media theory, that this linearity is misconceived and that receivers of communication, wherever they happen to be, and whether understood as audiences or users, are active interpreters and mediators of even the most consistent and dominant of media representations, it is still possible, reasonable and necessary to acknowledge the persistent power of our media's mediations. Media are nothing if they do not convey meanings, and even if we can (and we can) negotiate those meanings for ourselves and distance ourselves from those meanings we find unacceptable or unpalatable, in the absence of others – both other meanings and other realities – our perceptions of the world cannot but be increasingly and consistently framed by what is seen and heard through screens and audio-speakers.

The power of the media

The multiple negatives of the last paragraph are intended, and intended to be instructive. There is inevitably and necessarily a need for caution in

Regulation is not only about protecting our own security

any kind of moral position lest it be seen as, or become, moralistic. So it needs to be understood that the present argument is not for a new kind (or even an old kind) of censorship. On the contrary, at issue are the presumptions and preconditions for our understandable (perhaps even natural, at least sociologically speaking) concern for regulation. Perhaps it is time to recognise that regulation should not just be concerned with the protection of our own securities and of those we hold dear or for whom we have some formal, familial or even national responsibility.

From regulation to an ethically oriented education

Regulation should address the wider and, I have suggested, the much deeper issue of our relationships to others, to those for whom we have no formal responsibility, to those who are distant in space or culture, the strangers amongst us, our neighbours abroad, but for whom our basic humanity requires that we should care. This is of course a tall order. However it suggests a shift, and one that it might well be argued is long overdue. It involves a shift away from regulation as narrowly conceived in the minds and practices of parliaments and councils, towards a more ethically oriented education, and towards a critical social and cultural practice which recognises the particular characteristics of our mediated world. We once upon a time taught something called civics. It is perhaps time to think through what civics might be in our present intensely mediated century.

In one sense, perhaps, we could say that we have been here before, at least in part. The mid and late nineteenth century saw, certainly in the UK but also in Western Europe and in the USA, the rise of a political project, broadly speaking, to incorporate disparate and displaced populations into civic culture. The displacement was for the most part internal: populations leaving the land and traditional cultures and finding themselves in cities and within urban and popular cultures. Industrialisation was having profound social consequences, and the social consequences involved very significant and destabilising shifts in the communicative infrastructures of everyday life.

Stabilisation of power structures through cultural integration

Such destabilisation and the consequent danger of anomie amongst an increasingly concentrated population was clearly a source of anxiety amongst elites – both legitimate and paranoid. Nation states were being consolidated and any source of political resistance was clearly a focus of concern. At the same time democracies were maturing, and working-class movements were themselves encouraging the displaced and disadvantaged – the still excluded – to generate the necessary social and cultural capital to participate increasingly fully and meaningfully in the public affairs of the strengthening state. There were both campaigns for, and political commitments to enable, mass literacy. Workers' educational movements engaged the mature; increasingly universal primary and secondary education engaged the maturing.

All participation is double-edged. It is both enabling and constraining. The literacy of the book, the newspaper and the pamphlet brought with it both the means for incorporation into national culture and the means for the suppression of any alternative, but it also brought an increasingly informed, reflective and cultured citizenry. Vernacular literacy was a precondition of such participation and reflection. To pretend that this was not a regulatory project would be naïve. At the same time, however, it was also a liberating one – and in essence and in intent, very often, a genuinely moral one, whatever we might think about Victorian ethics. The focus of that first regulatory impulse was clearly that of the nation state, a state enabled initially by the Gutenberg revolution[12] and secured – at least for large slices of the twentieth century – by Marconi's and Baird's.[13] The focus now, arguably, is post-national, if by that can be meant the redrawing and puncturing of the boundaries around and between states in the face of globalising culture.

Participation as both regulation and liberation

Whereas the nineteenth-century civic project required the literacy of the written text, a literacy that was both literal and critical, the twenty-first-century civic project requires a literacy of mass-mediated, electronic texts – and this too needs to be both literal and critical. But there the similarity ends. For the twenty-first century brings with it a different cultural and political challenge, in which the different media, both analogue and digital, are differently implicated in the structures and dynamics of everyday life.

Critical capacity as a prerequisite for understanding

For most, the literacy of the book was a literacy of decipherment: to be able to read, to follow, to understand, to appreciate. It required considerable application and the acquisition of sophisticated skills. Media literacy in an age of broadcasting was much less demanding, and the ease of access to complex audiovisual texts was seductive. The mass media were seen as more powerful not just because they were mass, but because they dimmed critical skills, the skills of engagement and struggle with complexity.[14] It was not thought that literacy, at least in the terms where it was appropriately applied to the written text, was necessary. Indeed the mass media were seen to be destroying and undermining that kind of literacy. It is possible, of course, to argue that the Internet has created its own demands for a new kind of literacy, text-based but requiring new skills of organisation and decipherment, and that this is already transforming the structured illiteracy of the age of broadcasting. I would suggest that for the most part the literacy required for the Internet is still seen to be essentially technical, and is rarely approached as requiring more sophisticated skills.

The age of television and radio made different demands on media literacy

In both the new and the old media, therefore, very little attention has been given to media literacy as a critical activity. Very little attention has been given to media literacy as a civic activity. Very little critical attention has been given either to literacy or civics as an alternative to the blunderbuss of

Media literacy as a civic activity

---

12 See Eisenstein 1979
13 See Scannell 1989
14 See Rosenberg and White 1957

media regulation, or to the possibility of developing an ethical agenda which would inform such a project.

In a recent paper,[15] Rüdiger Funiok has addressed some of these questions through an interrogation of audience ethics, that is, the responsibility that users of the media can, and should, develop for themselves. He cites Cees Hamelink's conclusion[16] that "media consumption should be viewed, like professional media performance, as a social practice which implies moral choices and the assumption of accountability for these choices." This is a complex demand, of course, and extends way beyond the still limited framework that I am pursuing here. Yet the notion of responsibility is crucial, responsibility for oneself, and for others; in the context of the family, of course, but also in the context of neighbourhood and nation (imagined communities both) and, now, in the context of a global culture and a global imaginary, which the world's media are daily creating.

Media literacy in this context is a political project, just as media civics is a "literary" one. The former is a prerequisite for full participation in late modern society, involving as it does the critical skills of analysis and appreciation of the social dynamics and social centrality of media as framing the cultures of the everyday. Media literacy above all requires an understanding of the non-transparency of media and of the moral implications of that non-transparency. And it requires an understanding of mediation as a social and political process. Media civics, correlatively, depends on media literacy. Media civics, crucial to citizenship in the twenty-first century, requires the development of a morality of responsibility and participation grounded in a critical engagement with mediation as a central component of the management both of state and global politics and that of everyday life: both of the system and the life-world.

There is very little surprise in these observations, at least from the point of view of the academic study of the media, but equally there is very little surprise in the observation that these fundamental critical principles have hitherto for the most part failed to inform both the deliberations of policy makers, and the judgements of citizens.

Media use as involving a conscious moral choice

Media literacy as a political project, media civics as a literary project

---

15 See Funiok 2000
16 Hamelink 2000, p. 400

4.6.3
Conclusion

Our regulatory impulses need to be both informed and moderated by these concerns. Citizenship requires responsibility, and to exercise such responsibility well and thoroughly in turn requires the ability to see the world and to see through our media's limited and inadequate representations of it.

I have proposed the notion of proper distance as a framing device for such a project. Media civics has to burst the bounds both of the nation state and the narcissistic limits of concern only with the individual and the self. Its regulatory embrace should bring the other into its ambit. A sense of proper distance is a moral sense, one in which the relationship between proximity and distance is mediated by an effective measure of understanding, care and responsibility. We need to know about each other in a way that can only involve a constant critical engagement with our media's representation of the other. Such engagement is as important to our relationships to our neighbours as to the strangers both amongst us and far away. The everyday, hitherto the site of an unreflecting gaze, can, and should, be made more critically aware – for that is, after all, what our media can enable for us, if there is a mind to do so. Representational ethics, the ethics informing the production and reception of the images and stories of both old and new media, emerges from these discussions as a new and compelling concern.

Regulation is not, therefore, just a matter of production. And here as in other dimensions of media dynamics, production and consumption blur; the boundaries between them become indistinct. Equally, the full responsibility for a moral agenda informing media practices should lie not only with audiences and users. It is the interests and understandings of audiences and users, the urgent requirements of citizenship, which should continue to constrain and increasingly determine the regulatory process. We are, of course, responsible for ourselves. But, as Emmanuel Levinas insists, if we are to claim a full and proper humanity we must claim responsibility for the other. In this sense, as well as reading, we might need to regulate, against the grain.

Citizens must see through the flawed media representation of the world

The notion of proper distance

Representational ethics is required

Author Curricula

Stefan Bechtold
Fellow of the Center for Internet and Society at Stanford Law School.

Law studies at the University of Tübingen. Subsequently research assistant at the University of Tübingen and visiting scholar at the Law School of the University of California at Berkeley. In 2001 doctorate at the University of Tübingen and subsequently study visit to Stanford University (JSM degree).

Jean-Claude Burgelman
Head researcher of the ICT Unit of the IPTS in Seville.

Master in science and technology dynamics and doctorate in social sciences at the Free University of Brussels. He is Professor of Communication Technology Policy at the Free University of Brussels and was founder and head of the research centre SMIT (Studies on Media Information and Telecommunications).

Stephen Coleman
Since November 2002 Professor of E-Democracy at the Oxford Internet Institute of the University of Oxford.

Head of studies of the Hansard Society and head of the E-democracy Programme. Lecturer in Media and Citizenship at the London School of Economics and Political Science. Cabinet adviser for e-democracy. He is a member of the board and consultant for yougov.com, as well as international consultant for the OneWorld Foundation.

Benjamin M. Compaine
Research consultant of the MIT Program on Internet and Telecom Convergence.

Studies at Dickson College and at Harvard University (M.B.A.), Ph.D. from Temple University. From 1979-86 he was executive director of the Program on Information Resources Policy at Harvard University and from 1986-94 chief executive officer of Nova Systems, Inc. He was Professor for Telecommunications at Temple University from 1994-97 (founder and chairman of the Center for Information Industry Research). From 1997-98 he was Senior Research Professor for Communication at Pennsylvania State University.

Hardy Dreier
Since November 1999 research fellow at the Hans Bredow Institute in Hamburg.

Studies in journalism, politics and librarianship at the Free University of Berlin. From 1994-99 he was research assistant in economics and mass communication at the Institute of Journalism and Communication Science of the Free University of Berlin.

Ken Ducatel / Marc Bogdanowicz / Fabiana Scapolo / Jos Leijten / Jean-Claude Burgelman Members of the Futures Projects and the ICT Unit of the Institute for Prospective Technological Studies (IPTS) of the Joint Research Centre of the European Commission.

Valerie Feldmann
Since 2004 Associate with McKinsey & Company in New York.

Studies in business management, media communications, cultural anthropology and music science at the University of Münster. In 2003, doctorate at the Free University Berlin. 2001-03 lecturer at the Free University Berlin. Affiliated Researcher at the Columbia Institute for Tele-Information (CITI), Columbia University, New York.

Siegfried Frey
Since 1985 Professor of Communication and Media Psychology and head of the Laboratory of Interaction Research at the Gerhard Mercator University of Duisburg.

Previously at the Max Planck Institute for Psychiatry in Munich (1966-71), at the University of California, San Francisco (1971-73), and at the University of Bern (1974-85). Directeur d'Études at the École des Hautes Études en Sciences Sociales (E.H.E.S.S.), Paris, ongoing since 1982.

Valerie Frissen
Since 1999 head researcher and consultant of the Dutch research organisation TNO.

Studies in communication sciences and doctorate in social sciences (1992) at the University of Nijmegen. Subsequently lecturer and researcher at the University of Amsterdam, Faculty of Communication Sciences and Communication Research.

Jeffrey Funk
Since April 1996 Associate Professor at Kobe University, Japan.

Studies in mechanical engineering / engineering and public policy at Carnegie Mellon University, USA. Doctorate in engineering and public policy at Carnegie Mellon University, USA. Assistant Professor of Business Management at Pennsylvania State University, USA, and visiting assistant research scientist, industrial and operations engineering, at the University of Michigan, USA.

Hans Geser
Since autumn 1986 Extraordinary Professor at the University of Zurich, Switzerland.

Studies in sociology, social psychology and economics at the University of Zurich. Doctoral dissertation (1975) and postdoctoral thesis (habilitation, 1979) in sociology at the same university. From 1983-86 Professor of Sociology at Heidelberg. Head of a major research association as part of the national programme of selective measures "Demain La Suisse."

Berthold H. Hass
Since 2003 Junior Professor of Business Management (esp. New Media) at the Institute for Management of the University of Koblenz-Landau.

Studies in business management and economics at the Humboldt University of Berlin and the École des Hautes Études Commerciales Lausanne (Diploma in Commerce 1998). Doctorate (2002) at the Ludwig-Maximilian University of Munich with a dissertation on the business models of media enterprises.

Dominik K. Heger
Since 2000 research assistant to the chair of Prof. Dr. Dres. h.c. Arnold Picot, Ludwig-Maximilian University of Munich, and from 2000–2004 Managing Editor of the European Communication Council.

In 2003, doctorate at the Ludwig-Maximilian University of Munich.

Thomas Hess
Since October 2001 Chairman of the Institute for Business Informatics and New Media at the Ludwig-Maximilian University of Munich.

Studies in business informatics at the Technical University of Darmstadt, doctorate at the Institute for Business Informatics at the University of St. Gallen, and postdoctoral thesis (habilitation) in business management at the University of Göttingen.

William Lehr
Research consultant of the MIT Program on Internet and Telecom Convergence, research scholar at Columbia University's Graduate School of Business, and research associate at the Columbia Institute for Tele-Information.

Obtained a doctorate at Stanford University and an M.B.A. at Graduate School. Also has an M.S.E., B.S. and B.A. degree from the University of Pennsylvania.

Friedemann Mattern
Since 1999 Professor of Computer Science at the ETH Zurich (Federal Institute of Technology), Department of Distributed Systems.

Studies in computer science at the University of Bonn. From 1983-89 research assistant in the Department of Computer Science at the University of Kaiserslautern. Ph.D. in 1989, and from 1989-91 assistant lecturer in the same department. Professor of Practical Computer Science at Saarland University in Saarbrücken from 1991–1994, and Professor of Practical Computer Science and Distributed Systems at Darmstadt University of Technology from 1994–1999.

Lee W. McKnight
Associate Professor at the School of Information Studies of Syracuse University, New York.

Gained his Ph.D. in political science at MIT, has an M.A. degree from the Johns Hopkins University and a B.A. from Tufts University. He is also Director of the Murrow Center, founder of the MIT Internet Telephony Consortium, and President of Marengo Research. Until 2002 he was Associate Professor of International Communications at the Fletcher School of Tufts University in Massachusetts.

John Pavlik
Professor of Journalism and Mass Media at Rutgers University, New Jersey.

M.A. and Ph.D. from the University of Minnesota, and B.A. from the University of Wisconsin-Madison, USA. Faculty Research Fellow of the Columbia Institute for Tele-Information (CITI), Columbia University, and Faculty Associate of the Institute for Learning Technologies, Teachers College. Until 2002 he was Professor and Director of the Center for New Media, Columbia School of Journalism.

Arnold Picot
Since 1988 Chairman of the Institute for Information, Organisation and Management at the Ludwig-Maximilian University of Munich.

Doctorate and postdoctoral thesis (habilitation) at the Ludwig-Maximilian University of Munich. Subsequently assumed the Chair of Business Management at the University of Hanover. From 1984-87 held the Chair of General and Industrial Business Management at the Technical University of Munich. He is Chairman of the Board of the Münchner Kreis, a member of various research advisory committees, boards and commissions, as well as the (co-)editor of numerous journals, series and publications.

Klaus Schrape (1946–2001)
Director of Prognos AG, Basel, and head of the Media and Communication Department. Professor of Sociology and Media Science at the University of Basel.

Studies in sociology, psychology, economics and statistics at the Universities of Kiel and of Basel (doctorate in 1977). As a member of Prognos AG, the author of numerous studies for private and public institutions in Germany and Switzerland: e.g. *Digitales Fernsehen: Marktchancen und ordnungspolitischer Regelungsbedarf* (Munich, 1995) and *Künftige Entwicklung des Medien- und Kommunikationssektors in Deutschland* (in conjunction with DIW, Berlin 1996).

Hannes Siegrist
Since 1997 Professor of Comparative Cultural History / Modern Europe at the Institute of Cultural Studies, University of Leipzig.

Studies in general history, sociology, German literature and journalism at the University of Zurich. In 1976 doctorate at the University of Zurich. In 1992 postdoctoral thesis (habilitation) at the Free University of Berlin (on recent and very recent history). From 1976-96 research and teaching activity at universities and research centres in Zurich, Bielefeld, Berlin, Florence, Uppsala and Budapest.

Roger Silverstone
Professor of Media and Communications and Director of the Interdepartmental Programme in Media and Communications at the London School of Economics and Political Science.

Studies in geography and sociology at Balliol College, Oxford, and the London School of Economics and Political Science (B.A., 1966; M.A., 1979;

Ph.D., 1980). Numerous research projects for European and British institutions in the field of media and communication technologies.

Ilkka Tuomi

Since 2002 visiting scientist at the Institute for Prospective Technological Studies, Joint Research Centre in Seville.

Studied theoretical physics and obtained his doctorate in education at the University of Helsinki. From 1987-2001 he worked for the Nokia Research Center, and from 1999-2001 was visiting researcher at the University of California, Berkeley.

Martin Weber

Head of the Technology Policy Unit at the Austrian research centre Seibersdorf GmbH.

Studies in process engineering at the TH Aachen and the University of Stuttgart. Studies in political science at the University of Stuttgart. From 1993-97 doctorate in the field of the economics of innovation. From 1996-2000 research assistant at the Institute for Prospective Technological Studies, Joint Research Centre of the European Commission, Seville.

Axel Zerdick (1941–2003)

From 1980 Professor of Economics and Communication at the Department of Media Economics and Media Management of the Free University Berlin.

Diploma in commerce in 1968, doctorate in 1970. Research and teaching activities at diverse universities at home and abroad, co-editor of various academic journals. From 1975 management and policy consultant in Europe and Japan. Involvement in founding various enterprises. From 1996 founder and speaker of the European Communication Council.

References

Abernathy, W.; **Utterback**, J. (1978), Patterns of Innovation in Technology, in: Technology Review, Vol. 80 (July), pp. 40–47

Agre, Philip E. (2001): Changing Places: Contexts of Awareness in Computing. http://dlipp.gseipp.ucla.edu/people/pagre/hci.html

Ahlert, Dieter (2002): Integriertes Markenmanagement in kundengetriebenen CM-Netzwerken, in: Ahlert, D.; Olbrich, R.; Schröder, H. (Ed.): Jahrbuch Handelsmanagement 2001, Frankfurt am Main, pp. 15–59

Anderson, Benedict (1983): Imagined Communities: Reflections on the Origin and Spread of Nationalism, London

Anderson, Craig A. (2001): Violent video games and aggressive thoughts, feelings and behaviours. http://psych-server.iastate.edu/faculty/caa/abstracts/2000-2004/02A.jcc.pdf

Anon (1999): Hacker Journalism, in: The Economist, December 4th, p. 82

Anon (2000): Here, there and everywhere, in: The Economist, June 24th, pp. 115–118

Anon (2001): Public W-LANS Seen As Essential to 3G Services, Telecom A.M., Vol. 7, (132), July 10th, 2001

Anon (2002a): Lizenzbranche 195 Mio. schwer, in: LicensingMarkt 3/2002, p. 3

Anon (2002b): Vier Mrd. Dollar Handelsumsatz, in: LicensingMarkt 3/2002, p. 14

Armstrong, Arthur; **Hagel**, John III (1995): Real Profits from Virtual Communities, McKinsey Quarterly 3/1995, pp. 127–141

Arthur, W. Brian (1985): Competing Technologies and Lock-in by Historical small Events: The Dynamics of Allocation under Increasing Returns, CEPR Discussion Paper 43, Stanford University

Arthur, W. Brian (1989): Competing Technologies, Increasing Returns, and Lock-in by Historical Events, in: Economic Journal, Vol. 99 (3), pp. 116–131

Arthur, W. Brian (1994): Preface, in: Arthur, W.B. (ed.): Increasing Returns and Path Dependence in the Economy, Ann Arbor, MI

Arthur, W. Brian (1996): Increasing Returns and the New World of Business, in: Harvard Business Review, Vol. 74, pp. 100–109

Bachen, Christin (2001): The Family in the Networked Society: A Summary of Research on the American Family. http://stpp.scu.edu/nexus/Issue1-1/Bachen_TheNetworkedFamily.asp

Barlow, J.B. (1996): A declaration of the independence of cyberspace, in: The Humanist, Vol. 56 (May/June), pp. 18–19

Bauman, Zygmunt (1993): Postmodern Ethics, Cambridge

BBC News (2002): Bridging the digital divide.
http://newpp.bbc.co.uk/hi/english/special_report/1999/10/99/information_rich-_information_poor/newsid_466000/466651.stm

Bechtold, Stefan (2002): From Copyright to Information Law – Implications of Digital Rights Management, in: Sander, T. (ed.): Security and Privacy in Digital Rights Management, Berlin

Bechtold, Stefan (2002): Vom Urheber- zum Informationsrecht – Implikationen des Digital Rights Management, München, 2002

Beck, Hanno; **Prinz**, Aloys (1999): Ökonomie des Internet – Eine Einführung, Frankfurt am Main

Beckham, J.; **Huffstutter**, P. J.; **Oldham**, J. (1999): First-person game is a landmark, in: Los Angeles Times, May 1st 1999

Benhabib, Seyla (1992): Situating the Self: Gender, Community, and Postmodernism in Contemporary Ethics, Oxford

Benkler, Yochai (2002): Intellectual Property and the Organization of Information Production, in: International Review of Law & Economics, Vol. 22(1), pp. 81–107

Berger, Peter L.; **Luckmann**, Thomas (1966): The Social Construction of Reality: A Treatise in the Sociology of Knowledge, New York, NY

Berghel, Hal (1999): Value-Added Publishing, Communications of the ACM, Vol. 42(1), pp. 19–23

Bertrand, André (1999): Le droit d'auteur et les droits voisins, 2nd edn., Paris

Bertrand, Gilles, **Michalski**, Anna, **Pench**, Lucio R. (1999): Scenarios Europe 2010, Five possible Futures for Europe, Forward Studies Unit

Blumler, Jay G.; **Coleman**, Stephen (2001): Realising Democracy Online: A Civic Commons in Cyberspace, London

Böll, Karin (1999): Merchandising und Licensing: Grundlagen, Beispiele, Management, Munich

Bolt, David B.; **Crawford**, Ray A. K. (2000): Digital Divide: Computers and Our Children's Future, New York

Boltanski, Luc (1999): Distant Suffering: Morality, Media, Politics, Cambridge

Böning-Spohr, Patricia; **Hess**, Thomas (2001): Zum Veränderungsbedarf im Verlagscontrolling, in: krp, Sonderheft E-Business & Controlling, 2/01, pp. 40–51

Böning-Spohr, Patricia; **Hess**, Thomas (2002): Analyse der Wechselwirkungen zwischen Print- und Online-Angeboten mittels Wirkungsketten, in: Altobelli, C.F. (ed.): Print contra Online? Verlage im Internetzeitalter, München

Bosse, Heinrich (1981): Autorschaft ist Werkherrschaft. Über die Entstehung des Urheberrechts aus dem Geist der Goethezeit, Paderborn et al.

Bourdieu, Pierre (1977): Outline of a Theory of Practice, Cambridge

Bourdieu, Pierre (1993): The Field of Cultural Production: Essays on Art and Literature, Cambridge

Bowker, Geoffrey C.; **Star**, Susan L. (1999): Sorting Things Out: Classification and its Consequences, Cambridge, MA

Breemen, Alex van (ed.), (1999): Drenkelingen in de Digitale Delta. Dossier ten behoeve van de expertmeeting De digitale kloof in cijfers, BZK november 1999, Amsterdam

Breemen, Alex van; **Terstroot**, E. (1999): De informatiemaatschappij van en voor iedereen? Een onderzoek naar de adoptie en het gebruik van informatie-en communicatietechnologie door individuen. Doctoral thesis, University of Utrecht

Brenner, Walter; **Zarnekow**, Rüdiger (1999): Innovative Ansätze zur digitalen Bereitstellung multimedialer Inhalte, in: Schumann, M.; Hess, T. (eds.): Medienunternehmen im digitalen Zeitalter. Wiesbaden, pp. 33–50

Brooks, Dylan et al. (2001): Mobile Content and Applications: Monetizing Popular Interactive Services, Jupiter Vision Report Broadband & Wireless 08/2000, New York, NY et al.

Brotman, Stuart (2002): Creating the Digital Dividend: How Business Benefits by Closing the Digital Divide, MIT Technology Review. http://www.technologyreview.com/articles/brotman0302.asp

Brown, John PP.; **Duguid**, Paul (2000): The Social Life of Information, Boston, MA

Browning, John, **Reiss**, Spencer (1998): Encyclopedia of the New Economy (Part I), in: Wired, Vol. 6(3), pp. 105–114

Bruck, Peter A.; **Selhofer**, Hannes (1996): Sind die fetten Jahre vorbei? Zur internationalen Werbemarktentwicklung, in: Altmeppen, K.-D. (ed.): Ökonomie der Medien und des Mediensystems: Grundlagen, Ergebnisse und Perspektiven medienökonomischer Forschung, Opladen, pp. 179–202

Buhse, Willms; **Thiem**, Henning (2000): Kooperationen entlang der Wertschöpfungskette in der Musikindustrie: Status quo und Implikationen durch Electronic Commerce, in: Steinle, C. et al. (eds.): Vitalisierung: Das Management der neuen Lebendigkeit. Frankfurt am Main

Bundeskartellamt (2001): Das Untersagungskriterium in der Fusionskontrolle – Marktbeherrschende Stellung versus Substantial Lessening of Competition, http://www.bundeskartellamt.de/Proftag-Text.pdf

Bureau Veldkamp (1998): Mediagebruik onder etnische publieksgroepen: Onderzoek in opdracht van NOS, NPS en RVD, Amsterdam

Burk, Dan L.: **Cohen**, Julie E. (2001): Fair Use Infrastructure for Rights Management Systems, Harvard Journal of Law & Technology, Vol. 15(1), pp. 41–83

Burke, Peter (2001): Papier und Marktgeschrei. Die Geburt der Wissensgesellschaft, Berlin

Burke, Peter (2000): A Social History of Knowledge: From Gutenberg to Diderot, Cambridge

References

Burkhardt, Jochen; **Henn**, Horst; **Hepper**, Stefan; **Rindtorff**, Klaus; **Schäck**, Thomas (2001): Pervasive Computing – Technology and Architecture of Mobile Internet Applications, Munich et al.

Buxmann, Peter; **König**, Wolfgang (1998): Das Standardisierungsproblem: Zur ökonomischen Auswahl von Standards in Informationssystemen, in: Wirtschaftsinformatik, Vol. 40(2), pp. 122–129

Bygrave, Lee A. (2002): The Technologisation of Copyright: Implications for Privacy and Related Interests, European Intellectual Property Review, Vol. 24(2)

Bygrave, Lee A.; **Koelman**, Kamiel J. (2000): Privacy, Data Protection and Copyright: Their Interaction in the Context of Electronic Copyright Management Systems, in: Hugenholtz, B.P.; Aspen, P. (eds.) Copyright and Electronic Commerce, London

Carnoy, Martin (2000): Sustaining the New Economy: Work, Family, and Community in the Information Age, Cambridge, MA

Carvin, Andy (ed.) (February 2000): The E-Rate in America: A Tale of Four Cities, Benton Foundation, pp. 1–57

Castells, Manuel (1989): The Informational City: Information Technology, Economic Restructuring, and the Urban-Regional Process, Oxford

Castells, Manuel; **Hall**, Peter (1994): Technopoles of the World: The Making of 21st Century Industrial Complexes, London

Cavanaugh, Tim (1998): Royal Controversy, in: Wired, Vol. 6(9)

Certeau de, Michel (1988): The Practice of Everyday Life. Berkeley, CA

Cheskin Research (April 2000): The Digital World of the US Hispanic

Christensen, Clayton; **Rosenbloom**, Richard S. (1995): Explaining the Attackers advantage: technological paradigms, organizational dynamics, and the value network, Research Policy, Vol. 24(2), pp. 233–257

Christensen, Clayton M. (1997): The Innovator's Dilemma: When New Technologies Cause Great Firms to Fail, Boston

Christians, Clifford (2000): An intellectual history of media ethics, in: Pattyn, B. (ed.): Media Ethics: Opening Social Dialogue. Leuven, pp. 15–46

Clark, Kim B. (1985): The Interaction of Design Hierarchies and market Concepts in Technological Evolution, Research Policy, Vol.14(5), pp. 235–251

Coase, Ronald H. (1937): The Nature of the Firm, in: Economica, Vol.4 (16), pp. 386–405

Cohen, Hal (2000): The Price is wrong – And Customers couldn't be happier: Why Flat Rates und Fixed Prices rule, in: The Standard.com. http://www.thestandard.com/article/article_print/0,1153,20976,00.html

Cohen, Julie E. (1998): Lochner in Cyberspace: The New Economic Orthodoxy of "Rights Management", in: Michigan Law Review, Vol. 97(2), pp. 462–563

Cole, Jeffrey (2001): The UCLA Internet Report: surveying the digital future. http://ccp.ucla.edu/pdf/UCLA-Internet-Report-2001.pdf

Cole, Michael (1996): Cultural Psychology: A Once and Future Discipline, Cambridge, MA

Coleman, Stephen (2001): A Cyber Space Odyssey, London

Coleman, Stephen; **Gotze**, John (2001): Bowling Together: Online Public Engagement in Policy Deliberation, London

Collins, Harry M. (1975): The seven sexes: a study in the sociology of a phenomenon, or the replication of experiments in physics, in: Sociology, No. 9, pp. 205–224

Collins, Harry M. (1987): Expert systems and the science of knowledge, in: Bijker, W.E.; Hughes, T.P.; Pinch, T. (ed.): The Social Construction of Technological Systems: New Dimensions in the Sociology and History of Technology, Cambridge, MA, pp. 329–348

Collins, Richard; **Murroni**, Cristina (1996): New Media, New Policies, Cambridge

Communication on Interactive Policy Making: SEC/522, 2001

Compaine, Benjamin M. (1981): Shifting Boundaries in the Information Marketplace, in: Journal of Communication Vol. 31(1), pp. 132–142

Compaine, Benjamin M. (ed.) (2001): The Digital Divide: Facing a Crisis or Creating a Myth? Cambridge, MA

Compaine, Benjamin M.; **Weinraub**, Mitchell (1997): Universal Access to Online Services: an Examination of the Issue, in: Telecommunications Policy, Vol. 21(1), pp. 15–33

Cooper, G. (2000): The Mutable Mobile: Social Theory in the Wireless World, paper presented at the "Wireless World" Workshop, University of Surrey, April 7th

Coppel, Jonathan (2000): E-Commerce: Impacts and Policy Challenges, OECD Working Paper, ECO/WKP (2000) 25, Paris

Coulborn, Rushton (1959): The Origin of Civilized Societies, Princeton, NJ

Crang, Mike; **Thrift**, Nigel (2001): Introduction of Thinking Space, in: Crang, M.; Thrift, N. (eds.): Thinking Space, London

Curtis, Michael (1998): Introduction to the Transaction Edition, in: Lippmann, W. (ed.): Public Opinion, London.

Davied, Daniel J.; **Fisher**, James E.; **Arnold**, Mark; **Johnsen**, David (1999): Usage Profiles of Users of Interactive Communication Technology: An Empirical Investigation into the Significance of Selected Individual Attributes, Intellectual Property and Technology Forum. Boston, College Law School. http://infoeagle.bc.edu/bc_org/avp/law/st_org/iptf/commentary/content/19990-60510.html

Davies, Gillian (1994): Copyright and the public interest, Weinheim

Detering, Dietmar (2001): Ökonomie der Medieninhalte: Allokative Effizienz und soziale Chancengleichheit in den Neuen Medien, Münster

Dietl, Helmut; **Franck**, Egon (2000): Free-TV, Abo-TV, Pay per View-TV: Organisationsformen zur Vermarktung von Unterhaltung, in: Zeitschrift für betriebswirtschaftliche Forschung Vol. 52(9), pp. 592–603

Digitale Delta (1999): De Digitale Delta: Nederland oNLine. Interdepartmental ICT memorandum , http://info.minez.nl/kennisent/ict/

Dijk, Jan van (1998): Toenemende ongelijkheid bij het gebruik van nieuwe media, in: Frissen, V.; Molder, H. te (eds.): Van Forum tot Supermarkt? Consumenten en burgers in de informatiesamenleving, Leuven, pp. 113–128

Dornan, Andy (2002): The Essential Guide to Wireless Communication Applications: From Mobile Systems to Wi-Fi, 2nd edn., Upper Saddle River, NJ

Downes, Thomas A.; **Greenstein**, Shane M. (1999): Do Commercial ISPs Provide Universal Access? in: Eisner Gillett, S.; Vogelsang, I. (eds.): Competition, Regulation and Convergence: Current Trends in Telecommunications Policy Research. Mahwah, NJ

Dreier, Hardy (2002): Vielfalt oder Vervielfältigung? – Medienangebote und ihre Nutzung im digitalen Zeitalter, in: Müller-Kalthoff, B. (ed.): Cross-Media-Management: Content-Strategien erfolgreich umsetzen, Berlin et al., pp. 41–60

Dreyfuss, Rochelle C.; **Zimmerman**, Diane L.; **First**, Harry (eds.) (2001): Expanding the Boundaries of Intellectual Property – Innovation Policy for the Knowledge Society, Oxford

Drotner, K. (2001): Medier for fremtiden, Kopenhagen

Ducatel, Ken; **Bogdanowicz**, Marc; **Scapolo**, Fabiana; **Leijten**, Jos; **Burgelmann**, Jean-Claude (2001): Scenarios for Ambient Intelligence in 2010, Final Report compiled by K. Ducatel, M. Bogdanowicz, F. Scapolo, J. Leijten, . J.-C. Burgelmann; Februar 2001, JPTS-Seville. www.cordipp.lu/ist/istag.htm

DuVal Smith, Anna (1999): Problems of conflict management in virtual communities, in: Smith, M.A.; Kollock, P. (eds.): Communities in Cyberspace. London, pp. 134–163

Eberspächer, Jörg; **Hertz**, Udo (eds.) (2002): Leben in der e-Society: Computerintelligenz für den Alltag, Berlin et al.

Ducatel, Ken; **Bogdanowicz**, Marc; **Scapolo**, Fabiana; **Leijten**, Jos; **Burgelman**, Jean-Claude (2001): ISTAG – Scenarios for Ambient Intelligence, Office for official publications of the European Community

Ehrhardt, Marcus (2001): Netzwerkeffekte, Standardisierung und Wettbewerbsstrategie, Wiesbaden

Eisenstein, Elizabeth (1979): The Printing Press in an Age of Social Change, 2nd edn. Cambridge

Ekman, Paul (1993): Facial expression and emotion, in: American Psychologist, Vol. 48, pp. 384–392

Ekman, Paul; **Friesen**, W.V.; **Ellsworth**, Phoebe (1974): Gesichtssprache: Wege zur Objektivierung menschlicher Emotionen, Wien

Ekman, Paul; **Friesen**, W.V.; **Ellsworth**, Phoebe (1997): What the face reveals, Basic and applied studies of spontaneous expression using the Facial Action Coding System (FACS), Oxford

Elkin-Koren, Niva; **Netanel**, Neil W. (eds.) (2002): The Commodification of Information, The Hague

Engeström, Yrjö (1987): Learning by Expanding: An Activity Theoretical Approach to Developmental Work Research, Helsinki

Engeström, Yrjö; **Middleton**, David (1996): Cognition and Communication at Work, Cambridge

Erb, Hubert (2001): Die legale Filmleihe übers Internet kommt. http://www.heise.de/tp/deutsch/html/result.xhtml?url=/tp/deutsch/inhalt/kino-/9363/1.html&words=film%20Napster

Eurobarometer, 117, January 2002

Eurobarometer, 54, April 2001

European Commission (2000): Die neue Sozialpolitische Agenda bis 2005, June 28th

Evans, Philip B.; **Wurster**, Thomas S. (1997): Strategy and the New Economics of Information, in: Harvard Business Review, Vol. 5, 1997, pp. 71–82

Evans, Philip B.; **Wurster**, Thomas S. (2000): Blown to Bits: How the New Economics of Information transforms your Strategy, Boston, MA

Faulstich, Werner (1998): Medium, in: Faulstich, W. (Ed.): Grundwissen Medien, 3rd edn. Munich, pp. 21–98

Finkenzeller, Klaus (1999): RFID-Handbook. Chichester et al.

Fishburn, Peter; **Odlyzko**, Andrew M.; **Siders**, Ryan C. (1997): Fixed fee versus unit pricing for information goods: competition, equilibria, and price wars, in: First Monday. http://www.firstmonday.dk/issues/issue2_7/odlyzko/

Fisher III, William. W.(1999): Geistiges Eigentum – ein ausufernder Rechtsbereich. Die Geschichte des Ideenschutzes in den Vereinigten Staaten, in: Siegrist, H.; Sugarman, D. (eds.): Eigentum im internationalen Vergleich. Göttingen, pp. 262–289

Fleck, Andree (1995): Hybride Wettbewerbsstrategien, Wiesbaden

Fortunati, Leopoldina (2000): The Mobile Phone: New Social Categories and Relations, University of Trieste. http://www.telenor.no/fou/prosjekter/Fremtidens_Brukere/seminarer/mobil-presentasjoner/Proceedings%20_FoU%20notat_.pdf

Foucault, Michel (1979): Discipline and Punish, New York

Foucault, Michel (1984): Space, Knowledge and Power, in: Rabinow, P. (ed.): The Foucault Reader, New York, pp. 239–256

E-Merging Media

Frey, Siegfried (1993): Lavater, Lichtenberg, and the suggestive power of the human face, in: Shookman, E. (ed.): The faces of physiognomy. An interdisciplinary conference on the 250th anniversary of the birth of Johann Caspar Lavater, Columbia, S.C., pp. 64–103

Frey, Siegfried (1998): Prejudice and Inferential Communication: A New Look at an Old Problem, in: Eibl-Eibesfeldt, I.; Salter, F. (eds.): Indoctrinability, Ideology and Warfare: Evolutionary Perspective, Oxford, pp. 189–217

Frey, Siegfried (1999): Neue Wege in der Kommunikationsforschung, in: Ganten, D., et al. (eds.): Gene, Neurone, Qubits & Co, Unsere Welten der Informa-tion, Verhandlungen der Gesellschaft Deutscher Naturforscher und Ärzte, 120. Versammlung, 19.–22. September 1998 in Berlin, Stuttgart

Frey, Siegfried (2000): Die Macht des Bildes: Der Einfluss der nonverbalen Kom-munikation auf Kultur und Politik, 2nd edn. Bern

Frey, Siegfried (2003): The Pictorial Turn – A Shift from Reason to Instinct? In: Süß, S. (ed.) Form and Sign – Global Communication, Ulm

Frey, Siegfried; **Möller**, Carsten (2002): Dreamteam Mensch-Computer. Neue Wege zur nutzergerechten Gestaltung des Mensch-Technik-Dialogs, in: Kohnen, T. (ed.): Forum Forschung 2002/2003, Themenheft Kommunikation. Duisburg, pp. 44–50

Frey, Siegfried, et al. (1993): Mise en évidence du traitement cognitif et affectif du non-verbal. msh-informationpp, Bulletin de la Fondation Maison des sciences de l'homme, Vol. 70, pp. 4–23

Frey, Siegfried; **Hirsbrunner**, H.P.; **Florin**, A.; **Daw**, W.; **Crawford**, R. (1983): A unified approach to the investigation of nonverbal and verbal behavior in communication research, in: Doise, W.; Moscovici, PP. (eds.): Current issues in European social psychology, Cambridge: pp. 143–199

Friends of Europe, Report (2001), http://www.friendsofeurope.org/act_reportpp.asp?indexd=2001

Frissen, Valerie (ed.) (1997): Gender, ICTs and Everyday Life. Mutual Shaping Processes, proceedings from COST A4/GRANITE workshop, Brussels, EC/DG XII

Frissen, Valerie (1998): Ergens tussen forum en supermarkt. De toegankelijk-heid van de informatievoorziening voor postmoderne burgers, in: Frissen, V.; Molder, H. te (eds.): Van Forum tot Supermarkt? Consumenten en burgers in de informatiesamenleving. Leuven, pp. 159–170

Frissen, Valerie (1999a): De paradoxen van de digitale gemeenschap, in: Frissen, P.; Mul, J. de (eds.): Internet en openbaar bestuur, The Hague

Frissen, Valerie (1999b): Domeinverkenning 'De informatiesamenleving', by or-der of the ministry of social welfare, direction coordination for questions of emancipation, Amsterdam (unpublished research report)

Frissen, Valerie (in press): De participatie-paradox. Maatschappelijke en politieke participatie op het Internet, in: Van Cuilenburg, J.; Neijens, P.; Scholten, O. (eds.): Media in Overvloed, Over verdwijnende loyaliteiten en wisselende mediacontacten, Boeknummer Mens en Maatschappij

Frissen, Valerie (in press): ICT en arbeid in het dagelijks leven. Research commissioned by the Rathenau Instituut, The Hague

Frissen, Valerie; **Punie**, Yves (1998): Never mind the Gap; integrating qualitative and quantitative methods in user research. The case of busy households, in: Silverstone, R.; Hartmann, M. (eds.): EMTEL-Working Papers 6, May 1998, Brighton

Fröhlich, Jürgen (2002a): Busenfreundschaft, in: MCV 2/2002, pp. 82–84

Fröhlich, Jürgen (2002b): Gute Karten, in: MCV 7/2002, pp. 62–63

Funiok, Rüdiger (2000): Fundamental questions of audience ethics, in: Pattyn, B. (ed.): Media Ethics: Opening Social Dialogue, Leuven, pp. 403–422

Funk, Jeffrey (2001a): The Mobile Internet: How Japan dialed up and the West disconnected, Hong Kong

Funk, Jeffrey (2001b), Competition Between and Within Standards: The case of mobile phones, London

Garnham, Nicholas (2000): The role of public sphere in the information society, in: Marsden, C.T. (ed.): Regulating the Global Information Society. London, pp. 43–56

Garreau, Joel (2000): Home Is Where the Phone Is. Roaming Legion of High-Tech Nomads Takes Happily to Ancient Path, in: Washington Post

Geisler, Cheryl, et al. (2001): The Social Transformation of the Boundary between Work and Life, by It Gone Mobile, Rensselaer Polytechnic Institute, New York. http://www.rpi.edu/~geislc/Mobile/border.htm

Gershenfeld, Neil (1999): Wenn die Dinge denken lernen. Munich

Gesetz über Maßnahmen zur Förderung des deutschen Films (Filmförderungsgesetz – FFG) vom 6. August 1998 (BGBl. I PP. 2046) in der Bekanntmachung vom 6. August 1998 (BGBl. I PP. 2053–2070)

Getting The Message Across (2001): Friends of Europe's 10-point plan for improving the EU's public profile, Friends of Europe, Brussels, 2001

Giddens, Anthony (1984): The Constitution of Society: Outline of the Theory of Structure, Berkeley, CA

Giddens, Anthony (1991): Modernity and Self-Identity: Self and Society in the Late Modern Age, Cambridge

Gieseke, Ludwig (1995): Vom Privileg zum deutschen Urheberrecht. Die Entwicklung des Urheberrechts in Deutschland bis 1845, Göttingen

Gillard, Patricia (1996): Women and New Technologiepp. Information and Telecommunications Needs Research (SIMS). Monash University, Australia. http://www.infotech.monash.edu.au/itNo/reports/womentch.html

Gillmore, Dan (2001): HP backs off copyright threat against security researchers, posted in: Silicon Valley, http://www.siliconvalley.com

Global Reach, http://global-reach.biz/globstats/index.php3

Goffman, Erving (1959): The presentation of self in everyday life, Garden City

Gombrich, Ernst H. (1978): The Story of Art, 13th edn. London

Götz von Olenhusen, Albrecht (1982): "Ewiges geistiges Eigentum" und "Sozial-bindung" des Urheberrechts in der Rechtsentwicklung und Diskussion im 19. Jahrhundert in Frankreich und Deutschland, in: Herschel, W.; Hubmann, H.; Rehbinder, M. (eds.): Festschrift für Georg Roeber zum 10. Dezember 1981. Freiburg, pp. 83–111

Grassmuck, Volker (2002): Freie Software. Zwischen Privat- und Gemeineigentum, Bonn

Grice, Paul H. (1989): Studies in way of words, Boston

Groebel, Jo (1997): New Media Development: Stability and Change in Communication Behaviour, in: Trends in Communication, Vol. 1, pp. 5–17

Guibault, Lucie (2002): Copyright Limitations and Contracts – An Analysis of the Contractual Overridability of Limitations on Copyright, The Hague

Habermas, Jürgen (1989): The Structural Transformation of the Public Sphere: An Inquiry into a Category of Bourgeois Society, Cambridge

Haddon, Leslie (1998): Locating the virtual community in households of the future. Research report for NCR Financial Services (unpublished report about comparative research studies in five European countries)

Haddon, Leslie (2000): The Social Consequences of Mobile Telephony, Oslo. http://www.telenor.no/fou/prosjekter/Fremtidens_Brukere/seminarer/mobilpresen-tasjoner/Proceedings%20_FoU%20notat_.pdf

Hagel III, John (1996): Spider versus Spider, in: The McKinsey Quarterly, No. 1/1996, pp. 5–18

Halbert, Deborah (1999): Intellectual property in the information age: The politics of expanding ownership rights, Westport, Connecticut

Hall, Edward T. (1959): The silent language, Garden City

Hall, Peter (1998): Cities in Civilisation, London

Hamelink, Cees (2000): Ethics for media users, in: Pattyn, B. (ed.): Media Ethics: Opening Social Dialogue, Leuven, pp. 393–401

Hansmann, Uwe; **Merk**, Lothar; **Nicklous**, Martin PP.; **Stober**, Thomas (2001): Pervasive Computing Handbook, Berlin

Hardt, Peter (1996): Organisation dienstleistungsorientierter Unternehmen, Wiesbaden

Harvey, David (1990): The Condition of Postmodernity: An Enquiry into the Origins of Cultural Change, Cambridge, MA

Hass, Berthold H. (2002): Geschäftsmodelle von Medienunternehmen: Ökonomische Grundlagen und Veränderungen durch neue Informations- und Kommunikationstechnik, Wiesbaden

Hazlett, Thomas (2001): The Wireless Craze, the Unlimited Bandwidth Myth, the Spectrum Auction Faux Pas, and the Punchline to Ronald Coase's "Big Joke": An Essay on Airwave Allocation Policy. AEI-Brookings Joint Center for Regulatory Studies Working Paper 01-01

Helmholtz, Herrmann von (1867): Handbuch der physiologischen Optik, Voss, Leipzig

Henkel, Joachim (2001): Bezahlen auf Draht: E-Payment – Wie der Rubel ins Rollen kommt, in: C't 06/2001, pp. 270–281

Hess, Thomas (1999): Unternehmensnetzwerke, in: Zeitschrift für Planung, Vol. 10(2), pp. 225–230

Hess, Thomas (2002): Implikationen des Internet für die Medienbranche – eine strukturelle Analyse, in: Keuper, F. (Ed.): Electronic Business und Mobile Business - Ansätze, Konzepte und Geschäftsmodelle, Wiesbaden, pp. 569–602

Hess, Thomas; **Tzouvaras**, Antonios (2001): Books-on-Demand: Ansatz und strategische Implikationen für Verlage, in: Zeitschrift Führung + Organisation, 4/01, pp. 239–246

Hillier, Bill; **Hanson**, Julienne (1984): The Social Logic of Space, Cambridge

Hoenig, Joachim; **Scheerer**, Michael (2001): Die Reform der EU-Fusionsregeln nimmt langsam Konturen an, in: Handelsblatt, February 13th

Hoffman, Donna L.; **Novak**, Thomas P. (1999): The Evolution of the Digital Divide: Examining the Relationship of Race to Internet Access and Usage over Time. http://www2000.ogsm.vanderbilt.edu/digital.divide.html

Hummel, Johannes; **Lechner**, Ulrike (2001): The Community Model of Content Management – A case study of the music industry, in: Journal of Media Management, Vol. 7(1), pp. 4–14

Hutchins, Edwin (1995): Cognition in the Wild. Cambridge, MA

IDSA (2002): 2001 Game Industry Sales Data & Graphs. http://www.idsa.com/2001SalesData.html

Information Society Forum: first report, Brussels, 1998

Information Society Forum: second report, Brussels, 1999

IPTS: Information and Communication Technologies and the Information Society, Panel-Bericht zu IuK-Technologien, Futures Report Series 03, EUR 18730, IPTS, Seville

Jannidis, Fotis et al. (ed.) (1999): Die Rückkehr des Autors. Zur Erneuerung eines umstrittenen Begriffs, Tübingen

Jendraczyk, M. (1991): "Snap Judgments" in der Personenwahrnehmung, diploma thesis in the subsidary subject psychology, University of Duisburg

References

Jensen, E. (1999): Study finds TV tops kids' big diet of media, in: Los Angeles Times, 18th November, pp. A1, A29

Jones, Steven (ed.) (1995): Cybersociety: Computer-mediated Communication and Society, London

Jones, Steven (ed.) (1997): Virtual Culture: Identity and Communication in Cybersociety, London

Kant, Immanuel (1784): Beantwortung der Frage: Was ist Aufklärung? Berlinische Monatsschrift, No. 12, pp. 481–494

Kant, Immanuel (1991): An Answer to the Question: „What is Enlightenment?" In: Reiss, Hans (ed.): Kant. Political Writings, 2nd edn. Cambridge

Katz, J.E. (1999): Connections, Social and Cultural Studies of the Telephone in American Life, London

Katz, Michael L.; **Shapiro**, Carl (1985): Network externalities, competition, and compatibility, in: American Economic Review, Vol. 75(3), pp. 424–440

Katzenbeisser, Stefan C.; **Petitcolas**, Fabien A.P. (eds.) (2000): Information Hiding Techniques for Steganography and Digital Watermarking, Norwood

Kemp de, Arnoud (1999): Auf dem Weg zu einem integrierten wissenschaftlichen Informationssystem – die Entwicklung des wissenschaftlichen Springer Verlages Berlin/Heidelberg, in: Schumann, M.; Hess, T. (eds.): Medienunternehmen im digitalen Zeitalter. Neue Technologien – Neue Märkte – Neue Geschäftsansätze. Wiesbaden, pp. 249–265

Kempter, Guido (1998): Das Bild vom Anderen: Skriptanimation als Methode zur Untersuchung spontaner Attributionsprozesse, Lengerich

Kenney, Martin (2000): Understanding Silicon Valley: The Anatomy of an Entrepreneurial Region, Stanford, CA

Knorr-Cetina, Karin (1999): Epistemic Cultures: How the Sciences Make Knowledge, Cambridge, MA

Koelman, Kamiel J.; **Herberger**, Natali (2000): Protection of Technological Measures, in: Hugenholtz, P.B. (ed.), Copyright and Electronic Commerce, London

Kotler, Philip; **Bliemel**, Friedhelm (1995): Marketing-Management: Analyse, Planung, Umsetzung und Steuerung, Stuttgart

KPMG IT-Trends Institute (1999): De IT-antenne: volgen van ontwikkelingen in een dynamische markt. Resultaten van het grote IT-trends onderzoek 1999 binnen Nederlandse organisaties

Kraut, Robert; **Lundmark**, Vicki; **Patterson**, Michael; **Kiesler**, Sara; **Mukopadhyay**, Tridas; **Scherlis**, Willima (1998): Internet Paradox: A Social Technology That Reduces Social Involvement and Psychological Well-Being?, in: American Psychologist, Vol. 53(9), pp. 1017–1031

Krüger, Lorenz (1994): Universalgenie Helmholtz. Rückblick nach 100 Jahren, Berlin

Kummer, Hans (1971): Primate Societies, Chicago

Landry, Charles (2000): The Creative City: A Toolkit for Urban Innovators, London

Latour, Bruno; **Woolgar**, Steve (1986): Laboratory Life: The Construction of Scientific Factpp. Princeton, NJ

Lenhart, Amanda; **Rainie**, Lee; **Lewis**, Oliver (2001): Teenage life online. http://www.pewinternet.org/reports/pdfs/PIP_Teens_Report.pdf

Lenski, Gerhard; **Nolan**, Patrick; **Lenski**, Jean (1995): Human Societies: An Introduction to Macro Sociology, 7th edn. New York

Lessig, Lawrence (1999): Code and Other Laws of Cyberspace, New York

Lessig, Lawrence (2001): The Future of Ideas – The Fate of the Commons in a Connected World, New York

Levitsky, Serge L. (1964): Introduction to the Soviet copyright law, Leyden

Lichtenberg, Georg Christoph (1980): Schriften und Briefe. Erster Band. Sudelbücher I. Munich

Lichtenberg, Georg Christoph (1991): Schriften und Briefe: Zweiter Band, Sudelbücher II, Materialhefte, Tagebücher, 3rd edn. Munich

Lindsay, Greg (2000): Who's playing games online? in: Yahoo! Internet Life, No. 6(3), pp. 106–110

Ling, Rich (1997): One Can Talk about Common Manners: The Use of Mobile Telephones in Inappropriate Situations", in Haddon, L (ed.): Themes in Mobile Telephony: Final Report of the COST 248 Home and Work Group, Telia, Farsta. http://www.telenor.no/fou/prosjekter/Fremtidens_Brukere/publikasjoner.html

Ling, Rich (1998): "We Will Be Reached": The Use of Mobile Telephony among Norwegian Youth, Kjeller, Telenor Forskning og Utvikling, FoU Rapport 16/98

Ling, Rich (2000b): The Impact of the Mobile Telephone on Four Established Social Institutions, presented at the ISSEI2000 Conference of the International Society for the Study of European Ideas, Bergen, Norway, 14th to 18th August

Ling, Rich (2000a): Norwegian Teens, Mobile Telephony and SMS Use in School, Telenor Forskning og Utvikling, FoU Rapport 7/2000a

Ling, Rich; **Helmersen**, Per (2000): "It Must Be Necessary, It Has to Cover a Need": The Adoption of Mobile Telephony Among Pre-Adolescents and Adolescentpp, Telenor Forskning og Utvikling, FoU Rapport 9

Ling, Rich; Yttri, Birgitte (1999): "Nobody Sits at Home and Waits for the Telephone to Ring:" Micro and Hyper-Coordination through the Use of the Mobile Telephone, Telenor Forskning og Utvikling, FoU Rapport 30/99

Lippmann, Walter (1922): Public opinion, New York

Litan, Robert E.; **Rivlin**, Alice M. (2001): Beyond the Dot.coms: The Economic Promise of the Internet, Washington, D.C., pp. 101–119

Loader, Brian D. (1997): The governance of cyberspace: politics, technology and global restructuring, in: Loader, B.D. (ed.): The Governance of Cyberspace: Politics, Technology and Global Restructuring, London, pp. 1–19

Lorenz, Konrad (1942): Die angeborenen Formen möglicher Erfahrung. Zeitschrift für Tierpsychologie, No. 5/2, pp. 235–409

Lorenz, Konrad (1968): Vergleichende Verhaltensforschung, in: Lorenz, K.; Leyhausen, P. (eds.): Antriebe tierischen und menschlichen Verhaltens: Gesammelte Abhandlungen, Munich, pp. 15–47

Louis, Elaine. (1999): "If the Phone Had a Cord, You Could Strangle the User", in: *New York Times*, September 30th

Luhmann, Niklas (1981): Soziologische Aufklärung, Vol. 3, Opladen

MacIntyre, Alasdair (1981): After Virtue: A Study in Moral Theory, London

Macneil, Ian R. (1980): The New Social Contract – An Inquiry into Modern Contractual Relations, New Haven

Mahadevan, B. (2000): Business Models for Internet-Based E-Commerce: An Anatomy, in: California Management Review 42(4), pp. 55–69

Mander, Jerry (1979): Four Arguments fort he Elimination of Television. New York

Manning, P.K. (1996): Information Technology in the Police Context: The Sailor Phone, in: Information Systems Research, Vol. 7(1), pp. 52–62

Manz, Iris; **Fröhlich**, Jürgen; **Holowaty**, Christoph (2002): Schrecksekunde, in: MCV 3/2002, pp. 60–64

March, James G.; **Olsen**, Johan P. (1989): Rediscovering Institutions: The Organizational Basis of Politics, New York

Marks, Dean P.P.; **Turnbull**, Bruce H. (2000): Technical Protection Measures – The Intersection of Technology, Law and Commercial Licenses, European Intellectual Property Review

Marvin, Carolyn (1988): When Old Technologies Were New: Thinking About Communications in the Late Nineteenth Century, Oxford

Mathews, Joe (2001): Cell Phones on Campus Advocated, in: Los Angeles Times, Sept. 30th

Mayer-Schönberger, Viktor (2001): The authority of law in times of cyberspace, in: Journal of Law, Technology & Policy, Vol. 1(1), pp. 1–23

McLuhan, Marshall (1961): The Gutenberg Galaxy, Toronto

McLuhan, Marshall (1964): Understanding Media, London

Meffert, Heríbert; **Giloth**, Matthias (2002): Aktuelle markt- und unternehmensbezogene Herausforderungen an die Markenführung. In: Meffert, H.; Burmann, C.; Koers, M. (eds.): Markenmanagement: Grundfragen der identitätsorientierten Markenführung. Wiesbaden, pp. 99–132

Merten, Klaus (1999): Einführung in die Kommunikationswissenschaft, Vol. 1, Münster

Merten, Udo; **Grauer**, Manfred (1999): Speicherung und Verwaltung multimedialer Inhalte, in: Schumann, M./Hess, T. (Ed.): Medienunternehmen im digitalen Zeitalter. Wiesbaden, pp. 51–67

Meyer, PP.; **Schulze**, E. (1997): Womens acceptance of ICTs in the home. Theoretical considerations and empirical findings, in: Frissen, V. (ed.) Gender, ICTs and Everyday Life. Mutual Shaping Processes, Proceedings from COST A4/GRANITE workshop. Brussels, EC/DG XII, pp. 123–136

Meyer, Thomas (1992): Die Inszenierung des Scheins: Voraussetzungen und Folgen symbolischer Politik, Essay Montage, Frankfurt

Middelhoff, Thomas (1997): Entwicklung einer Multimediastrategie für Medienunternehmen, in: Die Betriebswirtschaft Vol. 57(3), pp. 411–422

Middelhoff, Thomas (1998): Wer bestimmt die Multimedia-Wertschöpfungskette? in: Picot, A. (Hrsg.): Telekommunikation im Spannungsfeld von Innovation, Wettbewerb und Regulierung. Heidelberg, pp. 47–57

Ministère de l'économie et de l'industrie (2000): Rapport Technologies-Clés 2005, Paris

Ministerie van OC&W (1999): Infodrome. Kennis en informatie in een veranderende samenleving: schaarste in overvloed? The Hague

Mitchell, William J. (1995): City of Bits: Space, Place, and the Infobahn. Cambridge, MA

Moore, Gordon E. (1965): Cramming more components onto integrated circuits, in: Electronics, Vol. 38, pp. 114–117

Morris, Charles W. (1938): Foundations of the Theory of Signs, in: Neurath, O.; Carnap, R.; Morris, C. (eds.): International Encyclopedia of Unified Science, Vol. 1, No. 2, pp. 1–59

Möschel, Wernhard; **Bechtold**, Stefan (1998): Copyright-Management im Netz, in: Multimedia und Recht, Vol. 1(11)

Mueller, Milton; **Schement**, Jorge R. (1996): Universal Service from the Bottom Up: A Profile of Telecommunications Access in Camden, New Jersey, in: The Information Society, Vol. 12, (3), pp. 273–291

Mustafayev, Arif (1996): Jawbones and Dragon Legends. Azerbaijan's Prehistoric Azikh Cave.
http://www.azer.com/aiweb/categories/magazine/42_folder/42_articles/42_azikhcave.html

Nalebuff, Barry J.; **Brandenburger**, Adam M. (1996): Coopetition – kooperativ konkurrieren – Mit der Spieltheorie zum Unternehmenserfolg, Frankfurt am Main

Nardi, Bonnie A. (1997): Activity theory and human-computer interaction, in: Nardi, B.A. (ed.): Context and Consciousness, Cambridge, MA, pp. 7–16

References

Nardi, Bonnie A.; **Whittaker**, Steve; **Schwartz**, HeiNoich (2000): It's Not What You Know, It's Who You Know: Work in the Information Age, in: First Monday, No. 5 (5). http://firstmonday.org/issues/issue5_5/nardi/

National Public Radio/Kaiser Family Foundation/Kennedy School of Government (2000): National Survey of American Adults on Technology. http://www.kff.org/content/2000/20000228a/TechnologyToplinepp.PDF

Nederlands Platform Ouderen en Europa (1998/1999): Toegang voor ouderen tot de Europese informatiesamenleving, 3 reports (September 1998, März 1999 und Juni 1999)

Negroponte, Nicholas (1995): Being Digital, New York, NY

Nelson, Richard R., **Winter** Sidney G. (1982): An Evolutionary Theory of the Firm, Cambridge, MA

Neumann, Manfred (2000): Wettbewerbspolitik. Geschichte, Theorie und Praxis, Wiesbaden

Neumann-Bechstein, Wolfgang (1996): Mediennutzung im Zeitalter multimedialer Möglichkeiten, in: Blind, PP.; Hallenberger, G. (eds.): Technische Innovation und Dynamik der Medienentwicklung (Arbeitshefte Bildschirmmedien 63). Siegen, pp. 106–126

Nilsson, Andreas: **Nuldén**, Urban; **Olsson**, Daniel (2001): Mobile Media, Viktoria Institute, Göteborg

Noam, Eli (1998): Spectrum auctions: Yesterday's heresy, today's orthodoxy, tomorrow's anachronism: Taking the next step to open spectrum access, in: Journal of Law and Economics, Vol. 41(2), pp. 765–791

Noam, Eli (2001): The Next Frontier for Openness: Wireless Communications: Paper presented at the Telecommunications Policy Research Conference 2001, Alexandria, VA

Nonaka, Ikujiro; **Takeuchi**, Hirotaka (1995): The Knowledge-Creating Company: How Japanese Companies Create the Dynamics of Innovation, Oxford

Norris, Pippa (2001): Digital Divide: Civic Engagement, Information Poverty, and the Internet Worldwide, New York

O'Brien, Daniel; **Charron**, Chris; **Grimsditch**, Tim (2000): Deconstructing Media, Forrester Report 03/2000, Cambridge, MA; Amsterdam

Odlyzko, Andrew (2001): Talk, talk, talk: So who needs streaming video on a phone? The killer app for 3G may turn out to be – surprise – voice calls, in: Forbes, August 20th, 2001

Oehmichen, Ekkehardt/**Schröter**, Christian (2000): Fernsehen, Hörfunk, Internet: Konkurrenz, Konvergenz oder Komplement? Schlussfolgerungen aus der ARD/ZDF-Online-Studie 2000, in: MP, Vol. 8/2000, pp. 359–368

Owen, Bruce M.; **Wildman**, Steven PP. (1992): Video Economics, London; Cambridge, MA

Palen, Leysia; **Salzmann**, Marilyn; **Youngs**, Ed (2001): Going Wireless: Behaviour & Practice of New Mobile Phone Users, Boulder, CO. http://www.cpp.colorado.edu/%7Epalen/Papers/cscwPalen.pdf

Parsons, Talcott; **Smelser**, Neil J. (1956): Economy and Society: A Study in the Integration of Economic and Social Theory, London

Pascal, B. (1972): Pensées, Paris

Patrizio, Andy (2000): Coming Soon: Pay-Per-Game, in: Wired News, http://www.wired.com/news/print/0,1294,39505,00.html

Pätzold, Ulrich, **Röper**, Horst (2002): Fernseh- und Filmproduktionsmarkt Deutschland. http://www.Now.de/medien/formatt_gutachten/formatt_gutachten.pdf

Peha, Jon; **Satapathy**, Durga: Spectrum Sharing without Licenses: Opportunities and Dangers, in: Rosston, G.; Waterman, D. (eds.) (1997): Interconnection and the Internet: Selected Papers from the 1996 Telecommunications Research Conference, Mahwah, NJ

Picot, Arnold (1982): Transaktionskostenansatz in der Organisationstheorie – Stand der Diskussion und Aussagewert, in: DBW, Vol. 42(02), pp. 283–286

Picot, Arnold; **Dietl**, Helmut (1990): Transaktionskostentheorie, in: Wirtschaftswissenschaftliches Studium, Vol. 4(04), 1990, pp. 178–184

Picot, Arnold; **Hass**, Berthold H. (2002): Digitale Organisation, in: Spoun, S.; Wunderlich, W. (eds.): Medienkultur im digitalen Wandel: Prozesse, Potenziale, Perspektiven, Bern et al., pp. 143–166

Picot, Arnold; **Neuburger**, Rahild (2002): Prinzipien der Internet-Ökonomie, in: Schögel, M.; Tomczak, T.; Belz, C. (eds.): Roadm@p to E-Business – Wie Unternehmen das Internet erfolgreich nutzen, St. Gallen, pp. 22–107

Picot, Arnold; **Reichwald**, Ralf (1994): Auflösung der Unternehmung? Vom Einfluß der IuK-Technik auf Organisationsstrukturen und Kooperationsformen, in: Zeitschrift für Betriebswirtschaft, Vol. 64(05), pp. 547–570

Picot, Arnold; **Reichwald**, Ralf; **Wigand**, Rolf T. (2001): Die grenzenlose Unternehmung, 4th edn. Wiesbaden

Piëch, Ferdinand (2000): Darstellung der Strategie von Volkswagen, ASSOCIATION OF EUROPEAN AUTOMOTIVE ANALYSTS' MEETING, 06.12.2000, http://www.volkswagen-ir.de/deutsch/08/html/piech_pp.html

Piller, Frank T.; **Schoder**, Detlef (1999): Mass Customization und Electronic Commerce, in: Zeitschrift für Betriebswirtschaft, Vol. 69(10), pp. 1111–1136

Pine, B. Joseph; **Gilmore**, James H. (1999): The Experience Economy: Work is Theatre & Every Business a Stage, Boston, MA

Pitroda, Sam (2001): Telecommunication and development in India: Speech to the Alcatel Foundation, Berlin, November 7th 2001

References

Plant, Sadie (2000): On the Mobile: The Effects of Mobile Telephones on Social and Individual Life.
http://www.motorola.com/mot/documents/0,102/8,333,00.pdf

Plinke, Wulff; **Rese**, Mario (2000): Analyse der Erfolgsquellen, in: Kleinaltenkamp, M.; Plinke, W. (Ed.): Technischer Vertrieb: Grundlagen des Business-to-Business Marketing, 2nd edn. Berlin et al., pp. 691–760

Plumpe, Gerhard (1979): Eigentum – Eigentümlichkeit: Über den Zusammenhang ästhetischer und juristischer Begriffe im 18. Jahrhundert, in: Archiv für Begriffsgeschichte, Vol. 23(02), pp. 175–196

Plurismus, August 2001

Polanyi, Michael (1998): Personal Knowledge: Towards a Post-Critical Philosophy, London

Porter, Michael E. (1985): Competitive advantage: Creating and Sustaining Superior Performance, New York, NY

Powell, Michael (2001) cited in: Ahrens, Frank (2001): The great deregulator, in: Washington Post, June 18, 2001

Price, MoNooe E.; **Verhulst**, Stefaan G. (2000): In search of the self: charting the course of self-regulation on the Internet in a global environment, in: Marsden, C.T. (ed.): Regulating the Global Information Society. London, pp. 57–78

Prodi, Romano (2000): Das Neue Europa gestalten: Speech to the European Parliament, Straßburg, February 15th 2000

Prümmer, Klaus von (1998): Wie das Internet die Arbeit von Verlag und Redaktion verändert, in: Fuhrmann, H.-J.; Pasquay, A.; Resing, C. (eds.): Zeitungen '98, Bonn, pp. 249–263

Püschel, Heinz (1986): 100 Jahre Berner Union – Gedanken, Dokumente, Erinnerungen, Leipzig

Quah, Danny T. (1996): The Invisible Hand and the Weightless Economy, Center for Economic Performance Occasional Paper 12, London: Center for Economic Performance, London School of Economics and Political Science

Quittner, Joshua (1999): Are video games really so bad? in: Time, May 10th

Rakow, L.F.; **Navarro**, V. (1993): Remote Mothering and the Parallel Shift: Women Meet the Cellular Phone, in: Critical Studies in Mass Communication, Vol. 10 (2), pp. 144–154

Raschèr, Andrea Francesco Giovanni (1989): Für ein Urheberrecht des Bühnenregisseurs, Baden-Baden

Rawolle, Joachim (2001): XML als Basistechnologie für das Content Management integrierter Medienprodukte, Dissertation at University of Göttingen (in press)

Rawolle, Joachim; **Hess**, Thomas (2000a): XML für das medienneutrale Publishing, in: IS Report, Vol. 4/05, pp. 40–43

Rawolle, Joachim; **Hess**, Thomas (2000b): New Digital Media and Devices – An Analysis for the Media Industry, in: Journal of Media Management, VOl. 4/09, pp. 89–99

Rawolle, Joachim; **Hess**, Thomas (2001): Ökonomische Aspekte des Einsatzes von XML-Standards in der Medienindustrie, in: Turowski, K.; Fellner, K.J. (eds.): XML für betriebliche Anwendungen – Standards, Möglichkeiten und Praxisbeispiele, Heidelberg, pp. 229–245

Raymond, Eric R. (1998): Homesteading the noosphere, in: First Monday, No. 3 (10). http://firstmonday.org/issues/issue3_10/raymond/ und http://www.tuxedo.org/~esr/writings/

Raymond, Eric R. (1999): The Cathedral and the Bazaar: Musings on Linux and Open Source by an Accidental Revolutionary, Sebastopol, CA

Rayport, Jeffrey F.; **Sviokla**, John J. (1994): Managing in the Marketspace, in: Harvard Business Review 6/1994, pp. 141–150

Reid, Elizabeth (1999): Hierarchy and power: social control in cyberspace, in: Smith, M.A.; Kollock, P. (eds.): Communities in Cyberspace. London, pp. 107–133

Reinhard-Karlmann, Susanne (2000): Crossmedia statt kreuz und quer: Dachboden Cyberland will jedem Medium den passenden Inhalt verpassen, in: Die Welt online. http://www.welt.de/daten/2000/12/14/1214mm209099.htx?print=11

Report of Working Group on Broadening and Enriching the Public Debate on European Matters, Brussels, 2001, p. 15

Rheingold, Howard (1993): The Virtual Community: Homesteading on the Electronic Frontier, Reading, MA

Ridder, Christa-Maria (2002): Onlinenutzung in Deutschland: Entwicklungstrends und Zukunftsprognosen, in: Media Perspektiven, Vol. 6(03), pp. 121–131

Rifkin, Jeremy (2000): The Age of Access: The new culture of hypercapitalism, where all of life is a paid-for experience, New York

Rogers, Everett M. (1995): Diffusion of innovations, 4th edn. New York

Rose, Mark (1993): Authors and owners: The invention of copyright, London; Cambridge, MA

Rosenberg, Bernard; **White**, David M. (eds.) (1957): Mass Culture: The Popular Arts in America, New York

Rosenblatt, William; **Trippe**, William; **Mooney**, Stephen (2002): Digital Rights Management – Business and Technology. New York

Roßnagel, Alexander (2002): Freiheit im Cyberspace, in: Informatik-Spektrum, Vol. 25(01), pp. 33–38

Ryan, James (1999): Stop the press, Business 2.0, Vol. 02(12), pp. 196–209

Salomon, Gavriel (1993): Distributed Cognitions: Psychological and Educational Considerations. Cambridge

Samuels, Edward B. (2000): The Illustrated Story of Copyright. New York

Samuelson, Pamela (1999): Intellectual Property and the Digital Economy: Why the Anti-Circumvention Regulations Need to Be Revised, in: Berkeley Technology Law Journal

Sander, Tomas (2002): Golden Times for Digital Rights Management? In: Syverson, P.F. (ed.): Financial Cryptography 2001, Berlin

Sawhney, Nitin; **Gomez**, Herve (2000): Communication Patterns in Domestic Life: Preliminary Ethnographic Study. Dept. of Ethnology and Comparative Sociology, University of Paris X Nanterre. http://www.media.mit.edu/~nitin/ethno/DomesticEthno.pdf

Saxenian, Anna L. (1994): Regional Advantage: Culture and Competition in Silicon Valley and Route 128, Cambridge, MA

Scannell, Paddy (1989): Public service broadcasting and modern public life, in: Media, Culture and Society, Vol. 11(2), pp. 135–166

Scheirer, Eric, et al. (2000a): Content out of Control, Forrester Report 09/2000. Cambridge, MA

Scheirer, Eric, et al. (2000b): Content Site Turnaround, Forrester Report 12/2000. Cambridge, MA

Schement, Jorge R. (1999): Of Gaps by Which Democracy We Measure, in: Information Impacts Magazine, Dec. 1999. http://www.cisp.org/imp/december_99/1299schement.html

Schmidt, Ingo (1999): Wettbewerbspolitik und Kartellrecht, 6th edn. Stuttgart

Schoegel, Kerstin (2001): Geschäftsmodelle: Konstrukt, Bezugsrahmen, Management. Munich

Scholz, Christian (2000): Strategische Organisation: Multiperspektivität und Virtualität, 2nd edn. Landsberg/Lech

Schumann, Matthias; **Hess**, Thomas (2000): Grundfragen der Medienwirtschaft, 2nd edn. Berlin et al.

Schumpeter, Joseph A. (1975): Capitalism, Socialism and Democracy, New York

Schwartz, Evan I. (1998): Webonomics: Nine Essential Principles for Growing Your Business on the World Wide Web, New York, NY

Screen Digest (2000): Release Windows and product lifecycles, in: Screen Digest

Sennewald, Nicola (1998): Massenmedien und Internet: Zur Marktentwicklung in der Pressebranche, Wiesbaden

Shafer, Scott T. (2001): The Blathering Storm: New Media offer Advertisers more Ways to talk to you, in: Red Herring, 20.03.2001, pp. 72–74

Shapiro, Carl; **Varian**, Hal. R. (1999): Information Rules: A Strategic Guide to the Network Economy. Boston, MA

Sherry, John; **Lucas**, Kristen; **Rechtsteiner**, Stephany; **Brooks**, Christi; **Wilson**, Brooke (2001): Video game uses and gratifications as predictors of use and game preference. Paper presented on the congress of the International Communication Association. http://icdweb.cc.purdue.edu/~sherryj/videogames/VGUG.pdf

Siegrist, Hannes (2001): Professionalization, Professions in History, in: Smelser, N.J.; Baltes, P.B. (eds.): International Encyclopedia of the Social and Behavioral Sciences, Amsterdam, pp. 12154–12160

Sihn, Wilfried; Klink, Joachim (ed.) (2000): Veränderungsmanagement im Verlagswesen: Bestandsaufnahme der Entwicklungstendenzen in der Verlagsbranche, Düsseldorf

Silverstone, Roger (1998): Talking about the Screen Machine: De toekomst van nieuwe media inEuropese huishoudens, in: Frissen, V.; Molder, H. te (eds.): Van Forum tot Supermarkt? Consumenten en burgers in de informatiesamenleving, Leuven, pp. 17–34

Silverstone, Roger (1999): Why Study the Media? London

Silverstone, Roger (in press): Proper distance: towards an ethics for cyberspace, in: Liestøl, G.; Morrison, A.; Rasmussen, T. (eds.): Innovations, Cambridge, MA

Silverstone, Roger; **Haddon**, Leslie (1996): Design and the domestication of ICTs: technical change and everyday life, in: Mansell, R.; Silverstone, R. (eds.): Communication by Design: The politics of Information and Communication Technologies, Oxford

Silverstone, Roger; **Hartmann**, Maren (Ed.) (1996-1998): The European Media Technology and Everyday Life Network (EMTEL) Working Papers, Falmer Brighton

Silverstone, Roger; **Hirsch**, Eric (eds.) (1992): Consuming technologies: Media and information in domestic spaces, London

Simmel, Georg (1908): Die Kreuzung sozialer Kreise. http://socio.ch/sim/unt6a.htm

Skiera, Bernd; **Lambrecht**, Anja (2000): Erlösmodelle im Internet, in: Albers, PP.; Herrmann, A. (eds.): Handbuch Produktmanagement: Strategieentwicklung, Produktplanung, Organisation, Kontrolle. Wiesbaden, pp. 815–831

Slevin, James (2000): The Internet and Society, Cambridge

Smith, Marc A.; **Kollock**, Peter (1999): Communities in Cyberspace, London

Smith, Michael D.; **Bailey**, Joseph; **Brynjolfsson**, Erik (2000): Understanding Digital Markets: Review and Assessment, in: Brynjolfsson, E./Kahin, B. (eds.): Understanding the Digital Economy: Data, Tools, and Research. Cambridge, MA; London, pp. 99–136

Sociaal Cultureel Planbureau (1998): Sociaal en Cultureel Rapport 1998, 25 jaar sociale verandering. Rijswijk

Soete, L., et al. (1997): Buiding the European Information Society for us all. Final policy report of the high-level expert group. Brussels: EC/DC V. http://www.ispo.cec.be/hleg/Building.html#1A

Sola Pool de, Ithiel (1977): The Social Impact of the Telephone, Cambridge

Sperber, D.; **Wilson**, D. (1986): Relevance, Communication and cognition, Oxford

Sproull, Lee; **Kiesler**, Sara (1991): Connections: New Ways of Working in the Networked Organization, Cambridge, MA

Stähler, Patrick (2001): Geschäftsmodelle in der digitalen Ökonomie: Merkmale, Strategien und Auswirkungen, Lohmar; Cologne

Suchman, Lucy (1987): Plans and Situated Actions: The Problem of Human-Machine Communication, New York

Szyperski, Norbert (1999): Mediendienste und Perpektiven der Medienwirtschaft, in: Szyperski, N. (ed.): Perspektiven der Medienwirtschaft: Kompetenz, Akzeptanz, Geschäftsfelder, Lohmar; Cologne, pp. 1–24

Thompson, John B. (1995): The Media and Modernity: A Social Theory of the Media, Cambridge

Thorngren, Bertil (2003): Profitability at any speed? In: Groebel, J.; Noam E.M.; Feldmann, V. (eds.): Mass media content for mobile communications, New Jersey

Timmers, Paul (1998): Business Models for Electronic Markets, in: Electronic Markets Vol. 8(2), pp. 3–8

Tolksdorf, Robert (1999): XML und darauf basierende Standards: Die neuen Auszeichnungssprachen des Web, in: Informatik Spektrum, 22/99, pp. 407–421

Townsend, A.M. (2000): Life in the Real-Time City: Mobile Telephones and Urban Metabolism, in: Journal of Urban Technology, Vol. 7(2), pp. 85–104. http://www.informationcity.org/research/real-time-city/life-in-the-real-time-city.pdf

Tuomi, Ilkka (2001): Internet, innovation, and open source: actors in the network, in: First Monday, No. 6 (1). http://firstmonday.org/issues/issue6_1/tuomi/index.html

Turecek, Oliver; **Grajzyk,** A.; **Roters**, Gunnar (2001) Videobranche im Umbruch: Video- und DVD-Markt im Jahr 2000, in: Media Perspektiven 5/2001, pp. 264–271

Turkle, Sherry (1995): Life on the Screen: Identity in the Age of the Internet, New York

Turowski, Klaus (2001): Spezifikation und Standardisierung von Fachkomponenten, in: Wirtschaftsinformatik, Vol. 43(03), pp. 269–281

Tushman, Michael L.; **Anderson**, Philip (1986): Technological Discontinuities and Organizational Environment, in: Administrative Science Quarterly, Vol. 31(03), pp. 439–456

U.S. National Telecommunications and Information Administration and the U.S. Economics and Statistics Administration (2002): A Nation Online – How Americans are Expanding Their Use of the Internet, February 2002. http://www.ntia.doc.gov/ntiahome/dn/index.html

UCLA-Internet-Report (2001): Surveying the Digital Future, UCLA Communication Policy

Utterback, James (1994): Mastering the Dynamics of Innovation: How Companies Can Seize Opportunities in the Face of Technological Change, Boston

Varian, Hal R. (1996): Differential Pricing and Efficiency, in: First Monday, URL: http://www.firstmonday.dk/issues/issue2/different/index.html

Wadle, Elmar (1996): Geistiges Eigentum: Bausteine zur Rechtsgeschichte, Weinheim

Wadle, Elmar (1999): Entwicklungsschritte des Geistigen Eigentums in Frankreich und Deutschland. Eine vergleichende Studie, in: Siegrist, H.; Sugarman, D. (eds.): Eigentum im internationalen Vergleich. Göttingen, pp. 245–263

Waesche, Niko (2003): Internet Entrepreneurship in Europe: Venture Failure and the Timing of Telecommunications: Reform, Cheltenham; Northampton, MA

Walsh, David (2000): Interactive violence and children. http://www.medianadthefamily.org/press/senateviolence-full.shtml

Wamser, Christoph (2000): Werbung und Electronic Commerce: Eine ökonomische Perspektive, in: Wamser, C. (ed.): Electronic Commerce, Munich, pp. 131–168

Wand, Peter (2001): Technische Schutzmaßnahmen und Urheberrecht – Vergleich des internationalen, europäischen, deutschen und US-amerikanischen Rechts, Munich, 2001

Want, Roy; **Fishkin**, Kenneth P.; **Gujar**, Anuj; **Harrison**, Beverly L. (1999): Bridging Physical and Virtual Worlds with Electronic Tags, in: Proceedings ACM CHI '99. Pittsburgh, PA, pp. 370–377

Watzlawick, P.; **Beavin**, J.H.; **Jackson**, D.D. (1967): Pragmatics of human communication: A study of interactional patterns, pathologies, and paradoxes, New York

Wayner, Peter (2002): Disappearing Cryptography, 2nd edn. San Francisco

Weijers, Thea; **Rijsselt**, Rene van (1998): Ouderen in de informatiemaatschappij; aan- of uitsluiting? in: Frissen, V.; Molder, H. te (eds.): Van Forum tot Supermarkt? Consumenten en burgers in de informatiesamenleving. Leuven, pp. 145–158

Weiser, Mark (1991): The Computer for the 21st Century, in: Scientific American, Vol. 265(9), pp. 66–75

Wellman, Barry (1999a): Networks in the Global Village. Boulder, CO

Wellman, Barry (1999b): The network community, in: Wellman, B. (Ed.): Networks in the Global Village. Boulder, CO, pp. 1–48

Wellman, Barry (2000): Physical place and CyberPlace: the rise of networked individualism, in: Journal of Urban and Regional Research. http://chaspp.utoronto.ca/~wellman/publications/individualism/article.html

Wellman, Barry; **Gulia**, Milena (1999): Virtual communities as communities: Net surfers don't ride alone, in: Smith, M. A.; Kollock, P. (Ed.): Communities in Cyberspace, London, pp. 167–194

Wenger, Etienne (1998): Communities of Practice: Learning, Meaning, and Identity. Cambridge

Werner, Heinz (1953): Einführung in die Entwicklungspsychologie, 3rd edn. Munich

Williamson, Oliver E. (1981): The Economics of Organization – The Transaction Cost Approach, in: American Journal of Sociology, Vol. 87(6), pp. 1537–1568

Williamson, Oliver E. (1983): Organizational Innovation – The Transaction-Cost Approach, in: Ronen, J. (ed.): Entrepreneurship. Lexington, pp. 101–133

Williamson, Oliver E. (1985): The Economic Institutions of Capitalism – Firms, Markets, Relational Contracting, New York

Winner, Langdon (1997): Cyberlibertarian myths and the prospects for community, in: Computers and Society, Vol. 27(3), pp. 14–19

Wirtz, Bernd W. (2001a): Medien- und Internetmanagement, 2nd edn. Wiesbaden

Wirtz, Bernd W. (2001b): Electronic Business, 2nd edn. Wiesbaden

Wissenschaftlicher Beirat (beim Bundesministerium für Wirtschaft und Technologie) (2001): Wettbewerbspolitik im Cyberspace. http://www.bmwi.de/homepage/download/doku/Doku495.pdf

Woodmansee, Martha (1998): The cultural work of copyright. Legislating authorship in Britain 1837–1842, in: Sarat, A.; Kearns, T. R. (eds.): Law in the domains of culture, University of Michigan Press, pp. 65–96

World Telecommunication Development Report (2002): "Reinventing Telecoms" & Trends in Telecommunication Reform 2002 "Effective Regulation". http://www.itu.int/newsroom/wtdc2002/backgrounder.html

Zacherl, Jürgen (2001): Die Power Rangers von Bandai: Erfolgreiche Lizenz-Synergiefelder als Wegweiser für die Spielzeug-Philosophie der Zukunft, in: Böll, K. (ed.): Handbuch Licensing, Frankfurt am Main, pp. 205–231

Zawel, Adam (2002): Enterprise Need for Public and Private Wireless LANs, Wireless/Mobilc Enterprise Commerce

Zerdick, Axel et al. (2001): E-conomics, Berlin et al., 2001

Zook, Matthew A. (1999): The web of production: the economic geography of commercial Internet content production in the United Statepp. Environmental Planning A (in press). http://ist-socratepp.berkeley.edu/~zook/pubs/Web_of_Production-Zook.pdf

Index

3G 114; 143; **165–180**
3G provider 169; 173; 174; 180

administration 46; 68; 204; 266; 331; 351
agents, intelligent 193; 195
Ambient Intelligence 144; **181–199**; 206–208; 211; 261; 265
anonymity 198; 282
anti-trust authorities 353; 354
anti-trust law 350; 351; 354
architecture, technical 304; 305; 307
artificial intelligence 193; 208
attention 26–31; 46; 47; 55; 73; 76; 79; 81; 86; 94; 127; 128; 135; 143; 155; 162; 198; 254; 256; 258; 280; 294–296; 299; 367; 377

backbone-networks 168
bandwidth 41; 48; 76; 103; 117; 121; 149; 151; 153; 167–169; 178; 196; 333; 397
"blogs" 21
body area networks 148; 153
broadband 25; 70; 76; 85; **101–103**; 126; 143; 165–171; 178–180; 192; 241; 277; 291
broadband cable 76
broadcasting 23–28; 32; 55; 69; 117; 190; 347; 363; 370; 377
business model 22; **33–39**; 49; 53–56; 76; 94–97; 112; 149; 156; 165; 166; 169–171; 189; 190; 199; 292; 331–337
business networks 65; 262
business webs 22; 28; 92; 190; 344; 349; 353
business-to-business 22

cable modem 77; 168
cable network 69; 70; 297; 350
capacity 24; 40–46; 70; 138; 149; 154; 169; 170; 176; 177; 213; 236–242; 245; 253; 257–260; 265; 291; 359; 361; 368–375
carrier media 34; 41; 42; 48; 52
CD 40; 58; 59; 75; 77; 86; 89; 109–111; 121; 122; 291; 292; 331; 334; 350; 351
CD-Rom 41; 61; 62; 121; 291
cell phone 170; **235–260**; 291; 350

citizen 117; 125; 138; 144; 149; 181; 199; 213; 232; 248; 261; 263; 264; 272–274; 279–283; 285; 288; 297; 300; 302; 314; 316; 327; 328; 357–379
collaborative filtering 70
competition 22; 27; 28; 44; 47; 56; 78; 91–93; 166; 173–180; 191; 231; 265; 269; 272; 292; 317; 318; 335; 338; **339–355**; **367–371**
competition policy **339–355**
competition law 339; 342; 349
connectivity 28; 117; 169; 170; 177; 219–221; 224; 226–232; 242; 244; 250; 271; 295; 296
content production, non-professional 21; 27
consumer protection 29; 161
content provider 47; 56; 76; **104–106**; 108; 110; 111; 115; 176; 178; 225; 334; 336; 338
content syndication 65
content, paid 22; 24; 25
convergence 23; 53; 54; 145; 150; 165; 181; 187; 267; 302; 346; 347; 354; 375
coopetition 345
copy management systems 332
copyright 19; 39; 46; 48; 50; 301; 311; 312; 314; 316–319; 322–329; **331–338**; 348;
copyright law 29; 41; 46; 50; 312; 316; 319; 323; 324; 326; 327; 329; **331; 335–338**
cost structure 46; 62; 352
creativity 217; 305; 312; 314; 316; 317; 320; 327
critical mass 21; 25; 189; 275; 345; 346; 351; 352
cross-media strategies 54; 55
customer-relationship-management 109
customisation 40; 53; 69; 104; 105; 117; 118; **125**; 190; 266
cyberspace 161; 220; 225; **304–306**; 345; 358; 364; 365

data protection 160; 162; 331; 335; 338
databank 57; 60; 61; 67; 68
de jure standard 64

decentralisation 246
de-communication 26
de-facto standard 64; 195; 348
dematerialisation 342
deregulation 242; 252; 329; 353; 370
diffusion 21; 25; 143; 144; **208, 209**; 230; 232; 248; 274; 303
digibetism 272
digital divide 162; 188; 213; 214; 224; 262; 265; **271–300**; 303
digital rights management 29; 178; 301; **331–338**
digital television 111
digitalisation 15; 16; 25; 27; 28; 31; 33; 35; 40; 56; 59; 65; 66; 69; 75; 82; 301; 316; 326; 328; 329; 342; 346
disintegration 31; **33–56**; 312
disintermediation 51; 52
disruptiveness 104; 105; 114
distance, proper 302; 373–375; 379
distance, social 373
distance, spatial 22; 215; 239; 254; 345
distribution 21; 24; 25; 27; 31; 33; 35; 36; 39–41; 44; 51; 53; 54; 58; 75; 76; 82; 89; 101–103; 124; 167; 185; 266; 269; 277; 299; 311; 313; 318; 319; 323; 328; 331; 342; 348; 350;
distribution channels 27; 31
distribution of knowledge 319
division of labour 205; 220; 221; 301; 316; 327; 328
DSL 168
DTD 60–63; 72
DVB-T 25; 28
DVD 23; 75; 77; 80; 84; 86; 87; 109; 110; 113; 332; 333

e-business 150; 266;
e-commerce 17; 21; 47; 57; 66; 77; 110; 114; 159; 165; 196; 264; 332; 333; 361
economic theory 224
economies of scale 41; 56; 190; **347**; **348**; 352
economies of scope 40; 43; 262; **347**
e-democracy 301; 302; **357–365**
education 85; 86; 187; 188; 190; 267–276; 296–298; 314; 316; 318; 323; 327; 329; 335; 364; 376
e-governance 309; 357

e-paper 23
e-paradigm **261–264**; 269
e-representation 363
e-society 202; 208
ethics, applied 367; 369
externalities 20; 105; 291; 293; 299
evolution 17; 28; 97; 98; 115; 144; 159; 165; 201–205; 208; 210; 212; 214; 235; 252; 259; 271; 286

face-to-face 209; 235; 237; 239; 259
fair use 337
film industry 25; 86; 90; 92; 93
first copy cost 58; 69; 347; 348; 352
flexibility 25; 165; 172; 173; 199; 219; 243; 263–265; 267; 334
follow the free 347

gaming **84–86**
globalisation 22; 44; 232; 262; 264; 326; 328; 329; 345; 370; 372
governance 262; 263; 270; 358–360; 365; 372
GPRS 115
GPS 112–114; 124; 147; 153; 156; 260

hardware 76; 77; 98; 179; 191–196; 207; 255; 259; 274; 275; 289–292; 332; 338; 339; 351
HDSL 347
HTML 60; 62; 77
hyperlinks 23; 32; **122**; **123**
hypermedia 118; **122**; **123**

immorality 370; 374
i-mode 105–110; 146; 147; 176
individualisation 31; **57–59**; **69**; **71–74**; 159; 240; 267; 280; 371
inferior goods 45
Information and Communication Technology 15; 33; 47; 50; 53; 201; 278
information overload 21; 184; 188; 196; 198
information products 40; 72; 74; 347
information revolution 271; 273
information society 75; 77; 144; 181; 199; 202; 205; 206: 214; 261; 271; 273; 274; 279; 283; 307; 317; 333; 336; 359
information supplier 281; 282
informatisation 159; 161; 162
infrastructure, backbone 171
infrastructure, network 168; 172; 179

infrastructure, social 217
infrastructure, technical 52
infrastructure, wireless 167; 174
infrastructure, wireline 166; 175
innovation 29; 94–96; 139; 149; 178–
    180; 189; 199; 203–205; 208;
    209; 216; 217; 231; 264; 265;
    273–279; 294; 301; 305; 312;
    315; 319; 329; 331; 335–337;
    350–354
innovation commons 305
institutions 15; 16; 21; 80; 188; 201;
    211; 232; 235; 237; 248; 251–
    255; 258; 262; 267; 296; 299; 303;
    312; 314; 317; 318; 323; 329; 344;
    357–363; 372
integration, social 245; 251; 328
intellectual property 19; 301; **311–
    329**; 333; 369
interaction 26; 41; 48; 52; 53; 58; 74;
    106; 124; 157; 179; 181; 183; 187;
    191; 193; 196; 198; 206; 213;
    216–220; 237–239; 243; 247;
    248; 254–259; 264; 305; 306;
    315; 334
interactivity **25**; **26**; 41; 117; 357; 358;
    360
interculturalism 328
intermediary 51; 52; 172; 253; 313;
    322; 359
internationalisation 326; 328; 345
internet economy 19–22; 28; 301; 302;
    339–344; 349–355
internet radio 24
internet revenue forms 22
internet service provider 291; 292
internet shopping 109
internet TV 24; 76
intimacy 244; 282
intranet 21; 23; 66
involvement 32; 98; 118; 124; 240;
    241; 254; 257; 279–283; 306;
    358;

journalism 32; **117–126**

legislation 301; 313; 323; 336; 347;
    352–355
liberalisation 315; 370
licensing 31; 55; 80; 81; 83; 87–92;
    172–174; 334
localisation 143; 147; 150; 154; 156–
    158; 193; 262; 345
location based services 112

logistical stream 37
logistics 158; 266; 298

machine-to-machine 156; 182; 193;
    198
man-machine communication 139
market domination 302; 341; 350–354
market penetration 347; 352
mass media 21; 27; 35; 226; 309; 367;
    377
mass media content distribution 21
mass media content production 21
mass production 154; 158
media competence 368
media culture 203; 367; 372
media integration 111
media literacy 117; 367; **375**; **377**;
    378;
media provider 23; 47; 66
mediation 215; 302; 328; 367–378
merger control law 341; 342
meso media 23; 24
micropayment 46; 106; 195
mobile Internet 32; **97–115**; 146; 170;
mobile phone 43; 84; 86; 97–115;
    143; 145–150; 153; 159; 160;
    176; 181; 213; 214; 230; **235–
    259**; 275; 287; 333; 350
mobilisation 282; 313
mobility 22; 28; 98; 165–168; 184;
    207; 215; 231; 236; 245; 257; 263;
    265–270; 301; 326
modernism 204–206
monopoly 167; 174; 318; 345–347;
    352–354
Moores Law 149; 151; 205; 290; 291
morality 371; 378
MP3 145; 350; 351
multiculturalism 328
multimedia 32; 58; 70; 75; 77; 93–96;
    117; 118; 123; 126; 165; 178; 216;
    236; 241; 283; 346
multitasking 78–80
music market 51; 52
music on demand 51

nanoelectronics 192
nanotechnologies 191; 192; 196
narrowband **101–103**; 169
network effects 20; 21; 24; 55; 63; 99;
    105; 106; 112; 113; 293; 337; 345;
    346; 351
network goods 20; 28; 351; 352

networking 17; 33; 59; 65; 66; 69; 94; 143–145; 154; 157; 165; 172; 174; 176; 180; 181; 192; 195; 196; 229; 230; 266; 269; 271; 358

nonverbal communication 32; 130; 133; 140

object-to-object 156; 198
offline 45; 78; 84; 95; 162; 216; 241; 350; 358
one-to-one marketing 47
online news 45; 117; 118
online newspaper 22; 23
online media 21; 27; 28; 42; 72; 73; 290

participation 19; 50; 59; 112; 187; 208; 213; 244; 248; 264; 267; 271; 273; 274; 279–284; 302; 306; 309; 357; 359; 376–378
pay TV 39; 48; 58; 80; 331; 333
pay-per-view 39; 48; 49; 80
PDA 98; 143; 147; 150; 155; 189; 259
personalisation 40; 41; 53; 71; 125; 159; 182
person-to-person 156; 213; 230
platform 21; 22; 27; 31; 32; 87; 92; 143; 166; 176–180; 190; 195; 196; 199; 271; 281–284; 305; 332; 337; 338
portability 98; 114
portals 32; 37; 47; 52; 66; 87; 106–108; 151; 266; 359–362; 371
positive feedback 105; 106; 112; 217
post-PC era 143; 150; 151
power of images 137
pricing policy 37
print media 23–27; 79; 111
product architecture 34; 37–40; 43; 46; 56
protection 26; 29; 46; 50; 160–162; 184; 188; 195; 229; 270; 301; 302; 313; 315–326; 331–338; 353; 369; 370; 376;
proximity 110; 148; 217; 235; 236; 255; 257; 259; 373; 379
public sphere 231; 252; 257; 301; 306–309; 313; 327; 370; 373

range 17; 31; 34; 47; 58; 75; 77; 79; 109; 118; 119; 147; 148; 158; 167; 182; 190; 191; 210; 237; 239; 241; 260; 263; 275; 283; 301; 316; 334; 336; 359; 368

rational passivity 25; 26
rationality 49; 51; 230; 308; 309
recipient 31; 32; 42; 47; 48; 55–58; 69; 72; 128; 139; 140; 240; 247; 248; 313; 314; 328; 365
regulation 68; 224; 259; 266; 268; **301–309**; 319; 326; 329; 333; 336–339; 345; 350; 367–372; 375–379; 392; 404; 410
reintegration 31; 33–55
reregulation 301
revenue forms 22; 24; 239; **48–50**
revenue model 24; 31; 34; 37–39; 44; 48; 56; 189
revenue stream 37
RFID 152
role-to-role 213; **230–233**

selection 26; 53; 79; 109; 110; 208; 232
self-regulation 213; 224; 304; 306; 338
service provider 26; 48; 99; 106; 115; 144; 166–180; 292
set-top box 290
SMS 115; 145; 176; 248; 251; 254; 259
social networks 213; 216–218; 225–231; 238; 240; 244; 277
social relationships 213; 237–239; 256; 258; 259; 280
social systems 203; 237; 243; 250; 252; 253; 256–258;
solidarity, transpatial 225; 226
special interest 297; 309
spectrum policy 169; 172; 177
standard 51; 60–68; 74; 81; 101; 119; 120; 123; 147; 157; 160; 162; 165; 179; 192; 195; 264; 266–268; 291; 293; 299; 332; **345**; **346**; 348; 351; 353; 370
standardisation 63; 64; 301; 332; 337; 345; 346
storytelling 32; 117–126
streaming media 169
sustainability 184; 188; 199; 208

telecommunication 17; 35; 51; 57; 140; 150; 160; 165; 166; 169; 179; 190; 215; 217; 236; 241; 263; 265; 266; 271; 286; 290; 294; 295; **298**; 302; 346; 347; 354; 370;
telephone networks 76
telephone services 165; 169

television 23; 25; 27; 28; 35; 48; 49; 55; 57; 59; 69; 70; 76–81; 85; 86; 98; 104; 111; 118–124; 137; 138; 226; 285; 290; 291; 294; 297; 299; 316; 347; 362; 363; 365; 371; 377
teleworking 267
tracing 137; 158; 332
transaction costs 41; 46–51; 205; 334; 344; 345
transformation 15; 21; 36; 77; 89; 94; 95; 117; 120; 202; 203; 206; 217; 218; 230–232; 243; 261; 262; 267; 269; 271; 307; 309; 317; 328; 373;
transmission media 41; 42; 48; 52; 53
TV set 209; 238; 290

ubiquitous computing 143; 145; 155; 157–163; 181; 261
UMTS 149; 153; 241
universal service 275; 289; 296; 297

value added services 26
value chain 25; 36–39; 50–53; 57; 168; 171; 172; 346

value stream 37
value structure 34; 37; 39; 40; 50; 53; 56
versioning 22; 25; 28
vertical integration 22; 28; 39; 50; 51; 178
virtualisation 215
virtuality 29; 219
visual information processing 134
visual perception 32; 137; 138

WAP 115; 146
wearable computing 100; 148; 153; 159
webcasting 23; 363
web logs 21; 23; 28
WiFi 146; **165–180**;
windowing 80; 81; 83
wireless technologies 165; 167; 178; 179; 296
WLAN 165–178
World Wide Web 119; 156; 292

XML 60–74; 155

Druck: betz-druck GmbH, D-64291 Darmstadt
Verarbeitung: Buchbinderei Schäffer, D-67269 Grünstadt